The Uruguay Round and Beyond

SIE *Studies in International Economics* includes works dealing with the theory, empirical analysis, and evaluation of international policies and institutions, in the area of international macroeconomics and finance, international trade theory and policy, as well as international legal and political economy.

Keith E. Maskus, Peter M. Hooper, Edward E. Leamer, and J. David Richardson, Editors
Quiet Pioneering: Robert M. Stern and His International Economic Legacy

Bjarne S. Jensen and Kar-yiu Wong, Editors
Dynamics, Economic Growth, and International Trade

Jagdish Bhagwati and Mathias Hirsch, Editors
The Uruguay Round and Beyond: Essays in Honor of Arthur Dunkel

Kala Marathe Krishna and Ling Hui Tan
Rags and Riches: Implementing Apparel Quotas under the Multi-Fibre Arrangement

Alan V. Deardorff and Robert M. Stern
Measurement of Nontariff Barriers

Thomas Cottier and Petros C. Mavroidis, Editors
The World Trade Forum, Volume I: State Trading in the Twenty-First Century

Rajesh Chadha, Sanjib Pohit, Alan V. Deardorff, and Robert M. Stern
The Impact of Trade and Domestic Policy Reforms in India: A CGE Modeling Approach

Alan V. Deardorff and Robert M. Stern, Editors
Constituent Interests and U.S. Trade Policies

Gary R. Saxonhouse and T. N. Srinivasan, Editors
Development, Duality, and the International Economic Regime: Essays in Honor of Gustav Ranis

Charles P. Kindleberger
Essays in History: Financial, Economic, Personal

The Uruguay Round and Beyond

Essays in Honor of Arthur Dunkel

Edited by
Jagdish Bhagwati
Mathias Hirsch

Ann Arbor

THE UNIVERSITY OF MICHIGAN PRESS

First paperback edition 1999

Published in the United States of America by
The University of Michigan Press
Manufactured in the United States of America
♾ Printed on acid-free paper

2002 2001 2000 1999 4 3 2 1

Library of Congress Cataloging-in-Publication Data

The Uruguay Round and beyond : essays in honor of Arthur Dunkel /
edited by Jagdish Bhagwati and Mathias Hirsch.
p. cm.
Includes bibliographical references (p.).
ISBN 0-472-10980-4 (cloth : alk. paper)
1. General Agreement on Tariffs and Trade (Organization)
2. Uruguay Round (1987–1994) 3. Commercial policy. 4. Foreign
trade regulation. I. Dunkel, Arthur, 1932– . II. Bhagwati,
Jagdish N., 1934– . III. Hirsch, Mathias.
HF1721.U837 1998b
382′.92—dc21 98-20651
CIP

ISBN 0-472-08647-2 (pbk.)

Acknowledgements

In preparing this Festschrift to honour Arthur Dunkel we have incurred many debts. Chief among them is to the authors who submitted their contributions on time and cooperated cheerfully in revising their manuscripts where needed.

Our thanks also go to Nestlé SA and MS Management Service AG for their generous financial support, which has made it possible for us to arrange with Springer-Verlag to publish the volume speedily and handsomely, and to present it to Arthur Dunkel at a celebration in St. Gallen, Switzerland, in May 1998.

We would also like to seize the opportunity to thank Richard Eglin, Helmut Maucher, Herbert Oberhänsli, David de Pury and Wolfgang Schürer. Without their constant personal support this undertaking would not have been possible. Michaela Eglin also deserves our thanks for editing the manuscripts with dedication and care in a most efficient way, and for producing a camera ready copy.

Jagdish Bhagwati
Mathias Hirsch
Editors

New York and Geneva, February 1998

Arthur Dunkel

Preface

This Festschrift is dedicated to Arthur Dunkel, who celebrated his sixty-fifth birthday in August 1997. As Director-General of the the General Agreement on Tariffs and Trade (GATT) between January 1980 and June 1993, Arthur Dunkel presided over what has since been recognized as the most innovative phase in the history of multilateral trade, the Uruguay Round of Multilateral Trade Negotiations. The Round began in 1986 in Punta del Este, Uruguay, and ended in December 1993 in Geneva. Arthur Dunkel strengthened the foundations of the GATT and paved the way for the creation of the World Trade Organization in 1995.

With a prophetic sense for the impending upheaval awaiting the world economy in the 1980s, Arthur Dunkel pressed ahead with his Uruguay Round agenda to defuse the economic and political pressure points that were swelling the ranks of the protectionists. He also went a long way towards softening the antagonism between north and south by giving the silent majority a voice and the wherewithal to benefit from, but also to assume responsibilities within, the system.

As the idea of this book to pay tribute to Arthur Dunkel's accomplishments took shape with authors' contributions flowing in, so did the certainty that such tribute was wanting to be paid with enthusiasm, candidness and even affection to Arthur, the D-G, and Arthur, the friend. The present volume is an illuminating account of trade history in the making by those most closely involved. When the Uruguay Round was launched, few people knew what challenges the negotiators would have to face and what the future trading environment would be. Few would have ventured to predict the fundamental changes that have taken place: the end of a bipolar world, the sharp increase in countries wishing to participate in the multilateral trading system and the greatly expanded coverage of trade, which now comprises services. It is only fitting therefore that the chief architect of the Round, and of the resulting WTO, is celebrated in this volume with several notable contributions by major players.

The task of putting together a volume for a man of such distinction as Arthur Dunkel posed some difficulty. In particular, it was very hard to choose the authors from among his many admirers and friends without risking offense to those who had to be left out. In the end, we decided that the best strategy was to have a well-defined topic that would both honour Arthur Dunkel by becoming a testimony to his accomplishments and provide a way of delimiting the legion of potential authors to a functional few.

The theme of the volume that we finally chose has turned out to be: *The Uruguay Round and Beyond: Essays in Honour of Arthur Dunkel.* Dunkel's career at the GATT was long and distinguished. But its crowning point was his masterly, and indeed invaluable, guidance of the Uruguay Round negotiations through many vicissitudes. His indomitable spirit kept the progress going even as many despaired: the Dunkel Draft, in the end, was what anchored the Contracting Parties down, providing the lifeline to an eventual agreement.

One would not pay due tribute to Arthur Dunkel, if one were to limit it to his role as Director-General of GATT. This is why we have asked his longtime friend Jean-Pascal Delamuraz to reveal the other side of Arthur in the first paper. Faced with the problem of translating the untranslatable, both the original article in French and what comes closest to it in English have been reproduced here. But it is not only Jean-Pascal Delamuraz's likening Arthur Dunkel to a cat that gives us a glimpse of the man behind the personality. Rubens Ricupero compares him to Moses, who was denied entry into the promised land. Roy MacLaren puts him on a level with the likes of Richard Cobden, and still others elaborate his manifold qualities.

In the first part of the book, insiders, like Geza Feketekuty, one of the architects of the General Agreement on Trade in Services; Marcelo Raffaelli, former Chairman of the Textiles Surveillance Body of the Multi-Fibre Arrangement at the GATT; Rubens Ricupero, UNCTAD Secretary-General; Clayton Yeutter, former US Trade Representative and Secretary of Agriculture, and B.K. Zutshi, at the time Indian Permanent Representative to the GATT, give their account, each recollecting beautifully the story of the negotiations. Robert Hudec's paper on the Role of the GATT Secretariat in the Evolution of the WTO Dispute Settlement Procedure wraps up this part.

In the second part, which deals with the effects of globalisation and the geopolitical changes, the European Commissioner for External Economic Relations Willy de Clercq, the Swiss Chief Negotiator during the Uruguay Round David de Pury, Canada's former Minister for International Trade Roy MacLaren, Chairman of Nestlé and President of the International Chamber of Commerce Helmut Maucher, the WTO's current Director-General Renato Ruggiero, and Arthur Dunkel's successor Peter Sutherland, explain how these changes affect the world trading system.

Lastly, given Dunkel's continuing interest in the new but unfinished issues that go beyond the Uruguay Round, we have been lucky to secure in the third part contributions on competition policy by the European Commissioner Sir Leon Brittan and on the proliferation of regional agreements and their potential threat to multilateral trade by the former Chairman of the Board of the Federal Reserve System Paul Volcker. Jagdish Bhagwati and Richard Eglin, formerly Director of the WTO Secretariat's Trade and Environment Division, show that policy issues such as labour standards, human rights and the protection of the environment have to be dealt with on an international level, but that there are more effective means than trade measures to achieve the desired objective. This part also benefits from contributions by scholars in international trade like Arvind Panagariya and T.N.Srinivasan, who analyse regionalism, and those in international law like Merit Janow, who looks into competition policy in the context of the multilateral trading system, and John Jackson who ponders the implications of the rules-based WTO for the concept of sovereignty.

We cannot do better than to conclude with the remarks of the former Indian Permanent Representative to the GATT and Chairman of the GATT Council, B.

K. Zutshi, given on two separate occasions in honour of Mr. Dunkel's departure from the GATT. They illustrate, just as Jean-Pascal Delamuraz has observed, that the man Arthur Dunkel inevitably–and fortunately–has influenced the Director-General Arthur Dunkel and vice-versa:

If I recall correctly, Arthur you made the point that you did not believe in getting emotional and that emotion did not have a place in the business of negotiations and, perhaps, by implication in the serious business of life... This set me to wonder about Arthur, the man behind the official. Not for long though. It was during 1992 as Chairman of the Council that I came to know Arthur a bit more closely, though still in the work-place and in the official context. Nevertheless, I did see Arthur's emotional side, his vulnerabilities and that was the basis of my comment the other day about his being human, all too human. Arthur, for that reason, you have earned my greater respect. All this is a long-winded way of saying that your heart is in the right place. For what is wisdom, except knowledge, tempered by feeling, thought informed by emotion. You have both in abundance except that while you cannot help revealing the one, you are good at concealing the other.

If I may turn now to Arthur, the man. From time to time I have disagreed with him, often mildly, but sometimes strongly. So, I am sure, have others, at some time or another, but still we all have been able to retain his friendship, goodwill and mutual respect. That is the hallmark of a gentleman. Nothing reflects this better than my own experience, if I may share it with you. Arthur has always given me the impression that India has a special place in his heart, not that I recall his saying so in many words, or in specific terms, but by way of a word here, a hint there and by his grasp of our problems and concerns he has created this impression on me. In the beginning, I thought this was unique for India, until I discovered, with a tinge of disappointment, but also with understanding and appreciation, that he had been able to convey the same impression to others also about them; not in the sense of being everything to everybody but in the sense of conveying a feeling of singular value to each contracting party and each participant in the Round. This is a reflection of the special quality of empathy he possesses, a rare gift. He may not always have been able to help, but he always understood and appreciated.

Jagdish Bhagwati
Mathias Hirsch
Editors

New York and Geneva, February 1998

Table of Contents

Part III: Globalisation and the World Trading System

Part I: Introduction

Arthur Dunkel

Jean-Pascal Delamuraz

Arthur Dunkel aime les chats. C'est dire qu'il aime l'intelligence, la ténacité à réussir, l'habileté, l'indépendance.

Au fait Arthur Dunkel est chat lui-même.

* * *

L'intelligence, en lui, consiste à appréhender le meilleur de ce que le milieu ambiant peut lui offrir. Ainsi conjugue-t-il, en claire harmonie, la robustesse déductive des Helvètes et la sensibilité latine–la sensibilité lusitanienne tout particulièrement.

Fertile est le terreau constitué par un quotient intellectuel que l'on s'accorde à reconnaître supérieur aux moyennes et par un instinct fulgurant. Ce terreau recevra en plénitude la semence universitaire puis l'enrichissement né de l'activité d'un jeune fonctionnaire voué au sacerdoce international–avec tout ce que cela comporte en rencontres humaines d'envergure et en situations politico-économiques défiantes. Le terreau Dunkel est le plus fructifiant qui soit; c'est quasiment de l'agriculture intensive (prescrite par ailleurs!).

On a connu et on connaît encore des gouvernements ou des généraux *en retard d'une guerre*. L'intelligence, c'est d'être *en avance d'une idée*. Arthur Dunkel est toujours en avance d'une idée–au minimum!–mais il a ... l'intelligence de ne point le faire éprouver (ou si rarement!) au bataillon qui chemine au jour le jour. Et quand le bataillon l'aura comprise, cette idée, elle sera devenue sienne. Elle passera la rampe d'autant mieux.

Et, ce jour-là, Arthur Dunkel sera noyé, comme toujours, dans les volutes de sa fumée, mais ce seront les volutes de la satisfaction. L'oeil malin sera mi-clos–toujours le chat!–, protégeant un jardin intérieur exubérant. Il continuera à nous rappeler Sisyphe...à cette différence près qu'Arthur, lui, s'est libéré du rocher. Il médite déjà l'idée suivante: l'idée d'avance!

* * *

Chez lui, l'indépendance est la condition d'être et de *fonctionner*.

Il a à exécuter un mandat public. Celui de son pays lorsqu'il est haut fonctionnaire suisse. Celui du GATT lorsqu'il en est directeur général.

Il excelle par sa fidélité absolue à la mission dont il est chargé.

Mais il met au service de cette mission l'indépendance d'esprit et de comportement qui en assurera le succès.

La négociation internationale laisse relativement peu de marge au négociateur. Arthur Dunkel ne cherche pas à élargir la marge. Mais il la remplit–et comment!

Il la remplit par sa force de conviction, par son habile savoir-faire, par son indépendance avant tout. Car l'indépendance seule vous permet de distinguer le phénomène des épiphénomènes. Elle vous libère des *a priori* formels souvent stérilisants et vous autorise ainsi à consacrer votre talent à la substance. Elle vous confère cette relativité indispensable à l'accomplissement fructueux de tout service.

Discipline de l'apostolat, indépendance dans son accomplissement.

* * *

L'intelligence et l'indépendance réunies dans le même homme ouvrent l'horizon. Un horizon qui n'est pas occulté par la seule perspective de la négociation en cours, si vaste soit-elle.

Non! Un horizon riche d'autres valeurs de civilisation, un horizon de culture, un horizon de grand air. C'est l'horizon d'Arthur Dunkel.

Et il cherche à en faire comprendre la dimension aux autres. Parce que la caution des autres, en société démocratique, sera finalement indispensable à tout accomplissement et à toute consolidation de l'édifice international.

Il le sait. Il connaît et pratique la solitude du pouvoir. Mais il sort à point nommé de cette solitude pour communiquer et pour conforter la base de toutes ses démarches.

Cette inéluctable quête de légitimité appelle le spécialiste à devenir généraliste. Mais on ne redevient généraliste qu'habité par la culture, la sensibilité, l'ouverture.

Arthur Dunkel, dans le maquis des tarifs douaniers, de la clause de la nation la plus favorisée, du *green box* de toutes les certitudes, sait la dimension humaine de nos démarches: là est la téléologie de notre engagement public.

* * *

Arthur Dunkel, talentueux négociateur–côté chat–et, au-delà, homme d'autorité, esprit infatigablement curieux, jusqu'à l'éclectisme.

Un grand citoyen.

Un grand citoyen qui, sur les traces d'Herriot, a accroché sa charrue à une étoile.

Arthur Dunkel

Jean-Pascal Delamuraz

Arthur Dunkel likes cats. In other words, he likes intelligence, tenaciousness, cleverness, independence.

In fact, there is something catlike about Arthur Dunkel himself.

* * *

In his case, intelligence has meant making the most of what his surroundings offer, resulting in this quite harmonious blend of sturdy Swiss sense and Latin–more specifically Lusitanian-sensibility.

Combine an I.Q. generally recognized as being well above average with a remarkable instinct and you start with a fertile soil indeed. It was bountifully sown with the seeds of university education, and then enriched by the activity of a young official dedicated to international service, with all that that implies in terms of significant encounters and challenging political and economic situations. How fruitful it has proved in Arthur Dunkel! One might even speak here (fittingly enough!) of intensive agriculture.

There have been, and there still are, governments or generals who are *still fighting the last war*. The hallmark of intelligence is being *one idea ahead.* Arthur Dunkel has always been at least one idea ahead, but he has had the intelligence not to rub it in on the plodding rank and file (or only very rarely!). And when the rank and file understand the idea and take it up as their own, it will be that much more easily accepted.

And when that day comes, Arthur Dunkel will be wreathed, as always, in smoke, but also wreathed in satisfaction, his clever eyes half-closed–catlike yet again!–screening off the fertile brain behind. He still reminds us of Sisyphus... except that Arthur has rid himself of the boulder. He is already pondering on the next idea–still one idea ahead!

* * *

For him, independence is the *sine qua non* of this life and work.

He has had to discharge public duties: on behalf of his country as a senior Swiss official, and for GATT as its Director-General.

He has been outstanding in his whole-hearted, unswerving devotion to his duties.

But he has bent his independence of mind and action to the service of those duties, thus ensuring their success.

International negotiations leave their participants relatively little room for manoeuvre. Arthur Dunkel has not sought to overstep that margin, but he has certainly made remarkably full use of the room available!

He has exploited it to the full with the strength of his convictions, his skilled know-how, and above all his independence. For it is independence alone that enables you to disregard the trappings and get to the heart of the matter. It frees you from formal *a priori* positions that often lead nowhere, and enables you instead to devote your talents to substance. It gives you the relativity without which results cannot be achieved.

He has the discipline of apostleship, together with independence of mind in carrying it out.

* * *

A man who possesses both intelligence and independence has a vaster horizon, a horizon that is not confined to the ongoing negotiations, however wide-ranging they may be. Rather, Arthur Dunkel's horizon is wide open, with room for other values of civilization, for culture.

And he has tried to make others understand the dimension of that horizon, because ultimately, in a democratic society, the endorsement of one's fellows is essential in order to achieve anything or add anything to the international structure.

He is aware of this. He has known and experienced the solitude of power, but at the right time he has emerged from that solitude to communicate, to strengthen the foundations of all his action.

In this unavoidable quest for legitimacy, the specialist must go back to being a generalist; but he can only do so if he is willing and able to be open to the outside world.

In the thick of the jungle of customs tariffs, of the most-favoured-nation clause, of the *green box* of certainties on all sides, Arthur Dunkel has remained conscious of the human dimension of our work, which must remain our guiding principle and purpose as public servants.

* * *

This, then, is Arthur Dunkel, the canny negotiator–his feline side–and beyond that a man of authority, a tirelessly inquisitive and even eclectic spirit.

A great citizen.

A great citizen who, following in Herriot's footsteps, has hitched his plough to a star.

Part II: The Uruguay Round

Integration of Developing Countries into the Multilateral Trading System

Rubens Ricupero

> *And the Lord spake unto Moses that selfsame day, saying ... Because ye trespassed against me among the children of Israel at the waters of Meribah-Kadesh ... because ye sanctified me not in the midst of the children of Israel,*
>
> *Yet thou shalt see the land before thee, but thou shalt not go thither unto the land which I give the children of Israel.*
>
> (Deuteronomy, 32: 48, 51, 52)

> *And Moses went up from the plains of Moab unto the mountain of Nelo ... And the Lord shewed him all the land ... And the Lord said unto him, This is the land which I sware unto Abraham, unto Isaac, and unto Jacob, saying, I will give it unto thy seed: I have caused thee to see it with thine eyes, but thou shalt not go over thither.*
>
> (Deuteronomy, 34: 1, 4)

The quotation about Moses and the Promised Land is unavoidable each time one deals with Arthur Dunkel and the Uruguay Round.

If there ever existed a collective endeavour made possible by the contributions of thousands of individuals, it was the Uruguay Round. Those different contributions were not, however, of the same weight and importance, and there is no denying that Arthur Dunkel's contribution was, by far, more crucial and decisive than that of any other individual.

This is true in two senses. No one was more closely associated–and for so long–than the former Director-General of the General Agreement on Tariffs and Trade (GATT) with each and every one of the many phases of the longest of all Rounds, from the drawn out preparations, through the launching at Punta del Este, and the frequently difficult and painful negotiations up until almost the end.

At the same time no one could possibly claim more credit than Arthur Dunkel in terms of playing a personally central role at every turning point in the Round, starting with the compromise of the Punta del Este Declaration, through the resolution of the two major crises–the Montreal Mid-term Review in December 1988 and the hoped for but frustrated conclusion in Brussels in December 1990–up to the drafting and presentation of the Draft Final Act, the basis for the final outcome.

Moses was luckier than Arthur because at least the Lord made clear the reasons for denying him entry into the Promised Land. In Arthur's case, after making him wander in the desert for 40 years, the modern demi-gods of commerce, with their characteristically Olympian non-transparency, have never deigned to explain to us common mortals the reasons for their edict.

This is not, however, an investigative article about the last days of the Round, a task for which I would not be qualified having left Geneva in December 1991 when my term as Chairman of the GATT Contracting Parties expired.

My purpose is instead to risk a few partial comments about the role played by developing countries in the negotiations. To that end, I believe it would be only fair to point out that Arthur Dunkel made a conscious and serious effort to ensure that developing countries participated actively in all relevant aspects of the process.

During a large part of the Round, I was responsible for coordinating the so-called Informal Group of Developing Countries in the GATT. As a result of that experience, I can testify that Arthur was not only always available and responsive to the Group's requests but often also took the initiative of suggesting that he should be invited to address the Group whenever he felt it necessary.

With his long and diversified experience in economic diplomacy and his personal involvement in UNCTAD and other multilateral forums, Arthur Dunkel was keenly aware of the importance of integrating the developing countries into a trading system that had remained for too long an almost exclusive club of industrialized economies. He can thus take credit for having helped to make the Uruguay Round the historic endeavour that finally brought about that long overdue integration.

I will try to describe that process in two parts. The first is a very personal and impressionistic account of my own partial and incomplete experience during the Round. The second is a more articulated attempt to assess the results of the Uruguay Round from the perspective of the challenges ahead for developing countries.

1. Introduction

The fact that the major trading powers were mainly responsible for the delay in concluding the Uruguay Round demonstrated what had been taking shape for some time: the transfer to developing countries of the difficult task of defending the multilateral trading system.

This situation involves a paradox that is difficult to resolve. Indeed, the reason why developing countries are interested in maintaining the system, i.e., their lack of power and their greater vulnerability, is the same that makes them unsuited to assume such a role in the absence of cooperation by the larger trading partners.

The present trade regime originated in an Anglo-American conception and was part of a major restructuring of the international order after the Second World War, together with the institutions created at Bretton Woods–the International Monetary Fund and the World Bank–and, in its political dimension, the United

Nations. This structure, particularly its socio-economic aspect, was able to be built only because there was a hegemonic economic power–the United States of America, which was determined to be the foundation of the institutional expression of beliefs regarding free trade that were deep-seated in the inherited values of the ruling Anglophile and internationalist elite of that country's East coast.

American citizens, who were the main beneficiaries of a system under which for a long time they were the leading exporters, gradually acquired the belief that it was their altruism and their wish for German and Japanese recovery–rather than their own interest–that had moved them in the direction of free trade. It was not too long before this ideologically distorted perception gained ground in the Congress and academic circles, and among public opinion makers. Facing a European Union caught up in consolidating its internal integration and a Japan unable to overcome its short-term pragmatism, the group for which there is no satisfactory alternative to multilateralism has now been reduced to a number of isolated and peripheral developed countries (Australia, New Zealand and the Scandinavian countries) and to developing countries.

The latter evolved in the opposite direction from the United States. During part of the post-war period, it appeared to these countries that the Bretton Woods system, including the GATT, should be radically reformed through multilateral negotiations in order to restore equality in the decision-making process and promote the cause of development. Unlike the Bretton Woods institutions, efforts to that end produced some concrete results (the Generalized System of Preferences or GSP) as well as institutions (UNCTAD and UNIDO) and, above all, results of a conceptual nature (the principle of special and differential treatment for developing countries and the major declarations of principle by the United Nations and UNCTAD). After reaching its climax in the 1970s, when some seemed to see the short-lived success of OPEC as an irreversible change in the balance of forces, the reformist tide diminished and then ceased. Among the shipwrecked left on the shore were those nostalgic about navigation on the high seas and a greater number of pragmatic individuals, resigned to trying to secure a place in GATT's ark, even third-class, which would allow them to nourish the hope of reaching the promised land of development.

I was in some way a privileged witness to that development, as I arrived in Geneva to take up my duties as head of the Brazilian delegation to the GATT in November 1987 and stayed there until towards the end of 1991. (I actually left Geneva in August, but as Chairman of the Contracting Parties during that year I maintained my links with the negotiations and came back to chair the Contracting Parties' December session). Given the circumstances that led in 1989 to my succeeding the eminent Indian representative, Ambassador Shukla, as coordinator of the Informal Group of Developing Countries, and given the duties I performed, for which I was elected by my colleagues, and also because of the required geographical rotation (I was Chairman of the Committee on Trade and Development in 1989, Chairman of the Council of Representatives in 1990 and Chairman of the Contracting Parties in 1991), I shall venture to make some remarks and to formulate my impressions about the participation of developing countries in the Uruguay Round negotiations.

It has become a commonplace to say that, unlike past negotiations, the Uruguay Round was outstanding because of the intensive and influential participation of developing countries. The trend in that direction derived from the Tokyo Round, but it was manifestly intensified by the discussions, sometimes extremely difficult, marking the preparatory phase to the launching of the Uruguay Round.

2. The Divergence at the Outset of the Uruguay Round

The United States proposal, supported by the OECD countries, that the negotiations focus on the so-called new issues (services, trade effects of intellectual property rights and investment measures, issues related to advanced technology, etc.) gave rise from the outset to doubts and reservations in many developing countries, and led them to organize themselves into the *Group of Ten* (Argentina, Brazil, Cuba, Egypt, India, Nicaragua, Nigeria, Peru, United Republic of Tanzania and Yugoslavia).

2.1. The OECD View

The OECD view was founded on the conviction that tariff reductions agreed in previous GATT Rounds, and hence the low (between 2.5 and 6 per cent) tariff averages prevailing in the industrialized economies had exhausted the potential for additional tariff reductions applied to goods as a dynamic factor in the multilateral trading system. To prevent the system from becoming irrelevant it would be necessary to extend it to the new issues that were supposedly determinant for the future expansion of the world economy, through the inclusion in the GATT system, for instance, of subject areas possessing great dynamism but lacking multilateral regulatory norms, such as services. In parallel, in the area of the traditional issues, the main concern of the United States and its partners was related to the problem of *free rider*. The question was one of integrating the developing countries into a system of which they were beneficiaries (especially those that were recently industrialized and were having considerable export success) by exerting pressure on them to abandon waivers, such as special and differential treatment, which exempted them from the ordinary norms and from the obligation regarding tariff reductions and bindings.

Another twist behind the quest for new areas and the diminished attractiveness of the traditional issues to the industrial countries' negotiators was the fact that within the two main components of the traditional issues, there was great resistance on the part of the developed economies (in the case of textiles) and profound disagreement among them (in the case of agriculture).

The doctrinal framework developed after the last stages of the Tokyo Round by economists and policy experts in the OECD countries and in the OECD itself was founded on these concrete facts. According to them, the globalization of production through the distribution of the various stages of the production chain to different geographical locations needed a greater uniformity of standards and patterns at the international level. If production had a tendency to become international, legislation should accompany this tendency and come closer to a more or less uniform general model. A cycle of world trade–one of shallow integration–limited to *border measures* (tariffs and quotas) had been exhausted and the era of deep integration was starting, extending to decisions which until then had been considered to be within the sole jurisdiction of sovereign states (legislation on patents and intellectual property in general, regulations on banking, insurance, and other services and on investment standards).

There were doubts about whether an organization such as the GATT, comprising more than 100 countries with very different levels of development, was the ideal forum for this much more ambitious type of integration. For that reason, before and during the Uruguay Round negotiations, suggestions were often made in favour of a more exclusive forum, restricted to the industrialized economies and to those willing to accept a more exacting integration–some form of enlarged OECD. There were instances when such suggestions were used as a threat to exclude recalcitrants from, for example, the *trade liberalization club*, referred to by the then United States Treasury Secretary, James Baker, to which only *like-minded countries* could be admitted. The various proposals on *non-application* (on services above all), i.e., clauses that would reserve the extension of concessions to countries accepting a minimum level of obligations, had similar origins. In other words, one of the fundamental pillars of the GATT system–the most-favoured-nation clause–was to be suspended in such instances.

2.2. The Developing Countries' View

In contrast to this approach, developing countries protested that previous Rounds had been practically limited to industrial tariffs, from which rich countries benefitted more, leaving out areas of great potential expansion for less developed countries' trade. Even worse, not only were these areas left abandoned in a sort of "no man's land," but in some areas, such as textiles and clothing, representing the first and most accessible step towards industrialization, a reverse mechanism was set up–the Multi-Fibre Arrangement–which discriminated solely against developing countries' exports, the only ones subject to quotas.

Another sector of interest to developing countries, agriculture, was almost totally excluded from the system, and "waivers" renewed since the 1950s frustrated whatever few rules were included in the GATT. The general lack of discipline therefore allowed the European Economic Community, previously a net importer of foodstuffs, to become one of the largest exporters of agricultural products together with the United States, thanks to the massive use of subsidies, as in the case of the United States, which drove from the market more efficient producers in the developing world.

Similarly, developing countries complained about the lack of progress in trade liberalization of tropical products; the persistence of tariff peaks–the fact that in spite of moderate averages in general on all products taken together, very high tariffs were applied to certain products considered sensitive (footwear, leather goods, textiles, clothing); and tariff escalation–by which in the ascending chain of product expansion (coffee, cocoa, for instance) industrial countries' tariffs increase in line with the degree of processing and value added.

Even in the industrial sectors for which concessions were made (iron and steel, vehicles and transportation materials, machinery), such progress was gradually attenuated by double-edged pressure. On the one hand, concessions were practically eliminated by the arbitrary application of countervailing duties against subsidies (the virtuous indignation with which those who preach free trade from university chairs and editorial offices of English-language publications is directed against industrial subsidies, neglecting agricultural ones) and anti-dumping duties were calculated in an unjustified and absurd manner. On the other hand, pressures were exerted on exporters, so that they could not derive full benefit from concessions, through so-called voluntary export restraints, orderly marketing arrangements and other weapons in the vast arsenal of grey-area measures.

While previous Rounds had been successful in reducing industrial tariffs, sectors capable of mobilizing political support and pressure found in non-tariff measures a frequently more effective substitute to the tariff protection that no longer existed. In addition to the erosion of concessions and norms, there was the tendency of the United States, the initiator and guarantor in the last instance of the multilateral trading system, to resort increasingly to unilateral measures under its own legislation, whose best-known expression is the prolific family of Section 301 legislation (Super 301, Special 301, Regular 301, and others).

That was the disturbing picture which, in full view of world public opinion, eroded and demoralized the GATT machinery, giving to many the impression that it was about to collapse. For the same reason, as argued by representatives of developing countries, the first priority of the negotiations should have been the huge backlog of pending and unresolved issues remaining from previous Rounds. What purpose would it have served, for instance, to add more floors (i.e., new issues) to a building whose foundations were likely to collapse at any moment? Moreover, it would have been difficult to organize adequate negotiations on services, where the lack of concepts and precise data, and the concentration of export capacity in a few countries, would have further increased the imbalance of world trade in favour of developed countries– the very same ones that were opposed to the inclusion of textiles and agriculture. Similarly, the modalities proposed for patents and intellectual property would have frozen the world distribution of comparative advantages by making access to new technologies difficult or excessively expensive. The bans sought by the United States on the use of investment measures aimed at encouraging industrialization (national content requirements) or exports (measures related to export performance) would have had an influence in the same direction.

The positions of the two camps were well defined, each camp having powerful arguments and a different perspective regarding the emphasis and priority that should be accorded to the various issues. It could not be concealed that the level of development was the determining factor that gave the confrontation a clear North-South connotation, in spite of the unwillingness in GATT circles to accept that fact.

2.3. The North-South Dimension of the Negotiations

I remember clearly that this was the perception I had, shortly after my arrival in Geneva in November 1987, at my first "Green Room" meeting, a peculiar consultative process by which the GATT Director-General gathered together some twenty delegations in order to adopt decisions that would be validated by others. It was a frightening experience for the newcomer, alone, without advisers, in an almost English Club atmosphere, where everyone addressed the others by their first name. Despite the codified language, however, it was not difficult to perceive how the dividing line closely followed the development level of the countries the delegates represented.

It is true, as the highly experienced head of delegation of the European Community, Ambassador Paul Tran, recalled, that what makes all the difference is that contractual obligations are negotiated in the GATT, while only declaratory documents are approved in UNCTAD and other United Nations organizations. There would be no place in GATT for the type of negotiations, which used to take place in UNCTAD, where the Group of 77 spoke on behalf of more than 100 countries so diverse that the task could be fulfilled only on the basis of a generic and abstract lowest common denominator. In contrast, when contractual obligations are negotiated concrete interests impose their own logic and cross group borders, undermining internal solidarity and sometimes generating the most unexpected alliances. Such a major difference and such unpredictability however do not mend the rift between developing countries and OECD countries. Developing countries, in spite of their differences regarding particular interests, have many more points in common than views that converge with those of advanced economies. In this regard, notwithstanding the taboo surrounding the term in the GATT, the North-South dimension pervaded all the negotiations, somewhat like sex in Victorian England–ostensibly ignored but nevertheless present everywhere.

The negotiating platforms described in some detail above, which from the outset characterized the two groups, finally determined the development of the Uruguay Round. Their component elements came to be embodied, in various combinations, in the main documents that mark the successive stages of the negotiations. The Punta del Este Declaration of September 1986, for instance, which was a real programme of activities and the constitutional charter of the Round, was the result of a difficult compromise that protected the positions and dominant interests of the two groups, clearly postponing decisions regarding their definitive incorporation into the GATT and the conditions and terms whereby this could be done. The more difficult matter of the new issues was eventually resolved by means of an ingenious formula under which the negotiations on services were to be legally separated from those dealing with goods, following a second path which would nevertheless receive the same administrative support from the GATT Secretariat. Another decision that was postponed was whether to accept negotiations on standards and guidelines in the area of intellectual property, and if such negotiations were accepted, which organization would administer their results.

The Uruguay Round, which emerged from a compromise solution that badly concealed the always latent, difficult to reconcile, conflict of priorities, concepts and interests, never ceased to be a strategic game, with some brief spells of rapid progress interrupted by long periods of calm and critical hours of stagnation, coming close to collapse.

In this difficult game, in which it is rare to discern something that could be considered of collective interest and in which each proposal is negotiated in exchange for something else, the developing countries played an indispensable role in setting up the equation of diverging interests, embodying the impetus for change or assuming the defence of the status quo.

In previous Rounds, such as the Kennedy and Dillon Rounds, devoted basically to industrial tariffs, the game was almost totally dominated by the developed partners–the principal demanders of reductions. It seems that the few developing countries which then were parties to the General Agreement had been confined to the reserve players' bench, while awaiting their turn to go on the field.

This time, however, the less advanced economies were the original source of requests for change: in the textiles area, on their own; in agriculture, through an alliance with the United States and some OECD members (Australia, New Zealand and Canada); in demanding stricter rules on anti-dumping, safeguards and the prohibition of grey-area measures, jointly with other developed countries (the Scandinavian countries and Japan); and on other issues that had remained unresolved since the Tokyo Round, i.e., tariff peaks, tariff escalation and tropical products. It would therefore be totally unjustified to repeat the frequently expressed criticism regarding the passivity of developing countries in the GATT, their alleged propensity to become merely beneficiaries of concessions obtained by third parties (the *free-rider* position), or their alleged tendency to adopt the negative posture of those who know what they do not want but do not know what they want.

A second equally indispensable factor in negotiations was resistance to change. Developing countries displayed this resistance by taking the lead in opposing the new issues, which was a logical and natural attitude to adopt since the demanders in this regard were exclusively the developed countries, the sole ones with relevant interests in this area. In this case also, the contribution of the less advanced countries was valuable and irreplaceable in pressing for more precise definitions and more reliable statistical data with regard to services, and for a better differentiation between rules on intellectual property and investment measures on the one hand and their possible distorting effects on international trade on the other. The new issues negotiations eventually became a truly educative process for the negotiators, with surely more balanced results than those that would have been produced by passive acceptance of the initial proposals.

Developing countries were among the main proponents of the *single undertaking* provision in paragraph B (ii) of the Punta del Este Declaration. The Latin American members of the Cairns Group, in particular, wished to pre-empt a recurrence of the situation in earlier multilateral rounds where the initiatives to liberalize the agriculture sector had simply been permitted to die during the course of the negotiations.

However, during the period between the Montreal and Brussels Ministerial meetings, the concept of *single undertaking* was altered, mainly at the initiative of the EC and Canada, but with ideas coming from the GATT Secretariat. They recognized that the multilateral trade agreements would considerably modify and increase multilateral obligations, but they also sought to repair the fragmentation of the multilateral system caused by the optional Code results of the Tokyo Round. In order to avoid the impossible task of amending the GATT Articles, it was proposed to incorporate the results of the Uruguay Round in a totally new instrument which would involve the establishment of a new institution to replace the GATT, designated the Multilateral Trade Organization by its proponents at the time.

Their approach was that those countries prepared to accept the results of the Uruguay Round would withdraw from GATT and join the new organization; those developing countries not prepared to so subscribe would remain contracting parties to a de facto defunct agreement. It was also clear to developing countries that if they remained outside the new organization they would have no means of defending themselves against Section 301 action, particularly Special 301 on intellectual property.

When the concept of *single undertaking* was agreed at Punta del Este, there was no thought of setting up a new institution (at least no government had suggested that such an outcome could emerge from the Round) nor were developing countries aware of the real intentions of the developed countries in the TRIPS negotiations.

3. The Contribution of Developing Countries

Highlighting the contribution of developing countries, which is the subject of these comments, is not intended to deny or undervalue the contribution of others, to reduce the complex web of negotiations to a simplistic North-South opposition or thus to distort a reality where the logic of interests does not always coincide with previously established categories. In fact, on questions vital to the success of the negotiations, such as agriculture, or certain aspects regarding services (audio-visual, maritime) and even intellectual property, the clash was often between the United States and the European Community, and occasionally with Japan or other developed economies. On the other hand, in what may be termed the more traditional aspect of the Round, i.e., the tariff negotiations, the almost arithmetical bilateral collation of gains and losses was predominant. The incidence of the issue of development level in the negotiations was reduced to questions of more systemic interest such as the improvement of rules regarding settlement of trade disputes or the setting up of a mechanism for the periodic examination of governments' trade policies and practices. In other instances, as already seen with regard to intellectual property, or as happened at the discussions on new arrangements to invoke the measures provided for in Article XVIII(B) regarding possible balance-of-payments difficulties, the development problem was very much the focus of the debate.

Developing countries' action during the Round was not limited to individual action by delegations, some of which were prominent in taking the initiative of presenting texts that became the basis for final drafting, nor was it insufficient, those countries' delegates having earned general respect through the balance and solidity of their convictions and the technical knowledge upon which these were founded. The high quality of the delegates was also manifest in the leadership of the negotiating groups, the setting up of alliances with developed countries on specific matters, and the collective action of the Informal Group of Developing Countries.

3.1. The Groups' Chairmanships

To ensure the balanced conduct of the negotiations from the outset, the chairmanships of half of the fifteen negotiating groups in the first phase (until the Brussels meeting) were entrusted to experienced representatives from the Informal Group. Among these, it is fair to single out those who, having remained chairmen of negotiating groups even when these were restructured and reduced in number after the Brussels meeting, were still able to make very valuable contributions during the final phase. They were experienced specialists in GATT matters: Ambassador George Alvares Maciel of Brazil, in the field of safeguards and rules in general; Ambassador Julio Lacarte Muró of Uruguay, in the field of dispute settlement and systemic issues; and Ambassador Felipe Jaramillo of Colombia, in the field of services. All three had been chairmen of the Council of Representatives and of the Contracting Parties.

3.2. The Negotiating Coalitions (Cairns Group)

Possibly the modality of action that contributed most in imparting a multiplier effect to the originally limited influence of the developing countries was the setting up of coalitions with industrialized countries with related interests. Some of these, such as the so-called Hôtel de la Paix Group, in the initial phase, which brought together the *moderates* and dealt with tariffs and correlated issues, had little visible impact. Others, which did not end in alliances, were nothing but attempts, especially by the European Community but in some cases at the initiative of other countries, to gather together informally a small group of important delegations with a view to influencing the development of the negotiations and exploring the boundaries of official positions. Nevertheless, some of them succeeded in playing a useful part in channelling controversial and intricate technical questions, such as anti-dumping, safeguards, technical barriers to trade, and services.

The most notable and influential of all the coalitions was the one formed by Australia with exporters of agricultural products, named after the Australian city where its first meeting took place. The Cairns Group was very diversified, even heterogeneous in its composition, and it is surprising that it kept its unity, for which flexibility and mutual tolerance were constantly needed. On the one side there were the former Dominions, of Anglo-Saxon culture, two of which–Australia and New Zealand–were clearly committed to agricultural liberalization, and a third one–Canada–which had a more ambiguous position because of its own difficulties with tariffication and domestic provincial problems. On the other side were five Latin American countries (Argentina, Brazil, Chile, Colombia and Uruguay), the Argentinians being without any doubt the most interested in these negotiations which were vital for them. In the middle were the Asian countries, almost all members of the Association of South East Asian Nations (ASEAN)– Malaysia, Thailand and the Philippines (plus Fiji) with their characteristic Confucian pragmatism and more diversified export interests. On its own was Hungary, which was communist at the beginning of the Group's existence and in an increasingly uncomfortable position as the negotiations progressed because of its application to join the European Community. In spite of these considerable differences in development levels and interests, the Cairns Group acted throughout the Round as a sort of agricultural conscience of the negotiations and as a barrier against the temptation always present among developed countries to give in to the Europeans and, as was done in the Tokyo Round, to postpone once more the reform of agricultural trade in exchange for advantages in industrial products and new issues. Australian leadership greatly contributed to the relative success of the Cairns Group, as it was not only well prepared and competent from a technical point of view, but also constantly willing to commit itself at the highest ministerial level. However, as was observed at critical moments in the negotiations, there were limits to the readiness of developed country members of the Group to venture to propose extreme measures disapproved of by their OECD partners.

3.3. The Informal Group of Developing Countries

The Informal Group of Developing Countries (so called to differentiate it from the official and institutionalized Group of 77 in UNCTAD and other United Nations organizations) could obviously not develop the same type of action directed towards specific subjects dealt with by its members individually or as parties to the negotiating coalitions. I assumed the coordination of the Informal Group at the beginning of 1989, shortly after the Montreal deadlock, replacing Ambassador S. P. Shukla of India who was unanimously admired for his broad and solid technical knowledge, the logical clarity of his arguments and, above all, the integrity of his ascetic nature, whose almost spiritual radiance imparted a sense of elevation and seriousness to the debates.

I then realized how delicate the task was of seeking the elusive point of equilibrium among countries with great disparities in levels of development. At one extreme was Hong Kong, generally represented by competent British civil servants of the colonial government, a bastion of free trade, heavily engaged in textile trade liberalization and the disciplining of anti-dumping measures, but perceived by others as a sort of Trojan horse because of its dangerous affinity with developed countries regarding the new issues. Inevitably, in moments of irritation, there were suggestions that it be expelled from the Group. At the other extreme were the remaining Group of Ten countries: India, Brazil, Yugoslavia, Egypt, Cuba, Nicaragua and Nigeria. Occupying an intermediate position were Singapore, Malaysia, Thailand and the Republic of Korea, always cautious and pragmatic. China, still inhibited by the unfinished process of accession to the

GATT, was generally a silent but assiduous associate. Argentina and Uruguay gave priority to agriculture; Colombia, to tropical products; and Pakistan, to textiles. Chile, for its part, was active though moderate and objective in its interest in diversified exports. Africans were, in general, more interested in a few subjects closely related to their limited foreign trade: tropical products, fears of the erosion of their preferences under the Lomé Convention, and trade in toxic products. Bangladesh was outstanding as the lonely champion of the least developed countries, while others silently engaged in learning the negotiation process.

Such diversity led only to the adoption of a position based on generalities, so as to avoid encroaching upon individual interests and to attempt to translate for all the unified common denominator: the Group's platform in the Punta del Este Declaration, the defence of multilateralism and the principle of special and differential treatment for developing countries. Nevertheless, the role of the Group was no less useful in expressing, in clear and concise terms, the concerns of its members during the crucial phases of the Round and as a forum in which the small delegations could put forward their views and receive information, these delegations being normally excluded from the *Green Room* meetings and from restricted negotiations. At times of intense stress, uncertainty and contradictory rumours, we held daily Group meetings; for example at the time of the Trade Negotiations Committee meeting in April 1989, which made it possible to break the Montreal deadlock and resume negotiations, and during the Brussels meeting in December 1990 when the negotiations almost entirely collapsed. On many occasions we benefitted from the enlightening participation of GATT's Director-General, Arthur Dunkel, who showed constant interest and receptivity with regard to the developing countries' wish to be accepted as active and respected partners in the Round.

The relations between the Informal Group and the Director-General were not always without some sense of irony, as I had occasion to point out, for instance, some days after the dramatic interruption of the Montreal meeting, speaking at a meeting of the Contracting Parties in Geneva. Referring to the false options that had been presented to us, principally in matters of intellectual property, I recalled the episode in which Calonne, the Finance Minister of Louis XVI on the eve of the Revolution, forced the aristocracy to comply with the unpleasant duty of paying taxes. In a contemporary cartoon, the minister, represented as a monkey dressed as a head chef, addresses the nobility, portrayed as hens, ducks and turkeys:

Calonne: *My dear friends, I have gathered you together in order to know the sauce you want to be eaten with.*
Reply: *But we do not want to be eaten at all.*
Calonne: *Do not depart from the subject ...*

The Director-General, whose patience was always put to the test but who never lost his, perhaps forgave me for taking such liberty.

4. The Two Moments of Truth

During the interminable years of its extension, the Uruguay Round had ups and downs and periods of hope and disenchantment. Its hour of truth, however, coinciding with the climax of the resolute action by developing countries (or at least some of them) occurred first at the Montreal meeting in December 1988, and was surprisingly repeated in a very similar manner exactly two years later, in December 1990 at the Brussels meeting, which was meant to be the culmination of the negotiations.

On both occasions there was little imagination as regards the scenario. Agriculture was always the bone of contention. In the face of the European Community's refusal to accept minimal satisfactory results in the agricultural negotiations, the dilemma was clear: to accept anything, concealing the failure, or to have the courage to refuse the consensus in order to make progress in other areas, which was equivalent to a real veto–a frequently mentioned but never used taboo instrument in the GATT Rounds.

In both cases it was left to a handful of Latin American members of the Cairns Group to take the necessary step and to say loudly that the king was naked. This conclusion was arrived at not by election but by exclusion. Since it was evident at the Montreal meeting that there would be no agreement on the agricultural issue, we tried from the outset to secure resistance from the Cairns Group, which clashed with the Anglo-Saxon refusal (although some New Zealanders and a few Australians later confessed in private their regret for not having lent us their support). We then turned to the Latin American and Caribbean Group, where Mexico and Jamaica showed later that they were neither disposed to adopt an extreme measure nor interested in doing so. It was thus by elimination that the core of the group of five was formed: Argentina, unquestionably the first to indicate that there would not be consensus if agriculture were excluded, as well as Brazil, Chile, Colombia and Uruguay.

It was not true, despite what was reported in the press, that the Americans were behind this move or that they were informed of it or even interested in its success. The truth being that at the beginning US Trade Representative Clayton Yeutter, who was engaged in capitalizing on progress being made on the new issues and other areas, reacted to the Latin American initiative with irritation and impatience. Moreover, the general incredulity gave way to resignation only after exhausting hours of pressure and exhortation, which prolonged the "Green Room" meeting of ministers and heads of delegation in Montreal until dawn. The deadlock was broken at a small informal meeting held by the Director-General with representatives of a handful of countries (the United States, the EC countries, Canada, Australia, Brazil and India), where agreement was reached on the conditions of an accord which made acceptance of progress achieved in eleven sectors subject to resolving the remaining difficulties by April of the following year, in the areas of agriculture, textiles, intellectual property and safeguards.

With only changes regarding details and personalities, the same scenario occurred in Brussels, clearly with much more worrying consequences since this time the Round was scheduled to be concluded. In spite of the impact caused by that second fiasco, the agreements reached in Geneva were gradually taken up again. The scheme of negotiation was reorganized by reducing the number of groups and replacing some chairmen, and the path that would lead, one year after Brussels, to the Draft Final Act presented by Arthur Dunkel–the basis of the final agreement of 15 December 1993–was gradually smoothed out.

Today, there is a practically unanimous view in the WTO (GATT's successor) and in world-trade-related circles that the episodes at Montreal and Brussels saved the Uruguay Round and the multilateral system from the worst of failures: a fraudulent *success*, distorted by a new sacrifice of the ever postponed expectations of agricultural and textile trade liberalization. Until recently, just before the final *goal*, it was not unusual to hear advice in the United States that the Clinton Administration follow the path of the Carter Administration in Tokyo and please the Europeans at the expense of agriculture. Moreover, the problem is not limited to agricultural trade and to issues of traditional interest to developing countries. As is increasingly recognized in Geneva, even as regards services and other new issues, the extension of the negotiations made it possible to avoid mistakes and guaranteed a relatively less unbalanced result.

The success of the action undertaken by the five Latin American members of the Cairns Group was due to particular circumstances that may be difficult to reproduce. The first factor that made the move possible was obviously the split between the dominant poles of world trade: the European Community on the one hand, and the United States on the other. The latter, which was the sponsor of the original proposal to remove all agricultural subsidies and barriers (Reagan's *zero option* for the year 2000), could not, for fear of external demoralization and domestic problems with the American Farm Bureau, abandon the Cairns Group's Latin Americans and cease to show solidarity with an action whose inspiration lay in the refusal to capitulate in the agricultural negotiations. Secondly, it was essential to have behind the five Latin American countries, the Cairns Group, a broad coalition of industrialized and developing countries held together by a common cause with an indisputable moral weight, namely the inclusion of agricultural trade in the GATT. The third reason was that the Latin American decision was legitimated by its perfect consonance with the culture of an organization founded on the belief in free trade in all goods as far as possible. This makes a veto based on the demand for the integration of a sector more easily acceptable than a veto to deny such integration: it places the onus of justifying opposition to liberalization squarely on the shoulders of the other parties.

5. A Preliminary Balance Sheet

This is not the appropriate place to present a systematic evaluation of the results of the Uruguay Round, because of the short time that has elapsed since its official conclusion. Nor do I have at my disposal the technical means to undertake an examination of this kind.[1]

Concluding formally the negotiations at the meeting of the Trade Negotiations Committee on 15 December 1993, the new Director-General, Peter Sutherland, uttered with a three-year delay the words anxiously expected by the negotiators weary of fighting so many battles: *With this strike of the gavel, I consider the Uruguay Round concluded.*

At the same meeting, the representative of Malaysia, who was the coordinator of the Informal Group, speaking on behalf of the Group, enumerated the following aspects as the main shortcomings of the Round.

- The lack of commitment on the part of the major trading partners with regard to the principle of special and differential treatment for developing countries;
- The weakness of the results regarding market access, particularly for textiles, tropical products and fisheries;
- The insufficient consideration given to developing countries' interests in agriculture;
- The reduction of sectoral coverage in services.

Notwithstanding these shortcomings, the Group's spokesman and representatives of nearly forty delegations who made statements on that occasion recognized that the results of the Round were generally acceptable, though not entirely satisfactory from the perspective of each of them.

In evaluations made so far, it is emphasized that the multilateral system will emerge considerably strengthened by the creation of the World Trade Organization, the improvement of rules on safeguards, anti-dumping, subsidies and technical barriers to trade, the dispute settlement mechanism and the institutional aspects of the functioning of the system, as well as the process of progressive integration of agricultural, textiles and services trade.

In the end, the results of the Uruguay Round were much less satisfactory than had initially been expected (it is enough to compare the original proposals in agriculture with what was eventually achieved with much difficulty). Nevertheless, the results were reasonable by themselves and especially in terms of strengthening the multilateral trading system. It would be hard to exaggerate the disastrous effect a collapse of the negotiations would have had on an already weakened system.

I was not surprised by the outcome, because it had always been clear to me that the major trading partners could not afford to cause the failure of negotiations from which they would derive the greatest advantages, as regards not only the new issues but also the traditional ones. Even at moments of uncertainty and pessimism, I had the opportunity in Geneva to publicly declare that a failure of the

---

[1] Interested readers may consult the following documents: *An Analysis of the Proposed Uruguay Round Agreement, with Particular Emphasis on Aspects of Interest to Developing Economies.* GATT Secretariat, MTN.TNC/W/122, MTN.GNG/W/30, 29 November 1993; *Proyecto de evaluación de los resultados finales de la Ronda Uruguay de Negociaciones Comerciales Multilaterales a la luz de los intereses de América Latina y el Caribe.* PNUD/UNCTAD/CEPAL/OES/SELA/BID, Latin Trade; World Bank (1994), *The Uruguay Round: A Preliminary Assessment.* World Bank, Washington DC

Round would go against the sense of history, the sense of a growing systemic convergence and of the unification of markets at the global level, made possible by the disappearance of *real socialism* and by the integration of its former practitioners into the Bretton Woods institutions.

Nor was it surprising that during the final stage, the disputes between major industrialized partners were the main reasons for the delay in the conclusion of the Round and the weakening of the final results as regards not only agricultural, textile and anti-dumping matters, but also even the new issues (remember, for instance, what happened in services). It was merely a repetition of what occurred during the Tokyo Round and became chronic afterwards: the disputes, quarrels and threats involving the United States, the European Community and Japan.

It was thus fully demonstrated that developing countries could not, as was claimed before and after the controversy surrounding the initiation of the Round, be held responsible for an eventual collapse of the negotiations and the system, not even with regard to the new issues, which, albeit unwillingly, they accepted in the end.

The truth is that during the early years of the Uruguay Round a tendency became evident towards an alarming disagreement between the major trading partners and the developing countries over the fundamental issue of multilateralism. At the very moment the latter countries were finally being converted to the virtues of liberalization (even unilateral) and of the multilateral system, the former seemed to increasingly apostatize from the faith which for years they had preached to developing countries.

These words should not be taken as a sign of sectarianism. It was not long ago that the OECD's chief economist himself recalled in an interview that unlike more than forty developing countries committed to unilateral liberalization programmes, only four members of his organization had reached the end of the 1980s with trade regimes that were more liberal than at the beginning of the decade–Japan, Australia, New Zealand and Turkey.

The Uruguay Round was originally proposed at the beginning of the 1980s, a time when most of the industrialized economies were just starting to emerge from the corrective recession following the oil crisis. At present, developed countries, with the exception of the United States (as in the 1980s), are still faced with sluggish growth of their economies and high unemployment rates, factors that generally do not augur well for trade liberalization.

5.1. Results of the Uruguay Round

As a consequence of the Uruguay Round, new export opportunities will arise for all countries, including developing countries. The outcome of the Uruguay Round significantly strengthens the multilateral trading system in a variety of ways. The main achievement has been to address those areas and sectors where the absence of international consensus and workable rules had resulted in mounting trade tensions undermining confidence in the system (agreements on safeguards, subsidies, anti-dumping duties, agriculture, and textiles and clothing). This has made market access more secure, transparent and predictable. At the same time the obligations contained in the multilateral trade agreements (MTAs) are intrusive in that they imposed disciplines over areas of economic policy previously regarded as belonging to the domestic domain. Another major result has been the extension of multilateral disciplines to intellectual property and trade in services (banking and investment, professional services, telecommunications). At the same time, significant tariff cuts and a marked increase in the coverage of tariff bindings have been achieved (including a notable increase in the proportion of imports enjoying duty-free treatment in major markets), virtually all non-tariff barriers have been brought under tighter disciplines and the momentum of trade liberalization has been maintained. Moreover, the dramatic extent of tariff reduction and binding in developing countries provides new opportunities for their mutual trade as well as for exporters in the developed world.

The multilateral rights and obligations of all countries have been increased to broadly comparable levels (all countries will have the same level of multilateral obligations by the year 2000), with differential and more favourable treatment for developing countries being delineated in a more specific, contractual manner. Another area of potential benefit for developing countries is increased transparency and stability in trade regimes, including their own; this increases efficiency, helps lock in economic reforms and enhances their ability to benefit from market access and attract foreign direct investment. Finally, the various agreements have been linked together within the formal institutional framework of the WTO through a common and much improved system for the settlement of disputes. It should be noted that the WTO dispute settlement mechanism has been used successfully by developing countries.

This positive assessment, however, is tempered by a number of caveats. First, special safeguard mechanisms and other *exceptional* provisions contained in key agreements (such as those on safeguards, agriculture and textiles) could lessen the liberalizing impact of the agreements, and might lend themselves to abuse if not kept under close surveillance. Second, tariff reductions on key products of export interest to developing countries–such as non-tropical agricultural products, textiles and clothing, fish and fish products, leather and footwear–have been considerably below the norm. Third, the least developed and other poorer developing countries have suffered from the erosion of preferential margins under the Generalized System of Preferences and the Lomé Convention, and may face higher prices for imported foodstuffs and an increase in the cost of foreign technology. At the same time, they are required to accept more stringent obligations and a considerable administrative burden. The TRIPS and Customs Valuation Agreements seem to impose the most onerous obligations in this respect, particularly on the least developed countries.

It should be noted that the enhanced opportunities will not occur at once. Trade liberalization in many areas is to be implemented in stages: equal reductions over five years for industrial tariffs, beginning in January 1995; a phase-out over 10 years of the quotas imposed under the Multi-Fibre Arrangement; tariffication of various non-tariff measures affecting agricultural trade, and the reduction of these and other agricultural tariffs over six years; and improved market access for a range of service activities that was agreed to in the Uruguay Round and included in the schedules of commitments containing important limitations, which will be progressively liberalized through subsequent negotiations. Continuation of sectoral services negotiations yielded major results in financial and basic telecommunications services, but a more modest outcome in areas of interest to developing countries. Commitments regarding the mode of supply of natural persons, which is of particular interest to developing countries, are of a very limited nature and contain major qualifications, notably economic needs tests. Particular attention needs to be devoted to the preparation of a positive agenda for the next comprehensive round of negotiations on all services sectors and modes of supply.

It is evident that many developing countries have difficulties in meeting their obligations, including with respect to their enforcement and the procedural requirements. There are more than 240 notification requirements under the WTO agreements. Despite the difficulties in the review of notifications, attempts have been made to impose further obligations in this area. Moreover, while much attention has been devoted to the improvement of compliance with the various notification requirements, less consideration has been given to the implementation of substantive commitments.

5.2. Ensuring Effective Implementation of WTO Agreements

The credibility of future efforts at liberalization will depend to a large extent on the experience with the implementation of the results of the Uruguay Round. The process of implementation requires close monitoring, particularly with respect to the implementation of market access commitments concerning reduction of tariffs and elimination of non-tariff measures; bringing contingency trade protection measures into compliance with the relevant WTO agreements; phasing out restrictions under the Multi-Fibre Arrangement and integrating the textiles sector into the GATT; implementation of the provisions of the Agriculture Agreement; implementing all the provisions relating to developing countries in the Agreements on Technical Barriers to Trade and Sanitary and Phytosanitary Measures in a manner which ensures that these agreements would not unjustifiably limit the types of products that could be imported and would not be used as disguised protectionism; and making GATS Article IV obligations operational in respect of increasing developing countries' participation in trade in services by effectively liberalizing market access in sectors and modes of supply of export interest to them and providing them with access to technology and market information.

Future negotiations will have to take into account some of the unsatisfactory aspects of the Uruguay Round results. These include less than average tariff reductions achieved for many products of particular export interest to developing countries; persistent tariff peaks and tariff escalation in a number of sectors of interest to developing countries; prohibitively high tariff rates for several of the agricultural products subject to tariffication, and a lack of clarity and transparency in the tariff quota allocation mechanism and procedures in the importing countries, which makes it difficult for exporters to assess opportunities; lack of appropriate multilateral disciplines on preferential rules of origin where the propensity to use them for protectionist purposes is particularly pronounced; and the application of special rules of origin for the implementation of anti-circumvention measures, which is aimed at preventing alleged evasions of anti-dumping duties.

A major area of concern for developing countries is the implementation of the integration programme under the Agreement on Textiles and Clothing (ATC). The first phase of integration has been very disappointing mainly because of the end loading feature of the integration process, frequent resort to the transitional safeguard mechanism, the lack of effectiveness of the Textiles Monitoring Body, the implication of regional integration and special arrangements, as well as matters related to the application of rules of origin in the area of textiles and clothing. Moreover, although the targets set by the ATC for product inclusion in the first and second integration stages have been met in volume terms as required, their value equivalents are well below the targets set.

The removal or reduction of traditional trade barriers such as tariffs and quantitative restrictions has led to more use being made of contingency protection measures, particularly anti-dumping measures. Such measures are becoming the main mechanism for protective action in developed and some developing countries. In 1995-96, 147 anti-dumping actions were initiated by United States, the European Union, Canada, Australia and New Zealand, and nearly 600 definitive anti-dumping duties were in force in those countries at the end of 1996. The sectors targeted by new proceedings in 1995-96 were food items, chemical products, iron and steel, non-ferrous metals, machinery and transport equipment, textiles and clothing, and other manufactured goods.[2]

6. Integration of Developing Countries into the Global Economy

The economic and institutional integration of developing countries is a major challenge for international cooperation. To foster such integration, concrete economic and social policy measures are required to promote competitiveness, stimulate investment, develop human capital and facilitate the exploitation of the trading opportunities resulting from the Uruguay Round agreements. Measures also need to be taken to strengthen the effective participation of developing countries in the multilateral trading system as it has emerged from the Round and to minimize the risks of new imbalances and instabilities, including in international financial markets, and the potential marginalization of the least developed countries and other weaker economies. The integration of developing countries into the world economy and trading system to ensure equitable and sustainable development must be seen as an inherent component of future trade initiatives.

At UNCTAD IX the international community recognized that UNCTAD's main role in the field of trade in goods and services should be to help maximize the positive impact of globalization and liberalization on sustainable development by assisting in the effective integration of developing countries into the international

---

[2] UNCTAD Document TD/B/COM.1/13 of 2 September 1997, para 14

trading system. As mentioned in our joint study with the WTO,[3] the degree of a country's integration within the international trading system can be seen in relation to its ability to (a) identify and take advantage of trading opportunities, (b) meet its multilateral trade obligations, (c) formulate and pursue development strategies within the framework of those obligations, (d) defend its acquired trade rights, and (e) set trade objectives and effectively pursue them in trade negotiations. Meeting these challenges effectively will require a substantial strengthening of institutions and human and financial resources in developing countries and countries in transition.

Integration of developing countries is also an issue of special interest to the developed countries. The gains to industrial countries from increased trade integration with developing countries are potentially larger than the gains from additional integration among themselves. Trade integration arising from the ongoing liberalization process and from its extension to new areas such as services is likely to generate dynamic gains from increased market size, competition and technology transfer. Since developing countries are forecast to grow about twice as fast as industrial countries, and as countries in transition develop stronger supply capacities and become more competitive internationally, the dynamic gains from increasing trade with them are likely to be especially important.[4]

The realization of these gains will depend on the extent to which the adjustments required by the process of integration are carried out. International trade can only fulfil its potential as an engine of global economic growth if the necessary reallocation of resources in line with countries' different and changing comparative advantage is allowed to take place, and if the inevitable frictions and protectionist pressures that will arise in implementing appropriate structural adjustment policies are resisted.

6.1. Improving Export Opportunities and Trade Policy Constraints

The process of globalization and liberalization could entail risks of instability and marginalization for weaker economies. Not all developing countries are equally successful in benefitting from improved market access. Over 80 per cent of the total exports of developing countries are accounted for by just 15 countries. The most important challenge for the international community is to remedy this divergent performance, which is due to internal problems, particularly supply-side constraints, as well as to the external economic environment. For developed countries, integration with developing countries would entail adjustment costs, for example, shutting down sunset industries.

Least developed countries will face a considerable challenge since they lack a highly diversified export structure to take advantage of improved market access conditions for products in non-traditional markets and will be affected by the erosion of preferential margins which gave them a potential competitive edge.

---

[3] *Strengthening the Participation of Developing Countries in World Trade and the Multilateral Trading System.* (December 1996), TD/375/Rev.1

[4] World Trade Organization (1997), *Annual Report. Volume 1.* Geneva, Switzerland, pp 2-3

However, the development of the regional market, maintaining and improving preferential access where there is scope to do so, and the faithful implementation of the Ministerial Decision on measures in favour of the least developed countries agreed in the Uruguay Round should provide a springboard for these countries to compete on the world market. With regard to the problem of dealing with the transitional costs of adjustment to the post-Uruguay Round trading environment, African and other least developed and net food-importing countries should benefit from a safety net for this purpose, including supportive measures for raising the level of competitiveness and export capacity to ensure that these countries derive concrete benefits from trading opportunities resulting from the Round.

The market access improvements arising from the Uruguay Round will increase the trading opportunities for developing countries in a number of products, particularly in non-traditional markets. However, in order to realize the full potential of trade it will be necessary to overcome the problems resulting from the low diversification of production, inadequate and inefficient telecommunications, storage and road, rail and/or air transport facilities limiting the scope of supply-side response, the need for introduction and integration into production structures of new technologies and skills, and factors inhibiting intraregional investment flows.

One issue that will have to be confronted is the impact of increased multilateral disciplines on the development process. There is considerable concern in many developing countries that the WTO has reduced policy options to the extent that the possibility of emulating the successful development strategies of other countries, notably the East Asian countries, will be diminished. On the other hand, it is recognized that these strategies were carried out in a different world, and may not be entirely adapted to the globalization process. In fact, developing countries accepted greater disciplines in the Uruguay Round in return for greater security of access to Northern markets.

The post-Uruguay Round multilateral trading system forces developing countries to rethink their development strategies and industrial and export policies. Many targeted policy measures will cease to be available to policy makers. Measures such as investment and export subsidies for specific industries or enterprises, domestic-content rules and export-balancing provisions will have to be phased out, and the setting of conditions for fostering the transfer and application of patented technologies will become more stringent. The developing countries will be obliged to shift to more general and broad-based policies in conformity with MTAs. Thus the strengthening of supply capabilities will have to be achieved much more through economy-wide approaches towards promoting savings and investment, research and technological development, a high level of small and medium-size enterprises, regional development and the building of a modern physical infrastructure. Trade policy reforms and trade liberalization have to be further pursued in order to help improve resource allocation and competitiveness, although they would need to be linked more effectively to policies that cushion the social cost of the reform process and provide a safety net for vulnerable groups.

Such a policy shift may prove to be much more difficult for less advanced developing countries. Their comparatively lower level of development may require more coercive and targeted government policies to overcome supply-side constraints, diversify production and trade, and expand exports. Therefore, most developing countries and particularly the least developed amongst them will continue to face the need to promote new industries with more focused measures such as above-average tariffs and investment incentives for a transitional period necessary to overcome start-up difficulties, acquire the capability to compete with foreign suppliers, undertake investments in export capacities and gain a foothold in foreign markets. While the MTAs make time available to developing countries, and in particular to least developed countries, to adjust their policies to the new multilateral framework, the phase-out periods (for example in the area of subsidies and TRIPS) may not be sufficiently long for individual developing countries to reach a satisfactory stage of development that would facilitate the termination of more specific and targeted support policies.

Given all the above-mentioned constraints on national policies, concrete international action, including the possible extension of phase-out periods and financial assistance to remedy supply-side constraints (such as production and export structures concentrating on only a few products, poor financial and human capital endowment, weak technological capacity, inadequate legal and regulatory frameworks, and bottlenecks in physical infrastructure), is therefore needed to integrate developing countries into the international trading system and to equip them with the necessary economic and institutional tools.

6.2. Capacity-building

The strengthening of human resource capacity and of institutional support for trade becomes an imperative if developing countries are to cope with complex multilateral trade agreements whose scope increasingly tends to encompass areas traditionally regarded as the exclusive domain of autonomous national policy-making. Increasing requirements for transparency in domestic trade and economic policies in such a situation would imply organized, systematic reporting structures and management practices that are not yet in place in many countries. The Singapore Ministerial Conference confirmed that the WTO might become a forum for continuous negotiations. The skills required to manage continuous trade negotiations and to analyse complex technical information and data would need to be strengthened in many countries. Therefore, substantial efforts will be needed to identify their trading opportunities and to enable them to take full advantage of such opportunities, to strengthen institutions for trade policy formulation, coordination and implementation in order to build negotiating capacities for effective participation in multilateral, regional and bilateral trade negotiations, to adapt domestic trade legislation to the new trading system and to provide those countries with access to trade information. In this regard, UNCTAD's long tradition of and expertise in providing technical cooperation to developing countries in the trade field as well as in other areas will be invaluable.

It should be borne in mind that while the multilateral agreements provide the framework for the conduct of trade relations, it is the national (or community) implementing legislation and regulations and administrative procedures with which exporters will actually be confronted. The ability of countries to successfully manage the transition to the new trading environment emerging from the Round will not only depend on domestic actions taken by governments to implement the results and the external assistance they obtain to support them in this process. Equally critical will be the extent to which governments create the conditions necessary for maximizing the opportunities of exporters in foreign markets. Consequently, governments will need to pay growing attention in particular to creating a domestic policy environment which strengthens the ability of private firms to compete in international markets. It follows, therefore, that the private sector should increasingly be engaged in the process of external trade policy formulation.

In preparing for trade negotiations, advanced industrialized countries mobilize considerable resources to identify negotiating objectives, analyse the positions of their trading partners and form a national consensus. This process draws heavily on the experience of the private sector and on studies undertaken by government or research institutes, and is tailored to the needs of the industry. Questionnaires are sent to enterprises, including transnational corporations with global operations, trade associations and chambers of commerce, to obtain an inventory of constraints on access to markets. Trade officials abroad verify the responses received, taking into account the consistency of such measures with MTAs. In some countries, information on barriers affecting their trade and investment is continually updated and published at regular intervals. The OECD also provides a forum for the refinement and coordination of developed country positions.

In this respect, developing countries find themselves at a disadvantage. The capacity of their private sector to provide useful information is limited, in particular because most enterprises are not exclusively involved in global operations. As a result, the private sector often lacks well-informed perceptions of both market access conditions and its own relative competitive strength in international trade, particularly in the area of services.

7. Unfinished Business and New Challenges

The MTAs contain an impressive built-in agenda, including specific provision for new negotiations, notably on agriculture and services, and recommendations for improvements in the rules or the review of the operation of the agreements, and new issues have been indicated for future consideration, such as investment and competition policy under the TRIMs Agreement. This agenda thus provides the framework for addressing most of what are now being termed *new issues*. It is scheduled to begin before the year 2000. The experience in the implementation of the agreements will indicate more clearly the objectives behind future trade intentions.

One might have thought that WTO Members had their hands full with implementing MTAs and preparing for the built-in agenda. However, there have been a number of largely unexpected developments since the Marrakesh Ministerial Meeting, which have important implications for the future development of the multilateral trading system and for the role of developing countries within that system.

First, the developing countries have made full and successful use of the dispute settlement mechanism. Dispute settlement has become the major business of the WTO. Of the 96 cases brought before the Dispute Settlement Body since the WTO began to function, developing countries have been complainants in 21 cases and made a total number of 31 requests for consultations. It is notable that the first dispute resolved by the WTO was in favour of two developing countries–Venezuela and Brazil–against the United States. However, one must not underestimate the major technical constraints developing countries face when using the dispute settlement mechanism (for example meeting the deadlines set for each stage of the dispute settlement procedure) and financial constraints (for example obtaining legal assistance at reasonable cost).

Second, more unexpectedly, the first biennial Ministerial Conference, unlike the annual sessions of the GATT Contracting Parties, took the form of a negotiating session rather than a stock-taking exercise. The developing countries would have preferred the latter approach, but the major developed countries saw the Singapore Ministerial Conference, held in December 1996, as an opportunity to pursue outstanding issues on their negotiating agenda. Their first objective was to incorporate into the future work programme of the WTO certain new issues which they had unsuccessfully attempted to include in the work programme in Marrakesh. These included labour rights, which had been the most controversial issue at Marrakesh and remained so at the Singapore Conference, as well as investment and competition policy (which was to be dealt with in any case under the TRIMs Agreement). To this were added the less sensitive subjects of government procurement and trade facilitation.

The preparation of the draft Singapore Declaration was the subject of intense negotiation in Geneva from early September 1996 until the meeting in mid-December. Developing countries made considerable efforts to avoid any reference in the text to labour rights and, to a lesser extent, to investment, while striving for commitments to accelerate work on certain elements of the built-in agenda in areas of interest to them, such as agriculture. However, the final text that emerged in Singapore differed little from the original working draft submitted by Mr. Ruggiero at the beginning of the exercise.

In parallel to these tortuous negotiations under way in Geneva, the Quad countries were working out an agreement to liberalize trade in information technology products among themselves, and this was subsequently introduced into the APEC context where it received the support of a number of developing countries with an obvious export interest in this sector. This agreement, already *pre-cooked*, was brought to Singapore for negotiation to secure the acceptance by an additional number of countries with the aim of gathering a critical mass to justify its entry into force.

I attended the Singapore Ministerial Conference in my capacity as Secretary-General of UNCTAD, and was struck by the fact that the representatives of Canada, the European Union and the United States, who addressed the Conference early during the first morning session, stressed that in their view the Information Technology Agreement (ITA) would be the major issue before the meeting even though this agreement had not been discussed in the Geneva preparatory process. At the end of the Conference, the conclusion of the ITA and the decisions to pursue negotiations to liberalize the basic telecommunications and financial service sectors were presented as the main elements of the success of the Conference.

This package–liberalization of the flow of information, money and the equipment necessary to ensure its transmission–has been presented as a dramatic step towards promoting globalization and enabling all countries to derive benefits. It further enhanced the contribution that the Uruguay Round had made to the globalization process, notably through the elimination of tariffs in many industrial sectors and through the GATS and TRIPS Agreements.

It is clear that the practice of working out the rules, principles and details of trade agreements among like-minded countries, to be brought subsequently to the multilateral forum, and the sectoral approach (i.e., negotiations on basic telecommunications) is likely to intensify in the future. The most evident examples are the recent OECD negotiations on an investment agreement among largely capital-exporting countries, which in turn have drawn heavily on the approaches developed in NAFTA. APEC is considering the new ITA-type initiatives. Agreements have been reached among major trading countries on avant-garde subjects such as electronic commerce and certification procedures, and groups of technical experts, strongly influenced by industry interests, draw up international standards and negotiate rules of origin. The question of the relationship between international norms regarding labour rights and multilateral environmental agreements as they relate to the trading system has already been raised.

It can be expected that there will be continuous pressure to expand the frontiers of the trading system, since the differences in the application of international norms are seen as providing unfair competitive advantages, while the possibility of recourse to trade retaliation under the WTO is viewed as the only credible sanction available to enforce such norms. Thus, more and more policy issues are seen as trade related.

In this situation, developing countries are faced with serious challenges in exerting influence over the process of setting the international trade agenda. The post-Uruguay Round scenario appears to be one of continuous negotiation within a variety of multilateral regional and plurilateral forums. As I have observed above, the developing countries were able to exert considerable influence during the Uruguay Round. This was due, first, to the fact that the agenda for the Round was set at a major diplomatic conference–the Punta del Este meeting–in the preparation for which they were able to mobilize their intellectual and diplomatic resources to ensure inclusion of issues of primary concern to them. Second, the Uruguay Round lasted long enough to permit the establishment of alliances among like-minded developing countries, and even developed countries, on specific issues. As I have noted, such alliances were instrumental in securing a satisfactory outcome in agriculture, the dismantling of the MFA, the inclusion of the movement of persons in the GATS, and many other results.

The post-Uruguay Round scenario would seem paradoxically less structured. I say paradoxically, because on paper the WTO Agreement is a model of democracy, with most decisions based on consensus. However, as I have pointed out on other occasions, I see a major potential strain on the system arising from the fact that this form does not reflect the underlying reality, i.e., that decisions are taken by a limited number of countries in closed groups or, as we have seen, outside the framework of the WTO altogether. Unlike the IMF and the World Bank, the WTO is structured on the assumption that all members are equal, whereas the reality is otherwise.

If developing countries are to maintain influence over the future international trade agenda consistent with their growing importance as import markets, they will have to make considerable efforts to prepare technically sound initiatives for action in their favour, as well as counter-proposals in respect of proposals emanating from developed country forums. This will require the re-establishment of the Uruguay Round alliances of like-minded countries. Recent successes in the process of sub-regional integration among developing countries may facilitate this process. It will also call for increased efforts in human resource development and institution-building in most developing countries.

The components of a positive agenda for developing countries could include initiatives to liberalize trade in sectors where a sufficient number of them share an export interest, along the lines of the ITA, but dealing with all barriers affecting trade in the sector. In addition, across-the-board formulas could deal with peak tariff rates which impede or often prohibit trade. A large part of their efforts will have to be focused on the built-in agenda, so as to develop proposals to further liberalize the temporary movement of persons or to address certain service sectors in a comprehensive fashion, taking account of social and cultural considerations. The revision process in the built-in agenda provides opportunities to modify aspects of the MTAs to enhance their development friendliness.

However, future trade initiatives by developing countries will require a clearer understanding of the impact of globalization on the trading system, which could alter traditional perceptions of national trade interests. One area of relevance is that of electronic commerce, which may open up substantial new opportunities for developing countries. Again, globalization and liberalization may oblige countries to focus not only on market access for their products and services, but also on the benefits in terms of value added and profits that they are deriving from such trade, as well as the need to ensure that the behaviour of the main players in international trade, i.e., the transnational corporations, coincides to the greatest extent possible with national interests and development objectives. For this reason, a coherent developing country reaction to the current proposals on investment and competition policy would seem a matter of top priority.

Finally, another major issue facing the WTO is the accession of the more than 30 countries seeking to become members. These are mostly developing countries and countries in transition to a market economy. The major trading countries seem to have adopted the position that the acceding countries should be required to adopt a higher level of obligation than the original Members, and this approach has been put into practice in the terms of accession of certain small countries. However, the real challenge will be the ability of the WTO to accommodate major trading powers such as Russia and China. Their accession to the WTO should serve to rebalance the organization's decision-making process.

8. The Post-Singapore Trading System

While the Uruguay Round negotiators were cognizant of the importance of new and intensified disciplines in the areas of services, intellectual property rights and subsidies, they did not visualize the extent to which global production would become a reality. Certain concepts upon which trade instruments are based may be progressively rendered irrelevant by the process of globalization, or may impede the ability of countries to derive benefits from this process. Concepts that assume that production takes place within national boundaries may need to be re-examined (the issue of the circumvention of anti-dumping duties is a case in point). Similarly, negotiations on future commitments in the areas of both goods and services, including investment and competition policy as envisaged under the TRIMs Agreement, as well as in other areas such as standards, mutual recognition of qualifications, rules of origin and subsidies, must take into account the realities of globalization and the need to maximize its positive effect on development. There should be emphasis on approaches that enable developing countries and countries in transition to improve their supply capacity, particularly by increasing their capacity to attract investment to support development priorities, and allowing persons from developing countries to more effectively participate in the global process of enhancing skills and knowledge through international movement and access to networks.

Although the costs of protectionism and the benefits of trade liberalization are obvious to all of us, one cannot help being concerned that the political consensus in favour of further trade liberalization is weakening. Many have stressed the continued validity of the *bicycle theory*, i.e., in the absence of trade liberalization initiatives, protectionist forces consolidate themselves and succeed in reversing the liberalization process. It would seem, however, that the phenomenon of globalization and liberalization has somewhat aggravated this problem, in that it is increasingly perceived that both within and among countries the benefits accrue to only a few, many being marginalized and unable to enjoy them.

A consensus in favour of ambitious trade liberalization objectives at the multilateral level can only be achieved if developing countries, countries in transition and the various economic actors and political interests are convinced that they will be able to improve their situations as a result. This will require the comprehension and assistance of the international community, as well as increased coordination with respect to measures to reduce marginalization.

Among the asymmetries of globalization is the fact that liberalization of the world economy has proceeded so far in a lopsided fashion. As a result:

- Liberalization has proceeded more slowly in those sectors where developing countries are more competitive;
- Freer trade in textiles, often the first step on the road towards industrialization, will be achieved only in the first years of the next century;
- Major trading entities continue to protect their agricultural sectors;

While liberalization has succeeded in removing many restrictions on the freedom of capital and highly skilled labour to seek the greatest remuneration worldwide, no attention has been paid to abolishing the many restrictions on the freedom of movement of lower-skilled labour;

International economic cooperation to promote equitable and sustainable growth worldwide should focus in particular on three areas:

- Evolution of international trading and financial systems that ensure stability in global markets, promote the progressive but balanced liberalization of trade and investment, enhance the mobility of other production factors, and provide all countries with access to markets in goods and services, investment and technology;
- Enhancement of the competitive supply capabilities of structurally weak economies;
- Provision of financial support and incentives.

There are undoubtedly benefits to be obtained by developing countries that participate in the more extensive division of labour which future globalization will bring about. Integration should be pursued so as to derive both static and dynamic benefits from openness. But at each stage this should be done from a position of economic strength.

Bringing TRIPS into the Multilateral Trading System

B. K. Zutshi

1. Introduction

Among the most significant post-World War-II developments, with profound implications for the future course of world history and global welfare, are the break-up of the Soviet Union, and the successful conclusion of the Uruguay Round negotiations resulting in the setting up of the World Trade Organization (WTO). The implications of both events are still unfolding and it will be decades before the full impact is realised. Only time will tell which of these two events had a profounder impact on the course of world history.

We are too near to both events to assess their absolute and relative impact. However, we can, with a degree of confidence, talk about how they came about. This article, dedicated to Arthur Dunkel for his outstanding contribution to the successful conclusion of the Uruguay Round negotiations, will tell in brief the story of how, as witnessed by the author from a favourable vantage point, the Agreement on Trade-Related Aspects of Intellectual Property Rights (TRIPS Agreement) became part of the new multilateral trading system.

An outline of the TRIPS Agreement is first provided. This is followed by a discussion of the background to the negotiations, during which it emerged that the most controversial issues related to patents. Then, a summary is provided of the crucial issues that were raised during the negotiations regarding patents. Finally, the main elements of the negotiations, including the various issues that were of concern to India (a major negotiator among the developing countries) in particular, are recapitulated, providing a basis to consider the main thrust of the TRIPS negotiations after the December 1990 Ministerial meeting in Brussels and to recall how a clutch of controversial issues in this area were finally settled. A few comments are offered at the end by way of concluding remarks.

2. Salient Features of the TRIPS Agreement

The TRIPS Agreement consists of a Preamble and seven Parts. Part I and Parts III to VII are common and applicable to all the seven categories of intellectual property rights (IPRs) which have been addressed in Part II with respect to their standards, availability and scope. The seven categories of intellectual property rights covered are: *copyright and related rights*, *trade marks*, *geographical indications*, *industrial designs*, *patents* (which includes IPRs regarding micro-organisms and plant varieties), *integrated circuits* and *trade secrets*.

In respect of *copyright and related rights*, parties are required to comply with the substantive provisions of the Berne Convention (1971) for the protection of literary and artistic works, except moral rights as stipulated in Article 6bis of that Convention. Computer programmes have to be protected as literary works under the Berne Convention, and this protection will also cover Compilation of Data. Important additions to existing international rules in the area of copyright and related rights are the provisions on rental rights. The Agreement requires that authors of computer programmes and producers of sound recordings be given the right to authorise or prohibit the commercial rental of their works to the public. A similar exclusive right applies to films where commercial rental had led to widespread copying, which was materially impairing the right of reproduction. The Agreement also requires performers to be given protection from unauthorised recording and broadcast of live performances (bootlegging). The protection for performers and producers of sound recordings is for no less than 50 years. Broadcasting organisations would have control over the use that can be made of broadcast signals without their authorisation. This right will be for at least 20 years.

In respect of *trademarks* and *service marks*, the Agreement defines what types of signs are eligible for protection as a trademark or a service mark and what the minimum rights conferred on their owners must be. Marks that have become well known in a particular country shall enjoy additional protection. In addition, the Agreement lays down a number of obligations with regard to the use of trademarks and service marks, their term of protection, and their licensing or assignment. For example, requirements that foreign marks be used in conjunction with local marks will be, as a general rule, prohibited.

In respect of *geographical indications*, the Agreement lays down that all parties must provide means to prevent use of any indications that mislead the consumer as to the origin of goods, and any use that would constitute an act of unfair competition. A higher level of protection is provided for geographical indications for wines and spirits, which are protected even where there is no danger of the public being misled as to the true origin. Exceptions are allowed for names that have already become generic terms, but any country using such an exception must be willing to negotiate with a view to protecting the geographical indications in question. In addition, provision is made for further negotiations to establish a multilateral system of notification and registration of geographical indications for wines.

Industrial designs are also protected under the Agreement for a period of 10 years. Owners of protected designs are able to prevent the manufacture, sale or importation of articles bearing or embodying a design that is a copy of the protected design.

As regards *patents*, there is a general obligation to comply with the substantive provisions of the Paris Convention (1967). In addition, the Agreement requires that a 20-year patent protection be made available to all inventions, whether of products or processes, in all fields of technology. Inventions may be excluded from patentability if it is necessary to prevent their commercial exploitation on grounds of public order, morality, health, or for environmental reasons. Other permitted exclusions are for diagnostic, therapeutic and surgical methods, and for plants and animals (other than micro-organisms) and essentially biological processes for the production of plants or animals (other than microbiological processes). Plant varieties, however, must be protectable either by patents or by a *sui generis* system (such as the breeder's rights provided in an UPOV[1] Convention). Detailed conditions are laid down for non-voluntary licensing or governmental use of patents without the authorization of the patent owner. Rights conferred in respect of patents for processes must extend to the products directly obtained by such processes; under certain conditions alleged infringers may be ordered by a court to prove that they have not used the patented process.

With respect to the protection of *layout designs of integrated circuits*, the Agreement requires parties to provide protection on the basis of the Washington Treaty on Intellectual Property in Respect of Integrated Circuits (opened for signature in May 1989), but with a number of additions: protection must be available for a minimum period of 10 years; the rights must extend to articles incorporating infringing layout designs; innocent infringers must be allowed to use or sell stock in hand or ordered before learning of the infringement against a suitable royalty; and compulsory licensing and government use is only allowed under a number of strict conditions.

Trade secrets and know-how which have commercial value must be protected against breach of confidence and other acts contrary to honest commercial practices. Test data submitted to governments in order to obtain marketing approval for pharmaceutical or agricultural chemicals must also be protected against unfair commercial use.

The final section in this part of the Agreement concerns anti-competitive practices in contractual licenses. It provides for consultations between governments where there is reason to believe that licensing practices or conditions pertaining to intellectual property rights constitute an abuse of these rights and have an adverse effect on competition. Remedies against such abuses must be consistent with the other provisions of the agreement.

Part III of the Agreement sets out the obligations of member governments to provide procedures and remedies under their domestic law to ensure that intellectual property rights can be effectively enforced, by foreign right holders as well as by their own nationals. Procedures should permit effective action against infringement of intellectual property rights but should be fair and equitable, not unnecessarily complicated or costly, and should not entail unreasonable time-limits or unwarranted delays. They should allow for judicial review of final ad-

---

[1] Union pour la Protection des Obtensions Végétales

ministrative decisions. There is no obligation to put in place a judicial system distinct from that for the enforcement of laws in general, nor to give priority to the enforcement of intellectual property rights in the allocation of resources or staff.

The Agreement establishes a TRIPS Council to monitor the operation of the Agreement and Members' compliance with it. Dispute settlement will take place under the integrated WTO dispute settlement procedures.

The implementation of the Agreement is subject to different transitional periods for various groups of countries to bring their legislation and practices into conformity; developing countries and economies in transition have a five-year period; least developed countries have eleven years. Developing countries that do not at present provide product patent protection in an area of technology have up to 10 years to introduce such protection. However, in the case of pharmaceutical and agricultural chemicals products, they have to accept the filing of patent applications from the beginning of the transitional period. Though the patent need not be granted until the end of this period, the novelty of the invention is preserved as of the date of filing the application. If authorization for the marketing of the relevant pharmaceutical or agricultural chemical is obtained during the transitional period, the developing country concerned must offer an exclusive marketing right for the product for five years, or until a product patent is granted or rejected, whichever is shorter.

Subject to certain exceptions, the general rule is that the obligations in the Agreement would apply to existing intellectual property rights as well as to new ones.

3. The Background

Of all the subjects negotiated in the Uruguay Round, IPRs and services were the two subjects with North-South dimensions. Hence, the controversial nature of these negotiations before and after the launching of the Round. While services proved controversial even before the Round was launched, IPRs became so during the course of negotiations when the Punta del Este Mandate in this respect was interpreted by developed countries to cover also the norms and standards of IPRs. Developing countries, as a group, held the view that norms and standards of IPRs *per se* were not trade related and, therefore, not covered by the Mandate.

This disagreement on the interpretation of the Punta Mandate on TRIPS could not be resolved at the Mid-Term Review in December 1988 in Montreal. This, along with disagreements in the areas of agriculture, textiles and safeguards, was subsequently resolved in April 1989 in Geneva. The compromise in TRIPS envisaged negotiations on five elements relating to the applicability of basic principles of GATT: provision of adequate standards and principles concerning availability, scope and use of trade related IPRs, enforcement of such rights, dispute prevention and settlement and transitional arrangements. The issue of whether any agreement on TRIPS would be implemented in GATT or in any other international organisation was left open. However, the issue was resolved in the negotiations themselves by the decision to set up the WTO under which the TRIPS Agreement would be administered by a separate council.

The rest of this paper is devoted to the patents issue as, in the area of TRIPS, it proved the most controversial. It may, however, be said in passing that the impression about developing countries in general and India in particular being opposed to the TRIPS Agreement in the Uruguay Round negotiations on account of their own laws in all areas of TRIPS is far from true. India, for instance, had a progressive world-class legislation in copyrights, which provided protection to computer programmes on a par with that of artistic and literary works in compliance with the Berne Convention (1971). India's opposition was to norms and standards of IPRs being brought into the GATT/WTO, as on a conceptual basis these were not trade related. However, in case of patents, particularly in the area of food, pharmaceuticals and chemicals, it had other and more substantive concerns. More about that later.

The genesis of the controversial nature of TRIPS is not difficult to discern. The reasons for the insistence of developed countries on bringing the subject of IPRs within the ambit of GATT are not hard to find. Technology was increasingly becoming a commercial and tradeable asset and a dominant factor in determining international competitiveness. Developed countries were also at the same time losing competitiveness in traditional manufacturing fields to the so-called low wage producing countries. Developed countries also believed that developing countries were acquiring non-indigenous technologies by means other than imports or license, which developed countries considered an illicit economic loss to them. They equated protection of technology with protection of their market power. They were dissatisfied with the implementation of the IPRs through the World Intellectual Property Organization (WIPO) as it did not have an effective enforcement system. The developed countries were seeking to use the leverage of access to their markets in goods for the purpose of enforcing IPRs.

This aroused great fears and concerns among developing countries. It had, in part, to do with the conceptual basis of the debate on IPRs. The debate on IPRs in general and on patents in particular has been sustained by two somewhat opposite points of view. According to one approach the state must support an adequate return on research and development costs and thus provide a socially commensurate incentive to entrepreneurs by establishing and enforcing temporary monopolies for inventors. This is the price that society pays for progress. Another view is that IPRs are not different from other monopolies and they confer abnormally high profits upon their owners, invite abuse and restrict the spread of technology and its benefits.

Historically, the evolution of intellectual property protection shows that except for the United States, the developed countries practiced different protection regimes commensurate with different stages of their economic development. Patents in chemicals and pharmaceuticals were not being granted in a number of OECD countries until recently: the Federal Republic of Germany (FRG) until 1967, Switzerland until 1978, Japan until 1976 and the Nordics until 1968 did not provide patent protection for chemicals; and pharmaceuticals were denied such protection in FRG and France until 1967, and Italy until 1979. In Spain and Portugal, chemicals and pharmaceuticals became patentable only in 1992.[2]

There is an impressive body of economic literature that shows that protection of intellectual property on a global basis causes welfare loss. The worries of developing countries in this area, therefore, had to do with their ability to pursue public policy that ensures access to health care to their people at affordable prices and the development of agriculture. This was the basis for denying product patents for food, pharmaceuticals and chemicals in these countries.

4. Crucial Issues Regarding Patents Raised during the Negotiations

When the negotiations resumed after the Mid-Term Review, substantive differences persisted between developed and developing countries on basic issues relating to standards and principles concerning the availability, scope and use of trade related intellectual property rights and on the applicability of basic GATT principles and of relevant international intellectual property agreements or conventions. In varying degrees developing countries persisted with their stance that norms and standards of IPRs were not trade related. The most comprehensive articulation of this point of view was India's paper to the negotiating group submitted in July 1989.[3] This covered patents, trade marks including service marks, copyright, integrated circuits and trade secrets. In the case of patents, the paper reflected core concerns of developing countries on such issues as patentable subject matter, working of patents, non-voluntary licenses (compulsory licensing including licence of right), duration of patents and abuse of patent rights.

As to patentable subject matter, the concern of developing countries related to the general category as well as specific sectors. Developed countries were arguing for limited exclusions (in the general category) on grounds of public morality and for security considerations, while developing countries were seeking exclusion also on grounds of public policy. There was a consensus on exclusion for methods of medical treatment for humans or animals and for plants and animal varieties or essentially biological processes for the production of plants or animals. The developed countries sought inclusion of micro-organisms and microbiological processes and products. The developing countries were opposed to this on the ground that since micro-organisms existed in nature, they could not be called inventions and, therefore, could not be covered by the definition of patentability itself. There was also a difference of opinion on the treatment of microbiological processes and products, among other things, on ethical grounds. This covered the entire area of genetic engineering and protection for plant varieties (whether under patents or a *sui generis* system such as UPOV).

---

[2] Chakravarti Raghavan (1990), *Recolonization, GATT, the Uruguay Round & the Third World.* Third World Network. Penang, Malaysia, p 123

[3] MTN.GNG/ NG.11/W/37

One of the core concerns of developing countries had been to ensure the exclusion of pharmaceutical products from patent protection in order to avoid the danger of monopolistic pricing with adverse consequences on the access to health care for a significant proportion of the poor population of these countries. To maintain access to medicines and health care at affordable levels, the developing countries had been following the route taken by the developed countries earlier in either excluding pharmaceutical from patentability or allowing only process patents.

Another core concern related to the working of patents by patent holders in the areas of pharmaceuticals. To remedy the possibility of non-working patents, developing countries were providing for compulsory licensing. India, for example, only allowed for process patents in the food, pharmaceutical and chemical sectors, with a provision for *a licence of right*, i.e., the automatic grant of non-voluntary licences, without recourse to any judicial review; the patent owner was entitled to compensation subject to judicial review in accordance with the provisions of law in that regard. Other concerns related to restrictive and anti-competitive business practices of IPR holders, and to ensuring that broad public policy objectives were not adversely affected by the IPR regime.

In September 1989, India submitted another important paper[4] on the applicability of the basic principles of the GATT and of relevant international intellectual property agreements or conventions. This paper argued that except for the principles of transparency and differential and more favourable treatment for developing countries, the generally recognised principles of GATT (most favoured nation and national treatment) were inapplicable to intellectual property rights. The Indian position was that the philosophy of GATT was the promotion of free trade and fair competition, whereas the essence of the intellectual property regime was its monopolistic and restrictive character. While GATT was designed to serve as a negotiating forum for liberalisation of trade in goods, the intellectual property system sought to confer exclusive rights on their owners. In respect of international agreements or conventions on intellectual property, India believed that their basic provisions, giving freedom on scope and level of protection to members, particularly with reference to patents, were extremely valuable for developing countries as it gave them the necessary flexibility to design their own IPR protection in keeping with their developmental needs and priorities. It was felt that the freedom granted by the Paris Convention to members to decide the criteria of patentability, whether the patents should be granted for products only, for processes only, or for both, and in which fields of industry and for what term, was right and justified as it recognized the principles of primacy of public interest in the matter of providing intellectual property rights. It may be mentioned in parenthesis that a paradox was noticed in the negotiating positions taken by the developed and developing countries on IPRs in the Uruguay Round, which was characterized in the following words:

> *On the one hand, the industrialized countries that subscribe to free-market principles at home want to impose a highly regulated market for intellectual goods on the rest of the world, one in which authors and inventors may 'reap where they have sown'. On the other hand, the developing countries that re-*

[4] MTN.GNG/NG.11/W/39

strict free competition at home envision an .... unregulated world market for intellectual goods, one in which 'competition is the lifeblood of commerce'.[5]
Consistency is not a virtue practiced by nations, particularly in trade negotiations.

5. The Negotiations

In May 1990, a group of developing countries comprising Argentina, Brussels, Chile, Colombia, Cuba, Egypt, India, Nigeria, Peru, Tanzania and Uruguay submitted a draft intellectual property agreement. Part I thereof related to intellectual property and international trade, and laid down objectives, guiding principles and norms and, border measures related to counterfeit or piracy. Part II covered standards and principles governing the availability, scope and use of intellectual property rights. This laid down the objectives and principles in regard to norms and scope and, in respect of patents, it provided a set of rights and obligations of the patent holder, use of patents for government purposes and a license of right. In its approach the paper was not very much different from the position obtaining in the prevalent laws applicable to patents in developing countries.

The United States, the EEC and Switzerland also put up draft agreements, which were totally different in approach to that adopted in the developing countries' paper mentioned above. The Swiss draft envisaged TRIPS being added to the GATT as an integral part thereof, while the US and EEC papers envisaged a separate agreement. In their broad outline, these papers were along the lines of what ultimately emerged from the negotiations.

There was not much movement in the negotiating positions of the two sides until the summer of 1990. In July 1990, in order to break the impasse, a draft text of an agreement was prepared by the Chairman of the Negotiating Group incorporating therein both approaches to negotiations as promoted by the developing countries on the one side, and, the developed countries on the other. This document became the basis for negotiations until the Brussels meeting in December 1990, when the Round was scheduled to be concluded. Among the key issues on which there were major differences, a large proportion related to the area of patents. In the final phase of the negotiations in 1991, which led to the tabling of the Draft Final Act (the Dunkel Draft) in December 1991, the various patent-related issues were considered as a package.

A crucial change in the situation occurred during the negotiations between 1991 and 1992. While India's position on most of the issues remained unchanged, most developing countries had, under bilateral pressure, substantially changed their negotiating position in regard to most of the contentious issues in the TRIPS Agreement. This was particularly true of patents. The developing countries'

---

[5] Quoted in J.H. Reichman (1993), *Implications of the Draft TRIPS Agreement for Developing Countries as Competitors in an Integrated World Market.* UNCTAD Discussion Paper Number 73, (November), p 2. As mentioned later in this article, there was virtually no change in the text of the Agreement finally adopted in comparison to the draft TRIPS agreement.

position had also changed on account of developments not directly related to the negotiations such as the collapse of the Berlin wall, developments in the former USSR and substantial liberalization undertaken by the developing countries unilaterally and autonomously. In addition, the developing countries were keen to conclude the Round, and for that purpose were prepared to make concessions to the developed countries in new areas of services and TRIPS against better access to developed countries' markets in the area of trade in goods, in particular liberalization of trade in agriculture. Moreover, the United States had resorted to the use of unilateral measures under their Super 301 and Special 301 trade legislation to try to open the markets of developing countries. Special 301 was used as an instrument against developing countries to persuade them to fall in line on intellectual property rights, on a bilateral basis. The United States was able to get commitments from developing countries not only on providing higher levels of intellectual property protection but also on granting retroactive protection to patents from 1986 onwards, the so-called pipeline protection.

Throughout the negotiations, India was concerned about eight interconnected issues in TRIPS, but owing to the developments described above, it was isolated on some of these issues by the end of the negotiations. A summary of the situation with regard to these eight issues is given below.

- *The scope of patentability*: It had become clear by December 1991 that India's stand on exclusion of food, chemicals and pharmaceuticals from product patentability did not enjoy any support. There was, however, a shared concern among developing country participants about the patentability in biotechnology and genetics. This concern was also shared by a number of activists and NGOs in developed countries. Until the very end (December 1993) India continued to press for exclusion of bio-technology from patentability. However, towards the end of the negotiations, partly because of negotiating fatigue and more substantively because of the firm position of developed countries, the developing countries (including India) were not able to get biotechnology and genetics excluded from patentability. In case of protection of plant varieties, because of this being perceived to be against the interest of farmers, there were fears of political opposition in India. Subsequent events did show that these fears were not unfounded. The choice to provide protection for plant varieties under an effective *sui generis* system was the best developing countries were able to obtain in this regard. In this, the European Union played a very helpful role.
- *Term of patents*: Although India wanted to reduce the term of patents as much as possible, it was becoming clear that there was an emerging consensus for a 20-year patent period. That consensus prevented India from being able to reduce the term of patents.
- *Compulsory licensing*: India favoured maximum flexibility in the area of compulsory licensing. Working of patents locally was a demand supported by many developing countries. The issue was whether the provisions of the Paris Convention on compulsory licensing should be tightened further. On compulsory licensing, formally called *Other Use Without Authorization of the Right Holder*, a compromise was reached to attach conditions to such use rather than

provide for grounds or reasons under which the use may be permitted. The conditions that emerged finally are no doubt stringent, but they are much less stringent than what the developed countries wanted since it has been left up to WTO Members to determine the grounds for compulsory licensing. Moreover, these conditions specifically permit the use of compulsory licensing in situations of national emergency or circumstances of extreme urgency or in cases of public non-commercial use.

- *Period of transition*: India wanted a minimum transition period of five years with no pipeline protection.
- *Pipeline protection*: India was totally opposed to the US version of pipeline protection. The Swiss version, unlike that of the US, was devoid of the concepts of extraterritoriality and retroactivity and envisaged protection to begin only at the end of the transitional period in respect of inventions made during the period of transition. The only requirement was to provide for a *mail box* in which applications for patents for such inventions could be filed, but which would become effective only at the end of the transitional period.

  Regarding period of transition and pipeline protection, India had its way for a 10-year transitional period for product patents in the field of technology where product patents were not being granted at the time of entering into force of the Agreement. However, subject to certain conditions, arrangements would have to be made for accepting patent applications from the date of entering into force of the agreement in case of pharmaceuticals and agrochemicals and applications accepted or rejected at the end of the transitional period and, in the interim, subject to certain conditions, exclusive marketing rights granted for a period of five years after obtaining marketing approvals.
- *Exhaustion*: India along with many other countries, notably Hong Kong, was opposed to *Exhaustion* being dealt with under TRIPS. Exhaustion of IPRs refers to the concept where once the IPR holder puts goods or services containing the intellectual property rights on the market for the first time, the intellectual property rights of an IPR holder are exhausted with regard to any subsequent sale or use of those goods or services. The issue of exhaustion was not included in the TRIPS Agreement, thus achieving India's objective in this regard.
- *Protection of undisclosed test or other data for marketing approvals*: India was opposed to protection of undisclosed tests and other data for marketing approvals. As the negotiations progressed, a consensus formed on a text that was less strict than the text favoured by those pushing for the inclusion of this matter in the TRIPS Agreement. Ultimately, the consensus prevailed for a somewhat diluted level of discipline in this area but left the text ambiguous on the duration of such protection.
- *Control of anti-competitive practices*: This issue was addressed only in the draft legal text tabled by the group of developing countries. The idea was to explicitly include in the text of the TRIPS Agreement, for the first time in an international agreement, a recognition of the rights of members to cover, in their national legislation, those practices that were deemed to be an abuse of

IPRs or to have an adverse effect on competition, and to adopt appropriate measures to prevent or control such practices. Another aspect was to commit each member to consult and cooperate with another member with regard to ensuring that the intellectual property right holders from the first member complied with the national legislation of the other member. India was in the forefront of such a move, and its objective on this issue was substantially achieved.

There were three other aspects which India addressed together with the package of controversial issues. One related to reservations made with regard to the provisions of the TRIPS Agreement. Another was the public policy concerns of India, and the third addressed the issue of non-violation complaints in dispute settlement.

Regarding reservations, although Article 72 of the TRIPS Agreement states that: *Reservations may not be entered in respect of any of the provisions of this Agreement without the consent of the other Members,* India managed to dilute this provision through its negotiation of the Marrakesh Agreement Establishing The World Trade Organization. The provisions of the latter Agreement override those of the TRIPS Agreement. This, combined with the waiver clause under Article IX of the Marrakesh Agreement, provides a basis to alter the impact of the TRIPS Agreement's provision, which otherwise rules out any reservations.

India's public policy concerns were reflected in Articles 7 and 8 of the TRIPS Agreement, which address the objectives and principles of that Agreement. At the end of the negotiations, paragraphs 2 and 3 of Article 64 were added, which rules out the use of non-violation complaints for a period of five years, with a possibility of deletion of the provision or its further extension after review.

The results of the negotiations were contained in the Dunkel Draft tabled in December 1991. The text that was finally adopted in Marrakesh in April 1994 was virtually the same as the Dunkel Draft. It contained only two relatively small changes of substance; one of them was the addition of certain text relating to semiconductor technology in Article 31(c), the other was the above-mentioned text that ruled out non-violation complaints for at least five years.

6. Concluding Remarks

Of all the issues negotiated under the Uruguay Round, TRIPS was and remains the most difficult and painful issue for India. The developed countries had themselves acquired technology under lax IPR regimes and, besides, there were sound economic reasons for developing countries to oppose the move to bring TRIPS into the multilateral trading system. However, the TRIPS Agreement that was finally accepted did impose several restrictions which the developing countries had opposed. This was due to a number of factors that accentuated the already existing unequal bargaining power between developed and developing countries. These included concerted pressure by developed countries as a group, regarding TRIPS; progressive erosion of the unity of developing countries on the issue through bilateral economic and political pressure by developed countries, principally by the

US; a process of reform in several developing countries under which a strong IPR regime was considered necessary for increasing inward foreign direct investment; conclusion of bilateral agreements on IPRs between the US and quite a number of developing countries including large ones like Brazil and the People's Republic of China. In addition, there was a growing perception that failure of the TRIPS negotiations could result in a failure of the Uruguay Round itself, which, in turn, was perceived as opening the way for a possible breakdown of the existing multilateral trading system. At the end of the day, it was the assessment of developing countries that they needed a multilateral trading system, based on principles of non-discrimination, much more than the developed countries and if inclusion of TRIPS in the system was the price for that, they would have to pay it. However, this should not create the impression that developing countries failed altogether in achieving their objectives relating to TRIPS in the Uruguay Round negotiations. As shown in this paper, there were several concerns of India for which the final outcome was in consonance with India's demands. Furthermore, much stricter IPR disciplines accepted by China in the bilateral context showed the efficacy of the multilateral system where even though India was ultimately alone in pressing its various demands regarding TRIPS, the final result was much more *developing-country-friendly* than that managed by China on its own.

In India, the TRIPS Agreement remains controversial even at present (January 1998). Two successive governments have failed to secure legislative approval for the implementation of its obligations on the *mail box* provision of the Agreement for filing applications for patents during the transition period. India has also lost an appeal, under the WTO disputes settlement procedures, against a panel finding on its failure to comply with its obligation in this regard. This issue will have to be addressed by the next government (expected to assume office in early March 1998) and some way found to bring its legislation in conformity with its obligation under the WTO for filing patent applications during the transitional period. However, this has been made difficult by the debate on TRIPS in India, which has often exaggerated the adverse effects of the WTO TRIPS Agreement, for reasons far more connected with the politics of the issue than its merit or the objective situation on the ground. The author is of the view that the agreement on TRIPS may have given India a handicap but has not put it under a crippling constraint. The adverse effects on drug prices have been highly exaggerated, safeguards provided in the TRIPS Agreement have not been adequately studied, nor is there any serious evaluation of how India's legislation can be crafted to safeguard its public policy objectives in this area while maintaining consistency with the TRIPS Agreement. Furthermore, as mentioned at the outset, the main problem of India relates to certain issues regarding patents. For a number of IPRs, India's policy regime is largely consistent with TRIPS requirements. Moreover, India has much to gain from intellectual property protection in several advanced scientific fields, such as plant breeding, where Indian scientists have made a mark, and in other areas such as copyright.

Developing countries, including India, were able to get their concerns in the TRIPS negotiations addressed only after they engaged in serious negotiations. A lack of focus on TRIPS in the initial phase of the negotiations meant lost opportunities for developing countries to adequately prepare for these negotiations. In the author's view, India's lack of membership of the Paris Convention itself meant that India was less able to influence the multilateral process on TRIPS as it was not able to participate in parallel discussions and consultations that were being held on technical aspects within the Paris Convention framework.

Lastly, there is little point in lamenting developing countries' lack of bargaining power. For developing countries in general, and India in particular, to enhance their bargaining power, the only way is to gain economic muscle and a greater share in international trade. Meanwhile, it is essential that developing countries prepare adequately, and in time, for negotiations and to identify their common interests. Common positions identified by them need not be limited only to the interests of other developing countries. The Uruguay Round negotiations demonstrated effectively that common positions could be found among developing and developed countries also, and that support for one's position could come from unexpected sources. Such an identification of objectives and timely preparations for negotiations is now more important than ever before because some of the agreements under the WTO will be renegotiated by the turn of the century, and several old and new issues will be reviewed in the next few years with a possibility of beginning negotiations on them.

Bringing Textiles and Clothing into the Multilateral Trading System

Marcelo Raffaelli[1]

1. Introduction

From the first discussions in 1981 on the crisis of the General Agreement on Tariffs and Trade (GATT) and on how 'to deal with outstanding problems', it was evident that textiles and clothing would have to be listed among the elements contributing to that crisis and must be included in any effort to resolve the outstanding problems. In reality, of the areas covered by the GATT, two had remained largely outside its disciplines during the first three and a half decades of its existence: agriculture, and textiles and clothing.

Two previous GATT Rounds had been preceded by the conclusion of agreements on special rules for international trade in textile products. In 1961, before the Kennedy Round, the Short-Term Cotton Arrangement was negotiated, followed in 1962 by the Long-Term Cotton Arrangement, which remained in force until the end of 1973. The launching of the Tokyo Round had been facilitated by the negotiation in 1973 of the Arrangement Regarding International Trade in Textiles (better known as the Multifibre Arrangement–MFA). As a matter of fact, conclusion of the MFA had been regarded by several developed Contracting Parties to the GATT as a *sine qua non* if a new Round were to take place. Moreover, notwithstanding assertions throughout its text about trade liberalization and special regard for the interests of developing countries, the MFA apparently had never been intended by developed Contracting Parties as a tool for liberalization, but rather as a waiver for the imposition of restrictions of a kind forbidden by the General Agreement. By 1981, the way the MFA had been implemented had shown that such was, indeed, the case.

Thus, in 1981 it was clear that any new Round would have to deal with a genuine liberalization of trade in textiles and clothing. Such liberalization should cover not only the MFA but also non-tariff barriers, other than those applied under

---

[1] The author wishes to thank Tripti Jenkins and Bob Shepherd for their helpful suggestions.

the MFA, as well as tariffs. Nevertheless, the MFA, recognized as a derogation from the General Agreement, was the main *problem* to be tackled.

2. A Thorny Problem

Fortunately for the GATT, Arthur Dunkel (both as Director-General and in his capacity of Chairman of the Textiles Committee of the Multifibre Arrangement) participated in the negotiation of the second extension of the MFA, in late 1981. He was able to witness on that occasion a confrontation between developing countries under MFA restrictions and the European Economic Community, which wished to keep the MFA more restrictive than under its original 1973 text, something it had already obtained in the first extension (1977). Thus, Dunkel had no doubt from the start on the necessity to bring meaningful liberalization to the sector.

One need not repeat here all the difficulties encountered in the preparation of the Ministerial Declaration of 1982 and of the Punta del Este Declaration of 1986, and in the following negotiations. Throughout, textiles and clothing was one of the difficult subjects, and the difficulties inherent in the sector were deepened in both 1981 and 1986 because of negotiations then taking place to extend the MFA for the second and third times, respectively. As in 1981, the 1986 extension was the object of a harsh negotiation in which Dunkel was deeply involved, in his rôle of Chairman of the Textiles Committee.[2]

The agreement finally issued from the Uruguay Round was arrived at after long, difficult, often acrimonious negotiations. Dunkel participated fully in all key phases of these negotiations. First, there were the negotiations preceding the Mid-term Review on the progress of the Round, then those during the Mid-term Review (Montreal, December 1988), which ended with textiles and clothing among the four areas left without agreement.

The Ministerial meeting in Montreal decided that Dunkel in his capacity of Chairman of the Trade Negotiations Committee (TNC) at official level would conduct high level consultations to try and resolve issues in the four remaining areas.

The TNC at the Ministerial level met in Geneva in April 1989. Thanks to Dunkel's forceful chairmanship and further consultations he conducted, a text was approved on textiles and clothing during that meeting. Dunkel continued to be deeply involved in the negotiations that led to the Brussels meeting in December 1990. When the latter ended in failure, the Ministers designated Dunkel to conduct the negotiations needed to conclude the Round.

To make a long story short, the text of the Agreement on Textiles and Clothing (ATC) issued from the Uruguay Round had not yet been agreed by the parties in December 1991, especially in relation to the so-called *economic package* (in-

[2] Throughout the period covered, Arthur Dunkel had the invaluable assistance of M.G. Mathur, the Deputy Director-General responsible for textile matters. Of course, Dunkel was always available when his personal presence and intervention were needed.

creases in growth rates of MFA or MFA-like restrictions, percentages of products to be integrated, and so on). On 20 December 1991, Dunkel told the parties that he would include in his proposed Draft Final Act the text containing an economic package he deemed to be realistic, and that this was being done on a *take it or leave it* basis. His proposal was accepted by all, excepting two delegations who reserved their positions. (A few minor issues were kept unresolved until December 1993, together with issues in other sensitive areas of the Round).

3. Trade in Textiles during the Round

During the more than one decade that passed between the first talks on a new Round and its conclusion, important changes affected international trade in textile products: a) changes in its structure; b) changes in the way importing countries applied the MFA; c) changes in the trade policies of countries subject to MFA restrictions.

Before dealing with such changes, however, one parenthesis to explain that in MFA jargon developed members were called importing countries (Austria, Canada, EC, Japan, Norway, Sweden, Switzerland and United States), while developing and East European members were called exporting countries. Nothing was said or could be read in the MFA about only exporting countries being subjected to MFA restrictions. The reality, however, was that–with the exception of Japan, which itself faced restrictions by several importing countries–all the countries under MFA restrictions were developing and East European countries. The restrictions were applied exclusively by importing countries. Japan and Switzerland were the only developed participants that did not invoke the Arrangement.

Regarding the *structure of the trade*, one could point out as changes occurring in the period:

- The appearance of several newcomers whose exports increased rapidly in volume and value, thus increasing their relative importance in the sector; China and Indonesia are cases in point;
- Japan, still a large net exporter in 1981, ended the period as a very large net importer;
- In regard to clothing, there was increased use by developed countries of outward processing traffic, i.e., assembly operations in developing countries where labour was cheap, for subsequent re-importation of the finished item. When the United States adopted, in the mid-1980s, special rules to encourage the use of fabrics of US origin as the basis for the finished product, a substantial increase of outward processing occurred in Central American and Caribbean countries. Some EC countries had been doing this in both North Africa and East Europe, and increased this kind of operations in the latter area in the early 1990s;
- Structural adjustment was supposed to be pursued by the developed importing countries, but only some of them took this commitment seriously;
- Several developing countries, which had suffered from inflation and followed monetary stabilization programs, started to lose competitiveness.

As to *the way the MFA was applied by importing countries*, some were more restrictive in the beginning, becoming relatively more relaxed later on, while others went the opposite way:

- The European Community and Sweden were extremely restrictive until the mid-1980s, the terms of many of their bilateral agreements being, in my view, difficult to consider as MFA-compatible. From 1987 on, however, the terms of EC agreements showed some improvement, and in relation to a few small exporting countries EC agreements were either much improved or completely eliminated. Sweden withdrew from the MFA and ceased to apply quantitative restrictions on 1 August 1991;
- The United States applied MFA restrictions widely, but always in very relaxed terms as to initial quota, growth rates, and so on. In its agreements concluded to cover the period of MFA III (1982-86), the US even eliminated some group limits and some restrictions on textiles. From 1983 on, however, the appreciation of the US currency as well as the elimination of group limits led to a large and rapid increase in imports into the United States, and a more restrictive policy–which included restrictions on textiles–started to be applied in 1984. This was kept in place henceforth, regardless of the ups and downs of exchange rates. Nevertheless, the more restrictive policy did not prevent a constant increase in US imports, for several reasons: for instance, as the quotas negotiated by the United States in its agreements had been generous, many suppliers held large quotas, most of which had a growth rate of 6 per cent a year. China had to be accommodated in the US market and, also for political reasons, such accommodation entailed large quotas. During the last years of the MFA, US policy regarding textile imports led it to become the only country applying restrictions to *all* exporting countries participating in the MFA, as well as a number of non-MFA participants;
- Canada, did not apply restrictions as widely as the United States, and applied them on generous terms as to initial quota level, growth rates and flexibility provisions. Canada, however, tightened considerably its restrictive system in the last years of the 1981-93 period.

Regarding the *liberalization of imports by countries under MFA restrictions*, it is enough to look at the picture in 1981, when in many developing countries imports of most products were either prohibited, under discretionary licensing or subject to quotas, while by 1993 many of the most recalcitrant protectionists, as well as several countries that had been suffering from severe balance of payments problems had opened their markets to imports, eliminating licensing and/or quotas and lowering tariffs without asking for reciprocity: a not exhaustive list would include Argentina, Brazil, Chile, Peru, Uruguay, Costa Rica, El Salvador, Jamaica, Indonesia, Korea, the Czech Republic and Hungary. Such opening of markets also benefitted, of course, international trade in textile products.

4. Moving Ahead with the Brakes on

Without detracting from the merits of the delegates involved, one can say that the entire negotiation of the ATC was conducted under instructions from governments who were looking more at the rear view mirror rather than at the road ahead.

Unfortunately for the exporting countries, most of them seemingly had no idea in the early and mid-1980s of what their trade policies would be a few years hence. Had they known that the liberalization that in 1982 seemed politically and economically impossible would be their goal in the latter part of the decade, they could perhaps have obtained more favourable terms in the Round and avoided using much ammunition to fight proposals and ideas which, by the time the Round ended, had become part of their policies. Such ammunition could have been better used to obtain better treatment in both the ATC and other areas under negotiation in the Round.

On the other hand, governments of several developed countries allowed themselves to be driven by worries born from the recessions of the 1970s and early 1980s, adhering throughout the Round to ideas that were defensible (at least in terms of domestic politics) in the early stages of the Round, but much less so in the early 1990s.

One has the impression that governments of developed countries were more interested in obtaining tough provisions that would be politically acceptable at home than in negotiating a text that took into account–at least as far as possible–the inevitable changes that would occur in textiles and clothing production and trade during the ten-year life of the ATC.

It is true that the seeds of the Uruguay Round were planted at a moment of world-wide recession: in both 1980 and 1981 world manufacturing production increased by only 1 per cent; in 1982, world trade decreased. But from 1983 onwards the situation changed and the Round took place under more auspicious conditions. According to the International Monetary Fund's *Annual Report of the Executive Board* series, world trade volume increased at the following rates: 1984 - 4.5 per cent, 1985 - 3 per cent, 1986 - 5 per cent, 1987 - 6.5 per cent, 1988 - 8.9 per cent, 1989 - 7 per cent, 1990 - 4.6 per cent, 1991 - 2.4 per cent, 1992 - 4.5 per cent. According to the same source, industrial output in industrial countries showed the following rates of growth: 1987 - 3.3 per cent, 1988 - 4.3 per cent, 1989 - 3.2 per cent, 1990 - 2.4 per cent, 1991 - 0.6 per cent, 1992 - 1.6 per cent. In the *Annual Report of the Executive Board for the Fiscal Year Ended April 30, 1991*, the following comment is found: "The global economic setting in 1990 was marked by the crisis in the Middle East and associated developments in world oil prices, and by restructuring in Eastern Europe and unification in Germany, as well as the continuation of the debt crisis." Two thoughts can be added: the first is that some of these factors continued to influence the world economic performance in 1991 and 1992; the second is that the governments of the developed countries must have been aware that these factors were not of a permanent nature.

Of course, hindsight is an exact science. But the truth is that all the signs were there to see, as 30 years of restrictions on textiles and clothing had not been the answer to the problem, which lay rather in the comparative advantage of countries with lower labour costs and in the fact that for many countries this is one of the few sources of export earnings. The same countries that maintained throughout the Uruguay Round that the new system of restrictions should remain in force for 15 more years had been opening their markets to textiles and clothing from China, North Korea, Vietnam and the former Republics of the Soviet Union, thus recognizing that for these countries to insert themselves in the world economy and expand their trade relations the industrialized countries had to become outlets to their textile and clothing products.

One should not forget, on the other hand, that many countries under MFA or MFA-like restrictions, fearful of unfettered competition, were not enthusiastic over a rapid elimination of the quota system, some of them defending a longer period for the phasing out of existing quotas than the ten years finally agreed upon.

All this said, one must recognize that the ATC "presents some definitive advantages over the situation prevailing before its entry into force:

- It put an end to the long life of the MFA;
- It shall bring the textiles and clothing sector under the same rules and disciplines applicable to all other industrial products; the sector shall cease to be a *special case*;
- It shall end definitively on 31 December 2004; it cannot be extended."[3]

Let us hope that these advantages will not be eroded during the life of the Agreement or by a reversion to protectionism when it expires.

5. The New Agreement

Because negotiators and their governments looked more to the past than to the future, and because many of them were obsessed by the MFA, the ATC bears some uncomfortable similarities to the MFA. The ATC however is not the MFA with a new name; significant differences exist between both agreements, to wit.

5.1. Improvements

The MFA was a derogation from the GATT, open to participation by Contracting Parties wishing to adhere to it and under certain circumstances by countries outside the GATT. The ATC forms an integral part of the Agreements negotiated in the Uruguay Round and is applicable to all Members of the WTO, including many who had never participated in the MFA, but it is closed to non-members of the WTO.

The MFA was a derogation from the GATT, so it could not lay down rules on how to bring trade in textiles and clothing under GATT rules and disciplines. The ATC, being part of the framework of the WTO, establishes rules on how to bring that trade under WTO rules (in ATC language, this is the *process of integration*

---

[3] Raffaelli M and Jenkins T (1996), *The Drafting History of the Agreement on Textiles and Clothing*, International Textiles and Clothing Bureau, Geneva, Switzerland

into GATT 1994). This shall be done in four stages: the first two occurred on 1 January 1995 and on 1 January 1998, the dates of the remaining two being 1 January 2002 and 1 January 2005. WTO Members wishing so, may integrate their textiles and clothing sector more speedily. Integration into GATT 1994 means that once integrated a product is no longer subject to the rules of the ATC; thereafter any restriction on that product must take the form of a safeguard according to the Agreement on Safeguards.

The MFA had no program for improvement of the terms of restraints, at least during the life of each bilateral agreement concluded by its parties. Once a quota was negotiated and a growth rate agreed, such rate would be applied until the expiration of the agreement. The MFA fixed minimum rates for annual quota growth and for flexibility, but also permitted in exceptional cases the application of lower rates. Some importing countries had applied this possibility so extensively that they made the norm into an exception: the EC and Sweden become notorious *exceptionalizers*; the United States applied the exception largely in regard to wool products, and then in regard to very large suppliers, such as Hong Kong and Korea. The ATC determines that restrictions inherited from the MFA, i.e., MFA restrictions that remain in force under the ATC, benefit from periodic increases in their annual growth rates; some improvement has also been laid down in regard to flexibility provisions.

As to restrictions introduced under the ATC, they shall necessarily (with the exception of wool products in the United States) be granted a growth rate of at least 6 per cent yearly, and the rates for flexibility shall be at least as high as those established (but frequently not applied) under the MFA.

While restrictions negotiated under the MFA could be applied for the whole period of each span of its life (four to five years), restrictions introduced under the ATC are limited to three years.

Under the MFA, the Textiles Surveillance Body (TSB) represented the first instance in a dispute, it being possible to appeal subsequently either to the Textiles Committee (another organ of the MFA) and then to the GATT Council, or directly to the Council. On only one occasion was a dispute taken directly to the Council; nothing useful to the solution of the problem resulted from this initiative. Under the ATC, the Textiles Monitoring Body represents the first instance, the next ones being the Dispute Settlement Body and the Appellate Body. Thus, the WTO treats disputes concerning the implementation of the ATC the same way as any other dispute. By June 1997, two disputes regarding the implementation of the ATC had already been brought to the Appellate Body and ruled on by it.

A last point needs to be made relating to the application of the ATC. The European Union and Canada, two frequent users of the MFA, did not invoke the Agreement during the first 30 months of its life. Let this represent a trend for a restrained implementation of the ATC, in opposition to the often abusive implementation of the MFA.

5.2. Remaining Problems

While these are significant improvements in relation to the MFA, not everything is rosy with the ATC; some problems still need to be faced and solved.

In the first place, the ATC obliges all WTO Members to participate, thus placing many countries under a special régime which may come to be applied to them. Since most of the Round's discussions on textiles and clothing centered on the MFA, many Contracting Parties that were not parties to the MFA did not become involved in the negotiation, or were not invited to participate in the small groups where the real negotiation took place. When it became clear that participation by all WTO Members would be mandatory in all Agreements, it was too late for such countries to express their views and interests. And more: the negotiators placed countries that had not participated in the MFA under 10-year restrictions through the inclusion (in Article 2, paragraph 1) of the words emphasized in the following phrase: "All quantitative restrictions within bilateral agreements maintained under Article 4 *or notified under Article 7 or 8* of the MFA..." This means that restrictions applied outside the MFA to a non-MFA participant, by the simple fact that they had been notified to the TSB *solely for its information*, under Article 7 or 8, would remain in force for the next decade, on the same footing with MFA restrictions.

Another disadvantage of the ATC in relation to the MFA resides exactly in the fact that the above-mentioned restrictions–excepting those rescinded because the product in question has been integrated–will continue in force for 10 more years. Even if the restricting Member stops producing an item under restraint, it is not obliged by the ATC to rescind the restraint, creating a situation of discrimination in favour of unrestricted Members.

The pace of integration might be another disadvantage. The first three stages will result in the integration of 51 per cent of the total volume of imports of all products listed in the ATC's Annex. On the date of termination of the Agreement, therefore, 49 per cent of the total volume of imports of each Member shall be integrated. Since such products may remain under restriction until the last hour, this could mean that such products are considered the most sensitive to import competition; in other words, these would be the products whose producers have the strongest clout with domestic politicians. If one wished to be pessimistic, one could imagine the outcry that would be heard from such well-connected producers, claiming that they still needed more protection (probably they would claim to need 'just a few more years'); one could also imagine the danger it would pose to the liberalizing process if their outcry found sympathetic ears. I put the whole argument in the conditional tense because with the annual increases in quotas mandated by the ATC, the level of most quotas by the tenth year of the Agreement should be so high as to be, in all probability, irrelevant.

If, however, the danger mentioned above is a possibility, it would be compounded by the fact that countries that are not efficient producers but have managed to become exporters because efficient producers have been kept under restrictions, would also join the outcry, claiming they cannot afford to see their industries disappear all of a sudden. A variation on this theme is the case of Brazil: while still under MFA restrictions, Brazil became one of the only two WTO

Members invoking the ATC in order to impose restrictions. (The other is the United States).

While the period of 10 years is long enough to prepare for the future, no one can guarantee the decade will be put to good use; such is the unfortunate lesson from the MFA, under which participating countries had 20 years for adjustment but only a few seriously pursued any such program.

Finally, the problems arising from the entry into the WTO of several large exporters or potential exporters will have to be dealt with. Terms for the exports by China, Russia and others will have to be negotiated. Could such terms include restrictions going beyond the life of the ATC? Solutions for rather difficult questions need to be found.

6. Concluding Remarks

Let us now try to sum everything up.

The ATC is not the dream of any defender of free trade, but it reflects a reasonable balance of very divergent interests. Its greatest merit resides in bringing textiles and clothing in from the cold where the sector had languished under the GATT. Even if this is done in stages, and even if the great leap toward integration on the last day of the Agreement requires a considerable act of faith, I believe that there is reason to expect that liberalization of international trade in textiles and clothing is a reality.

I have two main reasons for being optimistic as to the permanence of the liberalizing trend.

My first is the already mentioned increase that quotas inherited from the MFA would enjoy during the ten years of ATC life. My second reason is the following. The MFA was possible under the aegis of GATT's pragmatism, which in some cases amounted to no more than permissiveness. The ATC, and the whole textiles and clothing sector, are now part of the WTO, a more legalistic institution, under the aegis of which the kind of pragmatic solutions resorted to under the GATT are no longer tolerated. I would venture to say, and I sincerely hope I am right, that the rule of law for trade in textiles and clothing is here to stay.

Bibliography

Raffaelli M and Jenkins T (1996), *The Drafting History of the Agreement on Textiles and Clothing*. International Textiles and Clothing Bureau. Geneva, Switzerland

International Monetary Fund *Annual Report of the Executive Board* Series. IMF, Washington DC

Bringing Agriculture into the Multilateral Trading System

Clayton Yeutter

1. Introduction

Agricultural trade policy has long been enigmatic, often inexplicable, always exasperating, and frequently counter to the long-term best interest of a nation's own agriculturalists. For half a century it has provided more distortions to the multilateral trading system than any other segment of the global economy. That is truly ironic when one considers that agriculture is still the largest industry in most countries, and that food products are so crucial to the survival and well being of all of us. Why so many nations have worked so hard over so many years to impede agricultural trade is almost beyond comprehension!

For a time many of us wondered if the world would ever learn. But it finally did, and the intent of this paper is to put that learning experience in chronological perspective–to share with you the bumps and bruises, the highs and lows of what has happened in agricultural trade over the past half century.

2. Through to the Sixties

When the General Agreement on Tariffs and Trade (GATT) came into being in 1947, most nations had relatively little interest in agricultural trade rules. Though food security was of concern in areas of the world that were rebuilding after World War II, the focus of most nations was on re-establishing the viability of their own agricultural sectors. Food imports, like other imports, were considered something of a necessary evil.

The focus of the GATT itself was far more on industrial rules than on agricultural ones. In fact, at the insistence of the United States, agriculture in essence received a pass on the Article XI ban of quantitative restrictions (import quota programs) and on Article XVI disciplines of export subsidies. Those exemptions meant that nations could readily support their farm sectors (through production subsidies) and then protect their high internal support prices through both tariffs and import quotas. Agricultural export opportunities were a negotiation priority for very few nations. Even the United States, with its huge export potential, seemed then to be far more interested in protecting its own domestic market than in advancing the cause of free and open trade in food products.

That attitude prevailed for nearly four decades, through all the early rounds of GATT negotiations. Agricultural tariffs were reduced somewhat during those rounds, but almost as an afterthought. The *levelling of the playing field* that occurred in those early years was almost exclusively in industrial tariffs.

In the 1960s the United States finally began to awaken to its own export potential in agriculture. After having spent enormous sums of money in an attempt to shore up domestic farm prices, the US government as a *purchaser of last resort* had accumulated huge grain stocks. But those stocks constituted a cloud overhanging the market, and when stocks were unloaded domestically farmers were furious. Yet the government could not unload them internationally either–except at a huge loss, and only where markets were open to food imports. So the US government financed the construction of thousands of grain bins, at a time when stocks were building elsewhere in the world too.

Something had to change, for the cost of such folly was becoming unbearable. The first attempt at reform occurred in the Kennedy Round, with the negotiation of the International Grains Agreement. That was an effort to bring a bit of coordination and sanity to global grain trade, but it actually accomplished little. There was too much government in farming already, and adding still more internationally was not the answer! The Kennedy Round (1964-67) did provide meaningful progress on some agricultural tariffs, as did the earlier Dillon Round (1960-62), source of the commitment by the European Community to a zero binding on oilseeds imports.[1] But non-tarriff barriers still were not on the negotiators' radar screens.

The United States did begin in the mid-1960s to make its overall farm policy somewhat more market oriented, and US farmers began to prick up their ears when they heard the word exports.

Then the Russians came, and the world of agricultural trade changed forever!

3. The Early Seventies

In the early 1970s, the former Soviet Union entered world grain markets in a major way–as a food importer notwithstanding that nation's great potential as a food producer. The US, the European Community, Australia, New Zealand and other agricultural exporting nations were euphoric. But Japan and other major food importing nations were frightened at the prospect of food shortages. Consumers everywhere, even in the US, feared dramatic rises in food prices. Almost overnight, food security became a global public policy issue, and Malthusian prophets of doom moved to center stage. The self-proclaimed experts on this subject pon-

[1] That later created one of the major bilateral disputes (and delays) of the Uruguay Round, resolved finally in 1993 and incorporated in the Blair House Agreement.

tificated at a *World Food Conference* in Rome which garnered lots of headlines but had few policy solutions.

The US then exacerbated the situation by announcing an embargo on soybeans. Although price rationed supplies, so that the embargo was never implemented, it nevertheless stimulated food importing countries (especially Japan) to adopt policies that would make them (a) more self-sufficient in food production, and (b) less dependent on the US for their food supplies. That embargo, and the broader embargo on grain sales to the Soviet Union, which followed a few years later, distorted agricultural trade patterns for years to come (much to the disadvantage of US agriculture).

4. The Tokyo Round

All of this economic trauma did have an impact on the Tokyo Round of GATT negotiations, which was under way in the mid-1970s. The US and other actual or potential food exporters began to abandon their parochial, often protectionist, mindsets. Nearly 30 years after the GATT began, these nations finally shifted their emphasis to opening markets. *Let's help feed the world* became the rallying cry, and negotiators sought for the first time to attack non-tariff agricultural trade barriers as well as tariffs. And for the first time they sought to discipline export subsidies, which were becoming increasingly distortive to world trade–fostering competition among government treasuries rather than among farmers. By then the US and other nations were becoming visibly distressed by the actions of the European Community, which had begun to use export subsidies extensively as an element of the Common Agricultural Policy.

Not much, however, happened at the Tokyo Round negotiating table. The European Community skillfully isolated agricultural issues from the traditional negotiating agenda and successfully persuaded negotiators to focus nearly all their attention on the latter. The EC and other nations also attacked the absence of an *injury* provision in US countervailing duty law, and ultimately persuaded the US to adopt such a provision–one of its major concessions in the Tokyo Round. In return the EC and other subsidizing exporters agreed to a vague commitment not to use subsidies to capture *more than an equitable* share of world trade. That turned out to be one of the worst bargains the US ever made, and it led to a huge shift in global market share in the late 1970s and early 1980s. The EC's share rose dramatically; the share of the US and other traditional exporters declined just as dramatically, with predictable economic and political results.

Disappointments, disillusionment, and a lot of market devastation lay ahead.

5. The Mid-Eighties

So much happened to agriculture everywhere in the 1980s that for purposes of this discussion, I will split that decade into two parts.

Farmers the world around respond to economic incentives about as rapidly as anyone, and the food shortage scare of the 1970s provided the proof of that statement. Higher farm prices enticed American farmers, and others around the globe, to plant *fence row to fence row*. The Common Agricultural Policy (CAP) had the same effect in western Europe. As a consequence, the Malthusian fears of the 1970s disappeared within only a few years, and as the 1980s began much of the world was again awash in food surpluses, particularly in grains.

An overvalued dollar made the US increasingly uncompetitive in food products, industrial goods, and even in some of its service industries. America's bilateral trade deficit with Japan grew astronomically, and its global trade deficit began to set new records. The entire American business community became deeply concerned, as unemployment rose to double digit levels, inflation matched those numbers, and interest rates exceeded 20 per cent for the first time in anyone's memory. For the US this was a shocking and intolerable situation, and American politicians responded by calling for action at the GATT to correct whatever was awry.

Agriculture as an industry went through very hard times, in the US and many other countries. Conditions *down on the farm* were the worst since the depression years of the 1930s, and thousands of farmers were forced into bankruptcy. American farmers were infuriated as their global market share continued to decline in the face of massive European Community subsidies.

Notwithstanding the generosity of the CAP, even European farmers were becoming uneasy about all this, knowing that the relentless increase in CAP expenditures could not last forever.

In 1982 the US government made its first attempt to cope with this situation internationally. US Trade Representative Bill Brock, supported by a delegation of American Congressmen, recommended at a GATT ministerial meeting in Geneva that a new trade round commence as soon as possible. Ambassador Brock also suggested that agricultural trade be front and center in such a negotiation, in light of the deteriorating farm economy in the US and numerous other countries. But the US was rebuffed, and its delegation returned home bitterly disappointed.

As the decade unfolded, agricultural trade patterns became increasingly distorted, bilateral and plurilateral trade squabbles increasingly prevalent, and farm policies in many countries began to *break the bank*. By mid-decade many countries, including the US, had a farm crisis on their hands. The US Congress finally responded with a farm bill in 1986 that not only provided an unprecedented US$26 billion in financial assistance to American farmers but also was confrontational in tone. The US initiated its Export Enhancement Program (EEP) as a counter to European Community export subsidies, and the world braced for a subsidy war. The stage was set for the most combative agricultural debate ever in the GATT and in other fora.

6. The Uruguay Round

Two other phenomena added pressures for a renewed multilateral effort to improve trade rules in agriculture and on other subjects. One was improved G-7 coordination of monetary policy, culminating in the Plaza Accord. That accord facilitated a realignment of exchange rates, bringing them much closer to purchasing power parity than had previously been the case. The weakening of the dollar vis-a-vis other major currencies significantly boosted US competitiveness in agriculture and in many other areas.

That development was macroeconomic; the other was microeconomic, reflected in the US choosing for the first time to attack *unfair trade practices* unilaterally rather than through GATT dispute settlement. Trade officials of other nations were shocked by this disdain for GATT procedures, but many were sympathetic because of the obvious shortcomings of the GATT dispute settlement mechanism.

The US had been winning most, though not all, of its GATT cases, but that was irrelevant since the losing country was privileged, under the rules, to veto the GATT panel recommendation. In addition, the settlement timetable was nebulous, which meant that many GATT cases simply dragged on for years. The European Community took advantage of these institutional shortcomings to protect the CAP against GATT challenge, and other countries (including the US) averted challenges to some of their own dubious trade distortions.

Unilateral action has none of those shortcomings. Section 301 of the US trade law was a swift, decisive, powerful trade policy weapon. It began to have an impact in bilateral negotiations on agriculture and in other trade disputes as well. That motivated the affected nations to seek multilateral disciplines over such unilateral measures. Section 301 was instrumental in bringing about the US-Japan beef/citrus agreement, a number of other bilateral accords with Japan, and agreements with the European Community on several longstanding agricultural disputes.

By mid-l986 interest in a new trade round began to rise. The enthusiasm for such an effort was far from overwhelming, for it was already apparent that agriculture would be contentious. Perhaps so contentious that it would torpedo the process even before it got under way, as it did in 1982.

One of the benefits of history is that one can, if willing and perceptive, learn from the past. And those for whom agricultural trade reform was important did precisely that. The first evidence came through creation of the Cairns Group in August 1986. That represented the fine leadership of John Dawkins, then Trade Minister in Australia. Dawkins recognized that his predecessors and their counterparts in New Zealand had long been committed, but ineffective, proponents of agricultural trade reform. They simply had too few allies, which meant that their proposals–reasonable as they might be–were quickly isolated by opponents and then just ignored. The Cairns meeting supplied the allies, including Canada and a number of influential developing countries. Fourteen nations joined the Cairns Group at that time, and they've worked together with remarkable coherence ever since. On numerous occasions they have provided a balance wheel to the ideological tiffs between the European Community and the United States over agriculture, nearly always with a constructive outcome. The Cairns Group has been catalytic, sensible and pragmatic. Without question their input was critical to launching the Uruguay Round agricultural negotiations, and to bringing them to a successful conclusion years later.

By the summer of 1986, Preparatory Committee (Prepcom) activity on a possible new trade round was well under way in Geneva, and was generating momentum. Not surprisingly there was more enthusiasm in Geneva than in capitals, but the latter were being propelled inexorably towards a ministerial level meeting. That meeting occurred in Punta del Este, Uruguay in September 1986.

Agriculture was on the minds of trade officials as the Punta del Este meeting drew near, but it was by no means the feature debate. The potential agenda was now much broader than in 1982. There was Prepcom discussion of the need for GATT rules on services, a wholly new topic for that organization which had traditionally dealt with rules only for goods. Some even thought the GATT ought to begin to develop rules for foreign investment, another wholly new topic. Dispute settlement was also being discussed, for the reasons outlined earlier in this paper, and many felt that this topic should be broadened into a negotiation that would encompass overall institutional reform for GATT as an organization. In addition, the US was pressing hard bilaterally for intellectual property protection, and numerous delegations believed this to be an issue ripe also for multilateral rules.

Notwithstanding the legitimacy of all these issues, new and old, as delegations arrived in Punta del Este a consensus on the agenda for a new trade round was far from apparent. Some delegations favored a more traditional agenda, Others, such as Brazil and India, objected vehemently to some of the new topics, and especially to the creation of multilateral rules for services and intellectual property. Still others, such as the United States, felt that the GATT was already behind the curve in responding to the needs of international commerce, and needed a major jolt if it was to survive, let alone function effectively in the future.

Agriculture might well have been lost in that shuffle of potential agenda topics, but it wasn't. And it may even have benefitted from the debate on other areas of interest. Not being the primary focus of attention, it could be handled with more poise and calm than was possible four years earlier. Personal leadership and the willingness to take political risk helped too. The Uruguay Round owes its auspicious beginning to Enrique Iglesias, then the Uruguayan Trade Minister, who chaired the meeting magnificently (on what must have felt like a continual, 24 hours per day schedule), with the able counsel of GATT Director-General Arthur Dunkel. For agriculture specifically, accolades go to Willy de Clercq of the European Community, Dick Lyng of the US and John Dawkins of the Cairns Group. All three were determined to bring agriculture into the negotiating process in a meaningful but equitable way, and they succeeded.[2] The Uruguay Round was

---

[2] The language on agriculture called for *improving market access through, inter alia, the reduction of import barriers* and *increasing discipline on the use of all direct and indirect subsidies and other measures affecting directly or indirectly agricultural trade, including the phased reduction of their negative effects.*

launched, with agriculture and all the other *new* topics on the agenda, giving it the broadest negotiating mandate in GATT history, by far.[3]

Negotiators went home and caught their breath, pondering how to get all this done within the four-year time frame that was then contemplated for completion of the round. The Tokyo Round had taken nearly twice that long, but most veterans of that exercise felt that such a lengthy time frame was inappropriate and unnecessary then and even less appropriate now.

The GATT Contracting Parties were determined to finish the Uruguay Round on time, and to avoid the traditional US-European Community bickering that had been the source of delay in earlier rounds. Other delegations also wanted to make sure they would be *players* this time, and not just onlookers as the two big trade giants debated their positions.[4] Regrettably those good intentions were once again not to be fully realized.

A few months later, in July 1987, delegations submitted their *initial proposals* in agriculture, and those submissions provided the first bombshells of the Uruguay Round. The Punta del Este language on agriculture was necessarily skeletal. The initial proposals were much more comprehensive, and the US proposal was surprisingly bold–some would say startling! It advocated the phase-out of all trade distortive production and export subsidies within 10 years, the conversion of all non-tariff measures to tariffs, and dramatic improvements in market access.[5]

The US proposal sent shock waves through the Geneva negotiating teams, and those shock waves reverberated among the capitals of all GATT nations with an interest in agriculture. Some concluded that this was just a negotiating ploy and that the US was not really serious. That was wishful thinking, for the eventual elimination of trade distorting subsidies in agriculture is assuredly a laudatory objective. Anyone believing in the fundamental benefits of more free and open trade would reach that conclusion; it is the foundation on which the GATT was created and built. In trade policy terms the US argument was compelling and persuasive.

Opponents of the proposal were immediately placed on the defensive, relegated to arguing that the proposal was politically impossible, and totally unrealistic within a ten-year time frame. The US response was *if not 10 years, how many? 12? 15? 20?*

Did American negotiators realize that their proposal established an unreachable objective for the Uruguay Round? Of course. But the US felt it was imperative to let the whole world know that it meant business on agricultural trade reform, that it would not accept another *nibbling at the edges* outcome that had characterized both the Kennedy and Tokyo rounds. By seeking a full measure of reform the US not only had a position based on principle, but one that also provided maximum negotiating leverage and flexibility. The US always knew that to bring about closure of the Uruguay Round, an agreement on agriculture would need to be politically tolerable for the European Community (with the CAP still being the

---

[3] In all, 15 negotiating groups were established.

[4] In agriculture that was an obvious objective of the Cairns Group.

[5] Alternatively *by the turn of the century* or *by the year 2000* since the Uruguay Round was expected to conclude in 1990.

political glue that binds the EC) and Japan (because of the special sensitivity of rice) while also representing substantial export potential for the US and the Cairns Group.

Fundamentally the US objective was to halt the onrushing train of trade distorting agricultural policies that had gained credence in many countries over the prior decade or more, turn that train around, and get it moving in the direction of free and open trade. Upon full implementation of the Uruguay Round the hope was that this train would be gaining speed, and that the next round of negotiations would propel the train to its final destination, an open, competitive global marketplace.[6]

In terms of broad negotiating strategy the US felt it imperative that the Negotiating Group on Agriculture focus on four discrete areas of reform: (a) production subsidies; (b) export subsidies; (c) import access; and (d) sanitary/phytosanitary (food safety) measures. The first three were and are inextricably related; what occurs in one inevitably affects, either directly or indirectly, what happens in the other two. The sanitary/phytosanitary negotiations were handled separately, and there the challenge was to persuade all GATT Contracting Parties to recognize the importance of this topic to people everywhere. This was fundamentally a standards issue, with the standards to be based on sound science rather than on fright or emotion.

The US also sought a specific, definitive, precise agreement, not one that might be subject to varied interpretations. Nebulous agreements rarely produce reform; they simply produce additional, and sometimes bitter, follow-up negotiations. The US delegation was determined to avoid such an outcome. That is why the United States favored the use of a quantitative standard, the Aggregate Measure of Support (AMS), for production subsidies; export subsidy reform measured in both value and unit terms; and the tariffication (i.e., the conversion of non-tariff measures to tariffs) of all import restrictions.[7]

7. The Mid-Term Review

During the tenure of a multilateral trade round it is important that trade ministers meet informally from time to time, to identify and seek to remove major stumbling

---

6 That was one of the reasons the US insisted that the Uruguay Round Agreement provide for an additional tranche of agricultural negotiations to begin one year before the conclusion of the Uruguay Round implementation period.

7 The Cairns Group shared that philosophical view. Later in the negotiations Aart de Zeeuw, Chairman of the Uruguay Round Agricultural Negotiating Group, worked with each of these parameters as he sought diligently to bring about consensus within the Group, and Director-General Dunkel did the same in his own Final Draft at an even later stage of the negotiations. For most of the Round the European Community resisted this format for agriculture, but the arguments in its favor were simply too compelling. In all negotiations one must ultimately find solutions that fit the economic environment which spawned the debate.

blocks, and to simply move the process along. This is *preventive medicine*, trade style.

As the Uruguay Round negotiations moved beyond preliminary skirmishing, the ministers agreed it would be helpful to have a Mid-Term Review, in the hope of having an early harvest of agreements in some negotiating groups. Canada agreed to host it, in Montreal, and the meeting was to be a ministerial level stock-taking of what had been accomplished during the first two years, followed by agreement on a work program for the final two years of the Uruguay Round.

By then the Round had begun to drift a bit, and there were concerns that we might be entering a lull period similar to what occurred in the Tokyo Round. So there were high hopes that the Montreal Mid-Term Review would counter that threat and become a momentum generator for the remainder of the Round.

The Montreal session forced ministers to prepare on issues of importance to them, and that in itself was useful. But too many delegations were not yet focused on the crucial issues of that complex negotiation. Those of us who advocated the Montreal session were correct in assuming that a successful Mid-Term Review was a prerequisite to a successful conclusion of the Uruguay Round within four years, i.e., by the end of 1990. But we were incorrect in assuming that we would make a quantum leap forward in Montreal.

Nowhere was this more evident than in agriculture, where the US sought agreement on a negotiating framework comparable to that outlined earlier in this paper. The European Community was wary of this proposal, and negotiators ran out of time in attempting to find framework language acceptable to both. That was a costly failure for all participants, including the US. It gave the round a psychological defeat, when it needed victories, and it halted momentum in agriculture just when the effort needed to be accelerated.

An agricultural framework did not materialize until Director-General Dunkel brought the Geneva negotiators back together four months later to finish the Mid-Term Review. All parties then agreed to negotiate *substantial progressive reductions in agricultural support and protection, sustained over an agreed period of time.* The US viewed this language as embracing distortions in production and export subsidies, and also embracing import restrictions of all types.[8] Later it would become apparent that the EC had a different view.

After the disappointments of Montreal the negotiators had a good feeling about being able to *put Humpty Dumpty back together again* in Geneva. One might have expected some nations to abandon hope after Montreal. But none did so, and after the negotiators wrapped up the loose ends of the Mid-Term Review (not just in agriculture, but in other negotiating groups as well), an air of optimism prevailed. Perhaps the Uruguay Round, with its daunting agenda, would be a success after all. Soon the anticipated year of destiny arrived.

---

[8] In October 1989 the US submitted a comprehensive negotiating proposal as a follow-up to the Mid-Term Agreement in agriculture. That proposal, which called for a phase-out of all trade distorting subsidies and import constraints, became known as the Zero Option.

8. The Early Nineties

Unglamorous but essential preliminary negotiations continued into the first half of 1990, at which time all efforts began to point towards a final ministerial meeting to be held in Brussels in December, the target for concluding this four-year negotiation.

At mid-year, Director-General Dunkel asked the various negotiating group chairmen to submit outline agreements which would serve as a basis for the final negotiating push. Agriculture's talented and dedicated negotiating group chairman, Aart de Zeeuw, developed a bold outline using the four category format that had been advocated by both the US and the Cairns Group. The content of that outline instantaneously demonstrated that there was still a huge gap between the positions of those groups and those of the European Community. EC negotiators were distressed, for the de Zeeuw outline called for specific reform commitments far beyond any that had then been contemplated by the Community. The EC was by no means prepared to endorse language that would call for significant change in its domestic price support and export subsidy programs, the heart of the CAP. It wanted much more flexibility in whatever reforms it might undertake.

The de Zeeuw outline was ultimately modified somewhat, but its very existence made it obvious that agriculture would be a "splitting headache" in Brussels. Director-General Dunkel's intent in calling for outline agreements was that those documents would be used to narrow differences between and among the major participants in the remaining months of 1990.[9] The hope was that a number of the Uruguay Round negotiating groups would essentially finish their negotiations before the opening of the Brussels meeting. The further hope was that even in contentious areas such as agriculture, services, and intellectual property only a few major issues would remain for ministerial disposition in Brussels. The final trade-offs could then be made, and an overall agreement concluded.

The US Congress sent its own message in agriculture by adding triggers in the Farm Bill calling for the much more aggressive use of American export subsidies if a satisfactory agreement on agriculture was not reached.

As the Brussels meeting convened it soon became apparent that there was lots of discord, in agriculture and on other issues. For example, the negotiation on services, a key element of the Uruguay Round, had seemed to be on track in Montreal, but clearly had become bogged down since. For a number of countries trade-offs between these two subject matter areas were imperative, so it was almost impossible to reach agreement in one without the other.

---

[9] The US and the Cairns Group each made an attempt to do this by submitting responses that filled in the blanks of the de Zeeuw outline. The US for the first time sent a formal signal that it was prepared to accept something less than the Zero Option. The US proposal called for a 90 per cent reduction in export subsidies and a 75 per cent reduction in the other two categories, implemented over 10 years from a 1986-88 base. The European Community had great difficulty developing its own pre-Brussels proposal. Late in that preparatory period it finally proposed a non-specific 30 per cent reduction in supports (from a more favorable base period).

In agriculture the hope was that everyone would be ready for a grand compromise, one that would not only take the agricultural negotiations over the top but also be a motivating force to bring everything else to a successful conclusion. Since the European Community had sent up a non-specific 30 per cent trial balloon on reforms, Sweden's Mats Hellström[10] decided to launch a trial balloon of his own. Hellström used the 30 per cent number, but applied it to internal supports, export subsidies, and import restrictions–over a five-year time frame and with a different base period. When even that proposal, far more modest than had been contemplated by most negotiators, proved unacceptable to the European Community, other negotiating delegations (led by some of the Cairns Group) abandoned the meeting. There was to be no agricultural agreement in Brussels, and no final wrap-up to celebrate.

The entire Uruguay Round then had a shaky foundation indeed. Fortunately, all delegations had by then invested so much intellectual energy and negotiating effort in the round that few participants wanted to walk away. In addition, much had been accomplished in the individual working groups, including the one on agriculture. In the aggregate more had already been done than in any previous GATT round; it was 'closure' that proved illusive.

The US Congress extended its fast track negotiating authority. That provided a bit of breathing space. But negotiators struggled until Arthur Dunkel, in one of his final and most courageous acts as Director-General of the GATT, produced a Draft Final Text just one year after the breakdown of negotiations in Brussels. This was a brilliant stroke, for it told those who had lost confidence that an agreement was still achievable. Success of the Uruguay Round was there for the taking. Through his personal leadership and creativity the Director-General had assimilated all the efforts of the Uruguay Round in a final draft text. The missing element was now one of political will, and it was up to the GATT member nations to provide that ingredient. Mr. Dunkel had thrown down the gauntlet to more than 100 trade ministers, a test of their political fortitude and that of their chiefs of state. Fortunately for the world, most were finally ready for the challenge.

Ray MacSharry, the European Community's Commissioner for Agriculture, had earlier stepped forward with a CAP reform proposal that was highly controversial politically but economically sound. Enacted in 1992, after months of vigorous debate, it halted the EC's own onrushing train of ever expanding agricultural subsidies, turned it around and sent it off in the other direction. In the view of some of us it was still moving too slowly, for lots of trade distortions remained, but at least it was going in the right direction. The concepts and provisions of the MacSharry reform package were beginning to approach the US/Cairns Group/de Zeeuw framework, as well as that envisioned by the Director-General in his Draft Final Act.

By then the US was implementing its 1990 Farm Bill, the provisions of which were quite compatible with the Draft Final Act. Hence, one could finally begin to see the outlines of an agricultural agreement between the US and the EC.

At that point the other Uruguay Round participants saw little value in further pursuing any aspect of the negotiations until and unless the EC and the US were

[10] Chairman of the Agricultural Negotiating Group at the Brussels meeting.

able to resolve their differences over agriculture. As in the Tokyo Round, they were unenthused about sitting on the sidelines as observers. But they had little choice, and could only hope for the best.

Regrettably the two giants had to resolve a bilateral dispute over cereal substitutes (mentioned earlier) simultaneously with their Uruguay Round agricultural issues, and that was a formidable challenge. The bilateral hurdles were finally overcome, and the so-called Blair House Agreement was signed between these two great economic powers–friends and competitors always–in November 1992.

Two years delayed, that was the beginning of a successful end to the Uruguay Round. Not everyone was enthusiastic about the US-EC accord. A good many of the agricultural negotiating group members felt that the final outcome encompassed too little reform, but others breathed a sigh of relief that the end was in sight and that some of the benefits of this protracted effort would accrue to them. There would soon be more agricultural competition in the world than at any time in their memories.

9. Electoral Transition

But then the United States had a presidential election, resulting in a transition just as the remaining trade-offs of the Uruguay Round might have been made. Though President Bush had hoped for a final agreement prior to his departure from government in January 1993, some of the GATT member nations preferred to take their chances with a new Clinton Administration. So all was delayed one more time! That too had agricultural implications.

The government of France was not pleased with the Blair House Agreement. In particular France objected to the magnitude of export subsidy reductions, and to the heavy "front loading" of those commitments. France was also displeased with certain other elements of the Dunkel text, including the provisions on services (an area of considerable export potential for France). The French expressed their displeasure in clear and distinct terms, both in Brussels and in Washington, D.C. So the Uruguay Round was once again threatened.

Arthur Dunkel retired on June 30, 1993, after having tirelessly and patiently presided over these negotiations for nearly seven years. He was succeeded by Peter Sutherland, a highly regarded political and business figure in Ireland, and also a former European Community commissioner. Director-General Sutherland hit the ground running, immediately establishing a work program for the fall and a definitive objective of concluding the Uruguay Round by the end of the year. Mr. Sutherland provided splendid leadership at that crucial time, and he was a demanding but fair taskmaster. Negotiators stuck to their timetable, modest concessions were made to satisfy French objections, and some issues were extracted from the negotiations to be dealt with separately in a post-Uruguay Round exercise. The final trade-offs were made on schedule, and the Uruguay Agreement Final Act was concluded on December 15, 1993.[11] The Agreement was signed in

[11] Amendments to the Blair House Agreement had been finalized one week earlier.

Marrakesh, Morocco on April 15,1994, and a new World Trade Organization (WTO) was born. It had been a long ride, nearly twice as long as originally anticipated, comparable to the time frame of the Tokyo Round. But the final package far exceeded anything ever before achieved in a multilateral trade negotiation. The GATT bowed out in style!

10. The Agricultural Results

What was in it for agriculture? As Carole Brookins, a prominent agricultural consultant, has said:

> *The Agreement was a remarkable achievement, bringing agricultural trade under the rules and disciplines of the GATT for the first time. No one should underestimate the value of full tariffication, nor the initial steps made towards eliminating export subsidies. In fact, the great tragedy for the agricultural sector and for the world economy is the nearly half century of time lost in getting this job started. If we had begun this process in 1947 when the GATT began its work in reducing industrial tariffs, we would have had a 50-year 'adjustment' period to transition down to full open markets in agriculture by 1997. And what a difference that would have made.* [12]

Carole Brookins was correct. The agreement on agriculture was a fine achievement, though it could have come decades sooner and the reforms could have been more extensive. Here is what did occur:

- *Production Subsidy Disciplines*–A 20 per cent reduction in the Aggregate Measure of Support (AMS) in equal annual installments from a 1986-88 base. The discipline applies only to domestic policies that are considered trade distorting (in trade jargon, the amber box). Subsidies such as those for research and extension, food inspection services, environmental programs, food aid, pest control, and a number of others are in an exempted *green box*. Notably, most direct payments to farmers (provided they are based on a fixed area and yield or a fixed number of livestock) are also exempt.
- *Export Subsidy Disciplines*–A 36 per cent reduction in expenditures and 21 per cent reduction in volume (24 per cent and 14 per cent respectively for developing countries) in equal annual installments from a 1986-90 base. The commitments apply to individual agricultural products, but annual reductions can be made from a 1991-92 base if the subsidy levels then were higher than during the 1986-90 base period.[13]
- *Import Access*–Conversion of all non-tariff barriers (import quotas, variable levies, minimum import prices, etc.) to their tariff equivalents. The tariff equivalents must then be reduced by an average of 36 per cent in equal annual

[12] In her address to the International Agribusiness Management Association (IAMA), Jakarta, Indonesia, June 1997

[13] This ameliorates the *front loading* problem that was so troublesome to France.

installments over the six-year implementation period. Individual tariffs must be reduced by at least 15 per cent during that period.

A safeguard mechanism is available should imports exceed certain specified levels.

Since many of the tariff equivalents will be quite high, a minimum access of 3 per cent of consumption is to apply immediately, increasing to 5 per cent of consumption in the sixth and final year of the implementation period. If import access already exceeds the minimum level, that access must be maintained.

Minimum access commitments are to be achieved through the use of tariff quotas. There are some qualifications to this provision permitting aggregation in certain cases (e.g., dairy products); granting an exemption for one staple food in developing countries under specified conditions; permitting Japan to postpone tariffication of rice until the end of the implementation period; and a few others.

- *Sanitary/Phytosanitary Measures*–A separate agreement which seeks to harmonize international standards through the efforts of organizations such as Codex Alimentarius, the International Office of Epizootics, and the International Plant Protection Organization. The basic thrust of this agreement is that countries must base their sanitary/phytosanitary standards and regulations on credible scientific evidence. Should they not do so, their import restrictions will be subject to challenge in the World Trade Organization.
- *Dispute Settlement*–The dispute settlement provisions emanating from the Uruguay Round will be applicable, of course, to all products, not just agricultural ones. They deserve special mention here because they respond to decades of frustration within the global agricultural community. The new provisions insure a decisive outcome in a timely manner. They've already become one of the earliest and most noteworthy success stories of the World Trade Organization.

Other elements of the Uruguay Round Agreement are also important to agriculture, but I shall not delineate them here. The five just enumerated are at the top of my list of Uruguay Round agricultural achievements.[14]

11. Future Challenge

This is no time to rest on our laurels, for there are plenty of challenges ahead in agricultural trade reform. The next opportunity to propel that reform 'train' will

[14] As Milling & Baking News put it in a December 28, 1993 editorial: *When the Round began ... the commitment to bring agriculture under GATT for the first time was viewed by cynics as little more than an ambitious wish inserted to satisfy the Americans. That this opening commitment has become reality ... provides a new standing for agriculture .... The industry has been granted new freedom by the Uruguay Round, a freedom holding out wonderful promise....*

arise in 1999, one year before the six-year Uruguay Round implementation period expires. That second tranche of agricultural negotiations is already on the WTO agenda, and interested nations should already have preliminary preparations under way.

The first obligation of the WTO negotiators should be to make sure that both the spirit and the letter of the Uruguay Round agricultural agreement are being fully met. Not surprisingly there've been some disagreements already over the Uruguay Round agricultural commitments. Some (hopefully most) will be resolved informally; others will be resolved through WTO dispute settlement. But some may call for *clean-up* negotiations in 1999.

The second challenge for the negotiators will be to move the reform process forward, in all the areas mentioned in this paper. Export subsidies should be phased out completely, in all WTO member nations. The GATT accomplished that for industrial products; the WTO should be able to do the same for agriculture.

The negotiators should be able also to phase out *amber box* production subsidies, even in developing countries where those resources can typically be put to better use elsewhere. And they should be able to shrink the *green box* of permitted supports, making sure they've removed elements of support that should perhaps have been in the amber category (i.e., subject to WTO discipline).

Import access might well turn out to be the salient feature of the 1999 tranche of negotiations. Minimum access under tariff quotas should increase significantly and tariffs should be reduced dramatically. By the end of the implementation period for this new agreement all agricultural tariffs should be below an agreed maximum level. *Stratospheric* tariffs in agriculture should become only a memory!

Finally, the negotiators need to amend the Sanitary/Phytosanitary Code based on implementation experience under the Uruguay Round. People everywhere should have access to ample supplies of wholesome foods. Food safety will become an increasingly important issue, and that will put the WTO Sanitary/Phytosanitary Code in the limelight. We must insure that it does its job, and does it well.

If the next set of WTO agricultural negotiators can skillfully build on the record of their Uruguay Round predecessors, the world will benefit enormously. If all goes well, they'll reach agreement as this century concludes, and their accord will be fully implemented a few years later. By then we may well have a billion more people to feed than inhabit the world today. That formidable task will be made much easier if we then have a far more free and open trading system in global agriculture.

Bibliography

Brookins CL (1997), *Agricultural Trade Policy: Can We Achieve Food Without Borders?* World Perspectives Inc. Newsletter, Washington DC

Brookins CL (25 June 1997), *Opportunities and Threats on the Road to 2020.* Address to the Annual Congress of the International Agribusiness Management Association, Jakarta, Indonesia

Congressional Budget Office (June 1987), *The GATT Negotiations and US Trade Policy*. Congress of the United States. Washington DC

Consultative Group of Eighteen (October 1981), *Agriculture in the GATT*. Note by the GATT Secretariat. Geneva, Switzerland

de Zeeuw A (July 1990), *Framework Agreement on Agriculture Reform Programme, Draft Text by the Chairman*. GATT Secretariat. Geneva, Switzerland

Fischler F (1 July 1997), *EU Readies Change*. Milling & Baking News, Kansas City, MO

Foreign Agriculture Service, USDA (January 1994), *Agricultural Provisions of the Uruguay Round*. US Department of Agriculture. Washington DC

GATT Secretariat (15 December 1993), *Final Act Embodying the Results of the Uruguay Round of Multilateral Trade Negotiations*. Geneva, Switzerland

Herlihy MT, Glauber JW and Vertrees JG (September 1993), *US-EC Blair House Agreemen*. Washington DC, USDAIERS International. Agriculture and Trade Reports, Europe

Hillman JS (Summer 1993), *Agriculture in the Uruguay Round: A United States Perspective*. Tulsa Law Journal, Tulsa OK

International Policy Council on Agriculture, Food and Trade (May 1994), *Assessing the GATT Agreement in Agriculture*. Thirteenth Plenary Meeting. Seville, Spain

Jackson J (1989), *Law and Policy of International Economic Relations: The World Trading System*. MIT Press: Cambridge MA

Office of Economics, Economic Research Service, USDA (March 1994), *Effects of the Uruguay Round Agreement on US Agricultural Commodities*. US Department of Agriculture, Washington DC

Office of Economics, Economic Research Service, USDA (May 1991), *Economic Implications of the Uruguay Round for US Agriculture*. US Department of Agriculture, Washington DC

Office of the US Trade Representative (October 1989), *Submission of the United States on Comprehensive Long-Term Agricultural Reform*. Negotiating Group on Agriculture, GATT Secretariat. Geneva, Switzerland

Paarlberg RT (Fourth Quarter 1995), *Does the GATT Agreement Promote Export Subsidies?* Choices, US Department of Agriculture, Washington DC

Paemen H and Bensch A (1995), *From the GATT to the WTO: The European Community in the Uruguay Round*. Leuven Uni. Press: Leuven, Belgium

Petersmann E-U and Hilf M (1988), *The New GATT Round of Multilateral Trade Negotiations*, Studies in Transnational Economic Law, Volume 5. Kluwer Law and Taxation Publishers: Boston MA

Preeg EH (1994), *Traders in a Brave New World: The Uruguay Round and the Future of the International Trading System*. Center for Strategic & International Studies. Washington DC

Sanderson FH (1994), *The GATT Agreement on Agriculture*. National Center for Food & Agricultural Policy. Washington DC

Sanderson FH (October 1994), *Agriculture and Multilateralism. Bretton Woods Revisited*. Conference sponsored by the Institute for Agriculture and Trade Policy, Bretton Woods NH

Schott JJ (September 1996), *WTO 2000: Setting the Course for World Trade*. Institute for International Economics, Washington DC

Working Party on Agricultural Policies and Markets of the Committee for Agriculture (1994), *The Uruguay Round: A Preliminary Evaluation of the Impacts of the Agreement on Agriculture in the OECD Countries*. Organization for Economic Cooperation and Development, Paris, France

Yeutter C (June 1994), *International Trade in the Aftermath of the Uruguay Round–A Policy Overview.* Address to the International Symposium on Competition Law and Trade Policy. Brussels, Belgium

Trade in Services–Bringing Services into the Multilateral Trading System

Geza Feketekuty

1. Introduction

One of the most innovative and important accomplishments of the Uruguay Round of Multilateral Trade Negotiations was the negotiation of the General Agreement on Trade in Services (GATS) and the associated annexes and national schedules of commitments. The negotiations resulted in a comprehensive set of rules for preserving and expanding market access for internationally traded services, an integrated framework for addressing interrelated policy issues affecting the operation of global companies producing services, and significant commitments with respect to the rapidly growing trade in information-based business services.

In the not too distant past, services were considered non-tradable. This was partly a matter of definition, because services were defined as being produced where they were consumed. International transfers of services that took place through the movement of service providers from one country to another were considered an international movement of a factor of production, not trade. The computer revolution changed this fundamental dichotomy by making it possible to produce information-based services in one country and make the item available to a consumer in another.[1]

In order to fully appreciate what was accomplished, it is therefore necessary to understand three things:

- First, the emergence of intra-corporate telecommunications networks and the growth of trade in information-based services through these networks has been the major driving force behind the globalization of production in both the manufacturing and services sector. It has enabled global firms to rationalize the production of internal business services and to coordinate production schedules at widely dispersed facilities on a global basis.
- Second, the rapid growth of trade in services has largely involved the procurement of business services by global enterprises who have been in the best position to procure services inputs on a global basis.

[1] For a further conceptual discussion see Bhagwati (1984) and Sampson and Snape (1985)

- Third, the sale of consumer services, particularly infrastructure services and services sold to consumers through local establishments, has been highly regulated. In contrast, the sale of many business services has remained relatively free of government regulation, and businesses with a global presence can get around restrictions on local retail establishments by dealing directly with global suppliers.

In addition to the information revolution, two other long-term economic trends fundamentally changed the role and tradability of services. First, the microelectronic revolution opened the door to greater competition in the provision of infrastructure services. Modern computer technology enables competitive providers of infrastructure services to share network facilities such as cables or pipelines and to coordinate the interconnection of independent networks. Other technological advances have created alternative modes or channels for delivering infrastructure services, e.g., cellular phones. Second, changes in the technology of production have significantly increased the role and share of business services in the production process, while the increasing technological complexity and customization of products has forced businesses to concentrate on their core activities and to outsource many of their business services.

The most important accomplishment of the Uruguay Round negotiations on services in the near term was the establishment of a framework and a set of commitments for keeping international trade in information-based business services relatively unencumbered. This was crucial, because trade in such services has been the major source of growth in international trade of services, and has been at the core of the productivity enhancing globalization process in both manufacturing and services.

Over the long term, the GATS will be remembered as one of the major achievements of the Uruguay Round. It created the basic framework for the progressive liberalization of trade in services and the reform of sectoral regulations which now and in the past have retarded productivity improvements in the largest sector of the economy. Services not only account for the largest and most rapidly growing sector in most economies, but are increasingly the key to the maintenance of a high growth rate in the world economy. Inefficiencies in highly protected domestic service industries have become the major bottlenecks to economic growth in many of the more advanced developing countries While these countries managed to achieve high growth rates in the past through an export-led expansion of manufacturing, they failed to reform regulations which restrict competition and trade in the business services and infrastructure services which those manufacturing enterprises must use to compete in global markets.

The GATS also paved the way in establishing a comprehensive framework for dealing in an integrated fashion with a broad range of policy instruments that affect international trade and investment. The globalization of production is creating political pressures for an expansion of the range of issues addressed in the World Trade Organization (WTO), including issues such as investment and competition policy which are covered in the GATS. While the GATS undoubtedly can be improved as a legal document, it constitutes a working model for integrating a wide range of policy instruments in a coherent way.

Much has been written, particularly in the popular press, about the shortcomings of the Uruguay Round results in services. This pessimistic assessment is based in part on a lack of understanding of what was accomplished with respect to information-based business services. In part it is based on a correct assessment that little was accomplished with respect to fundamental reforms in domestic regulations that restrict international trade and competition in infrastructure services and consumer services sold through local retail establishments. The latter was not achievable under any realistic scenario. At the same time, the framework established in the Uruguay Round creates a solid foundation for addressing these sectoral regulatory restrictions in the future. This has already been demonstrated in the subsequent negotiation of the Agreement on Basic Telecommunications Services.

2. What was Achieved in the Uruguay Round

Fifteen years ago, most trade officials and economists would have denied that services had anything to do with trade. In fact, trade in services was considered an oxymoron. Policy measures affecting the production and sale of services were considered a domestic matter, and international discussions of services were largely seen as an exercise in resolving national regulatory conflicts. Little credence was given to international specialization in the production of services, and to the economic benefits that could be derived from trade in services. Against that background, the results of the Uruguay Round are significant.

- The negotiations served to legitimize issues affecting international transactions in services as trade issues and to establish a comprehensive set of international rules for liberalizing trade in services, and an initial set of market access commitments on services that will reduce the uncertainty facing foreign providers of services.
- The negotiators were successful in developing a comprehensive legal framework for trade in services, the GATS. The GATS covers the full range of issues identified in the original analysis as critical to the achievement of effective market access, including provisions covering domestic regulations, establishment of a local presence, foreign investment and labor mobility. While the provisions of the GATS do not establish substantive, across the board commitments on such issues as market access and national treatment, they provide a legal framework for the negotiation of such commitments, and spell out the obligations assumed by countries with respect to negotiated commitments.
- The GATS provisions establish an across the board obligation on the transparency of laws and regulations affecting trade in services. Transparency is important for several reasons. Full information about the laws and regulations that will apply to a particular transaction is critical for an assessment of the costs associated with that transaction, and therefore the economic viability of that transaction. Without such information, the potential risks associated with

the pursuit of an economic opportunity might be unacceptably high. Accurate information about current laws and regulations is also an essential prerequisite for any effort to change laws and regulations that create market access barriers for foreign businesses. Full knowledge of the conditions and costs associated with any particular international transaction is the first requirement for trade, because without such knowledge importers and exporters cannot calculate whether trade is likely to be profitable. The framework also explicitly obliges governments to inform private parties that have submitted requests for operating licenses of the precise status of their applications.

- The GATS also contains an Annex on Telecommunications that establishes significant commitments with respect to the use of telecommunications networks for the provision of services covered in the national schedules and for intra-corporate communications. Business users are assured access to public telecommunications networks and private leased circuits on reasonable and non-discriminatory terms and conditions. They are also given the right to acquire and attach equipment, to connect private leased line networks to the public switched network, and to use operating protocols of the service supplier's choice. This Telecommunications annex is one of the most important achievements of the services negotiations, since the most troublesome barriers to the expansion of cross-border trade in information-based services have been government regulations that limit access to state of the art telecommunications facilities at competitive prices.[2]

The Annex on Telecommunications to the GATS, and the more recent Agreement on Basic Telecommunications Services, have created a solid foundation for the international commercial use of the Internet. Electronic commerce represents the next major revolution in international trade. It will bring the economic advantages of globalization down to the level of small enterprises and households. The rapid expansion of electronic commerce will create both unprecedented opportunities for individuals and small businesses to market goods and services to smart buyers around the world, and to buy the most competitive and attractive goods and services available in global markets. It will also create enormous regulatory challenges, many of which will have to be addressed in future trade negotiations. The agreements on trade in services negotiated in the Uruguay Round and since then provide an essential foundation for both exploiting the opportunities and meeting the challenges of electronic commerce.

2.1. Market Access Commitments

Under the GATS framework, substantive commitments on policy measures that affect trade in services are incorporated in national schedules, which are negotiated with each country. Most developed countries and many developing countries have submitted national schedules that contain commitments on market access,

---

[2] For an expanded treatment of this subject see Feketekuty and Aronson (1984)

foreign investment, temporary entry by service providers, and non-discriminatory national treatment of foreign services and service providers. Overall, 80 countries submitted national schedules with initial commitments.

Generally, the commitments embodied in the schedules submitted in this first round of substantive negotiations guarantee foreign service providers existing levels of access to local markets in the sectors covered by the schedules. Commitments on market access within the constraints of existing regulations are of real value because they give businesses greater certainty. They reduce the risk that the potential gains from new investments or long-term supplier contracts might be adversely affected in the future as a result of new trade or investment restrictions.

Current government regulations create very few barriers to the cross-border provision of many information-based services purchased by businesses. By committing themselves not to introduce new, more restrictive regulations on trade in such services, governments are committing themselves to keep their market open to cross-border competition.

The schedules submitted by developed countries guarantee existing levels of market access for most information-based business services. The schedules submitted by developing countries are less comprehensive in their coverage, but nevertheless contain useful commitments in the area of information-based business services.

2.2. An Integrated Approach to Trade in Services

An increasing complaint from business is that governments have too many different approaches to regulations and policies that affect a company's ability to do business internationally. There are separate agreements and bureaucracies dealing with trade, investment, visa issues, international banking transactions, capital transfers, telecommunications, transportation, and they are not necessarily consistent with each other.

Concerns about this kind of fragmentation have substantially increased in recent years in light of the growing globalization of production. In a globalized business, decisions regarding trade, investment, movement of personnel, and the development of private intra-corporate communication networks are all part and parcel of a corporation's strategic plan for organizing the global production and distribution of its output.

The GATS, together with its annexes and the national schedules, provides an integrated approach for dealing with a number of different interrelated policy measures that affect the ability of service providers to do business in foreign markets. In the eyes of many business managers this represents a major advance over the GATT. Such an integrated approach provides the basis for a more informed dialogue between business and government regarding the effect of government policy decisions in areas such as trade, investment, work permits and domestic regulatory issues on business decisions concerning the location of production, research and distribution facilities, and on the development of markets. Government decisions on these issues are naturally motivated by a wide range of policy objectives and involve decisions by many different government departments and agencies. Bringing their impact on trade together under one roof nevertheless permits a more coherent analysis of trade-offs between trade policy considerations and different domestic policy objectives.

The structure of the national schedules also helps to focus on the alternative means by which a business enterprise headquartered in one country can choose to deliver a service to another: by transferring the service across the border to the consumer (cross-border supply), by establishing the means for producing the service in the importing country (commercial presence), by moving the person producing the service temporarily to the importing country (presence of natural persons), or by selling the service to a foreign consumer in the exporting country (consumption abroad). This approach has the added advantage of highlighting the options open to a business in a coherent way.

The preference by business for an integrated approach is also reflected in business support for regional trade agreements that encompass a broad range of government policy measures that can affect trade and investment. In the future, we can expect increasing support from the business community for an extension of the GATT into new areas such as investment as a basis for establishing a more integrated approach for trade in goods.

3. The Basic Structure of the GATS

The GATS establishes an across the board obligation of transparency for all internationally traded services. The transparency provision obliges member countries to publish all government measures which affect trade in services and to respond to requests for information on any of the above. The GATS also establishes a general MFN obligation, i.e., countries are required to grant all foreign suppliers the same treatment, unless the country involved excluded a particular sector from the MFN obligation at the time the agreement went into effect. Members of a free trade area, however, are allowed to give each other preferential treatment.

A number of provisions apply to all internationally traded services that fall within a sector covered by a commitment entered into a national schedule. With respect to all such services, governments are obliged:

- to notify service suppliers of any changes in government measures that affect trade
- to administer regulations in a *reasonable, objective and impartial manner* and to establish procedures that meet a due process standard
- to record in their national schedule all government measures that limit access to the domestic market through any of the four modes of entering the market, i.e., cross-border trade, consumption abroad, local establishment, or temporary entry by service providers, and
- to provide national treatment to foreign services and foreign service suppliers, i.e., to treat foreign services and providers no less favorably than domestic services and providers.

Unlike the GATT, the GATS covers not only cross border transactions, but also the supply of a service through a locally established foreign firm in the importing country. In sectors where market access commitments are undertaken, countries are obliged to avoid restrictions on foreign investment and to provide foreign investors national treatment unless the country takes a specific reservation. The measures covered by this provision include:

- limitations on the number of service suppliers whether in the form of numerical quotas, monopolies, exclusive service suppliers or the requirements of an economic needs test;
- limitations on the total value of service transactions or assets in the form of numerical quotas or the requirement of an economics needs test;
- limitations on the total number of services operations or on the total quantity of services output expressed in terms of designated numerical units in the form of quotas or the requirement of an economic needs test;
- limitations on the total number of natural persons that may be employed in a particular service sector or that a service supplier may employ and who are necessary for, and directly related to, the supply of a specific service in the form of numerical quotas or the requirement of an economics needs test;
- measures that restrict or require specific types of legal entity or joint venture through which a service supplier may supply a service; and limitations on the participation of foreign capital in terms of maximum percentage limit on foreign shareholding or the total value of individual or aggregate foreign investment.

A third set of provisions is applicable to individual services covered by specific commitments entered into the national schedules. Governments are required to ensure that any regulation which affects trade in these services (a) is based on objective and transparent criteria, (b) is not more burdensome than necessary, and (c) will not in itself constitute a restriction on supply in the case of licenses. Governments are also required to ensure that monopoly suppliers of services treat foreign customers of covered services like domestic customers, and that they avoid anti-competitive practices when supplying covered services on a competitive basis.

A separate Telecommunications annex establishes rights concerning access to and use of public telecommunications networks for services covered by commitments. Suppliers of such services have a right to obtain leased lines on reasonable and non-discriminatory conditions where they are available; to move, store and process information over the network; to use the network for intra-corporate communications and provision of services; and to buy or lease and attach customer premises equipment to the network, provided such equipment does no harm to the network. The Annex also guarantees users of leased lines the right to interconnect leased lines, to connect leased lines to the public network, to use their own protocols and to attach their own equipment.

Other provisions cover issues such as subsidies, recognition of licensing and certification standards and procedures, and dispute settlement.

The substantive commitments on market access are contained in national schedules, which are divided into two parts. The first section contains general commitments on laws or measures that apply to all industry sectors listed in the schedule. The second section contains detailed, industry-specific commitments.

The industry specific commitments address each of four possible *modes of supply*: (a) services supplied across the border, e.g., information-based services transmitted through telecom networks or the mail, various transportation services, and goods shipped for repair or processing; (b) services consumed abroad, e.g., tourism, education, and medical services purchased by travelers to other countries; (c) services sold through locally established businesses, e.g., services provided by locally established, foreign owned banks, insurance companies, or advertising agencies; (d) services provided by individual service providers who reside in the exporting country, but have gained temporary entry into the importing country for the express purpose of producing a service locally, e.g., services provided by foreign orchestras, sports teams, professors, doctors, or architects.

For each mode of supply, a country can offer either a full or partial commitment. A full commitment means that there are no industry-specific restrictions on market access and no limitations on national treatment, i.e.,, that all foreign services and service providers will be treated like their domestic counterparts in the application of domestic regulations. A partial commitment binds the country to a particular level of market access or to a particular degree of national treatment, i.e., the country commits itself not to adopt any laws or regulations that would be more burdensome than the laws or regulations bound in the schedule.

Subsequent negotiations on basic telecommunications services led to an agreement on basic telecommunications services. It accomplished what would have been difficult to envision only a few years back–a new international regime in telecommunications based on market competition. This constituted a major shift from the previous regime, which was primarily designed to preserve national monopolies and regulated prices. While individual countries have established their own transition schedules, and their own national conditions and reservations, the document clearly defines a new competition-oriented norm for international telecommunications.

The Telecommunications annex and the subsequent General Agreement on Basic Telecommunications Services (GBT) are among the most important achievements of the services negotiations, since the most troublesome barriers to the expansion of cross-border trade in information-based services have been government regulations that limit access to state of the art telecommunications facilities at competitive prices.

The more recent commercialization of the Internet has increased the importance of preserving open access to the telecommunications network by foreign service providers. For the first time, foreign services providers can have direct access to a retail distribution network for information and information-based services. The Telecommunications annex and the GBT provide an essential foundation for agreements that will need to be negotiated to permit the expansion of international economic commerce. Some ideas on the content of such an agreement are put forward in a separate section below.

While much was accomplished in the negotiations on international trade in services during the Uruguay Round, there is considerable room for improving the existing provisions of the various agreements, for expanding the coverage of commitments contained in the national schedules, and for eliminating restrictions to trade in services. The negotiators themselves identified a number of areas where they had failed to reach agreement, and where they felt negotiations needed to continue. These issues are examined in the first section below. Another set of issues concerns the coverage of commitments contained in the national schedules, and a third set of issues relates to constitutional shortcomings of the GATS.

4. The Unfinished Agenda

The Uruguay Round negotiators identified a number of areas where further negotiations were required over the near term. This, in essence, represents a consensus view that the negotiations fell short of expectations in these areas. These unfinished agenda items fall into three categories:

- cross-cutting issues such as subsidies and government procurement, which may need to be covered by rule-making provisions in the GATS;
- sectors such as shipping and financial services, where a sectoral annex was oncsidered necessary to achieve more substantive commitments in national schedules and the elimination of national reservations on most favored nation (MFN) treatment;
- functional policy areas such as labor mobility, where a functional annex is thought to be necessary to achieve more substantive commitments in national schedules.

4.1. GATS Rules

The negotiators identified three areas of rule-making where it had not been possible to agree on substantive provisions, and where the GATS therefore only contains procedural provisions that serve as place markers. The three areas are (a) emergency safeguard measures, (b) government procurement, and (c) subsidies.

Developing appropriate disciplines in these areas will require a careful analysis of the special characteristics of services in general, and of individual services sectors in particular. There are four difficulties in developing substantive rules in these areas:

- Uncertainty whether there is a sufficient problem to warrant the development of a discipline. The existence of GATT rules in these three areas for trade in goods leads some to conclude that parallel rules are needed in the GATS for trade in services. But there is little solid empirical data at this stage to build a persuasive case.
- Data on production, consumption, costs, and prices are available only for broad categories of services, not for detailed products. This makes it more difficult to prepare objective analysis of price and cost data than is the case for internationally traded goods.

- Significant differences in the industrial structure, method of distribution, and nature of various types of services. These differences make it more difficult to develop one rule that would cover all services in an equally effective manner, and may make a sectoral approach to the development of necessary disciplines more workable than a generic approach in some sectors.
- Market access commitments cover not only cross border trade, but also trade based on local establishment, movement of consumers, and movement of service providers. The coverage of all four modes in the GATS makes it necessary to decide whether a single set of rules should cover all four modes equally, or whether separate rules need to be developed for each mode.

Each of these four factors–uncertainty, measurement and data problems, sectoral differences, and complexity of the four modes–affects the rule-making effort in the three issue areas–safeguards, government procurement, and subsidies–somewhat differently. What they do have in common is the need for more detailed analysis of the issues that are likely to arise in the different sectors. There may also be a need for some empirical experimentation in specific sectors where the lack of discipline is most notable. With these caveats in mind, the following comments on each of the three issue areas might provide some further insights into the way forward.

4.1.1. Emergency Safeguard Measures.

The purpose of a safeguards regime is to facilitate the negotiation of binding commitments by helping governments to overcome uncertainties with respect to the possible future domestic impact of liberalization commitments. By allowing governments to withdraw commitments temporarily when a surge of imports threatens to injure the domestic industry, the existence of an emergency safeguard measure can encourage negotiators to undertake more substantive commitments.

There are two basic problems in devising an appropriate safeguard rule for services. The first is that there is very little empirical data to inform the rule-making process. This lack of empirical data may be due to a lack of analytical work in this area. However, there may be a more fundamental reason as well–namely that trade in services is less characterized by surges than goods, and that many domestic regulations restricting trade in services are less easy to liberalize through a series of marginal changes. Whatever the case, more information about real world situations where safeguard actions were either taken or could have been taken in a practical way would be helpful. It might also be useful to analyze how countries have managed the autonomous liberalization of internal competition of services, and the kind of transitional regulatory safeguards they found it necessary to adopt to manage the process in sectors such as telecommunications, retail distribution and transportation.

There are two possible interim approaches that could be adopted until the world community has gained more empirical data about the problems faced in managing the liberalization of trade in services. The first would be to encourage countries that hesitate to make a commitment to build an escape clause into their national commitment in the form of a reservation. The second approach would be to allow countries to propose specific safeguard measures when the need arises, subject to the approval of the WTO Council on Trade in Services.

The second problem in devising a rule for safeguards concerns the difficulty in devising an approach that could apply equally to all four modes of importing services. Unlike the GATT market access commitments on goods, the GATS market access commitments on services cover not only cross border trade but also trade based on local establishment and movement of either the consumer or the supplier of services. This raises a key question. Should a country be allowed to limit the activities of locally established suppliers when the import disruption is due to cross border trade or vice versa? Should a country in such cases be allowed to limit the temporary entry of service suppliers, or the consumption of services abroad by its own citizens?

One of the things that has limited the protective effect of safeguard measures taken on cross border trade in goods is that such measures did not prevent the foreign producers from expanding their investments in the importing country. The protective effect of safeguard measures taken by a number of countries in the steel and automobile industries, for example, were significantly cushioned by foreign investment in these industries. This would suggest that countries should be forced to justify safeguard actions taken with respect to any one mode in terms of the injury or threat of injury that exists from imports in that mode. In other words, safeguard actions should be mode-specific.

4.1.2. Subsidies

The rule-making effort on subsidies breaks down into two components–the possible discipline on subsidies and the nature of an appropriate remedy. Under GATT rules, subsidized imports are subject to countervailing duties, while distortions created in the home market of the subsidizing country or in third markets are subject to the potential remedies available under the dispute settlement system.

There are few, if any, instances of direct export subsidies in services. Following the example of the GATT in prohibiting direct export subsidies should therefore not pose an insurmountable problem. The bigger issue concerns domestic subsidies, which tend to be concentrated in a few sectors such as sea, air and land transportation, telecommunications, and in public goods such as health, education, and pension systems. This may lead one to conclude that the optimal approach would be to adopt a general subsidies discipline, with a carve-out for difficult sectors. The general subsidies discipline could follow the pattern of the GATT Subsidies Code. The sectors carved out from the general code could be covered by sector-specific commitments.

With respect to health, education and pensions, it needs to be recognized that most governments consider these activities as public goods that are legitimately subsidized by government. Sector-specific agreements on subsidies in these areas would have to give governments wide room to subsidize public services, while leaving room for the provision of privately provided services to those who can afford it.

With respect to transportation and telecommunications, any sector specific subsidy agreements would have to deal with two issues: transitional issues related to the adjustment of inefficient national champions in both industries and the subsidization of socially-desirable services such as the provision of telecommunications and transportation services to rural areas, the elderly or the poor, and the use of environmentally-friendly forms of transport.

The issue of an appropriate remedy is more complex. For a variety of reasons having to do with the special characteristics of services, it would be difficult to devise a workable countervailing duty. First, the invisible nature of many service imports would make it as impractical to impose a countervailing duty as it would be to impose a tariff on cross border trade. Second, the difficulty associated with identifying the production costs of an individual unit of services would make the imposition of a countervailing duty on the purchase of a specific service a completely arbitrary exercise. A more workable remedy might take the form of the remedies currently available under the dispute settlement system for subsidized competition in the home market of the subsidizing country or in third markets.

4.1.3. Government Procurement

The development of a discipline on government procurement will need to address two special characteristics of services. First, government procurement of many services is made on the basis of small contracts that would fall under the thresholds built into the Government Procurement Code for goods. While it would be possible to lower the threshold for services, it may prove too costly to impose the requirements associated with the Code on many small transactions.

The second issue is that the procurement of many services, particularly professional services, involves judgment calls about the quality of service. In fact, many professions have discouraged competition and marketing based on price, arguing that the choice of a professional is all about quality and reputation. Without pandering to that view, an approach to the procurement of professional services would need to address how judgments about professional competence can be factored into objective decisions.

There are a number of services where neither scale nor hard-to-quantify quality judgments are an overriding issue. It would make considerable sense to apply the procurement code to these services. Some prominent examples include transportation services, telecommunications services, construction, and financial services.

4.2. Sectoral Agreements

In four services sectors–telecommunications, financial services, shipping and professional services–the Uruguay Round negotiators decided that efforts to conclude a meaningful agreement on substantive commitments needed to continue. This decision was influenced by the absence of meaningful coverage of these sectors in the national schedules of many important trading nations, and by the decision of some countries, in particular the United States, not to apply the MFN provision to the first three of these sectors. The GATS also provided for further negotiations in professional services and for a future review of air transportation.

- Negotiations on basic telecommunications services led to a major breakthrough in the spring of 1997.
- Negotiations on financial services were concluded at the end of 1997.
- Negotiations on shipping failed to make any progress, and the negotiators have decided to postpone the resumption of these negotiations to the start of the next round of comprehensive negotiations on trade in services, which are scheduled to start in 2000.
- Negotiations on professional services have initially focused on accounting services.

Some comments are offered here on the challenges facing negotiators in the two sectors where negotiations will need to continue: transportation and professional services.

4.2.1. Transportation

Negotiations on all forms of transportation are likely to make more progress in the future if the negotiations were reorganized in terms of the different user communities. The current approach, which is to organize negotiations on the basis of sea, air and land transportation strengthens the hand of suppliers and regulators who would like to leave these sectors protected by restrictive national regulations.

A user-oriented approach to negotiations on trade in transportation services would focus the negotiations around each of the following four user communities: (a) global corporations who need to ship parts, components and assembled goods among their various facilities, (b) tour operators who provide organized leisure travel, (c) business users of express parcel and courier services, (d) users of scheduled public transport services. An organization of the negotiations along these four categories of users would make it easier to identify the requirements of users and to come up with provisions that will meet user requirements, and would force transportation companies to face up the needs of their customers. It would change the politics of the negotiations by making it easier for the different user communities to identify their common interests and to organize themselves politically, with the objective of breaking down national regulatory barriers to international competition.

The global corporation has special requirements for assuring a high degree of reliability and control over the transportation of parts and components between facilities located in different parts of the world. Depending on its needs, the corporation may need to be able to exercise control to assure timely delivery to meet just-in-time inventory control requirements, or they may need to assure customized handling of particular types of cargoes. They may also wish to have an ability to track the shipment of individual parts and components in order to empower them to reroute shipments if particular routes are blocked by strikes or natural disasters. In effect, these corporations need to be able to set up virtual transportation networks, or to entrust the management of such virtual networks to a global transportation manager. In either case, the corporation has to have some leeway to construct a network by linking together owned or leased facilities and modes of transport.

There is a close analogy with the need of these global corporations for control over their telecommunications with their various facilities around the world. Recognition of their telecommunications needs led to the negotiation of the user oriented GATS Telecommunications annex. The annex gives them the ability to lease and interconnect lines, and to use these lines freely for the transfer of information. A similar approach covering all modes of transport and warehousing facilities would generate similar benefits.

The second major, and politically powerful user community is represented by leisure travel. This community not only involves consumers of organized travel services, but also travel operators and the extensive network of travel agents. Charter services are already relatively free of many of the regulatory controls on scheduled public transportation, and it would not be a large step to negotiate an agreement providing for international competition in this area of transportation. Such an agreement would appeal to the public at large, and could be sold by every country as a measure to promote tourism, a financially attractive industry for most developing as well as developed countries.

The third group of users are business users of express package delivery and courier services. This highly competitive, international industry has developed in response to user needs. Resistance to the growth of the industry has come largely from the postal monopolies, and most regulatory restrictions are designed to protect these monopolies. An across-the-board approach to the problems faced by competitive providers of these services might prove more productive than the current piecemeal approach, and might enable these companies to better serve consumer needs.

That negotiations to liberalize international competition in scheduled public transportation will be the most difficult is clear from what is happening in the market place. Nevertheless, events are reshaping the industry. National airlines are reconstituting themselves into transnational transport companies through mergers, alliances, interlining agreements and other forms of cooperation. At some point the need for a new set of ground-rules for international competition among these mega companies will become obvious.

4.2.2. Professional Services

Efforts to create some sectoral guidelines for the liberalization of trade in professional services have focused on the development of a model agreement for accounting services. These negotiations are still under way. The basic goal is to expand on the provisions contained in Article VI(4) of the GATS. Negotiators are focusing, in particular, on three criteria built into this provision, namely that regulations be based on objective and transparent criteria, that they not be more burdensome than necessary to ensure the quality of the service, and that any licensing procedure in itself not restrict the supply of the service.

The basic issue for governments in accounting, as in other professional services, is to ensure the professional competence of the individual service provider, to monitor professional performance, and to discipline any lapses of professionalism. From a trade point of view the key issues are whether the standards and procedures adopted by individual governments constitute unreasonable barriers to trade. This can be the case if the standards or procedures established for evaluating qualifications unnecessarily discriminate against foreign practitioners, or unnecessarily restrict entry by both domestic and foreign applicants, serving to restrict entry into the field rather than ensuring professional competence.

In most cases the qualifications, regulations and procedures established for the licensing of a country's own professionals cannot be directly transferred to the licensing of foreign professionals–foreigners do not necessarily enter as apprentices, they may not have acquired a local educational qualification, their professional experience abroad may or may not be directly relevant, and the fact that they may not permanently reside within the country may require alternative approaches for disciplining unprofessional behavior. The establishment of a separate set of regulations and procedures for qualifying and licensing foreign professionals may thus actually facilitate trade. In fact, Article VI(6) directs Members to establish procedures to verify the competence of professionals from other member countries, thus implicitly recognizing the need for a specific procedure to license foreign practitioners.

The issue from a trade point of view is whether the qualifications, regulations and procedures established for foreign professionals are equivalent in their regulatory effect and not more burdensome than the procedures and standards imposed on a country's own professionals. Any rule-making under the GATS needs to establish some basic principles concerning the objectivity and equivalence of the qualifications and the procedures established for licensing foreign professionals. They should not get into substantive details, which are better addressed through bilateral agreements (as provided for in Article VII of the GATS) or international standards developed through appropriate international professional associations, (as provided for in Article VI(5)(b) of the GATS).

Non-discriminatory standards and procedures for ensuring the professional competence and professional performance of accountants can over time become barriers to entry if they are used to limit entry into the profession, thus raising the income of current members. The second issue from a trade point of view, therefore, is whether a country's regulations for the licensing of professionals are appropriate means for achieving legitimate social objectives, and whether they are not more cumbersome or restrictive than necessary to achieve that objective.

The best method of ensuring that professional licensing and qualification standards and procedures are not hidden devices to restrict competition is to require full transparency of both the regulatory objectives and the regulations. The rules should also stipulate that regulations achieve their stated objectives in the least burdensome manner. Transparency will enable everyone to test whether the objectives are legitimate and whether the regulations involved provide the least burdensome and least trade distorting method of accomplishing the objective. It may also be helpful to establish a link to established international standards in the field, by encouraging Members to make use of applicable international standards. In most professions, international professional bodies have emerged for the development of model standards or norms. The WTO Agreement on Technical Barriers to Trade adopts a similar approach by encouraging countries to adopt international standards where they meet the desired level of performance.

4.2.3. *Labour Mobility*

Negotiators at the end of the Uruguay Round failed to make substantive progress on a comprehensive agreement on the temporary entry of service providers, and few countries made any meaningful commitments in their national schedules. Subsequent negotiations failed to achieve much progress, and they have now been recessed until the start of a new round of negotiations on trade in services in 2000.

This lack of progress is regrettable, since most countries have visa regulations permitting temporary entry, and should have been in a position to make commitments based on current national visa regulations.[3]

4.3. Need to Expand Coverage of National Schedules

As previously noted, substantive commitments on market access and national treatment take the form of detailed commitments in national schedules under the GATS. The major goal of the first round of negotiations was to obtain binding commitments from countries to preserve the degree of openness and non-discrimination provided for in current laws and regulations. Maximum coverage was important because a number of disciplines incorporated in the GATS were activated by sector or product specific commitments in national schedules. Binding the existing degree of openness and non-discrimination was important because in most countries trade in information-based business services was relatively free of restrictive regulations.

The major disappointment was the limited coverage found in the schedules of the more advanced developing countries. The paucity of such stand-still commitments is particularly puzzling since many of the countries involved have unilaterally liberalized their policies in an effort to attract more foreign investment and to improve the performance of their economies. While many developing countries have traditionally viewed the services sector as the employer of surplus labor, some of them recognize that inefficiency and a lack of productivity in key services can stymie economic growth. It needs to be remembered, however, that these same countries have yet to bind tariffs in many goods, despite eight rounds of multilateral trade negotiations carried out over 40 years.

Some critics have complained about the absence of a substantial liberalization of trade as a result of these negotiations. While some degree of liberalization was generally considered a desirable outcome, substantial progress in dismantling restrictive regulation in the first round of negotiation was never considered a realistic goal by most negotiators and informed outside experts. Substantial liberalization in most countries and sectors would require major reforms in domestic regulations. This was clearly beyond what was achievable in an initial round of negotiations, particularly since there was little support from either the industries or the regulators in these industries for the negotiations. Nevertheless, the spotlight placed on trade in services as a result of the negotiations persuaded a number of countries to re-evaluate longstanding regulations that had outlived their purpose.

---

[3] For an expanded treatment see Feketekuty (1986) and Feketekuty (1988)

This led to a number of autonomous domestic reforms in the course of the 1980s, which were subsequently incorporated in commitments made in the national schedules.

The foremost challenge in the new round of negotiations on trade in services will be to expand the market access commitments incorporated in the national schedules. In approaching this task, the negotiators should prioritize their efforts by giving top priority to full coverage of information-based services, followed by as complete a coverage as possible across all services sectors. The objective should be to encourage as many countries as possible to commit themselves to maintain the current degree of access to their markets, through all four modes of accessing the market–cross border trade, establishment, consumption abroad, and temporary entry by foreign suppliers. Developed countries should commit themselves to bind the current degree of openness in all sectors and in all areas, and developing countries should set a percentage target for coverage.

The next level of priority should be to liberalize overt barriers to trade in services such as embargoes, quotas or other forms of discrimination against foreign suppliers of services. Generally, these barriers can be tackled without a major change in the regulatory regime of the countries involved.

Negotiators should consider the adoption of a *formula* approach to the market access negotiations, whereby countries would agree to a percentage reduction or elimination of particular types of market access restrictions such as quotas, citizenship requirements, and limitations on the allowed volume of activity by locally established foreign firms.[4] For certain types of barriers it might be possible to apply a formula to all sectors, while for other barriers it may be necessary to develop formulas adapted to the unique characteristics of that sector. Both horizontal and sectoral formulas could establish separate targets for developed countries, developing countries and least developed countries.

Achieving substantial liberalization of restrictive domestic regulations that do not overtly discriminate against foreigners will be difficult. To make progress in the heavily regulated sectors, governments most likely will have to address key regulatory issues on the basis of sectoral negotiations. This, of course, is already the case with respect to trade in telecommunications, financial services and accounting. To facilitate future negotiations in heavily regulated sectors, member countries should initiate a wider horizontal dialogue on the rationale and techniques for regulatory reform. They should also give serious consideration to a further amplification of the provisions on regulation contained in Article VI of the GATS. Some ideas on how this provision might be expanded is explored in another section below.

Negotiators should also consider ways and means of making the national schedules of commitments more user friendly to the business community. These schedules are very complex and difficult to read. Member countries should either revise the current scheduling rules or apply the existing scheduling rules on a more consistent basis. Member countries might also explore various presenta-

[4] A formula approach was first suggested by Sir Leon Brittan in a speech to a meeting of service industry representatives in Geneva, and was subsequently elaborated by Pierre Sauve in a paper published by the Coalition of Services Industries.

tional devices for organizing the information on a more consumer-friendly basis. The WTO is working on computer programmes that might aid users in identifying the national commitments in particular sectors, and this might go part of the way towards providing greater transparency of national commitments.

4.4. Constitutional Deficiencies

A number of issues may need to be considered with respect to the constitutional architecture of the GATS. The most commonly raised constitutional issues concern the absence of an across-the-board national treatment commitment in the GATS, and the scheduling of exceptions to the MFN principle in particular sectors.[5] Both of these issues, however, are transitional issues that will be self-correcting,

4.4.1. National Treatment–Top down or Bottom up

Cross-border trade in services is not easily controlled at the border since the actual cross border flow is invisible. Barriers to services instead involve the discriminatory application of domestic regulatory measures. The application of national treatment therefore is equivalent to committing countries to remove all barriers that favor domestic providers (though countries would still be able to keep regulations that protect incumbent firms from new domestic and foreign competitors). Most critics recognized the need for exceptions to national treatment, but would have preferred that countries be required to enumerate exceptions to national treatment rather than to assume the absence of a national treatment obligation unless a country schedules a positive commitment. This is self-correcting, however, because the national treatment provision in the GATS automatically applies to any sector in which a country schedules a commitment, and is binding unless the country enters a reservation in its national schedule.

4.4.2. MFN

Under the GATS, countries are allowed to enter reservations to MFN in individual sectors at the time they adopt the agreement. Countries are expected to remove these reservations, however, as a sufficient number of countries agree to a balanced package of reciprocal market access commitments. This has already happened with respect to basic telecommunications and financial services. As satisfactory agreements emerge in other heavily regulated sectors such as transportation, this problem too should be eliminated.

---

[5] See for example Hoekman (1995), Sauve (1995) and Snape and Bosworth (1996)

4.4.3. GATS and GATT–Forever Separate?

The more interesting constitutional question arises with respect to the relationship between the GATS and the GATT on issues that span both goods and services. The issue of how to handle cross-cutting issues has already arisen with respect to government procurement in the follow-up to the decision at the Singapore Ministerial to establish transparency in government procurement beyond the entities currently covered by the Code.

The issue of the relationship between GATT and GATS rules is likely to arise in a more pronounced way with respect to possible future WTO negotiations on an investment agreement. The aim of advocates of such an agreement is to develop a set of binding disciplines that would apply to all investments. The question is, would it make sense to have different rules for investment in service producing industries as against investment in goods producing industries? Can one even distinguish between goods and services producing firms when an increasing number of manufacturing firms also produce services?

A similar issue could arise if member countries were to conclude that any commitments on the movement of natural persons should apply not only to persons engaged in the supply of services, but also to persons engaged in the supply of goods. Once disciplines on investment cover both goods and services it will be difficult to make this distinction in any case.

Another area where an issue of overlapping disciplines might emerge is restrictive business practices.

There are three possible approaches that could be taken with respect to disciplines that apply to both goods and services. The first would be to maintain a complete legal separation between services and goods by carrying out separate negotiations under each umbrella, even if the issues are essentially the same. The second approach would be to maintain the legal distinction between the two agreements, but to combine the negotiations of common issues into a single negotiation and to insert the resulting language separately into the GATT and the GATS in parallel. The third approach would be to carve cross-cutting disciplines out of both the GATT and the GATS, and to place them under a combined umbrella. The third approach may well be the approach that should be taken, for a number of reasons.

First, the distinction between goods and services is already difficult to make in many cases. For example, the information that is contained in goods such as books, records, tapes or computer chips can be transmitted electronically, and in that alternative format would be difficult to treat as a good. Yet to apply different rules, depending on whether information was sold as a book or as an electronic transmission would not make any sense

Some have proposed to solve this problem by treating both the book and the electronic transmission of the information contained in a book as information products, subject to similar rules. This only raises new issues, such as whether the rules on goods or services should apply, and how one might distinguish between a book of architectural drawings and an architectural service. It has been suggested that a product is an off the shelf product sold as a commodity, while a service is a customized information supplied to a specific customer, which only raises different questions.

Disciplines concerning the treatment of enterprises as against the goods and services they produce create even more complex issues, because increasingly the same enterprises are engaged in both. An investment code that resulted in rights for the producer of a good would immediately raise the question of whether a particular enterprise that produces both goods and services should be treated as one or the other where different investment rules apply.

The second reason for developing a common set of disciplines is that over time trade in goods is increasingly taking on the characteristics of trade in services. As that happens, the need for different disciplines in goods and services will gradually disappear, and it should then be possible progressively to integrate the disciplines in the two areas into a common discipline. By splitting off individual disciplines that can apply equally to both goods and services, the transition could be managed as a step by step process.

The gradual erosion of the distinction between goods and services is due to both the effects of globalization and the increasing technological complexity of many goods. Manufacturing companies, as is true of services companies, increasingly have to be able to establish themselves in the importing market and to move technical, managerial and marketing personnel in and out of such markets. The need for disciplines on investment and the movement of natural persons thus is increasingly valid for both types of activities.

The more important impact of globalization, however, is the impact it is having on the whole structure of traditional trade measures, which are based on the assumption that products have a clear national identity. Trade measures such as tariffs, safeguards, anti-dumping duties and countervailing duties are imposed on the full value of a product entering a market, regardless of the national origin of its components and parts, and even if most of the value originated in the importing country. Countries have tried to get around the increasing illogic of this practice by circumventing it with various devices such as duty draw backs, free trade zones, etc., but each of these devices are complex and difficult to administer. The alternative response has been to eliminate duties altogether through sectoral free trade agreements or across the board regional free trade agreements. In the context of such agreements the distinction between goods and services tends to disappear.

5. Conclusion

The negotiations on services were a serious enterprise that yielded tangible results, however inadequate in some areas. Many services industries reported that the really important objective was to assure that new regulations would not block the growing volume of trade in information-based services over the telecommunications networks. As already noted, two issues were key to the achievement of this objective: (a) access to private leased line networks, and a commitment by governments not to interfere with transborder data flows through these networks; and

(b) a commitment not to introduce new restrictive regulations on telecommunications-based trade in these services, which for the most part was not covered by traditional regulatory structures. More recently, the agreement on international competition in basic telecommunications services has further strengthened the basis for what has been dubbed electronic commerce.

A solid foundation has been built for future negotiations aimed at the liberalization of trade in services. The reduction of regulatory and other barriers to trade in services will clearly take time. The GATS calls for comprehensive negotiations every five years, with the first such negotiation beginning in 2000.

A substantial liberalization of international trade in services will require substantial reforms of long-entrenched national regulatory systems. Considerable thought will have to be given on how best to address domestic regulatory systems that create barriers to expanded trade in services. The challenge is to devise principles and concepts for assuring international competition, while at the same time allowing diversity in national regulatory systems. Clearly, the objective cannot be the harmonization of national regulations. At the same time, different regulatory systems will have to offer similar competitive opportunities if trade in regulated services is to be liberalized further.

Bibliography

Bhagwati J (1984), *Splintering and Disembodiment of Services and Developing Countries.* The World Economy.7: 133-144

Feketekuty G and Aronson J (1984), *Meeting the Challenges of the World Information Economy.* The World Economy 7: 63-86

Feketekuty G (1986), *Trade in Professional Services: An Overview.* In: Barriers to International Trade in Professional Services. University of Chicago, Legal Forum, Chicago

Feketekuty G (1988), *International Trade in Services : An Overview and Blueprint for Negotiations.* Cambridge: Ballinger

Hoekman B (1995), *Tentative First Steps: An Assessment of the Uruguay Round Agreement on Services.* in The Uruguay Round and the Developing Economies. Will Martin and Alan Winters (eds), The World Bank: Washington DC

Hoekman B and Kostecki M. (1995), *Trade in Services.* In: The Political Economy of the World Trading System: From Gatt to WTO. Oxford University Press. Chapter 5

Sampson GP and Snape RH (1985), *Identifying the Issues in Trade in Services.* The World Economy 8: 171-181

Sauve P (1995), *A First Look at Investment in the Final Act of the Uruguay Round.* Journal of World Trade

Sauve P (November 1997), *Preparing for Services 2000: Buy Ten Commandments, Get One Free.* In CSI Reports: The Service Economy. Coalition of Service Industries, Washington DC

Snape RH and Bosworth M (1996), *Advancing Services Negotiations.* In: The World Trading System: Challenges Ahead. Jeffrey J. Schott (ed). Institute for International Economics:Washington DC

World Trade Organization (1995), *The Results of the Uruguay Round of Multilateral Trade Negotiations.* The Legal Texts. WTO, Geneva, Switzerland.

The Role of the GATT Secretariat in the Evolution of the WTO Dispute Settlement Procedure

Robert E. Hudec

1. Introduction

The dispute settlement procedure established by the World Trade Organization (WTO) represents a decision by the world's major trading nations to grant an unprecedented degree of power to a legal tribunal to enforce the various trade agreement obligations appended to the WTO Agreement. The WTO dispute settlement procedure provides that legal complaints by Members shall have automatic access to a neutral tribunal called a panel; it then sets forth a sophisticated litigation process leading to binding legal rulings by the panel, an appellate tribunal to review panel rulings, and a follow-up procedure ending in retaliatory sanctions for failure to implement such rulings. In the history of international law, it is rare to find a legal institution with this much regulatory power over significant areas of government economic policy.

The legal achievement represented by the WTO disputes procedure was not accomplished overnight. It occurred only after a slow–sometimes painfully slow–process of step-by-step developments beginning with the creation of the General Agreement on Tariffs and Trade (GATT) in 1947. It was only after the GATT had spent forty years to construct the basic elements of the present disputes procedure that governments were able to take the final leap to a fully binding procedure in the 1986-93 Uruguay Round negotiations.

Several generations of GATT Secretariat officials played a significant role in bringing GATT Contraction Parties to accept the key elements of that disputes procedure. The story of the Secretariat's contribution is an illuminating example of the difference that international civil servants can make in the evolution of international legal institutions. This monograph presents a brief account of that story, and how it all came out.

2. The Original Legal Design

Although modern governments have been negotiating trade agreements for several centuries, the use of third-party adjudication to enforce trade agreement obligations appears not to have received serious consideration until the 1946-48 negotiations that created the GATT. Before then, trade agreements had almost always been bilateral in form, and the two parties to such agreements typically did not look to any outside institution to adjudicate their legal disputes. If consultations failed to secure the conduct expected of the other party, the aggrieved party was left with no further recourse except declining to perform some or all of its own obligations. On the whole, governments seem to have been content with this rather weak form of enforcement, no doubt because experience showed that the mutual interest in trade liberalization was usually strong enough to persuade both governments to live up to what they had agreed to.

The plan for trade agreements after World War II called for the creation of a large international organization called the International Trade Organization (ITO) that would have one subdivision dealing with international trade in goods (the GATT), and several others dealing with employment, economic development, restrictive business practices and inter-governmental commodity agreements. The legal design of the ITO Charter provided for a rather elaborate procedure of third-party adjudication. Legal disputes could be submitted for a legal ruling by the ITO's eighteen-member Executive Board, followed by an appeal to the full membership in the plenary Conference of the ITO, and followed in turn by a further right to seek an advisory opinion from the International Court of Justice.[1] Unfortunately, by the time the Charter was finished and submitted for ratification in 1948, this relatively strong adjudication procedure no longer had very much domestic political support in some of the key member governments. The United States Congress refused to ratify the ITO Charter, and one of the main reasons for its refusal was a growing disenchantment with international legal institutions in the tense and suspicious climate of the early Cold War years.[2]

The GATT was negotiated in 1947, in the midst of the ITO negotiations, for the purpose of achieving an immediate reduction in tariffs among the twenty-three countries that were conducting the preliminary phases of the ITO negotiations.[3] Although the GATT was a separate agreement that came into force immediately, it was intended that GATT would be incorporated into the ITO when the ITO came into force in 1948 or 1949. Thus, the governments that negotiated the GATT in 1947 clearly intended that its obligations would eventually be enforced by the third-party adjudication mechanism of the ITO Charter.

In the GATT itself, however, the hurried character of the tariff-reducing enterprise led governments to fashion a considerably less ambitious dispute settlement procedure for the short period that the GATT was expected to stand alone. Several circumstances created the need to accept this more modest legal design. First,

---

1 See Brown, pp 227-234

2 See Gardner, Chapter 17

3 See Brown, pp. 131-134a

in order to fit within the rather limited negotiating authority of the United States, GATT had to be presented as a "trade agreement" rather than an international organization, and so it could not incorporate any organizational structures like the elaborate three-tier adjudication procedure of the ITO Charter. Under GATT, legal rulings would have to be made by periodic meetings of the signatory governments, with no further organizational structure provided for. Second, in order to avoid formal ratification procedures that would delay implementation of the tariff reductions, the nature of the legal commitment to GATT obligations was limited to a commitment, in a separate protocol, that governments would apply the obligations provisionally, a term that suggests something less than definitive and final legal commitment.[4] For the same reason, even this limited commitment was further reduced by granting governments an across-the-board reservation in the protocol for any existing legislation inconsistent with GATT obligations. And finally, because the ITO negotiations had not yet succeeded in defining the legal consequences of various kinds of legal claims that might be brought under a multilateral trade agreement, the GATT's own dispute settlement provision (still in force as GATT Article XXIII) had to be based on a much less precise draft text of the ITO disputes provision as it then stood–a text that applied to an extremely broad range of potential legal claims and that provided very little guidance as to their respective legal consequences. In sum, these several compromises with expediency left the GATT disputes procedure with hardly any legal foundation at all.

As things turned out, the weakness of the GATT's dispute settlement procedure proved to be something of an advantage in the more hostile political climate that greeted the GATT at the end of the ITO negotiations. GATT survived the demise of the ITO Charter, but it, too, was viewed with considerable suspicion by those domestic political interests opposed to any surrender of sovereignty to international institutions. In this climate, an elaborate and conspicuously legal adjudication procedure could have drawn more attention to GATT and subjected it to more intense opposition. The weakness and ambiguity of the GATT disputes procedure gave it a relatively low profile.

As often happens, however, the trade policy officials who negotiated the GATT and ITO agreements, and their ministries back home, were not willing to surrender their original legal design quite this easily. If an adjudication procedure had been a good policy before, then it was still a good policy, and it was up to trade policy officials to continue trying to achieve that policy in whatever way they could. They would simply have to be more careful, and perhaps a bit more creative, than was originally anticipated.

---

[4] *Protocol of Provisional Application.* GATT, Basic Instruments and Selected Documents (hereinafter BISD), Vol. I, p 77

3. The First Steps towards Third-Party Adjudication

Notwithstanding both the hostility of the external political climate and the internal weakness of the GATT adjudication procedure itself, some GATT Contracting Parties started submitting legal claims almost as soon as the GATT opened its doors for business in 1948. The leadership of the early GATT never seems to have contemplated not responding to these early legal claims. They simply set about trying to fashion a way of answering them.

Needless to say, the GATT's flimsy legal structure placed many obstacles in the way of an effective response. First, the GATT's lack of an organizational structure made it impossible for the Contracting Parties to do business on a continuing basis. Business had to done during periodic gatherings of GATT's membership, called *Sessions*. These early legal claims had to be disposed of, therefore, in the few weeks or months that the Contracting Parties remained in session.

A more serious obstacle to third-party adjudication was the fact that the GATT did not provide for any kind of neutral tribunal that could rule on legal issues. According to Article XXIII, rulings were to be given by the CONTRACTING PARTIES–the plenary meeting of all the signatory governments. An assembly of diplomats each representing his own government's interest hardly seems an appropriate forum for rendering an impartial legal decision.

The first few legal rulings overcame both the time pressure and the neutrality problem by the device of a ruling from the chair, which became a ruling of the entire membership when it was tacitly approved by silence.[5] This device was accepted as sufficiently neutral for two rather special reasons. First, the Chairman of the Contracting Parties during the first four sessions was L. Dana Wilgress, a senior Canadian diplomat who had also been Chairman of the 1946-48 GATT/ITO negotiations. Wilgress' key role in those negotiations lent an unusual degree of authority to his rulings, both because of his expertise as to the meaning of the agreement and because of the reputation for fairness he had earned in his work as chairman of the ITO negotiations. Second, and perhaps more important, in these early years most of the delegates to GATT meetings were also veterans of the GATT/ITO negotiations themselves. As such, they all felt they knew exactly what was meant by all of the provisions in the agreement they had drafted, and consequently saw nothing amiss in voting on authoritative legal interpretations. There was no problem of neutrality, they thought, when everyone in the room very well knew the right answer.[6]

The device of the chairman's ruling got the GATT past the first few legal claims, but it was clear to everyone that this device was not a long-term answer to the need for a neutral tribunal. The first, somewhat cautious step towards such a

---

5 See Hudec (1990), pp 75-76

6 To be sure, not every ruling by the membership came out looking quite so neutral. In 1949, Czechoslovakia brought a complaint against the Cold War trade measures taken by the United States. After a heated debate, the United States insisted on a vote. The vote dismissing the Czech claim was unanimous (except for Czechoslovakia), but there would have been no way to persuade Czechoslovakia that this legal ruling had been made by a neutral body.

tribunal was the decision to refer some of these early legal claims to a *working party*. In GATT parlance, the term working party refers to a smaller group made up of all those who have a direct interest in the matter, plus a representative cross-section of other governments. The normal function of working parties was to negotiate a political solution acceptable to the key parties with direct interests in the matter. On the face of it, the structure of the working party and the political orientation of its working procedures made it seem no more appropriate for handling legal claims than meetings of the entire GATT membership.

Without any formal changes, however, some of the early working parties to which legal claims were referred began to try to function as neutral fora anyway. The third-party members of the working party would try to arrive at a neutral view of the controversy. And then, contrary to normal working party practice of merely recording differences of position when there was no consensus, these working parties would report in a way that gave prominence to the views of the neutral members, and on that basis would offer a proposed recommendation and/or legal ruling for adoption by the Contracting Parties.[7] Like the early chairman's rulings, these attempts at third-party rulings by the neutral members tended to earn general acceptance despite their irregular origins. Once again, the main factor underlying their acceptance was the fact that most of the ITO veterans serving as GATT delegates were confident that they knew what the agreement meant. It also helped that most working parties had delegates from the United States, United Kingdom and France–the three most influential delegations that had not only done most of the actual drafting of the GATT/ITO agreements, but had in fact dictated most of their substance.

4. The Secretariat's Role in the Early Years

Because the GATT was a trade agreement rather than an international organization, it was unable to create its own secretariat. Instead, GATT member governments borrowed a secretariat from the secretariat that the United Nations had created to administer the ITO negotiations. The secretariat of the ITO negotiations had stayed in existence after the Havana Conference as the secretariat of an ad hoc organization called the Interim Commission for the International Trade Organization (ICITO) that had been created to prepare the ground for the ITO. After the ITO was abandoned in 1950, ICITO ceased to have any substantive function, but it nevertheless continued in existence for the next fifty years solely to provide a legal basis for the existence of the GATT Secretariat. The lending arrangement lasted until the WTO came into existence in 1995 and took over the GATT Secretariat as its own.

The first Executive Director of the GATT Secretariat was Eric Wyndham-White of the United Kingdom. A lawyer by training, White had been the director of the secretariat since the beginning of the ITO negotiations. He stayed on to lead the GATT Secretariat from 1948-68. Jean Royer, a trade diplomat from

---

7 See Hudec (1990), pp 76-80

France, served as Deputy Executive Secretary from 1948-58. The initial GATT Secretariat was quite small, and its volume of business during this period was small enough that Wyndham-White and Royer were able to participate actively on dispute settlement issues of any significance.

Although there is no record of the Secretariat's role in the plenary meetings that issued the first GATT legal rulings, it is likely that, as with all meetings of the Contracting Parties, the Secretariat in consultation with the Chairman had scripted each item on the agenda–that is, had consulted the relevant parties on their desires regarding the proper disposition of the matter and then prepared a script for the Chairman to follow in leading the meeting to the proper disposition. Given the extensive experience of the Chairman and the leading delegates, it is probable that they already had strong views on how they wanted these early legal issues to be handled, and would not have required much guidance from the Secretariat on that issue.

The Secretariat would have had a larger role in the working parties that were appointed to deal with some of the early legal claims. In addition to handling all the physical arrangements for meetings of the working party, the Secretariat is normally expected to supply the background information and other documentation needed by the working party. Usually, it also drafts whatever reports are needed to transmit the results achieved by the working party.

Once again, most of the individual delegates serving on the working parties would probably have needed relatively little guidance as to the merits of the legal problems before them. The drafting of the working party's conclusions was not so straightforward, however. Either the chairman of the working party or the Secretariat would probably have had to negotiate a bit with both parties in order to formulate a ruling that both could accept. Often the key was to find a verbal formulation which said enough to indicate the proper legal conclusion, but which did not say it so clearly that it would embarrass the losing government. The actual drafting of the decision was also quite important in protecting the GATT itself from the dangers of adjudication process. Given the uncertain reception that awaited GATT legal obligations in national capitals, it was important not to commit the GATT's full prestige behind rulings that governments might not be able to comply with. GATT would be better served by rather vague legal conclusions that left some room for manouvre if such difficulties arose. Finally, diplomatic obfuscation of these early legal rulings would also help to protect the GATT from attacks by hostile political forces in national capitals. Critics could not attack what their lawyers could not understand.

The early GATT legal rulings usually met these needs for kinder, gentler and more obscure legal rulings by resorting to the language of diplomacy rather than law. The art was to suggest the necessary conclusions with impressionistic brush strokes that, upon closer examination, never actually said in print what everyone knew they meant. The technique was particularly effective against lawyers, because under normal standards of legal analysis its was almost impossible to reach a satisfactory legal conclusion about what these decisions actually meant or required. Such vagueness did not cause problems within the halls of GATT, of course, because most of the veteran GATT delegates were accustomed to talking this way all the time, and their shared consensus about the meaning of the GATT left them in little doubt as to what these decisions meant. Indeed, the strength of this consensus was sometimes so strong that it hardly needed any written ruling at all. In one celebrated decision, the actual text of the working party report had followed the normal working party practice of merely stating the opposing views of the two sides to the legal dispute. In reality, the neutral members of the working party, and most other delegates, were firmly convinced that the complainant's claim of violation was correct. This point of view turned out to be so widely shared that, after about a year, all further GATT discussion of the case had simply assumed that approval of this very bland working party report had been an authoritative ruling of violation.[8]

According to the recollection of participants interviewed by the author many years ago, the Secretariat did most of the drafting of these artfully worded legal rulings in the early working party reports. The principal draftsman of the more important legal rulings was Deputy Executive Secretary Jean Royer, a role that he continued to fulfill until his retirement in 1958. Royer was not a lawyer, but he did have masterful command of the language of nuanced diplomacy. When those writing skills were coupled with his expert knowledge of the agreement, the result was a series of both penetrating and artful legal rulings that laid down some of the most important foundation concepts of present-day GATT law.

5. The Panel on Complaints

The GATT's procedure for third-party adjudication of legal claims took a significant step forward in 1952 when it was decided to refer all the legal claims on the agenda of the Seventh Session of the Contracting Parties to a body called a *panel on complaints* rather than a conventional working party.[9] The term panel in GATT parlance came from the term panel of experts–a term coined long before GATT to describe an ad hoc group of government experts (rather than policy officials) convened to render an expert opinion about some technical question that is capable of being answered objectively. The term thus connoted objective decisions based on expertise rather than political representation of one's government. The move to the panels was a natural next step. The need for a neutral and objective tribunal had been acknowledged from the beginning, and the early forms of decision-making had each tried in its own way to achieve such neutrality and objectivity. But it had to be clear to all participants that political bodies could never achieve the degree of neutrality and objectivity that would command the kind of respect needed for an effective legal system.

In the hostile political climate of the early 1950s, the *panel* initiative was a rather dangerous one. That was evident from the very cautious way the GATT went about it. The first version of the proposal merely called for creation of a single working party to handle all the Seventh Session complaints. When the decision was recapitulated a few days later, the name panel was slipped in without

---

[8] *Brazilian Internal Taxes*, 2 BISD 181-86 (1952). See Hudec (1990), Chapter 12

[9] See Hudec (1990), Chapter 9

explanation. Then, when the Seventh Session panel was appointed, its structure was defined in a way to suggest working party practice. Members of the Seventh Session panel were still identified by country, rather than the traditional panel practice of identifying the experts by name. And nothing was said about any changes in working procedure. Most delegations would have known and understood what was really going on here, but all seemed to agree that the less said the better.

The actual working procedure of the Seventh Session panel contained some quite significant changes from the procedure followed by working parties. The disputants were not voting members of the panel. All the panel members were in fact from countries that could be called neutrals. The panel would receive oral and written argument from the parties, but it would meet without the parties present to decide the case. The panel would still consult the disputants about ways to make the ruling more acceptable, but it was clear that the panel would reach its own decision in the end.

The panel ruled on four legal claims during the Seventh Session. In each case the parties accepted the new procedures without complaint, and all four cases were successfully resolved. The panel procedure then gradually came into the open during the next few years. Panel members were eventually appointed by name rather than country. The panel's working procedures were finally explained in GATT published reports, and the fact that panel members were to act in their personal capacity rather than on instruction from their governments was made explicit.

In the years between 1952 and 1963, panels resolved fifteen more legal controversies. The results were generally accepted by the disputants, and all produced some result that could have been called a success. By 1963, it could be said that GATT had succeeded in developing a quiet but effective mechanism for adjudicating legal disputes between members.

The leadership of the GATT Secretariat is generally credited with having initiated and managed the creation of the panel procedure. By 1952, the GATT's first acknowledged leader–Dana Wilgress of Canada, the first chairman of the GATT Contracting Parties after chairing the GATT/ITO negotiations–had left the scene, and Eric Wyndham-White's leadership of the Secretariat had by then earned him a role of considerable influence. Throughout his long tenure, Wyndham-White was always a staunch supporter of the panel procedure.

The basic elements of the Secretariat's role in panel proceedings were the same as for a working party–meeting arrangements, background information and documentation, and drafting. But the nature of the panel procedure worked to augment the influence that the Secretariat was able to exert on the content of legal rulings. With the parties out of the room when cases were being decided, the Secretariat would be able to take stronger positions on the merits. Likewise, the Secretariat would be able to use its role as principal draftsman more aggressively. To be sure, panel members would continue to exert an important check on the political viability of panel decisions, and their endorsement of decisions would still be critical to their perceived legitimacy. But as time went on, and particularly as new generations of GATT delegates replaced the original ITO veterans, the Secretariat's expertise and neutrality would become recognized by governments as the principal influence on the content of panel rulings.

6. The Anti-Legalism of the 1960s

The year 1963 marked a sharp breaking point in the development of the GATT dispute settlement procedure. From 1964 to 1970, the business of adjudicating legal claims simply stopped entirely. Moreover, the GATT's declared policy towards such adjudication took a sharply negative turn.[10]

The decline of GATT legal activity in the 1960s can be laid to two major changes that were taking place in GATT at that time. The first was the emergence of the European Economic Community. Though the Community achieved a surprisingly high degree of conformity with GATT legal requirements for creating a customs union, the Community was open to legal challenge in two important areas–its Common Agricultural Policy, and the preferential trade relationships it had established with former colonies. The Community met legal complaints about these deviations by lecturing the GATT membership about the injudiciousness of trying to solve sensitive economic and political problems by applying legal norms to them–norms usually referred to as wooden and legalistic. Instead, the Community argued, GATT should adopt flexible and pragmatic approaches to trade problems caused by these Community policies. Since it seemed clear that the Community was prepared to leave GATT rather than give up these important policies, the rest of the GATT members eventually agreed to set aside the adjudication procedure for these problems.

A second and broader reason for the declining use of GATT legal process in the 1960s was the expansion of GATT's membership to embrace a three-fold increase in the number of developing countries. By the mid-1960s developing-country members of GATT outnumbered the developed countries by more than two-to-one. Developing country members moved to make use of this majority power by organizing as a bloc that could present a long list of concerted demands for improved treatment. Many of these demands were presented as calls for enforcement of the legal obligations of developed countries, for in fact many of the latter's trade barriers impeding developing country access to their markets were GATT-illegal. Faced with these sweeping legal demands, most developed countries found that they had been converted to the European Community's philosophy of pragmatism. Even the United States took to lecturing developing countries on the injudiciousness of seeking legalistic solutions to sensitive political and economic problems. By the later years of the decade, observers could well describe the situation as the flowering of an anti-legalist movement within GATT.[11]

The anti-legalist movement continued in full force until the early 1970s. For the European Community, the anti-legalist position lasted a lot longer, because basic Community policies were still exposed to legal attacks throughout the 1970s.

---

[10] See Hudec (1990), Chapter 19

[11] See Hudec (1987), Chapters 3-4

Indeed, the Community's legal exposure became even more uncomfortable in the early 1970s when the United States launched a new round of legal attacks stimulated by trade losses due to the Community's Common Agricultural Policy. The Community continued to adhere to the anti-legalist position throughout the 1970s, and stood as a pillar of resistance to most of the efforts to revive GATT legal process that emerged during that period.

7. The US Effort to Revive the GATT Disputes Procedure

The United States deserted the anti-legalist camp in the early 1970s.[12] Broadly speaking, the change was triggered by growing concern about two parallel strains of increasing protectionism–the rise of protectionism in the US Congress and also a general increase in non-tariff trade barriers (NTBs) around the world. The US decided to attack this problem by seeking to launch a new round of GATT trade negotiations aimed at the NTB problem. Strengthening GATT's legal machinery became an essential element of that strategy for two reasons. First, the best legal technique for removing NTBs was to write more specific general rules covering the non-tariff measures in question, and such rules would require effective dispute settlement for their enforcement. Second, it was believed that the US Congress would not grant authority to negotiate new commitments on NTBs unless the Executive Branch could demonstrate the will and the ability to enforce those commitments. A visible and successful adjudication procedure was a familiar symbol of effective enforcement, particularly to an American audience.

The campaign for legal reform began with a trickle of US legal complaints in the first few years of the decade. The volume of US complaints gradually increased throughout the decade, and other governments were eventually induced to start using the GATT's legal machinery themselves. Then, towards the end of the decade, the United States used the Tokyo Round trade negotiations to press for a series of reforms that would strengthen the disputes procedure further. The European Community opposed most of the new reforms proposed by the United States and others, but did agree to a lengthy restatement of customary *GATT* practice.[13] This restatement had a greater effect than the Community probably anticipated. By codifying and legitimating the core elements of the adjudication procedure, it encouraged governments to employ the dispute settlement procedure even more frequently. The volume of dispute settlement activity continued to increase, and by the end of the 1970s the dispute settlement procedure had been restored to a central place on the GATT's regulatory agenda.

Although the re-emergence of the dispute settlement procedure in the 1970s was clearly based upon the precedent of the relatively successful disputes procedure of the 1950s, the 1970s procedure turned out to be something substantially

---

[12] See Hudec (1993), Chapter 4

[13] *Agreed Description of the Customary Practice of the GATT in the Field of Dispute Settlement (Article XXIII:2),* BISD, 26th Supp. pp 215-218, an annex to *Understanding Regarding Notification, Consultation, Dispute Settlement and Surveillance*, id, pp 210-215

different than the 1950s version. GATT had changed a good bit since 1960, with the result that the legal setting of the 1970s was quite different from the conditions that prevailed in the 1950s when the GATT had been a small and cohesive club staffed primarily by veteran trade policy diplomats from the ITO negotiations. The legal business of the 1950s had been a rather cozy affair conducted by this small group of like-minded diplomats. Government lawyers had had relatively little to do with the process. Diplomats had shaped the kind of legal claims presented, they had argued the legal claims with all the courtesy common to ordinary diplomatic discourse, and they had disposed of them with all the artful imprecision that diplomats are wont to employ in reconciling conflicts. The relative success of this diplomatic approach had persuaded most GATT participants of the 1950s that GATT was much better off without any lawyers at all in the GATT Secretariat. This anti-lawyer bias was made explicit Secretariat policy by Eric Wyndham-White himself, who saw to it that, in contrast to most other international organizations, the GATT Secretariat did not in fact have any positions for lawyers, as such.[14]

By the 1970s, the small and cohesive GATT of the 1950s had been transformed into a much larger collection of countries organized around several strong and frequently antagonistic power centers–the United States, the European Community, Japan, the developing country bloc, and an assortment of smaller developed countries. Moreover, the GATT delegations of the 1970s were staffed by an entirely different generation of trade policy officials, few of whom had even been on GATT delegations in the 1950s. The change in the United States delegation was particularly marked, for in 1962 the US Congress had taken responsibility for GATT affairs away from the trade policy diplomats of the US State Department and transferred it to a new agency–the Office of the US Trade Representative (USTR)–that was charged with undertaking a more aggressive pursuit of national economic interests.

The type of legal claims filed by the United States in the 1970s reflected these differences. The 1970s claims were shaped and prosecuted by lawyers–specifically, the USTR legal staff. In the tradition of much US domestic litigation, the US legal claims typically presented every legal argument that could be lodged against the trade measure being attacked, occasionally including many of rather dubious merit. In the GATT legal proceedings that followed, each of the many legal arguments was typically pressed as forcefully as possible, obliging panels to work their way through a sometimes bewildering array of not-always-consistent legal theories. The author has sometimes referred to this style of legal argumentation as *carpet bombing*–the military term for saturating a target with the largest possible number of bombs that can be dropped on or near it. Although most other delegations were still more disposed to handling legal claims in the old diplomatic

[14] A few staff members of the Secretariat had degrees in law, a university subject that is commonly taken by European students seeking entry into government service, but most had never used their legal training. Wyndham-White was himself a lawyer, a fact which seemed to increase the strength of his conviction that lawyers should have no role in GATT.

fashion, they had little choice but to copy the US legal techniques when facing US lawyers on the other side of a dispute.

The new type of legal claim, coupled with the greater degree of contentiousness among the GATT's Contracting Parties, presented a particularly difficult problem for the GATT's dispute settlement procedure. GATT panels continued to be *ad hoc* bodies consisting of three to five delegates from neutral countries. Individual panel members would usually have had a certain expertise about GATT policy in general, but were unlikely to have the detailed technical expertise needed to sort through the twenty or more esoteric legal issues raised by the legal debate between the parties. The Secretariat officials servicing the panel would have somewhat greater technical expertise in GATT law owing to longer contact with GATT, but in the absence of trained lawyers in the Secretariat, most Secretariat officials were also likely to be at a considerable disadvantage.

The 1970s Secretariat officials had a further disadvantage as compared with their 1950s predecessors. The 1970s Secretariat was a much larger organization with a much larger business agenda, which meant that the top leadership of the Secretariat were unable to devote the time and attention to panel proceedings that had been given by Wyndham-White or Royer. As a consequence, panel-service assignments were distributed among the subject matter *divisions* of the Secretariat, the assignment going to the division responsible for the subject matter area involved in the dispute. Distributing the Secretariat's legal work among a large number of different Secretariat officials, many below the level of Division Director, would deprive the Secretariat of the sustained contact with the panel procedure needed to build expertise and consistency. While some of the Secretariat officials assigned to panels were up to the task in some cases, it was inevitable that other panels would be less fortunate.

It was not long before some GATT panels began to experience difficulty in coping with this new and more demanding legal environment. The celebrated group of four *DISC* cases decided in 1976 produced the first significant failure.[15] These cases had elicited an dazzling display of the new style of tenacious (and tendentious) lawyering on the part of both US and EC lawyers, as both sides waged all-out legal warfare over both the procedures to be followed and the complex tax and subsidy issues in the case. The panel's ruling that the US DISC law was in violation of the GATT Article XVI:4 prohibition against export subsidies seemed correct to most GATT participants, but there was vigorous and widespread criticism of the panel's three companion rulings that the territorial tax systems of France, Belgium and the Netherlands were equally inconsistent with Article XVI:4. Many delegates suspected that the latter three rulings were in part a diplomatic effort to balance the result; if so, it was clear the panel has misjudged the room it had for diplomatic manoeuvre. The three contested *DISC* rulings became a very prominent black eye for the GATT dispute settlement procedure, because they continued to occupy a position of high visibility on GATT's legal agenda for the next five years, until the entire case was finally resolved by a 1981 settlement

---

[15] *United States: Income Tax Legislation,* BISD, 23rd Supp. pp 98-114. *France: Income Tax Practices,* id, pp 114-127. *Belgium: Income Tax Practices*, id, pp 127-136. *Netherlands: Income Tax Practices,* id, pp 137-147. See Hudec (1983), Chapter 5

that affirmed the European defendants' view of the law and essentially repudiated the panel ruling against them.

As the volume of GATT litigation began to accelerate towards the end of the 1970s, so did the number of problematic legal rulings. The next example was 1978 *MIPS* decision in which the panel's effort to answer a long list of esoteric legal claims made by the United States produced several rulings on collateral issues that were clearly in error.[16] Fortunately, criticism of the errors was not pursued when the case became moot due to termination of the challenged measures for other reasons. Next came a pair of related decisions in 1979 and 1980 which ruled that the European Community's export subsidies on sugar could not be found in violation of the qualified prohibition stated in GATT Article XVI:3.[17] Notwithstanding the problems in proving such a complaint, due to both an unsatisfactory legal text and a totally distorted international market, a substantial number of GATT delegations viewed the panel's inability to strike down these egregious export subsidies as a failure of either courage or legal skill or both. The panel did try to generate an alternative form of pressure on the Community's subsidy policy by finding that the Community was obliged to consult about the *serious prejudice* caused by its subsidies–an effort at a half-a-loaf compromise remedy typical of the 1950s diplomatic approach to difficult cases–but in the more contentious world of the 1970s this diplomatic attempt at compromise went nowhere. The Community consulted at length, but firmly refused to change anything.

The next problematic legal decision came in a 1980 panel ruling that European Community restrictions on imports of apples met one of the key requirements of the exception stated in GATT Article XI:2(1)(c).[18] The ruling was vigorously criticized by several governments at the time, and was eventually repudiated in two subsequent panel rulings nine years later.[19] The string of erroneous decisions finally came to a head with a 1981 panel ruling exonerating a series of Spanish internal measures that discriminated against imports of soyabean oil.[20] Many delegations suspected that the panel had been trying to fashion a diplomatic solution by cutting a little slack for a developing country, but, if that had been the purpose, it soon became clear that the GATT of the 1980s was no longer interested in diplomatic answers to legal claims. The United States organized a broad-based attack on the ruling in the GATT Council, and the ruling was formally repudiated when the Council voted merely to note the ruling rather than to adopt it. The Soyabean Oil case made it impossible to ignore the problem any longer.

---

[16] European Community: Program of Minimum Import Prices (MIPS), Licenses, Etc. for Certain Processed Fruits and Vegetables, BISD, 25th Supp. pp 68-107

[17] European Community: Refunds on Exports of Sugar, BISD, 26th Supp. pp 290-319; European Community: Refunds on Exports of Sugar, BISD, 27th Supp. pp 69-98

[18] European Community: Restriction on Imports of Apples from Chile, BISD, 27th Supp. pp 98-117

[19] European Community: *Restriction on Imports of Desert Apples from Chile*, BISD, 36th Supp. pp 93-135; European Community: *Restrictions on Imports of Apples*, BISD, 36th Supp. pp 135-167

[20] *Spain: Measures Concerning Domestic Sale of Soyabean Oil*, GATT Docs. L/5142 and L/5142/Corr.1, not reprinted in BISD

8. The Creation of the Secretariat's Office of Legal Affairs

Arthur Dunkel replaced Olivier Long as Director-General of GATT in 1980, just as the number of problematic panel rulings was beginning to draw attention to the Secretariat's lack of legal expertise. To many Secretariat officials and GATT delegates, the answer seemed obvious–the Secretariat would have to acquire a staff of professional lawyers to advise panels. But it was not that easy. The European Community, which was just then becoming the target of a new barrage of post-Tokyo Round legal claims by the United States, indicated it was strongly opposed to abandonment of the Secretariat's traditional no-lawyers policy.

Dunkel decided that the Secretariat had to move forward anyway. His problem was to find a solution that would improve the Secretariat's legal capacity in a way that would satisfy the Community's concerns as well. Dunkel's response was in the best traditions of the glacial gradualism that is typical of much GATT diplomacy. In January 1981, he created a Secretariat position entitled Director of Legal Affairs. He appointed to that position a very senior Secretariat official, a man widely respected for his archival knowledge of GATT history, and, more important, for the understanding and good judgment he had demonstrated during a long career as an international civil servant. To add further assurance to the *safety* of this position, the appointment was cast as a two-year experiment, a time limit that was guaranteed by the fact that the official himself was scheduled to retire in two years. Furthermore, the position had no staff assigned to it, limiting the amount of legal work it could do.

The two year experiment with the Director of Legal Affairs apparently caused no major problems for the Community. In the meantime, the volume and complexity of GATT litigation had grown even greater, making it all but essential that the Secretariat retain the position of legal advisor in some form or other. As for the Community, its opposition to legal staff had begun to soften a bit by 1983, but there were still considerable limits upon what it would accept. The search for a successor to the first Director of Legal Affairs brought forth a recommendation that the position be filled by someone with both the training and professional experience of a lawyer, possibly someone from outside the Secretariat. According to the recollection of participants, the Community vetoed the proposed appointment of one such *legal* candidate. Instead, the Community indicated that the most it could accept would be another very senior and very well respected member of the Secretariat, one who had a university degree in law but who had chosen a career as a diplomat and international civil servant, rather than as a lawyer. In January 1983, that official was appointed to the position.

This time, however, it was possible to take a series of additional steps over the next six months that eventually strengthened the position considerably. First, the position lost its temporary character. The title of the position was changed to Director, Office of Legal Affairs, with the Office being a permanent part of the Secretariat. Soon afterwards, additional staff was added–first a secretary, then a young lawyer that had been hired by another division for archival work, and a few months later another young lawyer who had been hired by another division as a trade policy counselor. The two additional lawyers had both the training and experience needed to cope with the kind of legal problems confronting the Secretariat. By mid-1983, therefore, a three-member Secretariat legal office with the requisite kind of legal expertise was up and running.

The Office of Legal Affairs did not bring about an error-free legal system. Panelists occasionally rejected Secretariat advice, and sometimes the panels were confronted with conflicting advice–one view from the Office of Legal Affairs and another view from the subject-matter Division assigned to the panel. And the Office of Legal Affairs itself stumbled a few times as well. In addition to these occasional legal errors, the dispute settlement process also produced a few other decisions that the losing governments simply refused to accept, and which, because of the requirement that rulings must be adopted by consensus, were never adopted.

Each time it suffered a disappointing outcome of one kind or another, however, the GATT dispute settlement process was able to pick itself off the floor and handle the next series of cases successfully. Eventually, the number of sound rulings and successful outcomes substantially outnumbered the disappointing results, and over the next ten years governments gradually acquired greater and greater confidence in the soundness and high legal quality of the GATT's dispute settlement process.[21] The Office of Legal Affairs was given most of the credit for these qualities.

The improved legal quality of the GATT's dispute settlement rulings had a major impact on the role of the disputes procedure in GATT affairs generally. The more confidence governments had in the procedure, the more they were willing to use it, and the more they were willing to submit difficult and sensitive cases to it. By the end of the 1980s, the dispute settlement procedure was handling the greatest volume of litigation in its history, and much of that work involved issues at the very center of GATT's policy agenda. The ultimate measure of government confidence in the GATT disputes procedure, of course, was their willingness to accept a major strengthening and enlargement of that procedure when transforming it into the WTO disputes procedure in the Uruguay Round. It is impossible to conceive of governments committing themselves to such a powerful disputes procedure without first having acquired a well-grounded confidence in the legal quality of the GATT procedure that came before it.

One must be careful not to overstate this last point, however. While governments did have confidence in the GATT procedure, they had not forgotten the errors and failures that had occurred on the long and difficult road to general acceptance. Also, it had to be recognized that the Secretariat's legal staff, however strong its influence in practice, did not have the legal or institutional power to control what panels actually did. Therefore, before governments would agree to grant the new WTO procedure power to issue legally binding rulings, they insisted on more solid institutionalized protection against legal error, and to this end they created the Appellate Body–a free-standing appellate tribunal with seven permanent judges appointed for renewable terms of four-plus-four years. Needless to say, the creation of the Appellate Body would inevitably dilute the dominant in-

[21] For a detailed analysis of the many cases that both advanced and retarded the success of the dispute settlement process during this period, see Hudec (1993), Chapters 8 and 10

fluence that the Secretariat legal staff had acquired over the legal content of GATT disputes procedure. Notwithstanding the critically important role it had played in bringing the GATT dispute settlement procedure to this point, it would now be necessary for the Secretariat legal staff to step back and let a more formal institution take over some of its responsibilities.

9. The Secretariat's Role Today: *Lawyers, Lawyers, Everywhere*

The GATT/WTO Secretariat has been almost unique among international secretariats in its commitment to a lean-and-mean personnel policy–a commitment to remaining as small as possible despite its increasing workload. The Secretariat's recent policy towards hiring additional lawyers stands out as an important exception to this policy.

The success of the three-person Office of Legal Affairs that began to operate in mid-1983 was eventually recognized in the form of increased staff. By the end of the Uruguay Round negotiations, the Office had grown to five lawyers. The growth of the Office has accelerated under the WTO. According the June 1997 edition of the WTO telephone directory, the WTO's Office of Legal Affairs now numbers eight lawyers and one depositary officer.

The same telephone Directory testifies to a creeping invasion of lawyers into other, subject-matter, Divisions of the Secretariat. Starting with a base of zero throughout the 1980s, the following is the present roster of legal affairs officers in those other Divisions:

Division	Lawyers
Market Access	1
Rules[22]	3
Intellectual Property	1
Services	2
Agriculture	0
Trade and Environment	0
Technical Cooperation[23]	2
Development	0
Accessions	1

[22] The Rules division covers the Antidumping and Subsidies/Countervail Codes, the Safeguards Code, State Trading and Civil Aircraft. A few years before the WTO was created, the Rules Division took over the responsibilities of the Office of Legal Affairs in supplying legal advice to panel proceedings involving Antidumping or Subsidy/Countervail measures.

[23] The Technical Cooperation Division is charged with advising and training developing country delegations, including supplying legal advice for dispute settlement proceedings.

Finally, of course, the Appellate Body created by the Uruguay Round reforms has its own separate legal staff, which, while not officially part of the Secretariat, numbers three more lawyers plus one Counselor.

The growing number of lawyers working in the Secretariat's Office of Legal Affairs and on the staff of the Appellate Body represents a major commitment of Secretariat resources to the process of dispute settlement. The resource commitment might be viewed as a measure of the importance that is accorded to dispute settlement in the WTO, but that interpretation could be a bit misleading. Whether or not WTO Members would have been willing to invest this much in order to reap the positive benefits of the new dispute settlement procedure, the fact is that they were pretty much compelled to make that investment to protect against the serious harm that poor quality legal decisions can cause now that the disputes procedure wields such power.

The addition of ten legal officers to the staffs of several subject-matter Divisions testifies to the growing share of WTO business that involves working with legal instruments of one kind or another. In the view of these Divisions, they cannot do the work expected of them unless they have access to their own legal counsel. One could venture a generalization about this increasing legalization of the WTO's business. It is said that societal institutions tend to follow a pattern of maturation according to which they progress from informal processes based on negotiation and accommodation of interests (diplomacy) to more formal processes based on settled norms (law). That clearly seems to be the case with regard to the evolution of GATT into the WTO. The changing character of the Secretariat is merely reflecting this larger tendency.

What role will the lawyer-ridden WTO Secretariat play in the WTO's new dispute settlement procedure? It has already been noted that the creation of the Appellate Body must necessarily diminish the influence of the Secretariat over the content of legal decisions. Neither the Office of Legal Affairs nor any other part of the WTO Secretariat legal staff is allowed to advise the Appellate Body directly. The Appellate Body's own three-person legal staff will undoubtedly have some influence over the work of the Appellate Body, and the relatively senior rank of the Director of that staff will probably insure a careful hearing for their views. But that legal staff will clearly not have the kind of dominant influence that the Office of Legal Affairs wielded over GATT panels in the 1980s and early 1990s. The institutional structure of the Appellate Body is designed to assure that the seven judges of the Appellate Body will develop their own legal expertise to the degree necessary to render independent judgments. All will have the professional training and experience needed to function as independent judges. They will normally serve for eight years, and their compensation indicates an expectation that they will devote at least half of their time to Appellate Body work. The Appellate Body has already decided to intensify the educational process built into to its workload by having all judges consult on every case.

The legal officers of the WTO Secretariat will have an opportunity to influence Appellate Body decisions indirectly through their work advising the ordinary panels that will render the first decision in the WTO's new two-tier dispute settlement procedure. A sound legal ruling by the panel, explained persuasively, can shape the way the legal issues will be presented on appeal, and the panel's legal reasoning will always have to be studied very carefully by the Appellate Body before it makes any decision of its own.

How much influence are Secretariat lawyers likely to have on the content of first-tier panel decisions? As long as panel members are drawn primarily from national delegations resident in Geneva, the relatively greater legal expertise of Secretariat legal officers is likely to continue to give them a considerable advantage in dealing with less expert panel members. A few recent WTO panels have shown a tendency to reach out for relatively more expert panelists, such as law professors or very well regarded former delegates with extensive panel experience. Panels composed of more expert panelists are likely to act with greater independence from their legal advisors. But such more expert panels are likely to be the exception rather than the rule, because of resource constraints. Resident Geneva delegates cost the Secretariat nothing, whereas the travel expenses of outside panel members from other parts of the world tend to be quite costly.

A factor that is more likely to dilute the influence of the Secretariat's legal advisers on first-tier panel decisions is what might be called the *balkanization* of the Secretariat's legal advising functions. Because of the growing number of legal officers in subject-matter Divisions, the Office of Legal Affairs will now have to share its own advising function with lawyers in the subject-matter Division appointed to service the panel. Legal advice emanating from a number of different parts of the Secretariat, each with its own institutional or subject-oriented perspective of GATT/WTO policy, and each with its own clientele of government ministries, is likely to lead to conflicting advice in a number of cases. When the two sets of advising lawyers are in conflict, several different kinds of results are possible. In some cases, one set of advisors may prevail over the other; when this happens, the panel decisions will probably have legal coherence, but they may well be inconsistent with each other as different decisions represent different approaches WTO to legal policy. In other cases, it is possible that the two conflicting sets of legal advice may cancel out each other's influence. In such a situation, some panels will just fall back on their own good judgment, but there could well be other cases in which the panel is so confused by the conflicting advice that they produce decisions that lack coherence altogether. On the whole, the sum of the different possible responses to conflicting advice will probably be that none of the Secretariat's legal staff will be able to exert a consistent influence on the content of first-tier panel rulings.

If the content of first-tier panel rulings does evolve as suggested, it will be up to the Appellate Body to do most of the work in pulling together a consistent legal policy for the WTO. This is not an impossible task, but it would obviously be better if the Secretariat's legal talent devoted to the first tier of the process were making a more systematic contribution to the development of that legal policy. At a minimum, some kind of procedure for coordinating legal advice to panels should be considered. Most governments have concluded that coordination alone is not enough, and that important issues of legal policy have to be controlled by a central ministry of justice that is separate from, and independent of, the subject-matter concerns of lawyers in other ministries. Whether the WTO Secretariat would be able to impose such a solution on its various subject-matter Divisions can be doubted.

The overall conclusion suggested by these observations is something of a paradox. We see that, not counting the Appellate Body, the number of legal positions on the WTO Secretariat has multiplied six-fold over the three lawyers in the 1980s Office of Legal Affairs. The result of this expansion, however, seems to be that the once-dominant influence of the Secretariat over the legal content of the dispute settlement process has declined. Part of this decline is due to the quite deliberate choice to create an Appellate Body to perform the error-control functions that had theretofore been exercised informally by the Secretariat's Office of Legal Affairs. But even the dispute settlement role that remains for Secretariat legal officials–advising first-tier panels–would seem to be diminishing in influence, due to the dispersion *(balkanization)* of the many new legal positions throughout the Secretariat. In this case, *more* seems to have meant *less*. The overall decline of the Secretariat's influence is undoubtedly a disappointing conclusion to a story of important achievement, particularly after the critically important role that the Secretariat played in bringing the GATT disputes procedure to the point where the present WTO disputes procedure could be built upon it. But such disappointments are often the fate of agents of change. Change agents are often the very first victims of the changes they have triggered.

What will happen to the Secretariat's role in WTO dispute settlement in the future? One possibility, mentioned above, is that the Secretariat will regain some of the lost ground by better coordination of its legal advising function, and perhaps even more ground by a greater centralization of the advising function under the Office of Legal Affairs. In the author's view, however, the resistance to this sort of coordination will probably be stronger than the desire to do it.

A more interesting scenario would unfold if the WTO were to contemplate making some more basic changes in the dispute settlement process. The present two-tier model, under which decisions by first-tier panels are reviewed by an Appellate Body, is somewhat awkward, and may prove even more awkward if conflict among the various legal advisers to first-tier panels begins to produce a significant number of inconsistent and otherwise unsatisfactory first-tier rulings. Strengthening the legal capacity of panel members themselves would be one way to avoid such a problem, but the resource cost of doing so would probably be prohibitive. And it would probably also be unnecessary. The same result could be achieved with a considerably smaller investment by turning the Appellate Body into a full time court that would handle all dispute settlement cases from beginning to end in a one-tier process. The workload is not so great–so far, anyway–that a single full-time tribunal could not handle it. Such a change would solve many of the other problems that are beginning to emerge with the two-tier process, such as the problem of time pressure that has already forced the Appellate Body on several occasions to function like a court of first instance in order to finish off cases within the time deadlines established by the new disputes procedure.

The choice to establish the present two-tier model was not really a choice based on a full and thorough examination of all possible models. In this case, as in all cases of GATT institutional reform, the political resistance to change forced governments to proceed in an incremental fashion–taking the existing model of the panel process that governments were comfortable with and making just enough changes to it to get the desired result. Once governments have lived with the new system for a few years, and particularly once they have become comfortable with the Appellate Body as a permanent and authoritative tribunal, they should be willing to entertain the kind of consolidation and simplification suggested in the previous paragraph.

What would be the consequences of such a change for the various elements of the WTO legal staff? The legal staff of the Appellate Body (which would probably have another name by then) would obviously grow. The large staff of the Office of Legal Affairs would no longer have any panels to advise, and so would have to concentrate on its other function of giving general legal advice to national delegations and to other branches of the Secretariat. At this point, someone might re-introduce the idea of creating an office of Avocat General in the Secretariat. Such an office would prepare an independent analysis of the legal issues in every dispute settlement proceeding from the viewpoint of overall WTO policy (as distinct from the necessarily parochial perspectives of the actual litigants), and would present that position to the tribunal. Many other legal systems, including the European Court of Justice, have found the institution of Avocat General to be a useful instrument for achieving highest quality results. It would be natural step at this point in the evolution of WTO law.

Bibliography

Brown WA (1950), *The United States and the Restoration of World Trade*. The Brookings Institution. Washington DC

Gardner RN (1956), *Sterling Dollar Diplomacy*. The Clarendon Press: Oxford

Hudec RE (1987), *Developing Countries in the GATT Legal System*. Aldershot, Gower for the Trade Policy Research Centre

Hudec RE (1990), *The GATT Legal System and World Trade Diplomacy*. 2nd ed, Butterworth, Salem NH

Hudec RE (1993), *Enforcing International Trade Law: TheEvolution of the Modern GATT Legal System*. Butterworth, Salem NH

Part III: Globalisation and the World Trading System

Whither the Trade System Next?

Renato Ruggiero

1. Introduction

The World Trade Organization (WTO) came into being in January 1995, making it the first new global institution of the post-Cold War era. This timing is significant. It reflects the fact that the multilateral trading system is rapidly moving to the centre of a new kind of international system that has taken shape since the fall of the Berlin wall and the increasing globalization of the world economy. Economics has replaced ideology as the main driver of world politics. Technology and liberalization are moving us towards a more integrated–even borderless–economy, blurring the line between domestic and foreign issues. And the ideological divisions of the last half century are fast disappearing, with the result that, for the first time in history, all major economies could soon be part of a single market system.

In this new international landscape, the WTO is emerging as a key pillar of our ever-more interconnected economy–defining the ground rules of trade relations, mediating economic conflicts, and supplying a much needed institutional link between an economy of global dimensions and the nation states that must direct it. As such, the WTO's influence is extending well beyond the trade arena itself. From investment and competition policies, to environmental, development, and even labour issues–more and more the WTO system will have to interact with a whole array of non-trade policies and values which increasingly spill across national borders and transcend national solutions. For these reasons the question "whither the trade system next?" can no longer be–if indeed it ever was–simply a technical question of adding a new rule here or removing a trade barrier there. It must be a broader political question about how to manage an increasingly global economic system. What should be its scope? How should it be led? And to what larger ends should it be directed?

It is a testament to Arthur Dunkel's vision and foresight that he understood that this transformation was already under way in the early 1980s–even though he could not have foreseen the end of the Cold War or the full extent of the technological revolution we see unfolding around us today. Dunkel inherited a trading system that was under considerable strain from a number of different directions.

Speaking to a London audience in 1981, just six months after his appointment as Director-General of the General Agreement on Tariffs and Trade (GATT), he warned that international trade relations were being held together by little more "than a kind of balance of terror."[1] Dunkel's use of the language of nuclear deterrence was not accidental. If by the 1980s trade had never played a more important role in the economic security of most countries, the post-war international system upon which this trade depended had rarely seemed less stable.

Many of the immediate sources of instability were readily apparent by the early 1980s. In 1971, the United States severed the long-standing fixed relationship between gold and the US dollar, which effectively ended the Bretton Woods system of fixed exchange rates. In a world of floating currencies, international capital movements became much freer and larger, while macroeconomic management assumed new and more complex dimensions. The early 1970s also marked the beginning of a protracted slowdown in the world economy brought on partly by the first oil price shock of 1973 and partly by deeper structural changes in industrialized economies. Stagnant growth, rising inflation, and falling employment rates had a destabilizing effect on international trading relations as governments faced growing pressure to protect domestic industries and jobs. This situation was further complicated by the emergence of new trading powers like Japan and, later, the *tigers* of south-east Asia in the 1970s and 1980s, which exposed large differences in relative growth rates, of exports in particular. More and more there was talk in certain industrialized countries of the need for fairer trade and a level playing field.

Behind these immediate challenges more profound changes were taking place in the underlying nature and balance of the world economy. Trade as a proportion of global output had been rising steadily since 1950, while liberalized financial and capital markets fostered the deepening of economic integration and interdependence. All of this was taking place against the background of profound technological changes in the international economy. Advances in informatics, transportation and communications were shrinking distances and erasing borders, first among OECD countries, but increasingly throughout the developing world, exposing national economies more than ever before to international trade and investment flows–a process that has come to be known as globalization. Certainly by the 1980s, if not much earlier, no major country could act in any economic policy area without considering the effects on other countries and their likely reactions, while many smaller countries were increasingly dependent upon the open trading system for their economic security.

This fundamental shift in the international system from geopolitics to geoeconomics would have far-reaching effects. Even before the end of the superpower confrontation, it was clear that commercial rivalries were rising in the shadow of existing military rivalries; and that these new tensions made the management of the international trading system more complex. The abrupt end to the Cold War in 1989 both reflected and reinforced this process. The Berlin Wall collapsed, in part, because of the profound technological and structural pressures

---

[1] Speech by Arthur Dunkel, (30 March 1981), *The GATT System in a Changing World*. Trade Policy Research Centre. London

unleashed by globalization. Television, telephones and fax machines revealed both the failure of socialism to deliver technological progress and the stark material differences between East and West, ending any pretence of a viable competition between state-planned and capitalist economies. The conversion of the former Soviet bloc economies to market-based systems suddenly opened up the possibilities of a single integrated global economy. But it also greatly increased the challenges of managing relations among economies that were at once highly interdependent and highly divergent.

Equally significant was the economic revolution unfolding in much of the developing world and the changing dynamic of the relationship between rich and poor countries, North and South. Countries in Latin America and Asia were at a stage where they were moving from a world of import substitution and protectionism, towards a world of freer markets and more open trade. This represented a sea-change in the orientation and scope of these economies for which the old GATT system, geared mainly to structuring relations among the industrialized countries, was largely unprepared. Many of the developing countries were still on the margins of the international trading system, while central and eastern European countries were operating under state-trading regimes that largely insulated their economies from world markets. Moreover, the GATT and its related agreements were not universal in scope; in particular, membership of the Tokyo Round agreements on non-tariff measures–the GATT *codes*–was far from complete. In the absence of broader and deeper rules, it was more the fear of the political consequences of trade conflict–Dunkel's *balance of terror*–rather than an underlying policy consensus, that was holding the system together.

In short, despite the advances of the Tokyo Round, the multilateral trading system had not kept pace with the rapid changes in the world economy. Many of the old flaws in the system remained: high tariffs were widespread, despite the reductions achieved in the Tokyo Round, and very few developing countries had bound their tariffs to any great extent. Non-tariff barriers to trade of all types were common. Agriculture in developed countries and industry in developing countries was increasingly protected from international competition by quotas, surcharges, variable levies and other distorting devices. And the GATT dispute settlement mechanism was incomplete, with Panel decisions easily blocked. But Dunkel's problems then were not just about old weaknesses in the system: new challenges had emerged. Regional trading arrangements were creating concerns, especially among non-participants, about trade fortresses and systemic fragmentation. Bilateralism and unilateralism–particularly as practiced by the United States through the use of its trade laws, in particular, Section 301–were serious concerns in trade relations. Added to this was the proliferation of voluntary export restraints (VERs), quantitative export targets, market sharing arrangements, and other so called *grey area measures*.[2] These trends raised the general question of whether economic relations between countries could be adequately managed any longer by a few rules on border measures and exchange rates. Much more was being ex-

---

[2] Croome J (1995), *Reshaping the World Trading System*. Publication Services, World Trade Organization, Geneva, Switzerland, pp 6-27; WTO (1996), *Annual Report*. World Trade Organization, Geneva, Switzerland, pp 28-29

pected from the trading system–subsidy practices, domestic regulations, and even fiscal and monetary policies were of growing international interest and the subject of trade controversy.

The Uruguay Round was Dunkel's answer to many of these challenges. New issues like trade in services, trade-investment links and intellectual property rights were brought into the ambit of the system's rules and disciplines, as were long-standing traditional–but no less critical–issues like agriculture and textiles. During the Uruguay Round, developing countries also accepted a range of new obligations, with special and differential treatment being confined mainly to transitional measures and the unique requirements of the least-developed economies. And the institutional foundations of the system were also strengthened with the creation of the WTO and the establishment of a binding dispute settlement mechanism.

But the WTO did not just represent a new chapter in international economic relations because the organization had a new name or new sectors of responsibility or a new dispute settlement procedure. It was a new chapter in the sense that the WTO brought together over 120 countries in a *single undertaking* and under a single system of rules shared by all. As such, it represented fundamental changes in thinking about, and attitudes to, global trade and investment around the world. Asking governments to embrace an ambitious plan for global liberalization as a *single undertaking* was effectively asking them to embrace a new approach to economic development: one which gave primacy to markets not governments, and to competition rather than protection. When combined with the end of the Cold War–an event unforeseen in the mid-1980s but crucial in changing the dynamics of the international economy–the Uruguay Round helped unleash a global economic revolution whose ripples can be seen in the continued momentum for liberalization throughout the world today. Dunkel did more than oversee the transition from GATT to the WTO; he helped oversee the successful transition from a world divided by ideology to a world increasingly bound together by trade and economics.

2. The Challenges of a Global Economy

Understanding this post-Uruguay Round world begins with an understanding of the pressures for integration–as well as the pressures for conflict–that have been generated by globalization. Greater integration means that trade, capital and information flow more freely than ever before across national borders. Greater integration also means that countries all over the world, and at all levels of development are under growing pressure to secure access to foreign markets, productive investment and advanced technology if they are to share in rising global production, employment creation, and technological advancement. The result is an almost universal drive, even competition in some regions, to liberalize markets–multilaterally if possible, unilaterally if necessary.[3]

Three major forces are driving this new world economy. One is the dramatic rise in trade flows over the last four decades. In 1995, world-wide trade exceeded US$6000 billion for the first time in history–a fourteen-fold increase compared to 1950. For the world as a whole, the ratio of trade to GDP roughly doubled between 1950 and 1974, from 7 to 15 per cent. In the past two decades it has increased to about 22.5 per cent, and there is every sign that it will continue to rise in the foreseeable future.[4] While there have been many factors driving this trend, the success of the multilateral trading system in helping to liberalize a widening circle of national economies cannot be underestimated. Over the course of eight major negotiating rounds, average industrial tariffs in developed countries have been reduced from more than 40 per cent to less than 5 per cent today, and well over 40 per cent of world trade will be tariff free when the Uruguay Round commitments are fully implemented. It is true that this process is far from complete: in many key areas, substantial tariff peaks remain; the Uruguay Round's final results in agriculture or textiles leave much to be desired; and negotiations are already scheduled to proceed in some of these and other key areas at the turn of the century. There is plenty on the liberalization agenda to keep us occupied well into the next century. It is also true that not all countries are equally integrated into the multilateral system. Liberalization has gone considerably further in Europe and in the Americas, than in parts of Asia or Africa. This is to say nothing of major economies like China or Russia which have yet to accede to the WTO. Yet, however imperfect our progress, the underlying trend is unmistakable. Multilaterally, regionally, unilaterally–all paths are leading to freer global trade.

The fast-expanding web of foreign investment is an equally striking sign of growing openness and integration. Several decades ago many countries sought to shut out foreign investment; now they compete for it. Foreign investment has become an even more powerful force for integration than trade in goods, as multinational firms attempt to extend their global reach by establishing a direct presence in foreign markets. After a sharp decline in the early 1980s, direct investment flows grew six-fold in the decade after 1986, from around US$60 billion to almost US$349 billion per annum, boosting the global stock of foreign direct investment to US$3.2 trillion, or double the level three years earlier.[5] Cross-border mergers and acquisitions alone were valued at US$263 billion last year–taking advantage in part of a world-wide wave of privatization valued at some US$83 billion. More and more trade takes place within companies or among related partners, as transnational firms seek out the most efficient global suppliers, customize products for different markets, and link into sophisticated distribution and technology networks.[6] More and more, trade encompasses the whole

[3] See, for example, Speech by the Honourable Roy MacLaren, Canadian Trade Minister (18 January 1995), *The Walls of Jericho Fall Down*. Toronto; Bergsten CF (1996), *Globalizing Free Trade*. Foreign Affairs (May/June), pp 105-120

[4] WTO (1995b), *Annual Report*. World Trade Organization, Geneva, Switzerland, pp 15-23

[5] The following figures are drawn from *World Investment Report,* September 1996, UNCTAD, and *Financial Market Trends,* June 1997, OECD

technology networks.[6] More and more, trade encompasses the whole spectrum of economic activity–from goods and raw materials, to components, services, and information. Production by foreign affiliates of transnational corporations now exceeds the total value of world trade–suggesting that investment has become an even more powerful vehicle than trade for delivering products and services across borders.

The global coverage of foreign investment flows is also changing. The bulk of direct investment still flows among OECD countries; for example, over one half of inward investment flows to just two countries, the United States and Great Britain. But the 1980s and 1990s have seen a dramatic surge in foreign investment flows to the developing world, and especially to South Asia and Latin America as firms continue to decentralize many aspects of the production process and locate them around the globe. Private capital flows to developing countries rose by one third to a record US$245 billion in 1996, six times the amount of official development assistance, and over a six-fold increase above the average inflows for 1983-89. Developing countries now account for 37 per cent of investment inflows, up from 30 per cent in 1995. These capital flows represented 4.5 per cent of developing country GDP, up from only 1 per cent in 1990.

As we approach the end of the 1990s, there are signs that a new dimension is being added to the global integration process–one where digital technologies and communications networks are creating the possibility of an increasingly borderless economy in key sectors. Over the last decade or so, the cost of telecommunications and computing has fallen dramatically, just as speed and capacity have risen. A transatlantic telephone call now costs just 1.5 per cent of what it cost 60 years ago. And the World Bank predicts that by 2010 the cost will have fallen by another two thirds–to about 3 cents a minute–making transatlantic telecommunications almost a free commodity. The cost of computing power has also fallen dramatically–by almost 100 per cent since 1960. A single transistor, which sold for US$70 in the mid-1960s, can now be bought for less than a millionth of a cent, in turn making computing power accessible to millions of ordinary people.

This increasingly borderless, information-based economy is perhaps best symbolized by the Internet. At once global and local, a communications tool and a knowledge resource, the Internet has been steadily doubling in size each year since its creation a quarter of a century ago. Already some 55 million people world-wide have connections to the Internet; by 2000 this number could grow to 550 million, approaching 10 per cent of the world's population. Nor is the Internet the only channel available. Other technologies like computerized financial markets, E-mail, telephone banking, and electronic data interchange are all moving us towards a more borderless, information-driven economy. Just as the globalization of trade and investment has changed the face of manufacturing since the 1980s, the advent of a borderless economy could transform services or *ideas-based* industries in equally dramatic ways–industries that already account for more than 70 per cent of GDP in many OECD countries, and up to 50 per cent in some developing countries. It was once assumed that most services were inherently non-tradable since the product was people–either their brawn or their brainpower–and

[6] WTO (1996), *Annual Report*. Geneva, Switzerland

exporting required a physical presence in foreign markets. For many services, this conventional wisdom has been turned on its head with the invention of the microchip. Now any service that can be digitized and transmitted electronically can be produced and delivered almost anywhere in the world in a matter of seconds. Computer software, medical information, educational programmes, data processing, legal and architectural services–all of these industries could become part of an increasingly borderless and competitive environment, where every country, every business operates in a virtual world market.

Several key features of this new borderless economy are worth noting. One is the increasing irrelevance of geography and time. Trade used to be shaped by the realities of geography as one element in a nation's comparative advantage. In important sectors, trade will take place irrespective of geographic considerations. The technological conquest of time and space will have far-reaching economic effects. Transaction costs for consumers and businesses will fall rapidly as many steps that intervene between buyer and seller–distribution, sales, retailing–are compressed. Transaction times will fall even faster, adding a whole new dimension to *just-in-time* production processes. Perhaps most significant of all will be the falling barriers and costs to market entry–or starting a new business–allowing a far greater number of suppliers to enter a market. Not only will consumers benefit from this increased competition, but small- and medium-sized enterprises as well as large multinational corporations will now be full participants in the global marketplace.

It is electronic trade that best demonstrates the waning relevance of geography, time and borders. The electronic exchange of software, services or information takes place in the closest thing yet to a single, world market–one defined, not by products, paperflows and border checks, but by electronic bytes and laser beams. Several years ago Robert Reich asked the question "Who is us?"[7] in an age of global integration. In other words, will economic nationality matter any more in a world where the web of global value added cannot be unravelled? Reich's question is even more relevant in a digital economy, one which operates in cyberspace and has no physical reality, let alone nationality. What, for example, is the nationality of a software package upgraded in Delhi for a corporation in Seattle and downloaded over the Internet in Beijing? And which government has jurisdiction over this kind of transaction? More and more of these kinds of questions will arise in the time ahead, posing significant policy challenges for national governments–from the relevance of rules of origin, to the enforcement of regulations and standards, to the collection of taxes from retailers and consumers operating in cyberspace.

A second feature of the borderless economy is that information is increasingly the critical resource and a major driving force of the integration process. Information is now key to the global economy. Just as surging trade and investment first fuelled globalization in the 1980s, now it is access to–and competition for–technology that is shaping the borderless economy. This diffusion of technology is of course not a new process–the story of human progress down the ages is in large part the story of the development and widespread application of technology.

---

[7] Reich RB (1990), *Who is us?* Harvard Business Review (January-February), p 53

What is new is the way an expanding network of computers, telephones, and fax machines is accelerating the process, and widening its scope. Unlike the classical factors of production–land, labour and even capital–information and knowledge are not bound to any region or country but are almost infinitely mobile and infinitely capable of expansion.

This knowledge-driven economy is not replacing other economic activities–factories and farming are not going to disappear, software is not going to become a substitute for the food we eat or the cars we drive. But technology is changing the way we produce things–sometimes in quite dramatic ways. Take even the most traditional of economic activities, farming, which has been with us since the dawn of time. Mechanization, biotechnology, transportation, and information technologies are utterly transforming agricultural production and distribution to the point where modern agriculture is sometimes closer to a service industry than it is to traditional farming. And much the same transformation is under way in mining, forestry, transportation, and other industries. This has resulted in the blurring of many of the old distinctions between manufacturing and services, products and processes, so-called high-tech economies, and more traditional industrial or resource economies.

This leads to a third characteristic: the borderless economy's potential to equalise relations between countries and regions. At the global level, old divisions between North and South are being superseded by new distinctions–between those countries embracing technology and globalization, and those that remain behind; or, as Jean-Francois Rischard of the World Bank suggests: *between fast and slow countries, learning and static countries, plugged-in and left-out countries, 100 per cent reliable countries and those that are not.*[8] Access to telecommunications is expanding rapidly–to one billion, or almost one in every five people, by the turn of the century–creating the real possibility of a telephone in every village. The dozen or so global satellite schemes now under construction will virtually eliminate bandwidth constraints and reduce connections costs to a few dollars per station in a decade. Many developing countries will be able to leapfrog entire stages of development into the latest generation of wireless telephony–avoiding the huge costs of building a copper-wire based infrastructure. Today more than 80 per cent of the world's population cannot make a telephone call; soon they will have access, not just to leading-edge communications, but to the educational programmes, medical services, and technical information that flow through cyberspace.

Already we are witnessing a significant shift in economic power towards the South and the East–a shift that will have as dramatic an impact on world politics as the collapse of the Berlin Wall. The World Bank projects that developing countries will grow by 5 to 6 per cent a year between now and 2020. This means that the developing countries will almost double their share of world output, from around 16 per cent in 1992, to 30 per cent in 2020. This year's UN World Economic and Social Survey notes that the circle of economic growth has spread to most parts of the world–and the IMF foresees world-wide growth of about 4.5 per

---

[8] Speech by Jean-Francois Rischard (Vice President of Finance and Private Sector Development, World Bank, Washington DC) at the 1997 Substantive Session of the Economic and Social Council (ECOSOC) High-Level Segment, 2 July 1997

cent a year over the next five years, compared with an average of 3.75 per cent over the past quarter century. What these numbers demonstrate, among other things, is the accelerating pace of development. A level of industrialization that took 150 years to accomplish in Great Britain, or 100 years in United States, is today capable of being achieved in less than a generation–the most rapid development process in economic history. With the spread of information technologies this process of industrialization is poised to accelerate and broaden even more.

This remarkable record of economic and technological progress is having a real impact on the everyday lives of people in many countries. The UNDP reminds us that poverty has been reduced more in the last 50 years than in the last 500. Since 1960, infant mortality rates have been almost halved. Malnutrition rates have declined by almost one third. By the end of the century, adult illiteracy will have been reduced by nearly three fifths and about 4 to 5 billion people will have access to basic education and health care. Even more remarkable, the UNDP talks about the potential for eradicating global poverty in the early part of the next century–a utopian notion even a few decades ago, but a real possibility today. The most striking feature of the late twentieth century is not the pain and dislocation produced by globalization and technological change, although these realities are certainly with us, rather it is the fact that billions of people have achieved a standard of living today that was attainable by only a fortunate few a century ago.[9]

3. Governing Global Interdependence

The huge transformation in the world economy over the last decade may in the long run prove to be more important than the dramatic geo-political shifts that accompanied the end of the Cold War. But if this process of economic and technological integration is to continue in an equitable and stable way, we will have to manage the many other challenges that accompany deepening interdependence. As national economies move closer together, the scope for friction also increases. Growing international competition for markets, investment and technology is already well under way. Indeed, one of the unfortunate paradoxes of the end of the Cold War is that the disappearance of overarching ideological and strategic imperatives has actually increased the political scope for trade and economic conflict among nations. For almost fifty years, the strategic imperatives of the Cold War meant that many trade irritants and frictions were overridden by foreign policy objectives. Some have even argued that the GATT/IMF system itself had less to do with a policy commitment to free trade than with the broader foreign policy objectives of the western alliance in a Cold War environment. But these pressures for economic cohesion have been lifted with the disappearance of the Soviet threat, with the less fortunate result that international trade has become a more prominent arena in which national interests and rivalries are played out.

---

[9] OECD, *New Global Age* (June 1997); World Bank, *World Development Report* (June 1997), IMF, *World Economic Outlook* (September 1997); UNDP, *Human Development Report*. (1997)

The reality of deepening global interdependence in the post-Cold War era has yet to dispel many of the myths associated with national security and national sovereignty. National competitiveness, however ill-defined, has replaced national security as a new acid test of strategic strength. In the 1970s the prescriptions for improving the economic performance of a country, so as to enhance its strength and influence vis-à-vis those of its rivals in world affairs, often focused on the use of industrial policies to promote strategic sectors of the economy. These strategic sectors have typically been high-technology sectors, with success in international *competition* consisting in the acquisition of technological mastery and production in sectors such as semiconductors, software, and aerospace.[10] The high-tech battles of the 1980s and 1990s foreshadow the even more complex technological rivalries that will be played out early in the next century over emerging trade issues like development subsidies, government procurement, competition policy, and intellectual property protection–all of which, it should be added, will be further complicated by the growing scope and sophistication of communications networks, and the advent of a borderless economy in many information technology products and processes.

Then there is the social adjustment challenge posed by rapid globalization and technological change. Periods of economic transition almost invariably produce losers as well as winners, and often the losers, at least in the short term, are those in society least well placed to defend themselves. Dani Rodrick, following Robert Reich's well known book, *Work Among Nations,* has argued that globalization is exposing *a deep faultline between groups who have the skills and mobility to flourish in global markets, and those who don't.*[11] Whether this social faultline *has* actually widened is a matter of intense academic debate. Even more relevant, for our discussion, is the debate over whether changes in labour markets can be attributed to liberal trade policies or to technological change–and whether technological change is itself being fuelled by globalization.[12] But one thing is clear: this challenge of social adjustment and cohesion is often occurring against the background of shrinking governments and diminished resources. For a variety of reasons, most of which have little to do with trade policy, the domestic systems that were put in place in this century to help share out the benefits as well as the burdens of

---

[10] This competition has been the subject of commentary by several observers. See, for instance, the analysis of such competition in Bhagwati J (1988), *Protectionism*. MIT Press: Cambridge Mass.; advocacy of such competition in Tyson L (1992), *Who's Bashing Whom? Trade Conflict in High Technology Industries*. Institute for International Economics, Washington DC; and a critical review of such advocacy in Jagdish Bhagwati's review of Tyson's book in the New Republic of 31 May 1993, *Rough Trade,* reprinted in Bhagwati J (1998), *A Stream of Windows: Unsettling Reflections on Trade, Immigration, and Democracy*. MIT Press: Cambridge Mass

[11] Rodrik D (1997), *Has Globalization Gone Too Far?* Institute for International Economics, Washington DC, pp 4-5

[12] There is an extensive scholarly literature on this subject. See, for example, the contributions by Bhagwati and Dehejia, and by Deardorff and Hakura, in Jagdish Bhagwati and Marvin Kosters (eds) (1994), *Trade & Wages: Levelling Wages Down?* American Enterprise Institute, Washington DC; and Susan Collins (ed) (1988), *The American Worker: Imports, Exports and Wages,* Brookings Institution, Washington DC

economic change–balancing the interests of efficiency versus equity, sunrise versus sunset industries, producers versus consumers–are increasingly under stress, in turn fuelling domestic pressure for protection from import competition and economic change.

Already these pressures are being felt by vulnerable sectors in the OECD countries. While it is true that the rapid industrialization of countries like China, Indonesia or Brazil represents enormous export and investment opportunities for developed countries, it is also true that the integration of these emerging giants into the mainstream of the world economy poses a significant adjustment challenge in advanced markets which can only be addressed with a coordinated policy response in areas like education and skills development. But this challenge of adjustment in the advanced economies pales in comparison to the major structural reforms that are needed in the developing world–and in a much shorter space of time. Although trade, investment, and technology move ever more effortlessly across borders, developing countries themselves often lack the basic infrastructure, financial or legal systems, or political foundations needed to cope with massive economic shifts. More importantly, many also lack sufficiently developed social and educational systems to meet basic living standards, let alone to prepare their citizens for a coming age of information economies and globally integrated markets. Then there are the many least developed countries which have simply been left behind by our fast-globalizing economic system, risking even further marginalization. Integrating these marginalized countries into the mainstream of the global economy must be one of the key priorities of the coming century. As the World Bank has recently underlined, we cannot expect to build sustainable free market systems on a global scale without also building the social and institutional foundations needed to sustain these systems.[13]

Deeper integration is also giving rise to other frictions based not on pressures for economic competition or protection but on clashes between distinct national systems–what Sylvia Ostry has called *systems friction*.[14] As integration moves deeper inside the border, the policy debate is shifting away from traditional arguments over tariffs towards non-tariff barriers related to fundamental differences between economic systems–investment rules, anti-trust and competition laws, taxation, and labour, environmental and cultural policies. It is precisely because these issues involve non-trade goals and cut deeply into traditional notions of sovereignty, that they could prove more difficult to resolve. Globalization is a great leveller. Fierce competition among economic systems for footloose capital, production and technology–and the jobs that accompany these investments–means that governments are coming under increasing pressure to streamline or harmonize their systemic differences. While it would be wrong to portray this process as a race to the bottom–indeed, the evidence suggests that it is usually the *absence* of adequate environmental, health, education, or social standards that is a major dis-

---

[13] World Bank (1997) op cit

[14] Ostry S (1990), *Governments and Corporations in a Shrinking World*. Council of Foreign Relations: New York

incentive to investment[15]–it is true that the relentless pressure for harmonization can itself be a source of tension when it challenges a nation's sense of identity, its sovereignty, and its control over its own destiny. Current domestic debates over foreign investment, labour standards, or culture can be seen as part of a much larger debate over whether globalization is shaping a world in which there are no differences.

Behind all this is the political challenge of managing an increasingly globalized economic system. As a rising share of national output is traded internationally and a growing volume of national savings is invested abroad, there is a growing role for multilateral organisations in providing institutional and legal frameworks for these crossborder economic activities. In other words, national security has taken on a new international economic dimension. And other dimensions as well. Jessica Mathews has recently argued that *a competing notion of 'human security' is creeping around the edges of official thinking, suggesting that security be viewed as emerging from the conditions of daily life–food, shelter, employment, health, public safety–rather than flowing downward from a country's foreign relations and military strength.*[16] For the critics of globalization, the vision of global free trade evokes images of a laissez-faire world unfettered by government, but this picture bears little resemblance to the complex needs of a modern international economy. Beyond the minimalist role in providing the regulatory framework, legal structures, and capital markets without which no market economy can operate–Adam Smith's *nightwatchman state*–the new international system also has a growing role to play in supplying public goods that are outside the economic realm, but nevertheless indispensable to global economic development and stability: environmental regulations, health measures, skills and educational development in many countries. More and more there is a need for international arrangements to deal with a growing list of transnational challenges, yet for the foreseeable future the nation state will–and must–be at the political centre of this system. At the same time, as global economic rules move inside the border there will be unavoidable clashes with traditional notions of sovereignty and the idea that there should be no interference in the domestic affairs of states. The tension between a political system that is local and an economy that is increasingly global will emerge as one of the key challenges all governments will face in this new era.

4. Institutional Oversight

All of this highlights the broader role of the WTO in the post-Cold War international system–providing an institutional link between a fast-globalizing economy and the national governments that must direct it. Modern economies work on a

---

[15] A survey by Deloitte & Touche Consulting Group says that in 1995, 76 per cent of total investment in the 10 foreign locations most favoured by US manufacturers was in high-wage countries, led by Sweden (US$9 billion) and Brazil (US$4 billion). The general conclusion is that a country's ability to meet world-wide best-practices is more critical for competing in the market than cheap labour.

[16] Mathews J (1997), *The Age of Non-State Actors*. Foreign Affairs (January/February) p 51

vast and complex network of interrelationships that in turn depend on an infrastructure of rules, laws, and institution to underpin and secure these relationships. As this fragile web expands across national frontiers–through rising flows of trade, capital, technology, information, and ideas, global stability will increasingly depend on the ease and security with which economic activity can move across borders to the benefit of industrial and developing economies alike.

John Jackson has described the WTO system as a *constitution* for global trade.[17] This constitution has always been expected to play two roles so as to facilitate the interaction among distinct and often widely different national economies and systems.[18] Firstly, to help move the international economy consistently in the direction of freer trade and secondly, to provide a coherent and non-discriminatory set of rules, resting on the twin pillars of national treatment and the most-favoured-nation principle (MFN). It is this astute blend of principle and pragmatism that gives the multilateral system its strength. This strength will be even more relevant to the emerging global age–as technology and economics continue to knit together very different countries, with very different backgrounds, at very different levels of development. While no list of future issues can be exhaustive, especially in the space available to us here, we can nevertheless assume that the agenda for the future will likely revolve around the following four broad themes:

4.1. Deepening the Rules

As global economic integration deepens, the need to deepen economic rule-making becomes more and more apparent, which in turn leads to the continued blurring of the distinction between domestic and foreign policies. The original GATT rules dealt largely with border measures as barriers to market access. But starting with the Tokyo Round, trade policy began to move inside the border by tackling issues such as subsidies, technical barriers to trade, and government procurement. And the Uruguay Round went much further still into the domestic regulatory arena to cover services trade, intellectual property protection, and trade-related investment measures. This process of moving inside the border has only continued since the Uruguay Round. At the WTO's first Ministerial Conference in September 1996, Ministers agreed to create a working group to consider whether investment rules should be brought into the WTO, and another group to consider whether the WTO should include multilateral rules on anti-trust and other competition policy-related issues. The recent Telecommunications Agreement–which creates an international regulatory framework for the global industry–pushes the frontiers even further by tackling issues like investment and competition policy from a sectoral approach. And candidates for further research in other sectors

---

[17] Jackson JH (1997), *The World Trading System: Law and Policy of International Economic Relations.* 2nd ed., MIT Press: Cambridge Mass., p 339

[18] Low P (1993), *Trading Free: the GATT and US Trade Policy.* The Twentieth Century Fund Press: New York, p 145

might include issues such as innovation policies, subsidies, regulatory policies, and product standards.

The nature of rule-making itself is also changing. The GATT's system of rules was traditionally concerned with products crossing borders, and the guiding philosophy was non-discrimination. Otherwise the GATT rules were largely indifferent to domestic policies and the way different economic systems operate. But this is changing. As we continue to strip away border barriers, the issue of how domestic policies and practices can distort competition and trade is inevitably coming to the surface. More and more trade conflicts will hinge on differing regulatory and legal systems. More and more trade rule-making will concentrate on cross-border coordination–even harmonization–of these domestic policies and regulations and efforts to devise global economic *rules of the road*; a process that in theory is not so much about what governments can't do but rather about what they can do together.

This represents a sea change in the underlying philosophy of the system, and could have profound implications for the way the global system unfolds. For fifty years, multilateral negotiations were focused almost exclusively on the removal of barriers at the border according to a score-card which was fundamentally mercantilist–the trading of one tariff concession for another. It is not clear that we yet fully understand how to be rule makers instead of tariff negotiators. Nor is it clear that, when negotiating services or standards or investment, we know how to measure market access or trade concessions meaningfully–or whether these concepts have much meaning any longer in a transnational economy.

4.2. Institutional Strengthening

The failure to establish the ITO in the late 1940s left the GATT without an institutional foundation on which to build future liberalization; even more significantly it left the system without a mechanism for binding dispute settlement. This deficiency has been rectified with the formation of the WTO. Two notable features of the new WTO are the provisions for biannual Ministerial meetings and the establishment of the Trade Policy Review Mechanism which, among other things, have sought to buttress the integrity of the rules of the trading system through regular surveillance. But without doubt the crowning institutional achievement of the WTO was the establishment of binding dispute settlement. The number of disputes that were subject to formal consultations rose to 42 in 1996 compared to 25 in 1995. While half of these cases involved traditional border measures, the other half involved consultations on anti-dumping or countervailing measures, or new disciplines resulting from the Uruguay Round. Equally important is the fact that a significant number of cases have been settled–that is, resolved at the consultation stage, which is an essential part of the dispute settlement procedure.

An important dialectic is at work here. As the scope of economic rule-making broadens and deepens, the role of dispute settlement is becoming correspondingly more important. Likewise, as legal remedies become more central to the functioning of the system, there is growing pressure to clarify and expand the rules of the trading system which, at least at the beginning of GATT's evolution, were sometimes designed more to facilitate diplomatic solutions and to paper over negotiating differences, than to provide a concise legal foundation for judicial outcomes. This movement from a diplomatic to a legalistic regime, and from consensus solutions to binding dispute resolutions, has greatly increased the institutional relevance of the WTO, and introduced a new dynamic into the rule-making process. But the increasing relevance of the dispute settlement procedures also raises important questions about the transparency of the system, and access to its processes. Especially as we begin to tackle new issues like investment or competition policy–issues that explicitly address private sector practices rather than just government policies–the question will inevitable arise as to whether (and how) private parties should have access to a dispute settlement process that remains limited to inter-governmental relations.

4.3. Broadening the Membership

The growing relevance of the WTO to the global economy has in turn exerted a huge gravitational pull on all countries to join the system–providing an important economic bridge between North and South, and developed and developing countries. Whereas the old GATT started out with just 23 members, most from the industrialized world, the WTO has rapidly expanded to 132 members, 80 per cent of which are developing countries or economies in transition. Nor is this participation limited to membership. Reflecting their rising trade power, developing countries are far more active players in the system than ever before. Just 10 per cent of GATT disputes involved developing countries between 1980 and 1994; but in the last two years alone, developing and transition countries have initiated about one third of the requests for WTO consultations or panels. And through their important contribution to the Singapore Conference and to the successful negotiations on telecommunications, financial services and the information technology agreement, developing and transition economies have demonstrated that they are not just active in the system, but indispensable to making it work. Nothing underscores this growing relevance of the WTO to the whole of the global economy more than the importance that China, Russia, and 26 other accession candidates attach to joining the system.

The single most important achievement of the Uruguay Round was the way it brought developing and developed countries into the fold of the trading system under one set of common rules. This *single undertaking* was critically important because it reinforced a fundamental change in attitudes of developing countries towards the global economy and the international trading system–a change which had already been foreshadowed by the decision of many Latin American and Asian countries to embark on a process of autonomous liberalization in the late 1970s and 1980s. For one thing, developing countries arguably benefit the most from the WTO's strengthened rules and dispute settlement procedures. Under the new dispute settlement system, even the smallest country can challenge the most powerful in defense of its trade interests–not on the basis of economic strength but on the basis of common and enforceable rules. Second, increasing market access–from the reform of agricultural policies, the reductions in industrial tariffs, the phase-out of quotas on textile and clothing imports, and the decision to phase out other bilateral quantitative restrictions–gives developing and least-developed countries more opportunity than ever before to increase and diversify their exports. Although developing and least-developed countries may have seen the erosion of some of the relative preference they enjoyed in developed markets under the Generalized System of Preferences or the EU's Lomé Convention, this is more than offset by the greatly improved MFN access to developed markets–and to fast-growing developing markets as well–resulting from the Uruguay Round's tariff cuts, and from the new initiative on information technology launched in Singapore. Third, the acceptance of multilateral trade disciplines can actually help reform-minded governments to resist and overcome domestic pressures to preserve the *status quo*. When special interests are strong enough they can often undermine public interests–especially in economic matters. The WTO agreements have helped to lock in economic reforms, reinforcing the internal liberalization process and encouraging domestic and foreign investment.

4.4. Linkages with Other Global Issues

One of the greatest challenges on the trade policy horizon does not involve trade at all, but revolves around the interface between the trading system and a number of policy areas such as the environment or labour standards, which are also spilling across national borders. There are several reasons why trade has moved to the centre of these debates. One is the proven success of the GATT system itself. Ahead of almost every other policy area, the international trading system has demonstrated that we are reaching a point where many of the policy frameworks that were constructed at the national level can now be more effectively constructed at a regional or global level. As John Jackson has pointed out, *the rules of product trade, centrally served by the GATT, are the most complex and extensive international rules regarding any subject of international economic subjects. As such it is natural that they would have some influence on the potential development of rules for other international economic subjects.*[19] Already the GATT template has been used to design a multilateral agreement for trade in service (GATS) and for trade-related intellectual property issues (TRIPS). There is now growing talk of a GATT for investment and a GATT for competition policy. This lesson has not been lost on other disciplines that have yet to achieve as successful a model as GATT for managing transborder issues and policy challenges. In the absence of a GATT for the environment, for example, many environmentalists have turned to the WTO for systemic support and leverage. Trade sanctions, in particular, are viewed by some as key to enforcing international obligations in an international system that is still a very long way from supranational rules and enforcement mechanisms.

---

[19] Jackson J (1989), *The World Trading System*. MIT Press: Cambridge Mass, p 21

But a deeper reason for the growing salience of the WTO is the role trade plays–or is alleged to play–in the process of globalization and transborder integration across a wide policy front. As a result of the diffusion and standardization of manufacturing technologies, countries at different levels of development, with different regulatory standards, labour markets and cultural norms are competing directly in world markets for the same products. Some groups, especially in advanced countries, see these systemic differences as conferring an unfair trade advantage, and stress the importance of achieving a level playing field. Still others worry about systemic competition in areas like environmental policy or health standards leading to a global race to the bottom. Then there are those who argue that trade agreements should serve goals beyond ensuring economic efficiency–such as human rights or environmental protection. The meaning and implications of these objectives are anything but clear. How to make the distinction between legitimate comparative advantages and unfair advantages? Whose standards, systems or cultural traditions represent a universal norm? And how to ensure that in pursuing ever deeper rule-making and harmonization we do not erase the very differences and comparative advantages that drive the trading system forward? One paradoxical result of this search for global solutions to non-trade issues is often growing pressure for unilateral actions, extraterritorial measures, and economic protection.

Still, these are not arguments for overlooking the many non-economic issues raised by globalization, or for ignoring the need for constructive linkages between trade and other issues in an era when the distinction between policies, as well as between countries, is often blurred. What an open, rules-based trading system provides is a necessary precondition–in partnership with the appropriate environmental, development, or social policies–for building a more globally coherent policy response to the challenges of globalization. The broader solution to environmental, social, and other challenges lies in reaching a global consensus in each of these areas; reaching enforceable global agreements and standards. And building the kind of global institutions needed to manage them. It lies, in other words, with developing global rules to address global needs–as we have done over fifty years with the trading system.

5. Towards a Universal System

Arthur Dunkel's achievement was to systematically link the role of trade to the establishment of the new international system which has taken shape in the post-Cold War era. This new international system that bears his imprint is unique in three broad respects. First, it is a system where geo-economics is now far more salient to inter-state relations than geo-politics. Today, international peace and security are just as likely to be defined in economic and trade terms, and to be determined in fora like G-7 or G-15 Summits, APEC, and the WTO. Second, this system is blurring the distinction between foreign and domestic policies, and between high and low politics. Trade issues will continue to move to the centre of public debate as trade policy continues to move beyond simple border tariffs, to involve deeper issues like investment policy, health standards, environmental regulations, and legal structures–issues that raise important questions about how we pursue legitimate economic and social goals in an increasingly borderless world. Third, the system's strength derives from its transnational rules rather than from international cooperation or coordination alone. This network of rules, embodied most notably in the WTO, not only give the trading system its resilience but also its great cohesion.

All of these factors make a post-Cold War international system centred on the WTO unique in another respect. We have the potential, for the first time in history, to incorporate all of the world's major countries and civilizations in a single community of interests. More and more countries are discovering that they cannot achieve economic growth and progress without embracing open trade and investment; that they cannot participate in a technology-driven economy without opening their societies to the flow of information and ideas; and that they cannot enjoy the benefits of the international system without at the same time accepting the reality and the validity of the rule of law–domestically as well as internationally.

Whither the WTO? The simple–and yet complex–answer its that we are headed towards a universal economic system. The WTO is fast becoming, if it is not already, one of the cornerstones of the post-Cold War international system. And in the foreseeable future, the WTO is destined to follow the path of globalization–that is to say, it must continue to grow in scope, complexity and ambition if it is to keep pace with a process of globalization which, in an almost literal sense, is moving with the speed of the Internet. The relevance of trade in general–and the WTO in particular–will only intensify in future years, as global economic integration continues, and as trade issues increasingly affect other policy areas and our day-to-day lives. And as the WTO grows in importance, we will have to grapple with the issue of how to interact with broader global goals and concerns–an issue that touches on the essential legitimacy of the new international order–without at the same time impairing the essential functions of the trade system.

Is this a cause for concern? The answer is both no and yes. It is vitally important that the widening and deepening of the WTO go hand in hand with maintaining its effectiveness and credibility. This means above all preserving the integrity of the rules–the source of the GATT's success in the past, and the WTO's strength in the future. It also means keeping the WTO Secretariat apolitical and the system contractual in nature. None of these challenges are insurmountable. At each stage of the GATT's fifty-year evolution, concerns have been expressed that the system is becoming unworkable; and the post-Uruguay Round era is no exception. Some observers have already begun to ask how an increasingly complex trading system of 160-plus members can be managed effectively. Others ask whether the growing diversity of the system will become a source of weakness–will the slowest ship set the convoy's pace. Still others worry that consensus decision-making will prevent the system from providing decisive leadership in an age of far-reaching and often breath-taking change.

Yet, what is most often forgotten in this rush to reform the system is the revolutionary nature of the original GATT idea itself. The process of bargaining for concessions among trade partners and then multilateralizing these concessions to the benefit of all countries, has proven a remarkable catalyst for trade liberalization. Moreover, the growing participation of developing countries in this system, far from slowing the process down, has introduced a new dynamic to the negotiating process, creating an even greater incentive for developed and developing countries alike to strike far-reaching market opening packages–a reality most recently demonstrated in the negotiations of basic telecommunications, financial services and the information technology agreements where the participation of developing countries was indispensable to success. Like Adam Smith's invisible hand, the genius of the GATT/WTO system lies in the way in which the individual pursuit of national self-interest can produce such extraordinary collective benefits in terms of more open trade and a coordinated international system.

Equally revolutionary is the core GATT principle of non-discrimination which has done so much to remove power politics from international trade relations, by guaranteeing countries equal rights, irrespective of their size and bargaining power. This has proved a remarkably cohesive force over the years, providing a unique and invaluable foundation for international cooperation and consensus in trade matters. And as developing countries, especially economic giants like China, become more deeply integrated into the global economy there is even more incentive to involve them more closely in consensus-based rule-making and institution building to ensure the stability as well as the inclusiveness of the system. By definition, the global challenges we face call for shared and cooperative solutions. And this can only be achieved by consensus. Marshalling the collective political will to address many of these challenges will not always be easy. It may even demand new negotiating techniques and new institutional reforms. Still, notwithstanding these difficulties, the reality remains that divisive approaches can only lead to divided outcomes.

The growing complexity of the system's rules and the diversity of its membership, far from weakening the WTO, has actually strengthened it. In moving from shallow to deeper integration and from narrow to far broader participation we have done more than add a new rule here or a new member there. We have created a new kind of economic system; a global web of interlocking rules and obligations which grows more indispensable to the management and stability of the world economy as it grows stronger. As we approach the 50th anniversary of the trading system this year it is increasingly clear that Dunkel's path-breaking work between 1980 and 1993 did not mark the end of a process, so much as the beginning of a whole new phase of international economic cooperation and rule-making. This year we have an opportunity to celebrate a unique–and uniquely valuable–exercise in global economic cooperation. This should be an occasion to send out a clear message about the opportunities of globalization and the unique role of the multilateral system. And it should be an occasion to look towards the future evolution of the WTO so as to ensure that it contributes significantly to prosperity and peace in the future.

Globalisation and the Uruguay Round

Peter D. Sutherland

1. Introduction

The successful conclusion of the Uruguay Round on 15 December 1993 and the subsequent creation of the World Trade Organization (WTO) on 1 January 1995 began a new era in world trade. Besides introducing the biggest trade liberalising deal in history, the agreements provide the world trading system with the means to confront the considerable challenges facing the world economy today. Arthur Dunkel played a vital role in making this happen. His vision and his unique capabilities have helped to bring about a defining moment in modern economic and political history.

2. Globalisation

The world has changed dramatically since Arthur Dunkel began the Uruguay Round negotiations in Punta del Este in 1986. It is no longer bipolar, conveniently divided between east and west. By becoming multipolar, power centres have become more diffused and increasingly complex. Indeed, many traditional alliances that were held together by the logic of the Cold War have been called into question as former allies searched for a new set of shared values and systems capable of enduring in a rapidly changing world. While the market economy system is largely agreed in principle, the mechanisms to make it work internationally are at an early stage of development.

The political fragmentation caused by extreme nationalism in many parts of the world is increasingly challenged by the process of deeper integration of the global economy and the participation of a greater number of countries in the world trading system. Driven by the liberalisation of trade and capital flows, reduced transport and communication costs, innovations in business organisation and the increasingly rapid diffusion of technological progress across borders, the pace of integration of the world economy, or globalisation as it is commonly called, has continued to accelerate since the middle of the 1980s.

2.1. Trends in Trade and Capital Flows

According to the IMF in this period the volume of world trade has "expanded almost twice as fast" as world output, while the rapid liberalisation of financial markets has seen international transactions in bonds and equities in major advanced countries increase to well over 100 per cent of GDP in 1995 compared with less than 10 per cent in 1980.[1] Largely driven by the stimulus of international trade, gross flows of portfolio investment and foreign direct investment (FDI) in the advanced countries more than trebled between the mid-1980s and the mid-1990s.[2] Despite a brief fall during the 1992-94 recession, FDI has shown rapid growth since the mid-1980s. This has been attributed to a number of factors. In particular, FDI is no longer confined to large firms. Even for small and medium-sized enterprises, production and distribution strategies increasingly span the globe as national and regional frontiers become less relevant for private sector decision-making. FDI has also increased considerably in the services sector which previously had been largely excluded from the process. In addition, there has been a considerable increase in the number of countries that are outward investors and/or hosts of FDI.

2.2. Developing Countries and Economies in Transition

Of course for much of the post-war period more than three quarters of the world population lived in countries whose governments were sceptical of–and in some instances, openly hostile to–the advantages of integration into world markets. That has changed with enormous implications for international economic relations. According to the IMF, the developing countries' share of world trade increased from 23 per cent in 1985 to 29 percent in 1995.[3] In addition, net private capital inflows increased almost sixfold in 1996 compared with the average annual inflow over the period 1983-89.

It must be conceded that the process of integration has not been without its difficulties. In some countries, particularly in the least-developed countries in sub-Saharan Africa, living standards have improved only slightly and the gap with the advanced economies has continued to widen. Over the past three decades, many in-depth studies of the trade and industrial policies of developing countries have established persuasively that functioning markets and open trade are associated with more rapid growth rates and hence should help these countries converge in their per capita incomes to those of the necessarily slower-growing OECD countries.[4] Indeed, the failure of some of these countries to participate in the benefits of globalisation can be attributed in some measure to the inadequate progress by

---

[1] International Monetary Fund (1997),. *World Economic Outlook.* IMF, Washington DC

[2] International Monetary Fund, ibid

[3] International Monetary Fund, ibid

[4] OECD Development Center, Paris. National Bureau of Economic Research, Washington DC. World Bank, Washington DC

their governments in improving the policy environment and the developed countries' policy of maintaining restrictions on imports in sectors, particularly agriculture, in which many developing countries enjoy a comparative advantage. The benefits of open markets and a truly global trading system do not provide a complete answer in addressing the issue of development but they are a vital part of the answer.

2.3. Protectionism

Clearly the globalisation of the world economy presents national economies and policy makers with enormous opportunities and challenges. As Arthur Dunkel has often stressed, by accentuating competition it produces wide-ranging benefits from innovation, new product and service development and greater specialisation in production. Although the majority of policy-makers and economic actors favour freer trade and greater economic integration in principle, in reality globalisation–and its implications for the future–is still far from being universally accepted. Business itself is not united in its welcome for the opportunities offered by globalisation or the rules that sustain it. For some sectors, especially where protection and government assistance have been used to muffle the signals of international supply and demand, the global market is seen more as a threat than an opportunity. Such interests–and they exist in most countries–frequently devote the energy and resources that should go into restructuring and becoming competitive to a frantic and doomed effort to resist change.

Unfortunately, their focused lobby groups find too often a sympathetic hearing from governments. Of course this reflects the lobbying power of old established industries which may be located in areas of high unemployment. While misguided political efforts to appease such sectional interests impose high costs on consumers and export-oriented businesses these are often not explained or understood. More generally, however, this phenomenon reflects the confusion and anxiety that characterise societies and governments in the developed world today. The rapid erosion of old barriers between economic and political categories–and between nations–has challenged established ways of thinking and established political attitudes. The result is a volatile and sometimes angry electorate and a tendency to look for simplistic solutions. The polemics of Le Pen in France have a certain seductive appeal, and similar incendiary rhetoric can be heard in other European countries. Though what these arguments generally have in common is denial–denial of international economic integration, denial of the economic potential of the wider world, denial of the need to compete.

As a result, public debate on the phenomenon of globalisation is too frequently focused on the perceived negative aspects, in particular, the effects of freer trade on employment and income distribution in advanced economies. The popular perception is that cheap imports from low-wage, developing economies are the cause of rising unemployment and falling wages among low-skilled workers and the decline of the manufacturing sector is one that must be addressed directly. Of course, a growing body of empirical evidence has shown that in fact globalisation contributes only marginally to unemployment or decline in real wages of workers in advanced countries. Most international economists who have studied the problem have concluded that the effect of trade with poor countries on the decline in real wages in the 1980s and 1990s is negligible; some have even argued that the effect has likely been favourable instead.[5]

It is also worth making the point that besides the undeniable advantages of freer trade to the advanced economies, there is a moral issue at stake. Labour cost differentials largely reflect the different endowments and technological capacity of countries and are in fact one of the main sources of comparative advantage that developing countries have vis-à-vis their rich counterparts. As such they are the catalyst for new growth in poorer countries. There is clear evidence that as productivity levels converge between developing and advanced countries so too do labour costs. A concerted effort must be made, therefore, to reduce the scope of interest groups to point to such nominal cost differences as a legitimate rationale for protectionism.

2.4. Interdependence and National Sovereignty

In addition, there is also the widespread perception that the liberalisation of trade and financial flows has increasingly restricted the autonomy of national governments in the field of economic policy, at a considerable cost to national welfare. There is little doubt that globalisation has increased policy interdependence and reduced national policy independence. As advances in communications and transportation shrink distances between people, and each country's activities become more intertwined with those of other countries, it is inevitable that countries will find that there are increased external influences on what used to be considered purely domestic policies. Indeed, the range of policies considered as trade-related has steadily grown from measures applied at the border on imported products to policies whose trade effects are incidental to their main purpose, such as production subsidies, taxation, investment, anti-trust and technical standards and domestic regulations. New areas of attention include the protection of the environment, investment and competition policy, which are accepted as being part of the future trade agenda. All of this must have implications for traditionally understood notions of the absolute nature of national sovereignty.

However, it is wrong to perceive globalisation as a game in which certain economies gain at the expense of others. If national policies respond adequately and in time to the pressures for structural adjustment in patterns of production, investment, and foreign trade that are generated by increasingly integrated and competitive world markets, then all countries will be in a better position to exploit their comparative advantages, enhance their long-run growth potential, and share in the benefits of the expansion of the world economy. While globalisation may raise the costs of economic distortions and failure to introduce adequate reforms, it has also increased the potential rewards for sound, outward-looking policies. This

[5] For a review of the recent studies, see Slaughter M, Swagel P (1997), *The Effect of Globalisation on Wages in the Advanced Economies*. Bhagwati J (1997) *Play it again Sam: Yet Another Look at Trade and Wages*. Columbia University, mimeographed

is clearly illustrated if we consider the impact of the liberalisation of financial markets on fiscal policy. While the global capital markets reward sound fiscal policy with lower interest rates and reduced exchange rate risk premiums, profligate governments are swiftly punished with currency instability and rising interest rates. As Richard O'Brien of the Global Business Network has argued, a liberalised and globalised capital market helps to limit the abuse by national governments of their power to raise taxes, print money, and borrow.[6] Although it might be said with some justification that financial markets tend to exercise discipline erratically, governments should not be tempted to respond to the excesses of financial markets by trying to restrict their power. Instead, governments are better advised to conduct policy in a such a way that it does not destabilise market expectations, and ensure that the markets are better informed.

2.5. Demographic Pressures

However, in recent years there have been other developments, which will increasingly shape the international trade and economic environment, that risk becoming a potential source of tensions. First, demographic trends in the developed and developing countries are markedly different. The global population, which has more than tripled this century, continues to increase at more than 80 million a year. Very low or zero population growth rates in the OECD countries are ageing the populations and bringing many attendant changes, not least of which are the financial implications for national pension schemes. As for the developing countries, over one third of the population is under the age of 15 and of the nearly two billion people who will be added to the world's population in the next 20 years, 95 per cent of them will be born outside the OECD area.

The consequence is that between now and the year 2015, the number of new jobs required to keep unemployment rates unchanged in the developing world will exceed the current populations of Western Europe and North America combined. Again the economic implications are manifold, including increased competition for capital and a continuing shift in competitiveness in labour-intensive activities to high population growth countries. Nor is it a coincidence that migration, and the linkage between the pressures for migration from low-income countries and trade barriers in rich countries, are moving rapidly up the international agenda.

2.6. The Risks of Strategic Trade Policies

Another significant development is that with the end of the Cold War competition has increasingly been refocused from the political-military sphere to the economic sphere with the result that national economic competitiveness has become the rallying cry. Of course, the notion of competition between countries and regions is rather simplistic in an era of greater global economic integration. Indeed,

---

[6] Quoted in Pam Woodall's *A Survey of the World Economy*. The Economist, 7 October, 1995

competition among enterprises is *the* issue in a global economy. Nonetheless, the concept of national champions has not lost its political appeal to some and it seems to influence policy-making to a growing extent. Moreover, as the interests that bound together traditional alliances have shifted, the cohesion that helped countries resolve economic problems can no longer be taken for granted, thus increasing uncertainty in the area of international economic relations.

3. The Uruguay Round

During the ratification process following the conclusion of the Uruguay Round there was a frenzied and sometimes somewhat unreal debate about winners and losers. Even the global effects were disputed. According to GATT Secretariat and later WTO estimates, real world income would increase by US$510 billion over the ten years to 2005 as a result of trade barrier reductions in the goods area alone. For OECD countries, merchandise trade would increase by 7 or 8 per cent; for developing countries the growth in trade was conservatively estimated at 14 percent. Even these figures made no allowance for services nor indeed the effects of the other 27 agreements that formed part of the Round. But the reality is that this type of analysis, valuable and relevant though it was, tells only a small part of the story. What we are witnessing is a global economic revolution that cannot be reduced to any meaningful statistical analysis.

With globalisation and indeed the contemporaneous phenomenon of regional integration (which I believe can be complementary) the interdependence fostered will ultimately have two fundamental effects. In the first instance it will reduce the possibilities of conflict between peoples. The mutual interest in harmonious relations will become a determining feature of foreign policy. Put at its most basic, when another provides a vital market for your goods and services, how can conflict with that other be in your interest? The second and related effect is that at a certain stage a reversion to isolationism becomes impossible. The counteracting force to any protectionist lobby becomes too strong to be resisted. This is already happening although we have not yet reached a stage where one can say that the process is irreversible.

3.1. Enhancing the Rules of International Trade

The growth of interdependence alone will not secure our future in the absence of a system to make it function effectively. This is the real achievement of the Uruguay Round. It has created a rules-based system. This is not some abstract or theoretical achievement. It is nothing less than a reinforcement of the rule of law in international economic relations, a reinforcement for which the need was both urgent and universal.

The GATT/WTO rules and disciplines reflect the view that a decentralised system of market-determined prices is the best way to ensure an efficient allocation of resources. They are designed for market-oriented economies, laying down the conditions of competition for a free enterprise system. In particular, the *tariffs only* principle aims to ensure that where protection exists, it does not block the working of the market mechanism, and the principle of non-discrimination aims to ensure that a country buys from the lowest cost foreign suppliers.

Once inside the border, goods are required to receive *national* treatment, that is treatment on a par with domestically produced goods. The binding of tariffs, countries' obligations to observe multilateral rules and disciplines, and the procedures for resolving disputes bring greater stability and predictability to the conditions of competition. But these fundamental principles are only valuable if there are mechanisms available to apply and enforce them.

International norms, such as those contained in the GATT play a critical role in enhancing freedom. In *The Constitution of Liberty*, the great Austrian economist F.A. Hayek developed further John Locke's very important idea of law as a guarantor of freedom:

> *The end of the law is, not to abolish or restrain, but to preserve and enlarge freedom. For in all the states of created beings capable of laws, where there is no law there is no freedom.*

At the international level, multilateral trade rules and disciplines not only ensure freedom for economic agents to operate in their commercial interest across national frontiers. They also enhance the freedom of governments in their trade policy interventions by defining the scope of actions permissible within the confines of international law. The behaviour of all governments becomes more predictable when the rules of the game are accepted by all and can be applied in practice.

A rules-based trading system is only as good as the credibility of its rules and procedures. For several years prior to the successful conclusion of the Uruguay Round, a number of developments had contributed to a steady erosion of the GATT's credibility. These included the failure to bring agriculture under GATT disciplines, the exclusion of textiles and clothing from the normal rules, the spread of bilateral quantitative restrictions imposed outside the GATT rules, the widely different levels of obligations among the member countries, and a perception that the rules including those governing the settlement of disputes had not kept pace with a changing world economy. As a result, the system was rapidly approaching a point at which even routine problems–let alone the new challenges outlined in the previous sections–threatened to overwhelm it.

4. The World Trade Organization

The crowning achievement of the Uruguay Round was the creation of the WTO. As the first international organisation to be created in the post-Cold War era it is unique. It is open to universal membership and its purpose is essentially to connect diverse national economies in a globalised market through the acceptance and observance of its rules by *all* its Members. This is in contrast with the Bretton Woods institutions, the IMF and the World Bank, which while they also have regulatory functions, were conceived primarily to manage resources and take decisions on the basis of weighted voting.

The WTO is a natural evolution of the GATT, or rather the fulfilment of its original aims. Based upon the same principles as the GATT–non-discrimination and reciprocity–the WTO extends these principles into the new rules on trade in services and intellectual property. As the legal and institutional umbrella both over these new agreements and the existing GATT the WTO constitutes a single undertaking.

This is an important change with respect to the Tokyo Round under which there was no obligation to accept the agreements covering anti-dumping, subsidies and countervailing duties, import licensing, technical barriers to trade, to name just a few. The replacement of the GATT legal system by the WTO means essentially the same rights and obligations for all Members, ensuring that the scope and depth of the multilateral trading system will be much greater than before.

To promote the credibility, acceptance and observance of its rules the WTO relies above all on two mechanisms. The first is the principle of transparency which is enshrined in Article X of the GATT 1947 and 1994 and reinforced by the Uruguay Round's Decision on Notification Procedures. Not intended to enforce specific agreements, the transparency principle is essentially a confidence-building measure which aims to restrain unilateralism.

The other important mechanism is the new multilateral dispute settlement system, created to avoid the unilateral interpretation of the WTO's rules. With the same procedure to be applied across all agreements, the dispute settlement system constitutes what Celso Lafer calls a "thickening of legality" which is essential to ensure the security and predictability of the multilateral trading system.[7] The principal changes with respect to the previous system are that under the new system the adoption of dispute settlement findings will no longer require the agreement of the losing country. In addition, the WTO introduces the possibility of an independent review by an appellate body before the panel's recommendations become legally binding. This is a safeguard against possible mistakes, ensuring that the greater automaticity is accompanied by a greater confidence in the results of the dispute settlement system.

The Uruguay Round negotiators realised that stability in trade relations can be attained only if the mutually agreed rules and market access commitments are backed up by procedures ensuring their proper enforcement and an institutional framework ensuring their proper administration. Both the enforcement procedures of the WTO and its institutional structure rest on more solid legal foundations than those of its predecessor. However, at the same time, the WTO does not create unwanted new obligations or threaten sovereignty of its member countries. It aims to administer obligations agreed mutually on the basis of reciprocity, and will serve as a forum for the negotiation of further such obligations. If anything, it will enhance the sovereignty of its Members, particularly the smaller ones, by providing them with a more stable international economic environment in which

---

[7] Lafer C (1997), *The Role of the WTO in International Trade Regulation.* Conference on The Impact of the World Trade Organisation on the Regulation of International Trade, World Trade Law Association.

to conduct their policies, and a clearer, more enforceable framework of rules to ensure their rights are respected.

4.1. The Future Role of the WTO

The WTO provides a vastly improved means of maintaining current commitments to trade liberalisation included in the Uruguay Round, as well as the possibility of extending the frontier of liberalisation more or less continuously. This is borne out by the intense activity of the WTO since the conclusion of the Uruguay Round. The long, protracted negotiations of the GATT rounds held once every decade or so today seem a thing of the past. In addition, the WTO provides a platform for developing a new global trade agenda; for improving international economic cooperation; for promoting sustainable development in developing countries and for supporting and consolidating the reforms of economies in transition. Furthermore, the WTO is a dynamic and expanding organisation within which regional initiatives can coalesce and evolve.

The new global trade agenda was tackled at the inaugural ministerial conference of the WTO in Singapore in December 1996 where it was agreed to establish working groups to study the linkages between trade and competition policy and trade and investment (already partially covered in the Uruguay Round agreements). On the controversial issue of labour standards it was agreed, correctly in my opinion, that although still a cause for concern they should not be linked to trade or used for protectionist purposes. The United Nation's International Labour Organisation was identified as the competent body within which a deal should be sought to ensure the observance of internationally recognised core labour standards.

The WTO is also of crucial importance for developing and transition economies undergoing radical and sometimes painful economic reforms. Significantly, in Singapore a plan of action was agreed that would help to improve the overall capacity of the world's 48 poorest countries to respond to the opportunities offered by the international trading system. Developing and transition economies make up the bulk of the 30 countries currently negotiating their accession or resumption of membership. It is also worth noting that a number of developing countries and economies in transition were among the most steadfast supporters of multilateral liberalisation through the Uruguay Round. This is in contrast to some developed countries which have at times wavered in their adherence to the principles that have made them prosperous.

The integration of the world economy has been accompanied by the proliferation of regional trade and economic co-operation agreements reflecting how individual countries, even the most economically powerful, realise that it is beneficial to pool resources in areas of common interest. Whilst recognising that such agreements are in conflict with MFN principles, I believe that they have generally been building blocks for the multilateral system. They have taken on the issues of protectionism first and have provided examples, used in the Uruguay Round, in the methodology of free trade. At the Singapore conference, the importance of regional trade agreements, particularly among developing and least-developed countries, was reiterated. It was emphasised properly that the multilateral trading system managed by the WTO should take primacy. This issue will remain with us but I am convinced that it can be handled.

The universal membership of the WTO means that it is ideally placed to contribute to new cooperative arrangements at the international level aimed at promoting global coherence in economic policymaking, not only in trade relations, but also more generally in other aspects of economic policy. The Uruguay Round decision regarding greater coherence in trade, financial and monetary policies states that: *the WTO should therefore pursue and develop cooperation with the international organisations responsible for monetary and financial matters* and the Director-General of the WTO is to pursue this question with the heads of the World Bank and the International Monetary Fund: *with a view to achieving greater coherence in global economic policy-making*"[8] The specifics of that cooperation were left open for the future. However, the task of developing such a coherence between the Bretton Woods institutions and the WTO has already commenced.

5. Conclusions

The increasing integration of the world offers unprecedented opportunities for improved growth, job creation and development. However, societies must be prepared to adjust, sooner rather than later, if the potential benefits of globalisation are to be fully realised. Moreover, I believe the challenges posed to the international trading system by the rapid integration of the global economy can only be managed collectively. With the creation of the WTO we are on the verge of completing a truly global trading system on principles that liberal democracies have promoted for fifty years or more–the system of collective economic security, which is the essential counterpart of political security.

However, if the multilateral trading system is to be a reality all the commitments that the WTO embodies must be implemented fully and effectively. Failure on the part of its Members to observe the rules on access to markets and conditions of competition to which they have contracted would quickly undermine the WTO's credibility. In particular, the major players must abide by the rules and procedures agreed. In this respect, it is vitally important that the US, the EU and Japan provide leadership. As during critical moments in the Uruguay Round negotiations national governments must overcome political hesitations and face down vested interests at home.

---

[8] WTO (1995), *The Results of the Uruguay Round of Multilateral Trade Negotiations. The Legal Texts*. Publication Services, World Trade Organization, Geneva, Switzerland, p 442

Bibliography

Croome J (1995), *Reshaping the World Trading System: A History of the Uruguay Round.* World Trade Organization, Geneva

Hoekman B and Kosteki M (1995), *The Political Economy of the World Trading System: From GATT to WTO.* Oxford University Press: Oxford

International Monetary Fund (1997) *World Economic Outlook.* IMF, Washington DC

Lafer C (1997), *The Role of the WTO in International Trade Regulation.* Conference on The Impact of the World Trade Organisation on the Regulation of International Trade, World Trade Law Association

Sachs J and Warner A (1995), *Economic Reform and the Process of Global Integration.* Brookings Papers on Economic Activity

Slaughter MJ and Swagel P (1997) *The Effect of Globalisation on Wages in the Advanced Economies.* IMF Working Paper WP/97/43 International Monetary Fund. Washington DC

Spero JE and Hart JA (1997), *The Politics of International Economic Relations.* St. Martin's Press

WTO (1995), *The Results of the Uruguay Round of Multilateral Trade Negotiations. The Legal Texts.* Publication Services, World Trade Organizaton,, Geneva, Switzerland

International Business Issues in View of Globalisation and Regional Integration

Helmut O. Maucher

1. Introduction

The change in world-wide markets, institutions and structures is accelerating. Products, services, technology and ideas are more and more traded in markets that are global. Competition between companies is more intense and far-reaching in a context of deepening economic integration. Labour and its cost, regions and, more generally, countries as places to invest (*Standorte*) are increasingly exposed to the same international competitive pressure as companies.

International companies are reorganising into new structures, some of them in response to the new situation and in order to catch up with these developments. Management of change has become a high priority for business leaders. Governments are also changing their policies, embarking on regulatory reform and looking for new ways of international and regional cooperation, sometimes in overlapping regional units. While change in public policies seems to be accelerating everywhere, it is now fastest in the countries of the developing world. They are autonomously opening up, deregulating, modernising and globalising their rules and institutions relevant for business, which gives room for an emerging new middle class linked to global market preferences and attitudes.

All this is creating prosperity and many new opportunities for people who never had this chance before. But people can take advantage of them only if governments take the right steps to adapt policies, to reduce the density of regulations and to create locally more room for manoeuvre for private initiative. A more effective help to those who are really in need must replace the hammock-type of social support. More generally, adjustments to economic change must be accelerated rather than slowed down. Further conditions for a positive outcome are peoples' attitudes, which in all countries must become more favourable to forward-looking change.

Today, there is also an urgent need to rethink the global framework for business and to adapt it to these new realities and requirements. A major change in strategy and the structure of international institutions should be considered, going beyond a reshuffling of existing international organisations and rules. New approaches to setting rules at the global level and different ways of thinking should be pursued, also able to address the next generation issues. There is a need to leave the world of *do ut des* behind. Opening an economy to private business is a win-win proposition; it should no longer be treated as a concession to other countries. New practical mechanisms such as public policy benchmarking (see below) should be tested in order to see whether they further the many positive developments briefly outlined above. Speed also matters. Long negotiations among bureaucracies more often have proven to be too slow to respond to the challenge of rapid global change. Finally and in particular, there is a need to set up a global framework for investment–as one of the elements of the new global setting.

The following quote puts these needs in terms of a programme:

> *Free trade, contestable markets and more global rules for investment and other business activities should also be seen in the context of the need to reorganise the overall political and international dimension. We have to adapt world-wide co-operation to the new structures and new dimensions of the markets and the world in general. I am thinking for instance of the necessary enlargement of the so-called G-7 to a G-10 or a G-14. I am also thinking of the role of the UN that needs to be adapted. The UN system and the organisations belonging to it were created at a time when the world was very much different from today. Change is urgent and here we expect a new impulse from the UN Secretary-General Kofi Annan and the reforms he has initiated.*[1]

This paper raises some questions about the framework from a business point of view. It cannot provide a comprehensive blueprint for the reform of global rule-making but proposes a work programme in a concrete perspective with selected elements which could become part of a new global design. Ideas and proposals are based on practical business experience and on deliberations in the European Round Table of Industrialists (ERT) and the International Chamber of Commerce (ICC). Above all, they represent common interests inasmuch as investors, the countries of origin of the investment and the country where the investment takes place should all gain from the new global framework for business.

2. Challenges for Public Rule-making World-wide[2]

Some people think that the main goal of public rule-making world-wide is to establish exactly the same set of rules everywhere. This is neither realistic nor efficient. We need common rules as far as possible; however, it is even more important to work globally with a common basic philosophy and some common principles, that is, to regulate only where necessary. But then we need for many of the

---

[1] ICC Congress Business Declaration and Resolution delivered by the author in his capacity as ICC President at the end of the 32nd ICC Congress in Shanghai on 10 April 1997.

[2] In his capacity as Chairman of the European Round Table of Industrialists (ERT), the author directed the working group reporting on investment in the developing world.

specifics also a variable geometry. In other words: a global framework should aim for the right balance between regulatory homogeneity and heterogeneity.

Any global scheme of rules and rule-setting must respond both to the reality of and to the need for constant change and take into account the huge diversity of situations between countries. What is best practice today may well be outdated tomorrow. More generally, when we aim for best practices we should no longer do this from an OECD countries' perspective. Where common rules are not feasible, we should look for ways of reaching mutual recognition.

The *contestability of markets* should become one of the major guiding principles of practical proposals for government policy, regulatory reform, harmonisation or mutual recognition and global regulation. To give more importance to *global competition* in *rules* as a means to gain overall competitiveness and efficiency is a further element of the proposed new focus for public policy. Both notions of *an overall enabling environment* for private businesses–foreign-invested and local–and contestable markets are also a key part of the proposed new international agreement on investment. All this is quite different from what has been negotiated up to now.

A contestable market is characterised by very low barriers to entry in all forms–exports, establishment of greenfield investments, acquisitions, alliances, full access to local factors of production and suppliers, possibility to establish relations of preferred supplier, and absence of exit restrictions (local and cross-border). It implies much more than simply eliminating border barriers, or guaranteeing the right of establishment. Instead, it addresses the broad range of *behind the border* impediments to effective access, presence and development in markets. Contestability as a concept is about the private sector in general, not only foreign private investment; there is less and less reason to make such a distinction. Contestability, like many other basic market principles, is a matter of degree; no market is fully contestable today.

2.1. New Focus of Global Rule-making

We should first understand how global rules develop. Today, there are a number of driving forces involved in establishing a more global setting for business. One such driving force is national governments, thinking global in their own national rule-making–we see this in the developing world, for instance in telecom regulations. A second works through competition on rules. A third is regional integration with common rule-making–as long as it is conceived as open regionalism this corresponds very much to the need for a variable geometry. A fourth is global negotiations among governments, usually with the support of an international organisation or secretariat (e.g., World Trade Organization (WTO), World Intellectual Property Organization (WIPO) or World Health Organization (WHO)). A fifth are efforts of global business to agree on certain rules (on marketing practices within ICC, or on international accounting standards within the International Accounting Standards Committee (IASC), for instance). And lastly, there are global rules set unilaterally and imposed on others through extraterritoriality.

Let me comment on just a few of these:
Competition in rules among countries and regions seeking to attract investment has become a strong and reliable engine for the present liberalisation process. It is one of the major new challenges and a big opportunity. Investors compare public policies and other facets of an investment environment before investing. Countries look at the policy changes in other economies from a perspective of improving their own environments for business. This new competition is becoming a global phenomenon, with developing countries taking a leading role. Their opening pace has accelerated considerably, and more and more often they are ahead of industrialised countries, for instance in allowing patents for biotechnology research, in giving access to foreigners to build telecommunication systems, or in moving directly to international standards when modernising rules, as for instance accounting standards.

Governments, seen by some as a *declining-growth-rate industry*, are now forced to become competitive with their respective sets of rules. Contrary to what is sometimes said in the press and by politicians, this competition is not leading to anarchy or to the destruction of institutions and societies. It separates the efficient from the inefficient and the competitive from the uncompetitive in terms of both rules and institutions, and it points to some serious rigidity in industrialised countries. As in any effective competition, the size of the home market matters less than before; big industrialised countries are affected by it too. American insularity in law, for instance, may no longer be sustainable under regulatory competition and the globalisation of rules and institutions. Some of the US's exaggerated reactions (extraterritoriality, etc.) may well be caused by an increasing awareness of this tremendous new global market challenge.

In order to use the potential of international organisations more efficiently, a *reorganisation of the UN system* and its parts must also be considered. Besides strengthening the political role of the UN (which is not the concern of this paper), the present reforms should aim for a service-minded organisation; the UN could even be empowered to take a leading role as a global coordinator of an increasingly complex institutional setting. There is, however, the precondition of first putting the UN house in order and using the present reform to make it internally more coherent. Different UN bodies still hold contradictory views on key issues for business (on the value of marketing, for example). International organisations should add value to the process of creating economic wealth and prosperity for people, and not look for redistribution in the first instance. While this is more and more accepted by many of the leading people in the UN system, some adherents to old ideologies are still active at lower ranks. Only a clear focus on the substance of reforms–instead of streamlining and cost-saving only, which is good but not sufficient–will help to prepare the UN system for the challenges of the 21st century.

We have seen on many occasions that the way global rules for doing business are set affects the competitiveness of our industries. This should be kept in mind when setting up the new global framework for investment and other global institutions. In other words, rule-making should not be dominated by the interests of one or only a few countries. Governments and industry should also start looking into the next generation of issues for the international economy. To contribute to identifying future needs and building appropriate strategies and structures for global rule-making that combines all these mechanisms (except extraterritoriality, which for obvious reasons should not be accepted) will be a major task of international business, and in particular of the ICC, when looking to the 21st century.

2.2. Investment and Property Rights–A Global Agreement

Industry needs a truly global agreement on investment as a major part of the new international framework for business. As outlined above in more general terms, this new agreement should aim to cover a broad range of different situations (Bangladesh as well as Argentina, for instance); it must also be specific enough to enable the efficient allocation of investment from a global perspective. The new agreement should be flexible to suit changing situations and at the same time actively stimulate and lock in progress in conditions for investment in a forward-looking and strategic manner.

In 1993, the ERT proposed moving quickly to a GATT for investment. The idea was further examined and adapted to the new institutional environment of the WTO in follow-up reports. Below are some ideas on what such an agreement might contain. We propose, for instance, that it should institutionalise international public policy benchmarking; provide instruments to lock in progress from competition in rules; and contain some supporting devices and minimum standards of protection for investment to prevent the bypassing of existing commitments. The idea is that this new type of agreement should accompany the present process of liberalisation in the developing world.

Before looking at the possible details of a new global framework on investment, a few basic principles and things of a practical nature need to be discussed and agreed on. They are:

- *Clarifying the perspective* of improving conditions for investment. Market opening and the globalisation of rules are not concessions to foreign investors. They are actually part of policies to increase economic efficiency and prosperity. Our proposals are based on ERT surveys of improvements in investment conditions. The empirical results show that there is already a highly efficient process of opening-up, deregulation, modernisation, and globalisation of rules and institutions relevant for conducting business. Opening-up no longer needs to be invented and initiated by negotiators, but understood by them, accompanied and nurtured by a more adequate global framework.
- *Maintaining the momentum* of liberalisation. We would like to see as many countries as possible move on to the fast track of opening up (Chart 2). The mechanisms of the new multilateral framework should stimulate continuous improvement (avoiding the stop and go of big rounds of negotiations), with steps taken in the right sequence (first steps before second ones in opening up and modernisation) and at the right pace, so as to avoid disruption.

Below is a proposal for an outline and practical elements of a future multilateral agreement on investment. Bearing in mind that this enumeration of features is illustrative, not exhaustive, the new agreement should:

- Provide rules and criteria for efficient *public policy benchmarking*, which consists of the comparison of measures for improving investment conditions with measures in force in those countries that perform best. The checklist for an enabling environment–briefly outlined in Chart 1–could be used as a reference, but is by no means an exhaustive list of criteria for public policy benchmarking. Effective benchmarking would also need a discussion about the optimum sequence of opening-up measures.
- Find ways to institutionalise *peer review* as a built-in device for continuous liberalisation and regulatory reform at global, regional, national and sub-federal levels.
- Offer the *flexibility* in form and substance that is needed to extend the coverage of the framework to additional areas relevant to contestability and an enabling environment whenever necessary.
- Apply the *most favoured nation principle* in all policies. Extend on a non-discriminatory basis to all investors–from all countries both developed and developing–any new investment liberalisation or protection offered autonomously, whether negotiated bilaterally or in regional agreements.
- Apply *national treatment* to foreign-owned firms in all relevant areas, including acquisitions for instance. At the same time, the agreement should aim for non-discrimination against local investors.
- Provide mechanisms to *lock in all progress* made in improving conditions for investment, such as notification procedures. The agreement should help improve the *transparency* of rules that apply to business.
- Contain rules to ensure *minimum standards* for global investment as well as the freedom and protection of private business and private ownership, in general, and in order to avoid the bypassing of commitments on free access by erecting new impediments in other areas. Minimum standards could involve adequate remuneration for capital without discriminatory taxation and its free transfer abroad, and adequate remuneration for the know-how and brand marketing transferred to a country.
- Foresee a flexible range of *dispute settlement* mechanisms with a clear order of priority and including *investor-to-state* dispute settlement procedures. These mechanisms should be unbiased and binding on large industrialised economies. A link to arbitration mechanisms might be foreseen.

The WTO will play a key role in building such a comprehensive new international framework for private investment, in co-ordination with the IMF and World Bank. At an early stage, existing *peer review* mechanisms should be used to test the proposed mechanisms on an extended range of issues. WTO or UNCTAD and for industrialised countries also the OECD should be invited to organise these test reviews on a one-to-one basis. Again, the proposed new instruments are not supposed to be used as a one-way street. Truly effective partnership also requires benchmarking of public policies in industrialised countries, which anyway would be in their own interest.

Industry also follows with great interest the progress made in the negotiation of a multilateral agreement on investment (MAI) at the OECD. Issues germane to industrialised economies are successfully addressed there, establishing a new and better level of market access for investment among members. It is important that a MAI is also open to non-member countries of the OECD. The approach proposed in this paper for a global agreement within WTO is different from, and in many respects complementary to, the MAI. It covers a broader range of issues and is supposed to help with the process of liberalising and creating an enabling environment. Benchmarks proposed will refer to countries at the same stage of economic development, not to OECD *best practices.* On some aspects, practical experience with negotiating and implementing a MAI or the peer review mechanism in the OECD Investment Instruments may be used to help design the new global agreement. However, this should by no means delay further substantive work on the issue in WTO.

2.3. Competition Policy

The focus on contestable markets proposed for the new agreement also encompasses *international competition policy.* Many of the aspects discussed in some detail here mainly concern industrialised countries; too often the business point of view is not sufficiently taken into account when designing new tools for competition policy. Any global instrument linked to an agreement on investment should be able to address structural impediments and restrictive business practices, for example in situations where local retail distribution is overly concentrated. According to the OECD, restrictive business practices are most frequent and damaging when the state, as a regulating authority, works together–openly or tacitly–with mercantilist local businesses. This illustrates the close link between global competition policy and regulatory reform. A global competition policy instrument should also try to reduce the risk of discrimination against foreign firms due to local political pressure on existing competition authorities, in merger cases for example, or of firms restricting or dominating markets because of the size and power of countries of origin. A global approach to competition policy may also help define the relevant market as global rather than, for instance, as between Hamburg and Frankfurt or between Paris and Marseille. Any clause on competition policy in a new investment agreement should establish a minimum set of rules that are binding on the existing competition authorities.

2.4. Social and Environmental Issues

Any transformation of an economy needs an effective solution to the social question. In the context of globalising markets and new rules on competition and investment, this means using the resources available for social support more efficiently. While the so-called European social system has come under scrutiny, I am convinced that the concept of helping those in real need is not in danger of being abandoned. However, we do need to find a novel support scheme, one that stimulates individual initiative and facilitates adaptation, instead of handing out entitlements indiscriminately.

Social coherence is also based on societal values. These values cannot be created by regulation, negotiated codes and the like; they have to develop in daily life. Pressures of the market will change values, but not jeopardise them, as long as we all share more values than just the so-called shareholder value.

Business should prepare itself to react appropriately to calls for more codes of conduct and more global control of companies as a counterweight to globalisation and the dogma of footloose firms. In the first place, international industrialists should continue to take advantage of the new and often unique opportunities offered by liberalising economies and *invest on a long-term basis*–this is the best way to contribute to world-wide prosperity. We see the need for European industry to become more active in those markets and to participate through investment in the growth of emerging markets. But while total FDI flows to the developing world are growing, European industry's share in total foreign investment in the developing world is falling behind. The share decreased from 37 per cent in 1983-84 to a level stagnating near 17 per cent in 1992-95, i.e., below Europe's relative share in world GDP. EU companies are losing investment market share, in particular in the most dynamic countries. A new global agreement on investment may help to correct this situation, but ultimately the main effort must come from European industry.

At the same time, practical solutions have to be found to alleviate local anxieties and to overcome problems created by investors on a case-by-case basis. The reports of the ERT highlight some of the concerns expressed by host countries, to which companies should try to find adequate responses. Basically, host countries confirm that a long-term engagement of the investor–rather than codes–is a good way to ensure environmentally sustainable development.

Requests for corporate commitments on ethics and *rules of good behaviour* (often imposed by activists or authorities) beyond practical self-regulation and in addition to, or in place of, public rules should be considered in the context of current global problems and priorities. Any discussion on societal values should go beyond the views of individual countries. Business should welcome some codes of conduct, but the problem is that codes general enough to be applied everywhere become meaningless and specific codes will not be applied by all countries and in all situations. As a matter of symmetry, global rules should also be considered for activists in order to anchor their legitimacy, their accountability and their liabilities.

3. European Union in a Global Context

Enlargement of the EU and the deepening of the integration without erecting a fence is the right response to the challenges facing Europe at present. And this process is well under way. But integration will progress further only if Europe focuses on the essentials for stability and competitiveness. From a business point of view, the following aspects are important:

- The free flow of goods and services, people, investment (including the freedom to organise a company efficiently) and finance in general. In many respects the Single Market is still in the making. In the meantime, we have a European standard for the form of a tractor seat, but electric trains still can not run across a border because countries have different types of electric current. The EU provides instruments to address many of the remaining practical problems, but no guarantee to solve them all.
- An effective common foreign and security policy, including a common immigration policy. Here, instruments still need to be developed. To make a meaningful contribution to the creation of a new global framework for efficient and competitive business, the EU will need more clout in the main areas of foreign economic relations. Several business groups already proposed a new formulation of Article 113 of the Treaty of Rome that goes far beyond the compromise reached in June 1997 in Amsterdam. A new formulation of this Article should not try to cover merely the issues of the negotiations that began 15 years ago and which in Amsterdam were added to trade in goods (i.e., services and intellectual property rights in a very restrictive formulation). It should invest the Commission with the negotiating authority for the new complex issues in all major areas of foreign economic policy and global rule-making. This is in everbody's interest because the EU can draw on its rich single market experience and use its acquired skills to handle diversity in an innovative way. Europe should take a leadership role in both bilateral and global negotiations.

In more general terms, we are in favour of rather less regulation, more subsidiarity and flexibility, as well as more rapid and efficient decision making mechanisms, including a wider role for decisions by majority.

Regulatory reform becomes urgent because policy changes providing better market access to foreign investors and more room for manoeuvre for local business people in the developing world are now transforming earlier weaknesses of these economies into a formidable competitive challenge. The challenge becomes even more powerful as in many areas these countries are moving ahead of Europe and other industrialised areas. Europe should start now with qualitative benchmarking of public policies to cope with this challenge and to work towards a positive-sum outcome in an ever-changing economic environment.

There is also a role for European business in global rule-making. In the first place, we should now look for ways to better coordinate the position of European industry and to constructively contribute to work in the ICC, similar to what we do in the International Accounting Standards Committee. Much will happen in international rule-making in the years to come, and industry should be a part of it to make sure these rules do serve our interests as well as those of others.

Once Europe has regained more self-confidence, European industry will make better use of its many existing strengths and improve its competitive standing. Among these strengths are its people, their experience in solving problems, the commitment to quality, the cultural diversity within Europe and cultural affinity in contacts with non-Europeans.

Special attention should be given to the trans-Atlantic partnership with its wide range of common interests on both economic and political grounds. The recent agreement on mutual recognition shows that there are many ways of moving towards more global rules and markets starting from regional integration.

4. Aspects Concerning other Regional Markets

Regional integration has become a successful feature in the opening-up of many countries. Approaches to integration differ as widely as solutions to the problems at hand. The North American Free Trade Agreement (NAFTA) with its relatively sophisticated instruments (including rules for foreign direct investment), should be expanded to form the Americas Free Trade Association (AFTA), comprising North and South America, ANDEAN and MERCOSUR.

ASEAN, the Association of South East Asian Nations, is more informal, less bureaucratic. Many of the solutions there are not the result of academic studies but of practical business requirements. the Asia-Pacific Economic Cooperation forum (APEC), is the most ambitious both in geographic terms and in substance. It also illustrates the fact that there may be a trade-off between size and homogeneity, and that political ambitions do not lead automatically to an optimum regulation area.

In Africa, with its many small and isolated economies, regional integration could mean a major step forward in economic development. SADEC in Southern Africa could become a case in point, illustrating the advantages of flexible regional integration for all participating economies.

Regional integration in Europe and elsewhere offers industry opportunities for a better utilisation of existing capacity, more efficient local sourcing (Argentina for packaging material for Brazil, for instance), economies of scale, etc. Also, local production of our goods in developing countries can get off to a quicker start because we rapidly reach the critical mass of consumer markets when several countries together establish a free trade regime, and a wider range of products can be offered to the consumer. In the early 1990s, for instance, we were able to demonstrate this with our ASEAN industrial joint ventures, with four new factories for different product groups in four different countries producing goods for the whole region, thanks to much lower tariff barriers between the ASEAN countries.

Integration is a process that helps business grow and be more efficient. It creates competitiveness and prosperity of an economy. The first step of the process is usually the reduction of customs duties; a further step is the reduction of non-tariff barriers, introducing common regulation and/or mutual recognition. Some of the new regions may follow the example of the European Union, but many of them are also successfully looking for new ways of joining forces.

As was said for Europe, we favour open regionalism everywhere. There is no need to build fences; on the contrary. New *national and regional rules should be conceived to meet global needs* (for instance, accounting rules or regulations for research and development in biotechnology).

5. Changes in Conditions for Investment in the Developing World

In 1989, the ERT, a grouping of business leaders from 43 major European companies representing a broad spectrum of industry, started discussion on changes in conditions for investment in the developing world. The ERT's objective is to improve Europe's competitiveness, strengthen the private sector and its efficiency in global markets, and contribute practical ideas and proposals for long-term solutions. The group sees this as a way to create wealth and jobs.

Within this overall set of goals, an ERT working group undertook two surveys on investment conditions in the developing world.[3] It provided systematic analysis to *describe the change*–the new focus, the wider scope, the quality and the pace of opening-up and modernisation–and to *evaluate* it from a business point of view.

Since 1989, the changes in these countries have been fantastic. Foreign investment in the developing world has increased fourfold compared to the preceding eight-year period. During the same time span, it developed from a one-way flow into a system of 'communicating vases' with industrialists from the developing world investing now more than US$50 billion a year abroad. Of equal importance was the fact that the share of private investment in total local investment increased significantly.

The questionnaire and the subsequent survey reports make no distinction between improvements in conditions for local and foreign-owned private sector companies. In a liberalising market, an effective local private sector is crucial for the long-term health and dynamics of the economy; local entrepreneurs have to mobilise the bulk of resources (human and financial) for competitiveness and growth. Local private sector strength is even a factor itself on the ERT checklist of conditions conducive to investment by foreign-owned firms. Any industrial investor from abroad needs open-minded, non-mercantilist local industrialists who view competition as being positive. Multinational companies need them as competitors in order to ensure their own efficiency as suppliers and distributors. There

---

[3] European Round Table of Industrialists: *Survey on Improvements in Conditions for Investment in the Developing World.* Brussels, May 1993; and European Round Table of Industrialists: *Investment in the Developing World – New Openings and Challenges for European Industry.* Brussels, December 1996. These reports can be obtained free of charge from the ERT Secretariat in Brussels, tel. +32 2 534 31 00 and fax +32 2 534 73 48

is a need for partnership between local and international private businesses, but a partnership of the market type that involves rivalry and competition.

The following two charts show the nature of change towards an enabling environment that took place over the survey period. Chart 1 shows that the improvements in investment conditions in the 28 survey countries are concentrated in areas of high priority to international investors (the darker areas in the chart).

The access for business to formerly restricted sectors was liberalised in a significant way (#11-4); the protection of intellectual property rights and the possibilities to pay for its use were improved (#11-6); overall import restrictions were considerably reduced (#12-3); privatisation and other measures meant to further strengthen the local private sector were initiated and successfully implemented (#21-1). All this happened while macroeconomic policies, the infrastructure, etc., underwent major improvements (#12). Chart 1 also compares the impact of improvement measures taken in 1993-96 and 1987-92: In all the areas of major change as listed above, the pace of opening-up accelerated.

The surveys also included a query on the kinds of problems that were being encountered with foreign investors. As we invest on a long-term basis, we try to avoid or to diminish any negative impact and ensure that the host country is a net beneficiary of an investment. Therefore, the response to this question was of great interest to us as an indication of where improvements in the conduct of investors were needed. In this context, none of the countries in our survey indicated that an international code of conduct might be useful.

Chart 2 shows the experience of different countries in liberalising their economies, according to our checklist. The vertical scale of the chart indicates the speed of opening; the horizontal scale shows progress made in creating an enabling environment for local and foreign-owned private businesses.

Three other ERT reports deal with the investment issue at a more general level. In particular, they point to the mutual benefits involved for investors and recipient countries from more and more countries joining the fast opening economies, irrespective of the degree of opening already reached. The practical policy proposals made in the present paper take this dynamic view into consideration.

6. Outlook and Conclusion

This article outlines some elements for a new international agreement for investment. The proposed framework aims at setting clear rules that facilitate global investment and at providing a built-in flexibility through mechanisms that facilitate adaptation to new situations. Our proposal is based on a comprehensive study of the experience of developing countries in opening up their economies and introducing regulatory and institutional change relevant to business. The proposal is built into today's international setting of the WTO and suggests the use of new instruments such as public policy benchmarking.

Chart 1 Improvements in conditions for investment in 28 countries

1993-96 (and 1987-92)

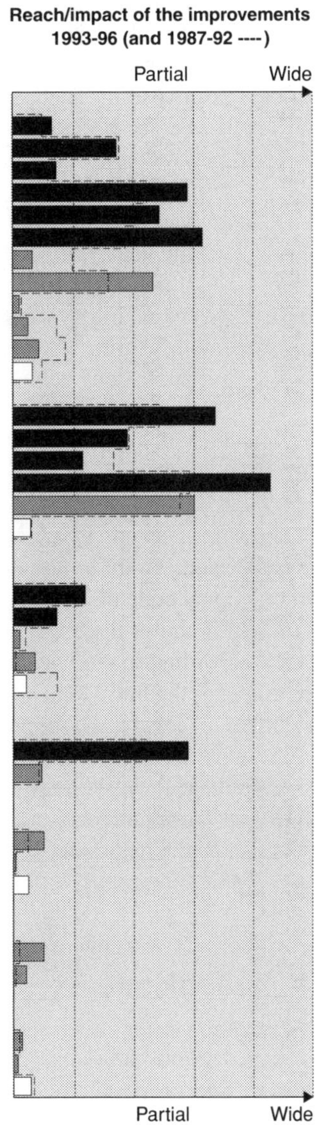

Impediment/improvement area:

11 Impediments for FDI

11-1 Management control
11-2 Ownership restrictions
11-3 Performance requirements
11-4 Sectorial licensing
11-5 Restrictions on foreign currency transactions
11-6 Intellectual property protection & remuneration
11-7 Inconsistent regulation
11-8 Ponderous control
11-9 Technology targeting
11-10 Personnel-related impediments
11-11 Nationalisation risk
11-12 Closing a business

 # 12 Macroeconomic (general)

12-1 Tax system
12-2 Price controls
12-3 Protectionism
12-4 Insufficient domestic finance
12-5 Restriction on marketing & distribution

13 Institutions

13-1 Legal system
13-2 Administrative inefficiency
13-3 Labour legislation
13-4 Corruption
13-5 Political stability & elasticity

21 Local private sector

21-1 Insufficient importance
21-2 Attitudes, quality

22 Labour

22-1 Qualifications; trainability
22-2 Attitudes
22-3 Politicised unions

23 Background - local population and tradition

23-1 Socio-cultural factors
23-2 Psychological factors

24 Various and living conditions

24-1 Environment; climate
24-2 Security; healthcare
24-3 War; other conflicts

Importance of each impediment/improvement area to foreign investors:

☐ Low ▒ Intermediate ■ High

Reach/impact of these improvements; horizontal scale.

The wider the reach of improvements and the higher the importance of the area to investors, the more positively size and efficiency of private investment will be affected.

Chart 2- **Survey on investment conditions – Speed of opening in 1993-96 and degree of openness reached end 1996**

Speed of opening 1993-96 ↑		The degree of openness achieved at the end of 1996 → Still partly closed	Moderately open	Quite open, some delays and costs remain	Quite open	Very open
	Countries on the very fast track		China India Egypt Nigeria		Brazil Indonesia Kenya Korea Mexico Turkey Thailand	Ecuador
	Countries opening with a high average speed	Vietnam		Pakistan Zimbabwe *average 28 countries*		Argentina Tunisia
	Countries opening with somewhat lower speed	Iran	Syria	Bangladesh	Colombia Saudi Arabia Sri Lanka	Guatemala

As in many other areas, speed matters. Authorities in some industrialised countries stress the complexity involved in negotiating an investment agreement; they first want to try out their own agreement in the OECD and then establish an exploratory analytical working group; they maintain that the results of the Uruguay Round of Multilateral Negotiations must first be implemented before the new issues can be addressed.

There is an urgency attached to instituting a new global agreement on investment, which will only cope with today's issues. But as the pace of change is accelerating, we already should think about the issues and the global architecture of the 21st century. The paper therefore points to the need to reflect on the strategy and the governance of a global regulatory setting for business in general in response to the multitude of new challenges.

At present, governments and business have no coherent overall strategy on global regulation. The approach is still piecemeal-sectoral, often along the lines of existing international organisations. Here, we may also need to consider fundamental changes in the UN system and its role in the international environment. While we need more global regulation, we also need global mechanisms to streamline and modernise all rules in a constantly changing world.

We should make prospective and innovative thinking part of the mandate of the leading international organisations, such as the WTO and the UN Secretariat. From both a European and a global viewpoint, there is a need for Europe to play a leading role and to put its rich experience to work. Europe will lose out if others continue to determine the basic philosophy and the substance of the rules of the game, and the world will lose out if there is no serious debate on innovations in regulations and institutions concerning investment and competition.

The demarcation line of responsibilities between governments, regional and global organisations and the private sector needs to be discussed further. We can glean patterns of change from the experience with accounting standards, with independent bodies being financed by the companies that set the rules and governments looking for ways to internalise these rules and reach mutual recognition.

However, when re-defining roles in global governance, business should clearly indicate that there is no intention to act as a judge on individual countries' behaviour in such areas as human rights for example, notwithstanding the fact that stability for business is linked to political and social stability. Indeed, business will contribute to this stability through the link between wealth, education and democracy.

Recently, in a meeting with leading politicians from central and eastern Europe, I emphasised that investment was very much a matter of trust. We should start to think about a new global institutional setting for international business where this trust stands at the very centre.

Drawing National Democracies Towards Global Governance

David de Pury

1. Lack of Progress towards Global Rules and Governance

Global governance is what is needed to make an increasingly global world economy function better and ensure sustainable world-wide growth and development. Just as a national economy needs adequate rules and institutions of governance to function properly, so does the world economy. And the more the world economy will integrate, the more the adequacy of its global governance will become a key element of its functioning.

This all sounds terribly banal at the end of the 20th century, in the age of globalization. It is not though if one considers that most of today's debate on globalization–a central political debate in most countries–is focusing on the nation state's governance. Last year, the World Bank Development Report[1] was about improving national governance, and the IMF's World Economic Outlook[2] focused on how nation states may best meet the challenges of a rapidly changing and highly integrated world economy. Neither report devoted much space if any to the improvement of global governance. Even within the European Union where international economic integration has gone further than in any other regional grouping in the world, the integration debate remains essentially a national debate on national rules. In Switzerland the question of how to deal with the European Union has not even started to be considered from the angle of what a future Europe may or should look like. The focus of the discussion remains on how Switzerland should develop as a nation and on how this nation should develop its bilateral relationship with the European Union. It is as if for the citizens of the world's democracies the only rule that will ever count is the national rule and the only political reality that

---

1 World Bank (1997), *World Bank Development Report: The State in a Changing World.* Oxford University Press

2 International Monetary Fund (1997), *World Economic Outlook: Globalization, Opportunities and Challenges.* May 1997. IMF, Washington DC

will ever be relevant is the national one. The recent Asian crisis has given us one more example of this state of affairs.

The gap between the economic reality of an emerging global market and the political reality of many national states is widening. This gap is dangerous. Jeffrey Sachs[3] draws a parallel between the end of the 19th century–a period in which a global market system eventually collapsed because of the absence of an international rule of law–and today. The present situation is less precarious than the one 100 years ago, mainly because today there exists an appreciable amount of international law and cooperation. Our global system nevertheless remains exceedingly fragile. Our national and international laws and institutions are ill-equipped to foster and sustain economic globalization.

The lack of interest and sense of urgency in establishing global institutions and rules explains the slowness of the international rule-making and governance-building process. Take the World Trade Organization (WTO) as an example. It is certainly true that the Uruguay Round was a major breakthrough. It moved trade negotiations from the traditional lowering of border tariffs to the ultimately much more relevant elimination of disparities between regulations of different nations. In spite of this step forward, the post-Uruguay Round trading system remains years if not decades behind the evolution of the real world. It still hardly takes into account the fact that an increasing number of products and services are researched, developed, produced, marketed and financed by processes taking place simultaneously in several countries. The present WTO system is still based on a world in which most products have a single national origin and a single national destination. It does not take into account the new reality within which–just to take one example–the US-based aircraft builder Boeing directly or indirectly accounts for 60,000 European jobs, while the European Airbus Group is responsible for 50,000 US jobs. In many areas the WTO *is* catching up with reality. Take the new WTO agreements concluded in 1996/97 and covering one trillion dollars worth of trade in information technology products, telecommunications services and financial services. Nevertheless, given the current slow pace of the WTO negotiating process and the explosive speed of economic integration, it appears highly unlikely that WTO rules will soon catch up with the requirements of the real world. That does not mean that the WTO system as it exists is not useful in fostering world economic growth. What it does mean is that its delayed reaction to what is happening in the market place is delaying and in some cases thwarting some of the growth it is supposed to foster.

This big lead of reality over the rule-making process is even more striking in the area of international money and finance. Take exchange rates. According to Paul Volcker[4] it seems strange indeed that we spend enormous amounts of negotiating energy and political capital to reduce already low tariffs by a few per cent only to see the effects of those lower tariffs swamped many times over by changes in exchange rates that very often seem to be unrelated to differentials in inflation

---

[3] Sachs J (1996), *Toward Peace and Prosperity*. World Economic Affairs (Summer issue) p 49

[4] Volcker P (1996), *Challenges Facing the International Monetary System*. World Economic Affairs (Summer issue)

rates or other competitive factors. In spite of this situation, Paul Volcker does not see an international monetary reform coming, even though he does see the necessity down the road of some sort of target zone system among the tripolar regions Europe, Japan and North America. Global monetary reform simply does not seem to be an issue today. This makes the European monetary reform all the more remarkable and noteworthy. Globally, most of the work taking place in the financial area is in the form of intergovernmental cooperation between national regulators or between the international financial institutions (IMF, IBRD) and national governments. It focuses mostly on areas like surveillance, exchange of information, transparency and, in the case of the international financial institutions, on credits linked to national adjustment programs. The Mexican peso crisis and the more recent East Asian financial turmoil have led to an increase in these activities. The G-7 Summit communiqué in 1997[5] is a good indicator of this tendency. Nevertheless and without belittling all of these efforts, the fact remains that on the monetary and financial front, no major breakthrough in terms of international rule-making is in sight. No WTO-like effort is being attempted in the direction of globally applicable rules. With the exception of the European Union, most if not all efforts undertaken are avoiding anything that smacks of supranationality.

2. Some Reasons for the Lack of Movement towards Global Governance and what to do about them

There are reasons why despite the rapid pace of economic integration we find it so hard to move, even timidly, towards a global system of public governance. Among these reasons, three seem particularly relevant:

- the insufficient perception of a need,
- the social backlash to globalization,
- the increasing tension between a national public sector and a multinational private sector.

2.1. The Insufficient Perception of a Need

The first reason for the slow progress towards global governance has to do with the insufficient perception of a need. The world economy is in better shape than it has probably ever been in our lifetime. In its Spring 1997 World Economic Outlook, the IMF states that: *economic and financial conditions are generally propitious for the global expansion to continue...*, that *there are few signs of the tensions and imbalances that usually foreshadow significant downturns in the business cycle...*, that *commitments to reasonable price stability are perhaps stronger than at any other time in the post-war era...*, that *fiscal imbalances are being reduced with increasing determination in many countries* and that *exchange rates among the major currencies appear to be generally consistent with broader policy*

[5] G-7 Economic Statement, 7 June 1997, Denver (Colorado) USA

objectives.[6] According to this description, it does not seem that the world economy is not functioning. In many ways it seems to function better than it has ever functioned. There is therefore not much talk about the need to improve global governance, and the G-7 is not much in the news any more. Among politicians the need to develop, to improve or to fix the world economic system is clearly not being felt with much urgency.

Can this sense of urgency be created, and will it do the trick in terms of improving global governance even if it is created? This is doubtful, particularly if we consider that we have had many emergency situations in the past–the oil crisis, the debt crisis, the peso crisis, the Asian crisis–and that none of them produced quantum leaps in the area of international rules and institutions.

For reasons to be explained later, national democracies and politicians rarely feel compelled to take political action outside their national framework. This is why politicians need to be brought to better understand that international rules and institutions can be of eminent help to them when it comes to making necessary but unpopular *national* policies palatable at the local level. As witnessed today in the European Union process towards a single currency, peer pressure can work wonders in this respect. The same goes for the WTO; when doing the right thing from a purely national point of view, like reducing import tariffs, in addition gives you the right to claim reciprocity from all your trading partners, you will have a much easier time to convince your national constituency that it really *is* the right thing to do.

2.2. The Social Backlash to Globalization

A second important obstacle to global governance has to do with the widespread belief that global competition destroys jobs and social welfare. This popular belief is particularly common in continental Europe but also exists in the Anglo-Saxon world. It leads many European governments to be exceedingly cautious when dealing with the issue of globalization and particularly with its welfare aspect. Rather than dealing with it openly and clearly, they often muddle it, for instance by making their constituents believe that Europe has always had and will continue to have a much more humane and social way to deal with competition and unemployment than the United States. The reality in most of continental Europe remains one of huge unemployment and of inefficient and unsustainable welfare programs, while the United States produces adequate growth and millions of new jobs. Fortunately, the Maastricht process towards a single European currency forces Europeans to undertake at least some of the economic steps that are needed to orientate Europe towards sustainable growth and globalization. The social climate has nevertheless considerably deteriorated in Europe and policies favourable to globalization have become decidedly less popular. Paradoxically, the election of social democratic governments in the United Kingdom and even in France could facilitate the necessary reforms. With nobody to their left, the social

---

[6] See footnote 1, p 1

democrats could possibly have an easier time to push through relatively unpopular economic and budgetary policies than their centrist or conservative predecessors. Furthermore, since the fall of the Berlin wall, some of the European social democratic parties have, by necessity, become more innovative and imaginative than their centrist and right wing rivals. It may well be therefore–this should at least be our hope–that the clash between those who somewhat naïvely believed that the disintegration of the USSR meant definitive victory for the free market and those who just as simplistically reject market globalization as a social nightmare, will end up producing an innovative policy breakthrough capable of saving at least some of globalization's economic, social and political golden eggs. The alternative scenario of a clash producing nothing more than political deadlock is of course also possible; but it would amount to a catastrophe, for Europe in particular.

How can this essential policy breakthrough be achieved? By building a consensus based on facts and by promoting acceptable social reforms. Both are difficult, but both have to be attempted.

As to the facts, they are well known. Most international organizations–the IMF, the World Bank and the OECD–have repeatedly stated that globalization contributes enormously to national and global prosperity. They have stated furthermore that globalization does not seem to be the principal force behind unfavourable developments in employment and income distribution observed in some advanced economies.[7] There is little indication for instance that increased trade with low-cost countries has contributed significantly to the declining share of employment in manufacturing, which is the principal tradable goods sector; nor does it seem to explain much of the relative decline of low-skilled wages. The fall in employment seems to be mainly due to the rapid growth of labour productivity in manufacturing, as a result of technical progress and capital deepening.[8] Most economists and economic thinktanks look upon globalization as a tremendous historic opportunity to generate sustainable growth and employment, an opportunity that must be seized by entrepreneurs, by corporations, by countries and, last but not least, by the international community. Market globalization alone of course is not like a miracle pill that cures all ills. To produce sustainable growth and employment, it needs to be embedded into an adequate global framework. Globalization and global competition in particular do not automatically create social justice, but they can provide the economic base for the development of the necessary social systems.

Governments have a particular responsibility to state the facts as they are, and not to shy away from them for fear of displeasing their constituents. Again, this sounds banal, but is not. Politicians are very good at ignoring the facts. International organizations like the IMF, the World Bank and the OECD have a key role to play in helping governments to state and recognize the facts. The 1997 annual reports of the World Bank and the IMF need to be commended in this respect.

As to social reforms, there exists a strong link between them and global integration and governance. Many governments particularly in western Europe will

---

[7] See footnote 2, p 1

[8] See IMF (1997)

need to reform their welfare policies by carefully weighing their social benefits and their economic costs. Without these reforms, countries will simply not be able to compete in the global market. However, these reforms will be politically feasible only if governments are perceived as remaining faithful to their fundamental social obligation. Dani Rodrik from Harvard University has recently written that a key component of the post-war social bargain in the advanced industrial countries was the provision of social insurance and safety nets at home in exchange for the adoption of freer trade policies.[9] Rodrik sees this bargain being eroded by increased competition and higher capital mobility. For him the key question is how to ease tension between globalization and political pressure to mitigate social risk.

There is no doubt that a new political bargain has to be struck in most developed countries. This bargain has to achieve two objectives. The first is to allow nations to remain on the globalization path and to get the maximum benefit out of it in terms of growth and jobs. The second objective is to reinvent a transparent social security system that efficiently protects the most vulnerable in society and is financially sustainable beyond our own generation. Both objectives have become more important than ever and in most European countries neither objective is being pursued with sufficient determination. Market reforms are being resisted with the argument that because of excessive market liberalization the number of needy people is increasing and that therefore the present social security systems should, if anything, be expanded, not restructured. Another argument used against social reforms is of Keynesian inspiration: in times of insufficient growth and unemployment, social security benefits should be increased, not reduced. All these arguments are fallacious. There will be no adequate growth and job creation without the new markets and the new competition that globalization offers. The inadequate rates of growth and job creation in most industrialized countries have to do with too little, not too much, liberalization. Deficit spending has not produced jobs as is evident in Europe today. And, last but not least, the objective of social reforms is not to offer less protection for the needy and vulnerable but on the contrary to render the social support system it more efficient and thus focus it more on the needy and vulnerable. To continue to spread it almost indiscriminately among all citizens will eventually kill it financially, and this to the detriment mainly of those who depend on it.

There will thus be no progress towards global governance without national governments renegotiating the political social bargain that exists with their electorate. This renegotiation implies not only deep reforms but also the reinvention and restatement of the bargain itself. Both are essential at a time of a potentially destructive clash between *globalists* and *isolationists*.

---

[9] Rodrik D (1997), *Sense and Nonsense in the Globalization Debate.* In: Foreign Policy, published by the Carnegie Endowment for International Peace (Summer issue)

2.3. The Increasing Tensions Between a National Public Sector and a Multinational Private Sector

The third reason for the exceedingly slow movement towards global rules and institutions has to do with increasing tensions between a public sector that has remained essentially national and a private sector that is becoming more and more international. Basically, these tensions should not exist because both nations and multinational companies need a well functioning world economy. The tensions exist though–they have even increased recently–because in a world undergoing rapid and revolutionary changes, the very different roles played by the state and the private sector have become much more apparent. The responsibility of the state is much wider than that of a corporation. It includes for instance all citizens, whether employed or unemployed. In times of high unemployment this naturally leads to tensions between firms that dismantle jobs and the state that has to deal with some of the social consequences. This tension exists even if down the road the economic advantages gained by the restructured companies will also benefit the state.

One of the main differences today between the private and the public sector is that the latter remains tied to national borders, while private firms are not. An increasing number of companies–tens of thousands of them all over the world–are not only multinational in terms of their activities, but are moving towards global systems of governance. As said earlier, all of their activities–research, development, production, financing, marketing, etc.–are increasingly being conducted through decentralized multinational processes. Every activity takes place wherever the conditions are the most favourable to the customer and this in terms of proximity to the market, economic and legal framework conditions, the macroeconomic climate, political stability, availability of research, development, brains, capital etc. It matters less and less where the center of these companies is located or where the top managers happen to be. Corporate boards are increasingly composed of directors of many nationalities. The same applies to management boards, whose members spend most of their time on airplanes anyway. For the private sector, at least for its most dynamic and innovative part, the global economy has become an almost endless source of competitivity. The name of the game today is to use this source to the fullest, to play the piano of the world economy not with one or two fingers, but with two hands and both feet. Businesses and business leaders thus increasingly use their influence globally, even if this influence is often overstated. Today, businesses have an international constituency in addition to their local ones.

Politics is a very different story. A politician is much more local or national than international. The power of a politician is based on local democratic legitimacy. If exercised outside national borders, it not only lacks this legitimacy, but it competes with power that has it. Politicians therefore have a clear preference for working on the national level, and this even in international matters. Those who elect them are at home.

The two worlds–the private sector and the governmental sector–are growing apart. This is by the way more the case in the developed world than in the developing world. In the latter, things have in fact become better. In the Seventies and the early Eighties, the multinationals were considered the enemy in many developing countries. The United Nations was organizing endless talks on how the multinationals had to behave in the developing world. All this has changed. International companies are welcomed, even courted, in many non-OECD countries. Deregulation and privatization efforts have created much more of a partnership between private corporations and governments of the developing countries, even if in many places these relations still leave a lot to be desired and have far to go. Ironically, it is in the developed world that the tensions between the private and the public sector are the most striking.

Why these tensions? With globalization and workforce dislocations progressing, governments tend to look upon multinational corporations with increasingly mixed feelings. Their influence on them is diminishing rapidly. Their contacts with them are less intense, as the multinationals spend less time worrying about the national framework conditions of their *homebase* countries, focusing instead on shopping around world-wide for attractive conditions. In several continental European countries business leaders have in fact lost hope of ever getting their governments to drastically improve their economic framework conditions. If anything, they are placing more hope on improving and developing the rules of the European Union. The European Roundtable of Industrialists (ERT) for instance is very active in this domain. Some multinationals have also become interested in a dialogue with global organizations like the WTO, even though this dialogue still lacks in intensity. Some large multinationals have in fact come to realize that they are the WTO's truest constituency, more than governments which, as examined above, have often kept some ambivalent feelings towards it. However, the problem that the multinational private sector faces when it comes to relations with international organizations and rules is that it has no direct role in them. Multilateral treaties and organizations apply to nations and are negotiated and governed by nations. Multinational companies, which have transcended national boundaries, have no direct access to these organizations' rulemaking talks or dispute settlement procedures. Their access remains dependent on nations, which may not share their views or their interest in making the global system function according to multinational criteria. So why bother with organizations and rules that only very indirectly affect them? Until more direct links are established between the multinational private sector and multilateral organizations like the WTO, these organizations are unlikely to enjoy the active support of multinational corporations.

An area of potential friction between nations and multinationals is highlighted in a recent article by Jacques Attali.[10] His point is that the market and multinational corporations, which have become global, are in the process of escaping democratic control, which has to a large extent remained national. Attali who goes as far as predicting the collapse of Western Civilization if the market triumphs over democracy, draws the wrong conclusions though. Rather than blaming the market, he should blame the inability of present-day democracies to extend

---

[10] Attali J (1997), *The Crash of Western Civilization, the Limits of the Market and Democracy.* In: Foreign Policy, published by the Carnegie Endowment for International Peace (Summer issue)

their rules and institutions of governance beyond their national democratic control. What is needed today more than at any other time in history are international rules and institutions capable of managing global interdependence. And this has to be done through systems of international cooperation that enhance and pool, not reduce, sovereignty and democratic control. This is of course easier said than done. But it would be an illusion to believe on the eve of the 21st Century that to resist the sharing of both sovereignty and democratic control with other democratic nations preserves national independence and sovereignty. The opposite is the case. Governments have to choose. They can either choose to open up their economies to the market, which today is a global force. This implies that they participate actively in building democratic global governance. Or they can choose to continue to manage what they wrongly believe to be under their total control, their national economies. That would imply that increasingly their activity would be reduced to dealing with the protection of those who will have lost out in the market, among them the corporations that have remained national.

If nation states and the multinational private sector want to make the world economic system work to their mutual benefit, they need to cooperate towards the same objectives, the setting of sensible international rules ensuring their application and establishing a dialogue within new types of institutions, national and international, where both sides have a voice. All three need to be tied to democratic control, because ultimately the world's democracies will not relinquish control over their economies.

3. Conclusion

Global governance is a key issue in today's globalized economy. It is being neglected, and when discussed, often with great passion, it is usually in a context of institution building. Politicians love to talk about the creation and the reform of organizations because it is easier than to deal with substance. It is symptomatic in this respect that the UN Commission on Global Governance has limited itself to proposing a new institution, the Economic Security Council. This proposal may be a very good idea. The fact remains, though, that rarely have breakthroughs in the area of international rules and cooperation been produced by the mere creation of new organizations. Breakthroughs have usually been produced by people and nations that had the political will and vision to change things, to make the world function better, whatever the organizational framework. The old GATT is a good example for that. In spite of the fact that it was temporary and that for nearly 50 years it failed to become a structured organization, it did more for world governance than dozens of highly structured and well thought out organizations.

What is needed is movement towards more global governance in terms of substantial global rules. If these rules don't materialize, if they do not catch up with an economic reality that has escaped the national framework, globalization with all its economic and social benefits and hopes, could well unravel. Because there is no sustainable freedom–and market for that matter–without rules. Freedom invariably carries with it the seed of its own destruction, if rules are not there to guarantee its development. It is therefore one of the most urgent tasks of our democracies to decisively move towards a truly global system of governance.

The Geo-political Changes during the 1980s and their Influence on the GATT

Roy MacLaren

When former Canadian Prime Minister Lester Pearson delivered his 1957 Nobel Peace Prize address, he entitled it *The Four Faces of Peace,* the first of which he identified as international trade: *The higher man sets his goals in this age of mass democracy,* said Pearson, *the more essential it is to political stability and peace that we trade as freely as possible.* Much the same sentiment had been expressed one hundred years earlier by Richard Cobden, the great British opponent of the Corn Laws. Cobden wrote in 1857 that *free trade is God's diplomacy and there is no other certain way of uniting peoples in the bonds of peace.*

This strong interconnection between trade liberalization and foreign policy goals–between global economics and geo-politics–has long been a central theme in the development of a rules-based international trading system. The General Agreement on Tariffs and Trade (GATT) had its origins in post-World War II institution-building, the primary aim of which was to secure a lasting peace among nations. The lessons of Smoot-Hawley and the Great Depression had taught only too well that peace must be built on prosperity and that prosperity depends, in turn, on an open and smoothly functioning international trade environment.

Although this vision of economic liberalism has been the foundation of the GATT, its engine of forward progress has been reciprocal bargaining of the most intense variety. Indeed, the contractual nature of the GATT, as a balance of concessions, embodies a considerable degree of mercantilist spirit while harnessing it to the noble objective of trade liberalization. This is the genius of the GATT–using the principles of most favoured nation and non-discrimination to extend the benefits of reciprocal bargaining on a multilateral basis. Yet the conceptual legacy of mercantilism remains very much alive in today's trade environment. Although we may have learned not to *beggar our neighbours*, we certainly strive to outdo them, particularly as trade performance becomes an increasingly important symbol of a nation's global strength and stature. Thus, the geo-politics of power and the geo-politics of peace continue to co-exist in the world trading system. Each played an important role in the drama of the Uruguay Round.

The seven years of the Uruguay Round negotiations, from 1986 to 1993, coincided with one of the most remarkable periods in modern history. This was a watershed, marked not only by the dramatic end of the Cold War but also by a technological, communications and industrial revolution which has fundamentally transformed the global economic landscape and shifted the balance of economic power. When the Trade Ministers of 117 countries met in Marrakesh, Morocco, to approve the Uruguay Round results in April 1994, the event had a significance far beyond what could be deciphered from the complex legal texts and detailed technical agreements being signed that day. As those of us at the meeting fully recognized, this was not merely the conclusion of another GATT round. The launch of the World Trade Organization (WTO) represented much more than a further stride in dismantling trade barriers. It symbolized a new departure for the multilateral trading system–the establishment of the first post-Cold War institution and the laying of a foundation stone for a new world architecture which is still being constructed.

The success of the Uruguay Round appears all the more impressive when viewed against the backdrop of its difficult origins. At the dawn of the 1980s, the prospect of another major round of GATT negotiations seemed almost as remote as the end of the Cold War. The Tokyo Round had only recently been completed after six years of difficult negotiation. In the tradition of previous GATT rounds, it had achieved the promise of additional tariff cuts by industrialized countries–an average of one-third reduction to be implemented in stages over the first eight years of the decade. Even more significantly, the Tokyo Round had added a series of new codes and framework agreements to the GATT aimed at bringing greater discipline to bear on non-tariff barriers such as discriminatory government procurement, subsidies and customs procedures. The Tokyo Round had also left an ongoing work programme for the GATT, including an agreement to continue negotiations on safeguards and to examine how greater progress could be made in reducing barriers to agricultural trade. There was a strong sense of negotiating fatigue, however, and the conventional wisdom was that the GATT would have much to absorb before attempting any major new trade liberalization initiatives.

Yet, even as the first tariff cuts of the Tokyo Round were being implemented, the international economic situation had begun to deteriorate. Widespread inflation and unemployment gripped the industrialized countries. The oil shocks of the 1970s had taken a heavy toll, particularly among oil-importing developing countries, many of whom would soon drift into serious debt crisis. Monetary instability and large balance of payments difficulties were a source of massive uncertainty. The engine of growth in world trade appeared to have stalled. In 1980, when Arthur Dunkel took the helm as Director-General of the GATT, world trade growth had dropped to only one per cent. Fortunately, the new Director-General had the foresight to recognize that the multilateral trading system was edging toward crisis. He quickly set out to respond to the challenge. Immediately on taking office, he initiated a series of brainstorming sessions with his senior staff. He traveled widely to Asian, European and western hemisphere capitals in order to assess and discuss the state of the world trading system. His diagnostic showed a system in turmoil. Although the Tokyo Round had made solid progress, it had been overtaken by events in the world around it. Suddenly, new strains were showing in the trading system which threatened to erase the positive Tokyo Round results even before they could be fully implemented.

The storm signals on the trade front were easily discernable: an ever-tighter application of the Multi-Fibre Arrangement (MFA) to restrict the textiles and clothing exports of developing countries; an increasing resort to so-called voluntary export restraint arrangements to manage trade in other sensitive sectors; a proliferation of anti-dumping and countervail cases aimed more at creating *process protectionism* than at dealing with genuine problems of unfair trade; and a mounting caseload of GATT disputes, particularly in areas such as agriculture where normal GATT rules were riddled with exceptions. The less developed countries (LDCs), many crippled by debt and searching for a New International Economic Order, saw the GATT as a rich man's club where LDC interests were frequently sidelined and where special and differential treatment had to be enhanced. The industrialized countries, on the other hand, were increasingly critical of *free rider* problems in the world trading system. Why should they open their markets to all comers on a most favoured nation basis when the developing countries, including those demonstrating growing export strength, had made no parallel market access commitments in the GATT?

With global economic performance in a downward spiral, the frictions increased. It was evident to Arthur Dunkel that a renewed sense of common purpose would need to be found for the GATT. In an important speech in London in March 1981, Mr Dunkel sounded a timely alarm bell. He warned of a world on the precipice of escalating protectionism, being held back only by a *kind of balance of terror*. He spoke of the urgent need to *establish new momentum in the right direction*–a goal that five and a half years later would be given concrete expression in the September 1986 launch of the Uruguay Round at Punta del Este.

The years leading up to Punta del Este were filled with tensions and disagreement among GATT members. This atmosphere and the trade frictions that underpinned it were symptomatic of fundamental shifts in the global order. Perhaps the most significant of these was the end of the bipolarity that had defined the world system for so many decades. The Cold War alignment continued to be dominant at the strategic and military level. In the economic sphere, however, the global structure was transforming rapidly into what became known as the Triad–a three-cornered world where the United States, although still paramount, was no longer unchallenged as Japan and Europe began to assert ever-greater strength as competitors. Nor were the Triad powers alone on the international stage. The OPEC countries had flexed their muscles with dramatic effect in the 1970s. The Asian tigers had not yet roared but were beginning to awaken. They were certainly showing their astonishing productive capabilities in a few sectors, most notably textiles and clothing, but increasingly in more sophisticated industries such as steel and electronics. The ground was shifting in the world's economy. The United States, in particular, was uneasy of its footing.

The US anxieties at the turn of the decade went well beyond economics. As the calendar turned on New Year's Day 1980, fifty American hostages were still held captive in Tehran. Moreover, in the last days of 1979, the Soviet Union had invaded Afghanistan, while the United States looked on in outrage but was powerless to prevent it. By April 1980, there had been the further spectacle of US helicopters incapacitated in the Iranian desert–a botched rescue attempt broadcast to the world and evocative of scenes only five years earlier when other US helicopters had fled from Saigon rooftops at the end of the Vietnam War. The impotence of superpower status was evident and highly frustrating. The election in 1980 of a new US President, Ronald Reagan, was one of the outcomes. He pledged to restore American primacy and, with Alexander Haig as Secretary of State, his early years earned him the reputation as the Great Cold War Warrior–rejecting Salt II and sponsoring the neutron bomb, MX missiles, the B-1 bomber and the Star Wars Strategic Defence Initiative.

The restoration of American greatness was an equally emotional issue in the economic sphere. Between 1940 and 1980, the US share of world GDP had declined from 40 per cent to just over 20. The Japanese economic miracle was both inspiring and frightening to American observers as Japan's share of world exports soared from 5.5 per cent in 1965 to over 11 per cent by 1980. The East Asian economies (China, ASEAN, Hong Kong, Korea, Taiwan) were not far behind, increasing their share of world exports from 1.6 per cent to 6.8 per cent during the same period and poised for a further doubling of their share to 13.5 per cent during the course of the 1980s. Haunted by the threat of de-industrialization, the United States feared that its so-called strategic industries, such as automotive, steel, electronics, machine tools and textiles, would be lost forever to import competition, with millions of workers idled as a result. For the first time, a strong preoccupation with the US merchandise trade balance took hold. After decades of large trade surpluses, the United States had experienced six deficits during the 1970s, the highest being US$34 billion in 1978. By 1986, the year in which the Uruguay Round was launched, the US merchandise trade deficit had been a fixture for eleven straight years, and had ballooned to a level of US$145 billion. This growing deficit was in fact a sign of relative strength in the US economy, as well as a consequence of an overvalued dollar and a soaring budget deficit attributable in part to the Reagan Administration's heavy defence expenditures. Nevertheless, the negative trade balance served as a rallying point for swelling protectionist forces. It was portrayed increasingly both as a symbol of relative US economic decline and as a symptom of unfair trade practices by trading partners of the United States.

Driven by strong political pressures, the US Administration began to yield more frequently to the temptations of protectionism and managed trade, perhaps the most notorious examples being the automotive and semiconductor restraint agreements with Japan. To its credit, however, the United States neither abandoned its fundamental free market philosophy nor abdicated its leadership responsibilities in the world economy. On the contrary, the challenge of a changing world was met with bold new initiative. The Reagan Administration, led by Bill Brock as US Trade Representative, became an early advocate of a new round of multilateral trade negotiations aimed at reshaping the GATT system and addressing a new agenda of trade issues.

A new round, it was felt, would serve as a beacon for a world economy dangerously close to foundering on the shoals of protectionism. For the United States, such a round was also seen as an opportunity to redefine the parameters of the world trading system–to reshuffle a deck which many US interest groups felt was stacked against them. This was, in part, a response to the *fair trade, not free trade* constituency–the view that, if the United States were to continue to keep its own market open, its exporters would need to enjoy a greater degree of access in other markets, including in developing countries.

The eagerness of the United States to engage in new GATT negotiations was driven by the search to find new comparative advantage for its exports. With rust-belt industries in evident decline, attention had turned increasingly to the service sector and to the high technology and knowledge-based industries where innovation and intellectual property rights were key to competitive strength. The agricultural sector was regarded as another area of US comparative advantage which had to date been largely excluded from the discipline of GATT rules and distorted by massive subsidization, particularly under the European Community's Common Agricultural Policy. Added to this was the area of investment flows, where US companies still dominated the globe, accounting for over 40 per cent of the world stock of foreign direct investment in 1980. In fact, even the massive US trade deficit of the day would have been erased if one excluded from it the inflows and outflows attributable to intra-company trade by US multinationals. Washington's agenda for a new round was fashioned within this strategic context. In broadening the GATT system to cover trade-related investment measures (TRIMs), trade-related intellectual property (TRIPS), services and agriculture, the United States saw an opportunity to counterbalance an apparent declining competitiveness in the more traditional industrial sectors.

The first serious attempt at achieving consensus on the launch of a new GATT round proved to be a notable failure. The United States pressed hard at the 1982 GATT Ministerial meeting but encountered strong resistance from not only the G-77 developing country bloc but also the European Community. The 1982 Ministerial Declaration stuck largely to the GATT work program inherited from the Tokyo Round, calling for further analysis and information-gathering on sensitive issues such as agriculture but studiously avoiding any implied commitment to launching new negotiations. The other major multilateral institutions fared no better that year in addressing the deteriorating world economic situation. The Versailles Summit was dominated by US-EC frictions over the Soviet pipeline dispute, while the IMF meeting in Toronto was marked by considerable hand-wringing about the looming international debt crisis, but there was no agreement on measures to avert it. Echoing Arthur Dunkel's speech in London a year earlier, OECD Secretary General Emile van Lennep warned in the 1982 Economic Outlook that: *the danger of a chain reaction of beggar-thy-neighbour policies, with particularly disastrous consequences, is now greater than at any time since the Second World War.*

The concerns about systemic collapse deepened as the protectionist pressures continued to escalate, spurred by rising job losses in the industrialized world. By 1982, the average unemployment rate had reached 9 per cent in the OECD countries–nearly double the rate only three years earlier. As the recession spread, 1982 also saw the first shrinkage in international trade since World War II. With a desperate need to reverse the downward spiral, an important initiative came from Arthur Dunkel. On his own authority, he proposed at the 1983 Annual Session of the GATT Contracting Parties that a "wise men's group" analyze the problems of the world trading system and propose solutions for the rest of the decade. Chaired by Fritz Leutwiler (Chairman of the Swiss National Bank and President of the Bank of International Settlements), the group brought together industrialists, academics and legal experts, as well as influential politicians such as US Senator Bill

Bradley. The seven-member committee laboured until 1985 and the Leutwiler Report, once released, played a significant role in fostering support for the launch of the Uruguay Round.

The commissioning of a wise man's group was but one example of the strenuous efforts made by Arthur Dunkel, sometimes under intense criticism, to build a new consensus that would move the GATT forward. In the tense trading environment of the early 1980s, the Uruguay Round proved to be as difficult to initiate as it would eventually be to conclude. Brazil and India led a chorus of developing countries in voicing strong opposition to a new round, particularly one that aimed at widening the GATT agenda to embrace new areas such as services, investment and intellectual property. Concerns over agriculture made the European Community almost as cautious. Gradually, however, consensus was built, through a series of high-level meetings, including the May 1983 Williamsburg Summit and the first Quadrilateral Trade Ministers' meeting chaired by Bill Brock in February 1984. By the time of the November 1984 GATT Contracting Parties session, both the United States and European Community were calling for a meeting of senior trade policy officials to explore the possibility of a new round. By 1985, the concept had been endorsed at the G-7 Summit in Bonn and in the OECD Ministerial Communique. Although a handful of hardliner developing countries continued to fight a rearguard action, others such as Korea, Chile and the ASEAN countries had begun to join the consensus.

A series of informal trade ministers' meetings, involving both developed and developing countries, played an important role in solidifying this broadening support. For instance, it was at such a meeting among twenty-four ministers in Stockholm in May, 1985 that consensus was achieved on a two-track negotiating approach separating goods and services, thereby setting the stage for the procedural outcome at Punta del Este. Once the November 1985 session of the GATT Contracting Parties took the formal decision to establish a Preparatory Committee, the platform from which to launch the new round had been fully constructed.

Between the GATT Ministerial in 1982 and the Punta del Este meeting of September 1986, the international economic situation had changed significantly. The patient and persistent consensus-building on a new round had been aided by a strong economic recovery. After reaching a low point in 1982, annual GDP growth for the twenty-four OECD countries had strengthened to between 2.5 and 5 per cent for each of the years between 1983 and 1986. World trade growth had also been restored, reaching a high of 8.5 per cent in 1984. This had enlarged the scope for political manoeuvre and created a more positive setting for the Punta del Este meeting.

At the same time, it was clear that the prospects for sustainable growth in the world economy continued to be threatened by the developing country debt crisis and by serious currency misalignments and structural imbalances among the major trading powers. The engine of world trade growth had been US imports. As a result, the US trade deficit had escalated from US$25 billion in 1980 to US$145 billion in 1986, with Japan and West Germany in large trade surplus positions. The threat of a US backlash became the single most preoccupying issue on the international economic agenda. With dozens of protectionist bills emerging in the US Congress, concerns increased about what Jagdish Bhagwati has called the diminished giant syndrome–the prospect that US anxieties over loss of economic dominance in a multipolar world would lead to unilateralism and disengagement from the multilateral trading system. The 1985 Plaza Accord, engineered by new US Treasury Secretary James Baker, was in part a response to this concern. It was aimed at addressing currency misalignments, and thereby easing the US trade deficit, through a deliberate appreciation of European and Japanese currencies against the dollar. The theme of macroeconomic coordination and multilateral surveillance began to take on more prominence at the G-7 Summits, partly as a code-word for US efforts to encourage greater stimulus in the domestic economies of Japan and West Germany. It was against this backdrop that the launch of the Uruguay Round took place, as yet another manifestation of a broad effort to re-shape the international economic system and to ensure that the United States, in particular, remained committed to its maintenance.

It was apparent from the outset that the new GATT round would be different from anything previously attempted. The agenda was the most ambitious ever undertaken. It would go well beyond the border measures normally dealt with in earlier GATT rounds and would penetrate deeply into the realm of domestic regulatory policy. Moreover, in addition to addressing a new agenda, it was clear that a new negotiating dynamic would pervade the GATT. The large number of active participants at Punta del Este, and the intensity of debate among them, signalled that GATT deals would no longer be made by the few and accepted by the many. The developing countries would play a major role in all aspects of the negotiations. Moreover, new alliances would be forged which cut across north-south lines. A portent of this in the month prior to Punta was the first meeting of the Cairns Group of agricultural exporters, including Canada, Australia, New Zealand and several developing countries. With a new agenda and new negotiating complexities, it was clear that the Uruguay Round would be a long haul.

The boiler room of the Uruguay Round negotiations soon became the Green Room, run by Arthur Dunkel. Through his artful chairmanship and intricate manoeuvring, the negotiations moved forward, gradually widening the areas of consensus toward a comprehensive package. However, the over-ambitious nature of the initial four-year timeframe quickly became apparent, as did the difficulty of the negotiating dynamics. At the Montreal mid-term review in December 1988, the prospect of an early harvest in certain areas, such as tropical products and dispute settlement, was blocked by the five Latin American Cairns Group members as a result of dissatisfaction over the state of the agricultural negotiations. Although this problem was subsequently resolved, it provided further evidence that GATT negotiations could no longer be settled among the dominant players. The agricultural dispute between the United States and Europe remained until the end of the Uruguay Round the major impediment to a successful conclusion. However, many other issues such as services, safeguards, intellectual property, tariffs and anti-dumping, took their turns as potential deal-breakers. After three years of almost ceaseless negotiating effort, the logjam remained so complete that Lester Thurow made his hyperbolic pronouncement in 1989 that *the GATT is dead.* His assessment gained credibility in the following year when, at the Brussels Ministerial meeting of November 1990, the GATT negotiations reached perhaps their lowest ebb. With US fast track authority about to expire, this meeting, which had been intended to bring the Uruguay Round to a conclusion, ended instead in yet another deadlock.

During the four years between the Punta and the Brussels Ministerial meetings, however, the world had witnessed two important new developments that would alter fundamentally the geo-political landscape. The first was a proliferation of regional trade agreements; the second, the sudden and dramatic end of the Cold War. Each of these developments gave rise to new anxieties about the potential impact on the future of the international trading system. Yet, in the final analysis, both proved to be extremely important factors in providing the necessary impetus to conclude the Uruguay Round.

The motivations underlying the impulse toward regional trade agreements were as varied as the countries engaging in them. One key factor for all players, however, was a recognition that the international marketplace was becoming more globalized and more competitive. For smaller and medium-sized countries, this triggered a search for greater economies of scale through securing open access to larger markets. This was a key consideration for Canada in engaging the United States in a bilateral free trade negotiation in the latter part of the 1980s, as well as for Mexico in joining with Canada and the United States to create the North American Free Trade Agreement (NAFTA) in 1993. Many other regional trade agreements were also spawned or strengthened in the late 1980s as countries around the world took stock of the globalization challenge. They often concluded that it could best be met collectively and in tighter cohesion with their closest trading partners. From MERCOSUR to ASEAN to the European Economic Area, there was a rush to find new mechanisms to deepen economic integration. While the Uruguay Round continued to flounder, regional trade agreements were being rapidly concluded. A negotiation of just over one year to conclude the NAFTA contrasted sharply with the six years already invested in the Uruguay Round without any conclusive result. Soon, heads of government were glibly projecting regional free trade deals of immense proportions: free trade in the Americas by 2005; free trade in the APEC (Asia-Pacific Economic Cooperation forum) area by 2020.

For some, the attraction of regional free trade was as much geo-political as it was economic. The foreign policy underpinnings of the 1985 United States-Israel free trade agreement, for instance, were highly evident. They were also a major factor in the NAFTA which, for the United States, was as much about the US-Mexico political relationship and the management of illegal immigration problems as it was about achieving free trade. Similarly, the December 1990 Enterprise of the Americas speech by President Bush–the precursor to the Free Trade Agreement of the Americas initiative–was reminiscent of John F. Kennedy's Alliance for Progress and even of the Monroe Doctrine spirit of US hemispheric hegemony. To the economic superpowers jostling for position within the Triad, regional trade agreements conveyed a sense of expanding spheres of influence. When the NAFTA was concluded, the United States took pride in proclaiming that it had surpassed the European Community by creating the world's largest free trade area. Then it was Europe's turn to congratulate itself as it once again leapfrogged into the lead by merging the EC and EFTA into a tighter-knit European Economic Area. On both sides of the Atlantic, the drive toward deeper and wider regional trading arrangements was seen as a means of increasing economic strength and competitiveness, not only vis-a-vis one another but even more importantly with respect to Japan. The Europe 1992 internal market initiative, for instance, was a direct response to the perceived Japanese threat–a product of European introspection about how it had lost a competitive edge to Japan and how it could strive to regain it by removing internal obstacles to economic efficiency.

The growing enthusiasm for regional free trade engendered concern about an erosion of the multilateral trading system. A tiresome and sterile debate began over the issue of regionalism versus multilateralism–a formulation that failed to recognize the synergy and complementarity of the two approaches to trade liberalization. In retrospect, however, it is clear that the robust trend toward regional free trade provided important impetus to concluding the Uruguay Round. The regional free trade initiatives helped to condition national psyches to the realities of globalization and to usher in additional competitive forces which accelerated the pace of structural adjustment in a large number of countries. This new trend also served to increase the stakes in the Uruguay Round by underscoring the need for the multilateral trading system to move forward or to risk losing relevance in a changing world. Above all, every step forward on regional free trade helped to push back the forces of protectionism and to strengthen the political commitment to trade liberalization. For instance, the US Administration's fight to implement NAFTA was instrumental in giving it the resolve to push for Congressional approval of the World Trade Organization. Having gone to the ramparts to defend the NAFTA against the likes of Ross Perot, US President Clinton and US Trade Representative Kantor were much more prepared to take on the protectionists when the political crunch came in the Uruguay Round.

Although the regionalism of the 1980s was a significant new feature on the geo-political landscape, its impact was dwarfed by the dramatic events within the Soviet bloc. In 1986, the year of Punta del Este, a new Soviet leader, Mikhail Gorbachev, had appeared on the international stage, engaging in an historic handshake with US President Reagan at the Reykjavik Summit and speaking of glasnost (openess) and perestroika (economic reform). By 1988, the year of the Montreal Mid-term Review, a major US-USSR disarmament treaty had been negotiated on medium-range nuclear missiles in Europe and the USSR had initiated its military withdrawal from Afghanistan. By the time of the Brussels Ministerial meeting in 1990, the Soviet dominos had fallen in central and eastern Europe, the Berlin Wall had been razed, and Germany was reunited. Within another year, by December 1991, the Soviet Union itself had disintegrated and Boris Yeltsin had emerged as the new leader in Russia.

These sudden and remarkable developments meant that the denouement of the Uruguay Round would be played out on an international stage, the setting of which would have been impossible to imagine at the time of Punta del Este. The phrase paradigm shift has been much over-used, but is quite apt when one considers how fundamentally different our world has become since the collapse of the Soviet system and the end of the Cold War. This has been a change of such magnitude that Francis Fukuyama has called it *the end of history,* at least in the Marxist-Hegelian sense of history proceeding by a dialectic of conflict. After decades of ideological cleavage, we have witnessed a widespread convergence of systemic values around the model of political democracy and market-driven economics.

The end of the Cold War opened enormous new opportunities for expanding the ambit of economic liberalism. It also made for greater uncertainty, however, even as the world became more secure. One such uncertainty during the the late 1980s revolved around the question of what impact the end of the Cold War might have on the multilateral trading system. There were many who feared that, in the absence of a common enemy, the western powers would be more prone to serious frictions arising from trade disputes. This was founded on the belief that, during the Cold War, the United States had been willing to pull its punches in the trade arena so as not to lose the support of its allies. Similarly, the European nations, in particular Germany, were seen to prefer compromise on economic issues to risking a possible erosion of the US strategic commitment to Europe. Fred Bergsten warned in a June 1991 presentation to the Royal Institute for International Affairs in London, that the end of the Cold War had pulled the strategic security blanket away from the multilateral trading system. With the disappearance of the unifying Soviet threat, there was a strong concern that the trans-Atlantic links would weaken. The political will to resolve trade problems might become, as a result, more difficult to muster.

Developments in the immediate wake of the Soviet system's collapse lent credence to this view. The United States was displaying a growing tendency toward unilateralism, as manifested in the aggressive Super 301 provisions of the US Omnibus Trade Act of 1988. The European Community, on the other hand, seemed to be drifting toward increasing inwardness, preoccupied with its own constitutional issues, its plans to absorb new members from EFTA, and its ambitious 1992 Internal Market project. The favourite media image of the day was of Fortress Europe and Fortress North America glowering at each other across the Atlantic. With the Uruguay Round mired in a seemingly endless negotiation, there was growing apprehension that the post-Cold War scenario would be one where economic conflict among the Triad came to replace military confrontation between the nuclear superpowers. In particular, there was concern that, with the Cold War behind it, the United States would no longer be prepared to act as the standard-bearer and agenda-setter for the multilateral trading system.

While the attention of the world focussed on central and eastern Europe, the need to restore confidence to the multilateral trading system was becoming increasingly urgent. Recession had again gripped the industrialized economies, with the level of world trade declining for three straight years between 1988 and 1991. There was also an escalating danger of a major trade war erupting between the United States and the European Community, particularly in light of the 1991 GATT Panel on oilseeds which had found against the European Community and led to US threats of retaliation on up to US$1 billion in EC exports. Spurred onward by impending crisis, and by the timeless shuttle diplomacy of Arthur Dunkel, US and EC negotiators redoubled their efforts to break the agricultural impasse, with the Blair House Accord finally being achieved in November 1992. Elections in the United States and France and an EC referendum on the Maastricht Treaty meant that 1992 was hardly a propitious year to bring the Uruguay Round to a close. Nevertheless, the nature of the deal had by then become clear. When Arthur Dunkel left office as GATT Director General in June 1993, the Draft Final Act–otherwise known as the Dunkel Text–had already defined the outcome of the Uruguay Round and the shape of the new trading system about to emerge. Although there would be further fine-tuning in the final months, what remained was the still formidable task of summoning the necessary political will to approve the deal and to defend it against the inevitable onslaught of protectionist attack.

Contrary to concerns about the end of the Cold War destabilizing the world's trading system, it was the geo-political sword that eventually cut through the Gordian knot of the Uruguay Round negotiations. By the late 1980s, the United States and the European Community had begun a close coordination of their response to the developments in the former Soviet bloc, including through concerting their economic assistance efforts in the context of the G-24. The focus at the highest levels had turned toward building a new trans-Atlantic and global architecture appropriate to the post-Cold War era. In 1989, US Secretary of State James Baker had made a landmark speech in Berlin calling for a *new Atlanticism.* The motivation was strong on both sides to achieve this–the United States concerned about losing its role and relevance in Europe, and the Europeans concerned about the United States losing interest. By November 1990, on the margins of the Paris summit of the Conference on Security and Cooperation in Europe (CSCE), the United States and the European Community had signed a Trans-Atlantic Declaration in order to reaffirm their shared commitment to common security, political and economic goals and to reinforce their close consultative arrangements. Moreover, the signature of this document came only a few months before the United States and Europe sent troops together into the Gulf War. Against this backdrop, the US-EC disagreement over agriculture in the Uruguay Round began to pale in significance. It was clear that the victory over communism had been an economic, not a military one. It would, however, be little more than Pyrrhic if it were followed by a breakdown in the multilateral trading system. Unless the GATT remained strong, the new Cold War architecture would rest on rocky foundations. The situation required decisive action to conclude the Uruguay Round and to disprove the doom-sayers such as Lester Thurow.

US Trade Representative Mickey Kantor, well known for his determined negotiating tactics, sensed the historic importance of the moment. In a May 5, 1993 speech to the National Press Club in Washington, he spoke of three decisive turning points for the world trading system:

> *After World War I, we raised trade barriers, with disastrous results. After World War II, we lowered tariffs and built global institutions to expand trade and investment even as we held communism to a standstill. The end of the Cold War is the third decisive moment in this century. We have a chance to build a new future and to make it the brightest and most enduring of all. Instead of a doomsday clock, with hands pointing toward a nuclear midnight, we want a 'growth clock' with hands pointing to noon. Instead of mutually assured destruction, we will strive for mutually assured growth.*

As was evident from Mr. Kantor's remarks, the world trading system was at a crossroads. The Uruguay Round had become much too important to allow it to fail.

The new imperative for success in the Uruguay Round was indicative of the fact that geo-economics had now replaced geo-politics on the top of the global agenda. This was also reflected on the domestic political scene. One need only recall the slogan of President Clinton's first election campaign: *It's the economy, stupid!* Political fortunes would soon depend much more on economic policy than on foreign policy. Moreover, foreign policy would be increasingly about economics as the reality sunk in that, just as all politics is local, all economics is international. In the post-Cold War era, economic diplomacy had moved to centre-stage. We now lived in a world where trade deficits were more important than missile gaps; where the roar of the Asian tigers had replaced the growl of the Russian bear; and where even spy networks were reported to have shifted their focus to economic intelligence.

The successful conclusion of the Uruguay Round began the work of constructing a modern architecture appropriate to this new world of geo-economics, including the creation of the World Trade Organization as a strengthened guardian of the rules-based trading system. In tactical terms, the Uruguay Round was about the intricate negotiating trade-offs related to tariff levels, non-tariff barriers and the myriad technical rules which define the complex legal environment for international trade. It was yet another chapter in the hard mercantilist bargaining which continues to propel the multilateral trading system forward. In strategic terms, however, the Uruguay Round represented a major systematic adjustment. It was about redefining the international trading system in a multipolar world, expanding its frontiers to take account of changing economic realities, integrating new markets and protected sectors into the rules of the system, and ensuring an ongoing multilateral commitment by the world's last remaining superpower.

The legacy of Arthur Dunkel must be seen in this context. The Dunkel Text became the blueprint for a new trading system, the design for the new architecture of the World Trade Organization. The Uruguay Round, however, merely laid the foundations. In the meantime, the pace of change has continued to accelerate. With the end of the largely static Cold War chess game, a new fast-paced free-for-all of global economic competition has brought additional waves of adjustment to the world economy. With globalization fast subsuming the Triad, regionalism, and trans-Atlanticism, the centrality of the WTO has become ever more important. At the same time, the political vision that emerged at the end of the Cold War and that contributed so importantly to the conclusion of the Uruguay Round is in danger of fading. Just as global developments in the wake of the Tokyo Round required the early launch of a further negotiating effort in the GATT, so the Uruguay Round needs to be followed by a new round which will continue to build on the WTO foundations. Although much has been accomplished, even more remains to be done–on agriculture, market access, trade remedies, investment, services, intellectual property, competition policy and trade and environment.

The so-called built-in agenda for the WTO covers much of this territory. It has already achieved important results in areas such as information technology and telecommunications, where private sector interests have pushed the trade liberalization agenda forward. It is becoming increasingly evident, however, that the launch of a new round will be necessary in order to achieve more progress on such a broad and comprehensive set of issues. This will be demanded by the mercantilist streak that remains embedded in the multilateral trading system–the need to show a balance-sheet of reciprocal concessions which, in some areas and for some parties, will only be achievable through cross-sectoral and inter-issue trade-offs. A new round will also be essential to instill once again in WTO Members the over-riding political vision necessary to move the trading system forward–the free trade vision that variously inspired Richard Cobden, Lester Pearson and Arthur Dunkel–on which our peace and prosperity will continue to depend.

The End of History for Free Trade?

Willy De Clercq

1. Introduction

A couple of years ago Francis Fukuyama, former aide of the Bush administration and now a senior advisor to the RAND corporation, published his famous (some might say notorious) book *The End of History*.[1] In it he addressed the question whether, after the collapse of the Soviet Union and of communism as a form of government, the ideological triumph of liberalism was complete; or in other words, does there still exist an ideological adversary who might seriously threaten liberalism and free market capitalism?

I would like to raise a somewhat similar issue. With the successful completion of the Uruguay Round negotiations and the establishment of the new World Trade Organization (WTO), is the triumph of global free trade complete and secured for the future or do there still remain some pitfalls that might confront it, in practice or in principle, with serious difficulties? In other words, what are the strengths and weaknesses of the current multilateral trading system and what was the role of the Uruguay Round in the whole picture?

From a historical point of view, the odds seem to be against the continuance of global free trade: *Taking a long historical perspective, we can observe recurrent swings in commercial policy from protection towards free trade and then back again towards protection.*[2] Or as Douglas Evans asserts: *It is now* (in 1974) *more than thirty-five years since the world has last experienced a protectionist dominated world economic system and we have grown accustomed to living under a liberally orientated world economic order. We should remind ourselves that historically speaking there have been only relatively short periods when the world has enjoyed the benefits of a relatively liberal system. Even a brief survey of modern history confirms that protectionism in some shape or form is the rule rather than the exception. Furthermore, we should not be surprised if protectionism, which we have previously mentally discarded as a product of the 1930s, rears its head again in a new guise which broadly fits the description of modern mercan-*

---

[1] Fukuyama F (1992), *The End of History and the Last Man*. Free Press: New York

[2] Ingram JC and Dunn Jr RM (1993), *International Economics*. John Wiley & Sons Inc: New York, NY. p 177

tilism, sometimes lablelled the new mercantilism (...) since the days of the early classical economists, protectionist instincts have always persisted like some economic equivalent of original sin.[3] We might even claim that throughout history, free trade has indeed been a very rare phenomenon. Only as a result of the theoretical legitimacy of free trade when measured against widespread mercantilism provided by David Ricardo, John Stuart Mill and David Hume, Adam Smith and others from the Scottish Enlightenment, and as a consequence of the relative stability provided by the UK as the only and relatively benevolent superpower or hegemon during the second half of the nineteenth century, was free trade able to flourish for the first time.

So, free trade is definitely a result of policy making which, as we know, is in turn a consequence of politics, of political pressures and ideologies. Therefore international trade, even in theory, can never be separated from political economy or more specifically from the theory of Public Choice. The topic can now be narrowed down to the following question: What are the internal and external political interests and forces that may strengthen or weaken the cause of global free trade, and how has the Uruguay Round affected them?

2. Public Choice Theory

Our current economic system is very much determined by politics, political interests and pressure groups, and *vice versa.* Government intervention and different types of regulations that interfer with economic life have indeed reached enormous proportions. It is within this political framework that profit-seeking market forces operate. Companies and other players in the market know that, and therefore invest huge amounts of money in lobbying to influence government regulations to their advantage. So we can claim that there is no such thing as a totally free market anywhere in the world–not even in the United States or the South East Asian countries, as many Europeans believe.

My own reaction is, so much the better. Even the original defenders–or should we say inventors–of the free market system during the Scottish Enlightenment advocated a free market with a strong government and strict public regulations. According to nobel laureate Douglas North, economic history shows us that basic supply and demand forces and the price mechanism cannot work without an efficient protection of property rights; putting this in place is, in the end, the primary task of any useful government. In other words, state intervention is a necessary condition for the proper functioning of the free market system and of free trade. However, this of course does not mean that every state intervention is correct or that it needs to be extensive; on the contrary.

A few decades ago–a short time in the history of economic ideas and science–a new breakthrough occurred in the way government, its organisation and actions are analysed. I refer to the rise of public choice theory, stimulated by economists

---

[3] Douglas E (1974), *The Politics of Trade–The Evolution of the Superbloc.* Macmillan:London, p viii

such as Mancur Olson, James Buchanan, Gordon Tullock, Anthony Downs, William Niskanan and Bruno Frey. Their theoretical and empirical research has been about non-market decision-making by democracies and bureaucracies, which they study with tools and principles from neoclassical economics such as methodological individualism, relative scarcity and consistent rationality.

The theory of public choice came up with a number of conclusions that at the time seemed astonishing but nowadays are quite self-evident. First, according to Olson, the smaller the group, the easier it is to organize individuals and their interests well. This may cause a disequilibrium: small, well-organised groups may systematically receive benefits from the state at the expense of larger, less well organized or not-at-all organised groups or even the entire population. As a result, smaller groups, focussed on their own interests in redistribution, may have a negative influence on the efficiency of political processes, on social benefits and on the growth of national income, since as they mature they push the government into producing more complex and extensive regulations to satisfy their demands.

Another important insight, suggested by Downs, is that politicians and voters are far more concerned with their own interests than with the public interest. This may sound obvious, but until recently most economists–the Keynesians, for example–believed that the state, and more specifically politicians and civil servants, actually served the public interest. In fact, in order to enhance their personal, and perhaps even altruistic interests, politicians need votes, and voters vote for those from whom they think they will benefit the most individually.

The problem for society is that although the average voter realizes the (usually short-term) benefits he receives, he does not understand the longer-run costs to society and even to himself resulting from his behaviour. This mechanism can result, for example, in the danger that politicians will offer short-term benefits to secure votes while shifting the costs to be paid, in the form of huge public debts, into the distant future. Belgium in the early 1980s, for instance, had a finance minister who proclaimed that the budget deficit had grown up just like that, and would therefore disappear later on ... just like that. His motto apparently was *Après nous le déluge.*

Small well-organized interest groups, who may know very well what the costs and benefits are to them of a particular policy choice, make it a point, therefore, to function efficiently as vote-raising machines for politicians who will address their particular interests, even if this comes at the expense of the rest of the population.

3. The Link between Public Choice and International Trade

The Public Choice theorists have, of course, much more to say than this, but even with only this insight from their work we are able to explain already a great deal about the past and present system of international trade, as did the Swiss professor of economics Bruno Frey: *Indeed, international economics is probably the field within economics in which the interaction between economic and political factors is most intensive. To everyone concerned with such issues, it is obvious that the international economy is strongly influenced by political factors.*[4] So, in the domain of international trade, the two different spheres of human behaviour (political and economic) are fundamentally interlinked.

Now, as Krugman and Obstfeld points out, the problem with this is: ... *the political boundaries between countries are artificial and may have little to do with the natural lines of commerce. Instead, political boundaries have been set by historical processes driven by war and diplomacy, which often produce geographical units that are peculiar when viewed in economic terms.*[5] Nevertheless, once these boundaries are set, governments want to create national economies they can control. In order to exercise control effectively, and therefore eliminate foreign economic interferences they cannot control, governments have throughout history invented many barriers to trade. These are, I fear, still numerous and often ingenious : tariffs, quotas, 'red tape' costs, customs checks, differences in national currencies, different regulations and standards, and so on, all in different sorts, types and measures. All these barriers have caused national markets until now to be far more integrated with far more economic advantages than international markets. That is why there remain so many opportunities for economic growth and wealth accumulation as a result of the integration of different national markets, and that is why pressure groups will grow within nation states to open up these opportunities.

From this perspective, we may argue that nation states, because they are a result of politics (the desire to maintain control over their territory, population and activities), remain an obstacle to a truly integrated world market. The question is: which political forces resist the emergence of truly free world trade and, as a result of their obstruction, produced roughly 22,000 pages of dense legislation in order to formalise the Uruguay Round when, as Susan Dentzer, economic columnist of US News and World Report, puts it: *If free-trade agreements really did free up all trade among nations, they would have to be only one sentence long.*[6] The answer to this question, or at least one of the answers, falls into two parts: one small and abstract, the second more elaborate and concrete. The first deals with the future of the nation state as such within our radically changing world and has a more abstract or theoretical content. The second deals with the actions, reactions and counter-reactions of nation states and their pressure groups towards the GATT, the Uruguay Round and the new World Trade Organization.

4. The End of the Nation State

An argument that is advanced by some is that this situation of national resistance to free trade will not persist because nation states will dissolve as a result of the

---

[4] Bruno BS (1984), *International Political Economics*. Basil Blackwell Ltd: Oxford

[5] Krugman PR and Obstfeld M (1994), *International Economics: Theory and Policy*. New York, NY, Harper Collins College Publishers: 175

[6] Dentzer S (1994), *A new tapestry of protectionism*. (December 5), US News and World Report: 83

pressures of a global economy. As Drucker writes: *Since talk of globalization of the world's economy began 35 years ago, the demise of the nation state has been widely predicted. Actually, the best and the brightest have been predicting the nation state's demise for 200 years, beginning with Immanuel Kant in his 1795 essay Perpetual Peace, through Karl Marx in Withering Away of the State, to Bertrand Russel's speeches in the 1950s and 1960s. The latest such predictions by eminent and serious people appear in a book called The Sovereign Individual by Lord William Rees-Mogg and Davidson who assert that for all but the lowest earners the Internet will make avoiding taxes so easy and riskless that sovereignty will inevitably shift to the individual, leaving the nation state to die of fiscal starvation.*[7]

Another popular defender of this thesis nowadays is the former Japanese company consultant Kenichi Ohmae. He claims that the engine of the economy in future will be the dynamics of regional states, not the nineteenth-century nation states.[8] He is convinced that these regional states will be shaped by successful local economies with common tastes and preferences, economies of scale and dynamics. Ohmae is not speaking of regions encompassing a number of existing nation states; on the contrary, he sees new opportunities in bridging the borders of nation states, which now limit growth. Could Karl Marx's theory that the economic base determines the political superstructure be right after all?

Others like Samuel Huntington claim that the international political future lies in the rise of one big world state or a limited number of super states, based on shared civilizations or ideologies. He sums up three causes why nation states as the basic units of geo-politics are becoming less dominant and less independent than they were during the nineteenth century.[9] We may find these causes in: a) economics, where international trade, capital movements and foreign direct investment lead to a faster and sometimes more efficient discipline on public finances; b) military matters, where defence technology has produced weapon systems that may hit targets anywhere in the world with devastating force and against which there is no real defence (e.g., nuclear missiles); and c) technology, which makes information and knowledge, now the engines of economic and socio-cultural progress, no longer controllable by national governments. Finally some, such as Richard Rosecrance, Professor of Political Science at UCLA, even assert that the future lies in the virtual state: *In economies where capital, labour, and information are mobile and have risen to predominance ..., the virtual state–a state that has downsized its territorially based production capability–is the logical consequence of this emancipation from the land. ... Rather than amass land,*

---

[7] Drucker PF (1997), *The Global Economy and Nation State.* Foreign Affairs (September/October) Volume 76, No 5, pp 159-171

[8] Ohmae K (1995), *The End of the Nation State: The Rise of Regional Economies.* Free Press: New York

[9] Quoted in The Economist: *The Shape of the World: The Nation State is Dead. Long Live the Nation State*, 23 December 1995-5 January 1996: 17-20

capital and labour, virtual states set strategy and invest in people. ... Hong Kong will be the model for this.[10] But this thinking seems a little bit too radical to me.

Although The Economist recognizes these forces as weakening the 19th century strength of nation states, it does not believe that nation states will disappear, and that for two reasons. First, because there are no viable alternatives to the nation states, in spite of conclusions about the emergence of one world government some might have drawn after reading Francis Fukuyama's book. In the words of The Economist: *Such people reckoned that most countries would no longer have any serious differences of opinion with each other about politics and economics; that they could therefore, seeing things in broadly the same way, use the United Nations as their instrument for solving minor disputes and so keeping the world tidy; and that in this way the foundations would be laid of an eventual system of global government. But,* The Economist continues, i*t could not be. Countries have long quarrelled, and will continue to quarrel, about many things besides ideology.* The nation state proves to be an excellent, highly tangible, rallying point on which people can recognize and base their own identity. In the words of The Economist: *A nation state is a place where people feel a natural connection with each other because they share a language, a religion, or something else strong enough to bind them together and make them feel different from others: 'we', not 'they'.*[11] These feelings can always be strengthened by state nationalism, which makes the nation state even stronger.

The basis for continued clashes lies within the apparent basic need of man to distinguish himself from other beings. Though man is by definition a social being, he is not a 'collective' being like the ant. Bertrand Russell, one of the greatest philosophers of this century, has illustrated this human quality to distinguish himself quite effectively by his World War II experience. He once described the behaviour of the population of London during the German bombardments in terms of every Londoner feeling himself as part of one big family, but when the external threat was over these feelings of connection quickly vanished: there were, for example, no more heartfelt conversations between strangers during bus rides. That is why Russell did not believe in a unified world or in one government. Only if Martians or some other alien race were to attack earth could he see an opportunity for the opposite to happen.

A second illustration of this is to be found in the apparent ethno-cultural reaction against economic and technological globalisation. Confronted with external pressures for change (and openness towards the world economy will inevitably lead to changes in traditional ways of living and doing business), people who are less adaptable to change will feel their existence threatened (humans are by definition cultural beings, which means that the culture in which they live is an integral part of their personality) and will therefore reject the changes. This is one reason, as the supporters of this argument assert, why the European Union, which indeed changes much within Europe, finds it so difficult to gain popularity.

---

[10] Rosecrance RR (1996), *The Rise of the Virtual State*. (July/August), Foreign Affairs: 45-61. Another interesting article on this issue has been written by Jessica T. Mathews (1997), *Power Shift.* Foreign Affairs (January/February):50-66

[11] see footnote 9

The second reason why The Economist believes that the nation state will not disappear in the future is that there are still too many political forces within the nation state whose existence depends on the survival of these states. Similarly, Drucker thinks that: *Despite all its shortcomings, the nation state has shown amazing resilience (...). So far, at least, there is no other institution capable of political integration and effective membership in the world's political community. In all probability, therefore, the nation state will survive the globalization of the economy and the information revolution that accompanies it. But it will be a greatly changed nation state, especially in domestic fiscal and monetary policies, foreign economic policies, control of international business, and, perhaps, in its conduct of war.*[12] During the 200 year-old history of the nation state, a lot of political forces and pressure groups have attached themselves to the nation state and will therefore, for the sake of their own survival, defend the survival of the nation state with every power they have–and indeed they do have power. With this somewhat Machiavellian vision, we can identify the actual forces for and against free trade

5. Forces in Favour of or Against Free Trade

The central element in the discussion between nation states and the WTO is national sovereignty, still a very important concept of power. Classical politics, and especially world politics, are played out in terms of zero-sum games, which means that one player wins at the cost of someone else. That contrasts with the funtionsing of the free market economy, where all players can end up winners, even if only after a while. What many governments continue to fear about the fundamental idea of the GATT/WTO is their loss of political power. We can see this throughout the history of the GATT. As Dunn and Ingram put it: *Regulation of external trade through tariffs, quotas, and other means has long been a prominent aspect of national sovereignty.*[13] Only under pressure from the public, the media and pressure groups do political leaders reluctantly give away parts of their national sovereignty to international organisations, including the WTO. Let us now see how this happened.

5.1. In the Beginning...

The political story of the GATT started even before World War II. President Franklin D. Roosevelt saw that the notorious Smoot-Hawley Tariff Act, imposed by Congress in 1930, had disastrous effects on international trade and after a while–and more importantly to an American president who still needed to be re-elected on domestic issues–on American economic growth and employment.

---

[12] Drucker PF, op cit, pp 159-171. A very interesting article regarding this subject can be found in The Economist, *Survey of the World Economy*, 20 September 1997

[13] Ingram and Dunn, op cit, p 177

Nowadays, some economists even believe that the Great Depression was caused primarily by these tariffs. President Roosevelt understood the economic and political importance of a sharp reduction in tariff rates. He persuaded the US Congress to authorize a new approach to tariff policy, and in 1934, Congress agreed to delegate to the President the power to fix tax rates on imports: *The reason for this was a simple, practical one: US tariff reductions were to be made in exchange for reductions made by other nations, and there is no way the necessary bargaining could be done in Congress.*[14] As a result of this and of many bilateral negotiations from 1934 to 1947, the average US tariff was reduced by about one third.

All this shows clearly the analytical usefulness of Public Choice theory. The individual members of Congress proved indeed to be more vulnerable to small, local pressure groups. As Dunn and Ingram note: *Initially, the primary purpose of the new tariff legislation was to provide some relief and assistance to American farmers, but the stock market crash and early signs of a slide into an economic slump led to calls for protective tariffs on numerous products. Members of Congress (representatives face elections every two years, so they have to respond quickly to their homefront) began to trade votes with one another and finally produced a tariff bill that sharply increased the level of protection all round.*[15] On the other hand, President Roosevelt, newly elected in 1932, was much more preoccupied by protests from abroad. In fact, *...its emergence after World War I as a world power and a major factor in world trade caught the US unaware and unprepared. The angry response to the Smoot-Hawley Tariff Act in the rest of the world took the country by surprise. Now the obligations of a world power began to make themselves felt.*[16] This made it possible for the President to withstand the pressures from domestic lobbyists. However, the problem for Roosevelt remained that during the 1930s the isolationist tendency within Congress was still dominant.

World War II changed this situation dramatically not only in international politics but also in domestic American politics. The United States emerged as the sole political, military and economic power in the western hemisphere, replacing the United Kingdom. The European countries were still weak and, maybe reluctantly, looked to the US as their leader (which stimulated the always latent messianic soul of the Americans), and the rising threat of the Soviet Union gave the isolationist tendency in American politics a severe blow. All this, among other things of course, caused the presidency to gain in political power and authority at the expense of the Congress. As a result, the General Agreement on Tariffs and Trade, concluded in Geneva in 1947, became fact because formal congressional approval was no longer needed. Moreover, the shift to multilateralism later on, based on the most favoured nation clause and the principle of non-discrimination, so central to the GATT, became possible. However, the establishment of an International Trade Organisation (ITO) still appeared politically impossible. One reason was that the Congress was opposed to the fact that the President would be able to decide arbitrarily whether or not the US would join the ITO, thereby abdicating a part of America's trade policy sovereignty. As a result, domestic American oppo-

[14] Ingram and Dunn, op cit, p 184

[15] Ingram and Dunn, op cit, p 182

[16] Ingram and Dunn, op cit, p 183

sition to a fully institutionalised, international trade body proved to be too strong: one could say that the ITO was, in the eyes of the numberous supporters of the sovereign nation state, a bridge too far.

5.2. Supranational Legal Order

The GATT nevertheless survived, and although it had originally a provisional character, it started to grow in every sense, including institutionally. In 1993, when the GATT had acquired diplomatic strength and had more than proved its usefulness, it was able finally to transform itself into the WTO with a limited, although growing, form of supranational legal order. Crucial to this legal order is that: *the new system of rules and enforcement would be more legalistic than the old GATT and also more automatic in areas such as dispute settlement.*[17] This phenomenon of international institutions growing in strength occurs everywhere around the world, especially in Europe, and somewhat frightens most of the larger countries (smaller countries see, on the contrary, in these international organisations possibilities to increase their diplomatic influence). This may be one reason why the larger countries tried first to slow down the growth of the GATT, and later on tried to monopolize the discussions.

The importance of the still small but ever growing supranational legal order of the WTO must not be underestimated. Look for an illustration at the development of the United States as a federal state or at the present situation within the European Union. In both cases, it is the (federal) courts–especially the Supreme Court in the US and the Court of Justice in the EU–and their jurisprudence about interstate commerce and trade that paved, and in the European case still paves, the way towards fully integrated markets. This is of course not yet the case for world trade, but: *the removal of veto power over adoption of reports and over retaliation should make it more embarrassing for governments to defy the system than was now the case, and that would create some pressure.*[18] In all events, the new dispute settlement mechanism has reduced the threat of unilateral sanctions by WTO Members. This has somewhat improved the certainty for those enterprises that depend on international trade. It may therefore be safe to presume that they will continue to lobby for even more certainty, by improving the authority of the WTO dispute settlement body.

5.3 GATT Moves on...

Coming back to the history of the GATT, the agreements reached in 1947 were based very firmly on the principle of free trade but unfortunately the list of exceptions to that principle proved to be lengthy, and indisputably all those exceptions were inspired by national interests. The participating countries were clearly not yet

---

[17] Raby G (1994), *Introduction*. Report of the OECD Workshop on the New World Trading System, pp 13-24

[18] Raby G, op cit, p 18

totally convinced of the advantages of free trade, or they were too afraid of the radical changes that free trade might have caused in their still war-torn countries.

First of all was the well known grandfather clause. This stated that exceptions to the regulations of Part II of the GATT were allowed when these regulations proved to be inconsistent with existing national regulations. Moreover, the participating countries continued to have the possibility to set tariffs on imports in order to protect their balance of payments, and to take trade restricting safeguards (quotas or tariffs) when confronted with imports that distorted their home-markets. Articles XX and XXI of the GATT summed up some other exceptions to international trade, among them public morals, health, intellectual property rights, trade in national artistic, historical or archaeological treasures, natural resources, and conditions of short supply nationally, as well as reasons of national security for which UN economic sanctions were permitted. Furthermore, the participating countries could decide through waivers to exempt a country from some of its GATT obligations: it was on the basis of this exception that the European Coal and Steel Community became legitimate in the eyes of the GATT. These waivers show, however, more than anything else that the GATT treaty was in those days strictly inter-governmental.

In 1947, during the first round of GATT negotiations, import tariffs were reduced by 44 per cent. However, during the following four rounds of negotiations (Annecy, France, 1947; Torquay, United Kingdom, 1950-51; Geneva, Switzerland, 1956 and 1960-62), tariffs were reduced further by only 3 to 15 per cent. These low reductions were due to the negotiation technique used, which was bilateral and by individual tariff line and which made strong pressures from protectionist lobby groups not only possible but also very successful. This way of negotiating also enabled the large countries with their huge internal markets to make trade deals between themselves, which were not always in favour of global free trade. On the other hand, it seemed clear that the small countries, which depended more heavily on free international trade, did not have enough impact to secure bigger reductions. Therefore, in 1962 the need for negotiations on a multilateral basis became very clear, and the Kennedy Round (1962-67) was the turning-point for solving these problems.

5.4. The Kennedy Round

The establishment of the European Economic Community (EEC) altered Washington's reluctance to engage in large tariff reductions. The Trade Expansion Act of 1962 allowed the President to agree to tariff reductions of up to 50 per cent and over a period of five years on the condition of reciprocity (notice the return of this mercantilist notion). New external developments, in the form of the creation of the EEC, seemed to have pushed the protectionist forces in Congress a little further backwards, or at least to give members of Congress the opportunity to pass the hot potato on to the President. The big tariff reductions of the Kennedy Round were also, however, a consequence of important changes in negotiation techniques. First, negotiators searched for linear or across-the-board reductions for all products, and they laid down the list of goods that did not fall under the agreement. Afterwards, the participating countries consolidated, one product at a time, the list of the applicable tariffs agreed upon. This resulted in an average tariff reduction of 35 per cent over a period of five years, and it laid the basis for new drastic reductions later on.

However, in the field of agriculture the situation worsened. The United States had used already in 1955 one of the GATT exceptions to protect their market from the import of agricultural products. During the Kennedy Round, the EEC's Common Agriculture Policy (the CAP) was in full development. Moreover, a mutual reduction of tariffs on agricultural products proved difficult because the US and the EEC differed significantly in the way in which they subsidized their agricultural sectors, complicating any possible exchange of concessions. The result was that the agriculture and fishery sectors were treated as exceptions, remaining outside the field of application of the GATT and leaving the way open for protectionism. Needless to say, under the pressure of lobbies these exceptions were interpreted extensively.

This proved to have dramatic consequences for the developing countries (LDCs) which relied then, and still rely heavily today, on exports of their agriculture products towards the markets of the industrialised world, and whose voices were almost never heard during the negotiations. In order to ease the pain, new principles were proclaimed to stimulate the export of industrial goods from the developing countries. First, the industrialised countries had to allow that developing countries could in some cases no longer be bound by the reciprocity principle. Second, the industrialised countries were obliged to stimulate the integration of the LDCs into international trade. Unfortunately, this proved to be the wrong policy approach, but at that time a lot of economists believed sincerely in the usefulness of stepped-up, centrally planned industrial modernisation schemes for the LDCs.

The last important result of the Kennedy Round was the principle that the fight against tariffs had to be combined with the fight against non-tariff barriers. This resulted for example in the drafting of the Anti-Dumping Code in 1968–dumping and subsidization were considered to be non-tariff trade barriers. This meant that additional tariffs could be levied on dumped products when they were imported into another country, but this had to happen under the supervision of the Committee on Anti-Dumping Practices. Here we see one of the first examples of the progressive development of a supranational GATT legal order.

5.5. In Tokyo

The next round of negotiations, the so-called Tokyo Round (1973-79), grouped together a bundle of trade issues for multilateral negotiation. The results were produced in a variety of different agreements. Theoretically, each stood on its own merits and had its own content, but in practice it was necessary to reach agreement on all the issues before the Round could be concluded successfully. All this, however, made the GATT very complicated. Even more damaging to the coherence of the GATT and to the principle of free trade, it gave the member states the opportunity to pick and choose the side agreements (with tariff concessions for new products that were not yet subject to previous GATT-regulations) and the codes (which contained agreements on non-tariff barriers) they wanted, and to leave aside the ones they thought to contain more painful obligations. *GATT à la carte* was a reality.

Nevertheless, once again important tariff concessions on industrial products were made–an average reduction of 33 per cent over eight years–and there was also some progress in the field of agricultural and tropical products, aircraft and aircraft components. The latter illustrates the impact of economic reality on politics; it remains very difficult for politicians to stifle the promising increase in trade in new high technology products, as was the case for aircraft in the 1970s. Also important in the Tokyo Round was that the negotiators reached an agreement on uniform criteria by which to value imports, because most tariffs were and still are *ad valorem* (i.e., levied as a percentage of the value of the product). This uniform interpretation prevented many disputes from arising.

Above all, the Tokyo Round became famous for its handling of non-tariff barriers. With the steady decline in tariffs, these were becoming increasingly attractive to lobbyists and to governments as potential protectionist measures, especially since the GATT already contained extensive exceptions to the prohibition on the use of quantitative trade restrictions, which could accommodate non-tariff barriers in one form or another.

The Multi-Fibre Arrangement (MFA)–renewed and prolonged once more in 1993–was a perfect illustration of those non-tariff trade barriers. On the basis of the MFA, the industrial countries gained control over the export of textiles and clothing from the LDCs, one of the few domains where the LDCs had a comparative, and even an absolute, competitive advantage over the industrialised countries, which the protectionists from the textile lobbies of the industrial countries made sure they blocked. It cannot be denied, that the MFA was a flagrant denial of basic GATT principles.

The same holds for voluntary export restraint agreements (VERs), orderly marketing agreements (OMAs), and restrictive business practices. In the latter case, the initiative comes from enterprises, in the case of VERs and OMAs the initiative comes from states and is related to other states. But what these three measures have in common is that they restrict or hinder exports and therefore trade. Because they are bilateral and do not involve third countries, the GATT rules did not apply and these agreements were therefore legal in the eyes of the GATT. The danger nevertheless existed that as they multiplied they would erode the GATT and compound existing trade barriers. The US or the EU could, for example, promise not to attack before a GATT-panel the closed Japanese rice-market in exchange for Japan *voluntarily* agreeing to restrain its exports of automobiles towards their markets.

The GATT has calculated that there are at least a thousand different forms of non-tariff trade barriers: technical trade barriers, public enterprises with local or national monopolies, discrimination against foreign companies in the case of government procurement, unnecessarily complex import clearance procedures, and so on. During the Tokyo Round, the GATT started to deal with these trade barriers by negotiating a series of special Codes. One was the Agreement on Technical Barriers to Trade, better known as the Standards Code, which stimulated the harmonisation of different national technical standards. A second was the Procurement Code, which made government procurement subject to basic GATT principles. A third was the Code on Subsidies and Countervailing Measures. In total, nine special agreements and arrangements resulted from the Tokyo Round negotiations, serviced by nine special GATT committees to ensure they would be lived up to. Notice once again the slowly growing GATT legal order.

5.6. The Big Breakthrough: the Uruguay Round

The Tokyo Round certainly had its successes, but in many areas the process towards free world trade was on the wrong track. First of all, not all GATT Contracting Parties signed on to the Tokyo Round Agreements and Arrangements (in some cases membership was limited to industrialized countries and only a handful of developing countries) with the result that there was a sharp fragmentation of the legal framework of the GATT. Second, it proved to be impossible to amend the GATT itself: doing so would have touched directly the interests of the bigger states who therefore refused to do so. Third, the GATT continued to be applied without ratification on only a provisional basis, causing it to have serious institutional weakness. Fourth, more and more member countries began to voice criticism over the way the large trading powers, the US the EEC and Japan monopolized the negotiations. And finally, the effectiveness of the GATT dispute settlement mechanism still depended far too much on achieving the consensus of all members to adopt panel findings, even those who were parties to a dispute.

Besides that, there were also numerous shortcomings with regard to content. Reference has already been made to the grandfather clause, creative interpretation and/or improper use of exceptions, waivers, *de facto* protectionist misuse of technical standards, VERs, the Multi-Fibre Arrangement, problems in agricultural trade, and all those areas that did not yet fall under the rules of the GATT such as services, trade-related intellectual property rights, environmental and social issues, and foreign investment.

Finally, by the mid-1970s the international trading system was beginning to show signs of strain. The industrialized countries suffered several severe shocks. First there was the collapse of the Bretton Woods fixed exchange rate system, which allowed countries to protect their industries through competitive devaluations of their currencies. This was followed by two oil shocks, serious external imbalances, and a period of creeping inflation accompanied by economic stagnation. Stagflation caused uncertainties amongst economists and policy makers, forcing them to abandon the Keynesian paradigm. All this made it possible for the industrialised countries to pay only lip service to the principle of free trade: protectionism was on the rise again.

These were the circumstances in which Arthur Dunkel came into office as Director-General of the GATT in 1980: there was no time for a honeymoon. With his never-ending energy and diplomatic skills, and the inspiration he brought to the somewhat demoralised GATT staff, he set to work. His dynamism showed up in the results. He brought the GATT member states back to the negotiating table in order to revitalise global free trade.

This made the launching of the eighth GATT Round (the Uruguay Round) possible through the Declaration of Punta del Este of 20 September 1986. The Declaration summed up what negotiators wanted to accomplish during the negotiations: a significant reduction or abolishment of some tariffs and non-tariff trade barriers, the application of GATT rules to the farm and textiles sectors; the establishment of international respect for intellectual property rights; the integration of trade in services and foreign direct investment into the GATT-framework; the enlargement of GATT membership towards new countries, and the improvement of the functioning of the GATT in the fields of efficiency and jurisprudence. Finally, some Tokyo Round Codes, especially the Subsidies Code, needed to be adapted to the new circumstances.

At the start it seemed that these goals could never be fully met. The LDCs resisted the integration of trade in services or any other new sector into the GATT framework. They feared that this would make cross-retaliation against them possible in fields that would hurt them the most. For example, were they to be found in violation of a GATT rule in the area of intellectual property, because of their production of counterfeit goods, they could face the withdrawal of trade benefits in other trade sectors where their export interests were concentrated. What the LDCs wanted in fact were the advantages of free world trade but not the obligations that go with that.

5.7. After Seven Years of Negotiations

Completing the Uruguay Round negotiations successfully was a very close call. Agreement was eventually reached in the fields of industrial goods, services, investment, intellectual property, agriculture, textiles, in the fields of international rules concerning customs valuation, government procurement, standards, dumping, subsidies, and safeguards, and finally in the domains of special treatment for LDCs, dispute settlement and the establishment of the WTO.

A lot of agreements indeed, but some countries were not and still are not happy about the way they were reached. In fact, the US and the EC first agreed bilaterally between themselves and then imposed their agreement on the other, less powerful or less well-organised states. For instance, in the Blair House Agreement on agriculture, the EC and the US both secured first their own interests: each agreed to allow the other to continue its own particular form of compensating its farmers, and the so-called *peace clause* contained in the Agreement ensured that for a certain period at least the European Common Agricultural Policy would not be challenged through GATT/WTO dispute settlement by the US. Inevitably, however, this happened at the expense of other agricultural exporting countries. Moreover, one can question why the EC and the US agreed to return, at the request of the US, to the negotiating technique used prior to the Kennedy and Tokyo Rounds of bilateral tariff concessions on a product-by-product basis. As we have already seen, this made the negotiations particularly vulnerable to pressure from protectionist lobby groups and caused, therefore, some serious delays.

That apart, the results of the Uruguay Round were indeed impressive. First, the grandfather clause was finally deleted (except for the US 'Jones Act'), which meant that WTO Members have had to adjust their domestic legislation to WTO rules. Second, tariff concessions averaged about 38 per cent. Some of the biggest tariff cuts were made by Asian and Latin American LDCs, an excellent change in policy direction after decades of import substitution.

In spite of resistance from some LDCs, a lot of new sectors of trade were brought under the wings of the WTO, including most important of all Trade in Services which was made subject to the classic GATT principles of transparency and non-discrimination. The Agreement on Trade-Related Investment Measures (TRIMs) banned local content requirements and a number of other trade-distorting measures attached typically to the activities of foreign investors. The Agreement on Trade-Related Aspects of Intellectual Property Rights (TRIPS) stipulated that an intellectual property right, registered in one member state applies also in all other member states. These states therefore have the obligation, if necessary, to change their legislation and to enforce these property rights. This may result in the destruction of imitation goods or imprisonment of those who deliberately violate these rights. Another important statement in the Agreement is that intellectual property rights are individual. The WTO does not recognize inventions that belong to the human heritage and that should therefore be open to anybody. The European Parliament, on the contrary, claimed until recently that genetic material is part of the common heritage of humanity and therefore cannot be patented. Unfortunately, the TRIPS Agreement contains no clauses to ban or sanction misuses in the establishment of intellectual property rights: some American companies for example want to patent the body cells of Indians without their knowing! Finally, the TRIPS Agreement stipulates some rules with regard to copyrights and patents.

The progress with regard to the liberalisation of trade in agriculture may seem minimal in comparison to the intentions set out in the Punta del Este Declaration, but the green light has been given for the reform of national agricultural policies. The Agreement on Agriculture consists of four elements: market access (the transformation of non tariff barriers into tariffs and a general tariff reduction of 36 per cent); export subsidies (reduction of 36 per cent in budgetary terms and of 21 per cent in quantitative terms); domestic support measures (reduction of 20 per cent, but the US and the EU are excluded as are the *green box* policies–policies that have no or only little impact on farm production or trade), and a timetable for the change (starting in 1995 and ending in 2000 for industrialised countries and 2004 for the LDCs).

As we have already seen, the Uruguay Round also made possible important improvements and additions to the rules of the trading system in areas such as customs valuation, pre-shipment inspection, rules of origin, import licensing, technical barriers to trade, anti-dumping and countervailing measures, and safeguards (banning VERs and OMAs). One other agreement worth mentioning is the Plurilateral Agreement on Trade in Civil Aircraft: no wonder that it was plurilateral and not multilateral when you realize that one American producer, Boeing, and one European producer, Airbus, monopolize the aircraft market and that each firm is supported by its government. So what do these governments do? They make deals between themselves.

Finally, besides the enlargement of the number of Members who will be bound from now on by WTO rules, a whole new mechanism of dispute settlement has been worked out. Its importance has been well summarized by Geoff Raby, as follows: *Participants [of an OECD workshop on the results of the Uruguay Round] agreed that progress in strengthening the dispute settlement procedures was one of the most important achievements of the Round. A good dispute settlement system was the key to the credibility and efficiency of the multilateral trading system. [But] in large measure, this would hinge on the quality of the panels and on the commitment by larger countries to respect panel decisions.* Although this dispute settlement system may be the true beginning of a WTO supranational legal order, caution is necessary in not pushing it too far. *This is to avoid the WTO dispute settlement system getting too far in front of the political systems of national governments.*[19] Because in the end, sovereignty still lies with the nation states and they can withdraw from the WTO whenever they want.

6. And the Answer is...

Now that we have seen where the GATT came from and where it stands today, we might give some possible answers or at least some considerations to our original question: is the principle of global free trade under the wings of the WTO secured for the future or not? As long as nation states remain the central elements in international politics, the answer lies to a great extent in the will, convictions and commitment of national politicians in promoting free world trade. As the participants of the OECD workshop on the New World Trading System put it: *In view of the complexity and extent of the new Agreements to be implemented, participants cautioned that if undertakings were not executed in the spirit of trade liberalisation, as well as in the letter, the WTO may not be able to realise its full potential. Vigilance would also continue to be necessary.*[20]

However, the problem national politicians face is three-fold. First, domestic firms in competition with foreign firms supplying the home market have the strongest interest in tariff protection, and generally oppose free trade policies. They are joined by the workers and the trade unions of that economic sector, who know that they can share the rents achieved by the tariff protection. Firms producing complementary products and supplying inputs to the import-competing firms are another group favouring protection (provided they do not themselves strongly depend on imported raw materials).

The protectionist groups usually have strong political interests, because the effects of a change in protection are visible and direct, and therefore carry a lot of weight in the political debate. These groups can easily argue that a tariff reduction would result in a direct loss to them, reducing output and employment, while favouring foreign interests. Increased protection, on the other hand (so they will claim), would obviously increase the employment of nationals and the output and

---

[19] Raby G, op cit, p 18

[20] Raby G, op cit, p 14

profits of domestic producers. These arguments are particularly forceful, and are actively promoted by trade unions, when there is an abnormally high level unemployment in the domestic economy.

The main group in society favouring trade-liberalizing policies and opposing protection are export suppliers. Firms offering their products on foreign markets realize that increased protectionism at home may lead to retaliation by foreign countries, threatening their sales. They cannot expect to widen their access to foreign markets if their own country is not prepared to reduce its protection. It is, however, quite difficult to translate these export interests into effective political action. The damage suffered through import restrictions is indirect; it has the characteristics of a foregone opportunity, which is difficult to quantify.

Among the firms opposing tariffs are the multinationals. They tend to favour free trade because they are able to compete efficiently on international markets. Also, protectionist tendencies may lead to restrictions in their own activities, in the extreme leading to the nationalization of their property in the foreign country in retaliation for protectionist actions in the home country.

Domestic firms using imported inputs for their production comprise another group interested in trade liberalization. Such firms, however, often belong at the same time to the import-competing sector, which has an interest in protection, so that their political position becomes equivocal or even pro-tariff.

Consumers and their organizations (as far as they exist) also have an interest in low tariffs. Trade barriers burden consumers, who find they have a smaller choice of products and have to pay higher prices for what's available. Consumer groups, however, have little effect on trade policy. One reason is that consumers are normally employees and workers. Their income is usually exclusively from this source while expenditures are distributed over many different goods, some of which are not (directly) affected by tariffs. As a consequence, it is individually rational for consumers to pay most attention to their position on the producer side, which often benefits from import protection. Another reason why consumers have little impact on trade policy is that the loss of consumer welfare through the imposition of tariffs is rather difficult to identify. It is hard to determine what the prices of the various products would be if tariffs were reduced or abolished, particularly when there is inflation, which easily overwhelms the small income effects. The 'invisibility' and indirectness of the opportunity cost of tariffs hardly motivates consumers to fight politically for tariff reductions. This lack of engagement only partially compensates the importers and distributors of foreign-produced consumption goods (such as retail chains, mail-order houses and discount firms) which have an obvious interest in a lessening of trade restrictions.

Whether the pro-tariff or the anti-tariff interests prevail in a country depends on the political weight of the corresponding groups, and the intensity with which they raise their demands in the political process. So we may conclude that protectionism has an absolute competitive advantage over a policy in favour of free trade.

The second difficulty that politicians confront is that the message about the advantages of free trade seems to be hard to get across to their voters, much harder than apparently simple but very wrong-headed notions about the so-called benefits of mercantilism. This is well illustrated by repeated instances of US politicians and the American public treating imports as a bad thing and exports as a good thing and as a result becoming periodically obsessed by US bilateral trade deficits, notably with Japan. In fact they are confusing a country with a private enterprise. Yes, for a company, the value of the outputs has to be bigger than the value of the inputs in order to stay in business, but the inputs of an enterprise cannot be compared with the imports of a country, and likewise outputs and exports. They are totally different notions.[21] Paul Krugman once said that *competitiveness* was, at best, a meaningless word when applied to national economies and, at worst, it encouraged protectionism. By and large, he was right, but, mercantilist trade policies can make for seductive political speeches.

Third, problems may arise with the regionalism of free trade agreements (FTAs) versus the emergence of world free trade: *While some claim to see regionalism and globalism as complementary, others see them as contradictory. These critics say that, belying their name, FTAs (the EU included) will make world trade less free.*[22] One of them is Jagdish Bhagwati, Professor of Economics at Columbia University and co-editor of this volume, who chides the Clinton administration for being...*infatuated with FTAs.* If he and his friends are right, this infatuation presents a real danger to global free trade. Only if:...*the WTO's member states (that is to say, the very governments who create FTAs) truly want to commit themselves to freeing trade multilaterally,*[23] may FTAs function as a step-up for a truly world free trade.

6.1. In the End, it is all about Idealism...

When one reads about all these threats to free trade, it is quite normal to start wondering how it has been possible for the principle and the practice of free trade to survive since World War II. That question cannot be answered by Public Choice theory, and it seems that even the protagonists of this theory are quite happy that it cannot. In an interview, James Buchanan stated that at the basis of his entire argument lay the hope that people and politicians will one day start to realize the dangers of short-sighted and greedy political behaviour, and will therefore change their behaviour and make Public Choice obsolete. For that to happen, we need pressure from lobbyists who benefit from free trade. But above all, we need the never-ending efforts of idealists, like Arthur Dunkel, who can convince the people and reluctant politicians in the world of international diplomacy, where eventually it all has to happen, of the advantages of free trade.

---

[21] The Economist, *Economics Focus*, June, 1996

[22] The Economist, *Regionalism and Trade*, 16 September 1995, pp 27-33

[23] ibid

Part IV: WTO and *New* Issues

Regionalism and the World View of Arthur Dunkel

Paul A. Volcker

Ten years ago, Arthur Dunkel greatly honored me by asking that I–a man mostly involved in money and finance–deliver a lecture[1] reflecting on the first 40 years of the GATT, the central official body for trade. He forced me to think about the inter-relationships and the directions in which we were moving. And it was a critical time.

GATT, looked at in perspective, surely could be pronounced a success. Tariffs had been reduced to a small fraction of their 1947 levels, and growth in trade helped stimulate the post-war economic expansion.

But in the 1980s there was also a perceptible loss of momentum in the drive for freer trade. Indeed, in some countries, including the United States, there was a sense of retreat, however grudging.

Fortunately, just a year earlier, in 1986, officials of the main trading countries meeting at Punta del Este had the courage to take the offensive. The agenda was set for the most ambitious set of multilateral negotiations aimed at liberalizing trade that the world had seen, negotiations that were to reach far beyond tariffs to other areas of trade in goods and services.

That agenda–with its vision of open trade and investment right around the world–came to define Arthur Dunkel's mission as Director-General of the GATT. No doubt, the so-called Uruguay Round took longer than even Arthur could have anticipated. The conclusion was reached only after his time in office. But there is no doubt that it was his sense of commitment, his persistence and his intellectual leadership that provided the basis for the final agreement. The agreement was crowned by the creation of the World Trade Organization (WTO), with an extended range of resources and responsibilities. The organizational triad perceived by the post World War II visionaries of three strong multilateral institutions for trade, for money, and for development was complete.

Far from yielding to protectionist pressures, the 1990s have turned out to be years of triumph for the ideal of open markets and liberalism. Trade, after slowing in the 1980s, has again been at the leading edge of economic growth, most especially among the emerging nations of Asia, Latin America, and Eastern Europe.

---

[1] *The GATT under Stress - Is There Life after 40?*: Address by Paul A. Volcker on theoccasion of the fortieth anniversary of the GATT. Geneva, November 30, 1987

But amidst all this progress, something else has been happening. In that GATT lecture a decade ago, I drew attention to two closely related areas of concern, both largely neglected in multilateral negotiations. One of those areas was the volatility of exchange rates. The other was the incentives and temptations to form regional trading areas. And one of those incentives was to build defenses against the disturbing impact of extreme exchange rate changes.

At the time, the European Community was the only important regional trading area in existence. But others were being discussed. Yet, little or nothing was done about reviewing or strengthening the GATT rules discouraging such inherently discriminatory agreements and minimizing their impact on the principle of most favored nation tariffs.

The European Common Market was not new and by the late 1980s was clearly a part of a larger intent to foster economic–and a significant degree of political–unity on the European continent. It had a natural monetary counterpart in monetary stability and a common currency, an objective now apparently on the way to fruition.

Europe could be, and always has been, considered something of a special case. With the glaring exception of the Common Agricultural Policy, its progress toward a European Union always fit comfortably within stated GATT rules for regional trading areas: i.e., that there would be no increase in external tariffs, and that the agreement would cover substantially all trade. Moreover, by implication if not by explicit language, there were clearly broader political objectives.

Now, Europe is not alone. What seemed ten years ago a temptation has become a reality. We can now count close to a dozen regional agreements in being, developing, or proposed. Most significant of all, given past attitudes and pride as the guardian of multilateralism, the United States has not just joined in the process, it seems to have advanced to the leading edge. Within the 1990s we have moved rapidly from the Canadian/American Free Trade agreement to the North American Free Trade Agreement (NAFTA), justified on the basis of geography, close existing trading relations, and political ties. Recently, there has seemed to be something of a consensus in Washington among those supporting freer trade about including far away Chile as a step toward Hemispheric arrangements. Regional free trade pledges have been made for all APEC (Asia-Pacific Economic Cooperation), and there is even talk about TAFTA, a Transatlantic Free Trade Agreement.

What is going on here? Have the concerns that I and others[2] had in mind been overblown? Should we relax and enjoy, as the Treasury Deputy Secretary Lawrence Summers puts it, any 'lateralism' - multi, regional, or even bi? Are we simply on a more practical road to global free trade?

The point can and has been made that there is a large difference between relatively closed preferential trading areas and regional agreements that really welcome and encourage extension, or that going much further would extend regionally negotiated reductions or elimination of trade barriers to all countries. Some have interpreted the Hemispheric or North Atlantic initiatives in that manner. But

---

[2] Perhaps most forcibly and persistently by Professor Jagdish Bhagwati of Columbia University, who is co-editing this volume.

I am skeptical of that approach. The idea of reciprocal bargains is well entrenched, and closed regional agreements gain political support precisely because they are, if not entirely closed, regional.

Those agreements, by their nature, discriminate. The basic principle of most favored nation, fundamental to the GATT-WTO, is violated. Conceptually the gains from free and open competition over the widest possible area are sacrificed. Smaller countries without economic or political clout and far from a major economic center are particularly at risk. Left out of new or existing blocs, and with natural markets obstructed, they are at a plain competitive disadvantage. But the concern is not just for relatively isolated and smaller countries. Ultimately, large regional arrangements carry the threat of dividing the world into three or four or five large trading blocs, with political as well as economic consequences.

It's worth recalling that in American post-war thinking, preferential agreements were not only economically discriminatory, they were remnants of a colonial and imperialistic frame of mind. As such, that particular concern may be anachronistic; the possibility that preferential arrangements might be associated with political rivalries as well as economic inefficiency is not.

The empirical question preoccupying economists is whether, in fact, the regional arrangements have led to a large diversion of trade. The evidence is pretty clear that trade within regional areas has been growing faster than trade with those outside. The dramatic collapse of trade within the Comecon bloc after the fall of the Iron Curtain is a dramatic reflection of the extent to which highly protectionist agreements divert trade at the expense of efficiency. But the agreements springing up recently have not been so rigid and insular. Trade generally–outside as well as within regions–has again been growing more rapidly than GNP. Moreover, regional trade seems to be growing faster even where there is no special stimulus of formal trade agreements. That is particularly true in Asia, presumably reflecting the rapid economic development of that part of the world.

All this strongly suggests we have not crossed some kind of economic Rubicon, reversing the progress toward freeing trade multilaterally that was the hallmark of Arthur Dunkel's work. Regional trade agreements have been relatively benign. In good part, however, that has been true precisely because of the simultaneous drive to reduce tariffs and other obstacles to trade on a multilateral basis. When tariffs are low and declining, the possibility of really dangerous trade diversion is limited.

The continuing challenge lies elsewhere, beyond the question of tariffs that have traditionally been at the center of the GATT's efforts to liberate trade. Protection more and more has taken the form of non-tariff barriers. Apart from quotas and other explicit restrictions, regional trade agreements give rise to complicated, controversial, and difficult to enforce *rules of origin*. Those rules are designed to prevent circumvention of national tariffs or other restrictions by, in effect, *laundering* an export from outside the region through a regional partner without equivalent or greater restraints. They are a by-product of FTAs, but hard to design, complicated in administration and potentially a tool of covert protectionism.

Politically, when regional trade arrangements include low income countries, they may also be used as justification for restricting imports from other low income, low cost developing countries outside the region. Health and security rationales for extra-regional restrictions may be reinforced. The acceptance of regional discrimination with respect to trade in goods can easily be extended to preferences for services and direct investment.

Significantly, regional currency arrangements, formalized or not, are a natural complement of FTAs and common markets. That is one consequence of the demonstrable lack of stability in market exchange rates in recent years. And the volatility of values among the principal currencies tends to reinforce the incentives for focusing trade on regional partners.

As a recent Report sponsored by the Carnegie Endowment states, all of this points to *both an important challenge and a unique opportunity.*[3]

Left to their own devices, and responding to internal political forces, regional trade agreements that seem relatively benign today may well drift into more restrictive approaches. In the world of monetary affairs, a certain drift toward definite currency areas is already present: formalized in Europe with ties to Africa; loose and informal in North America, but nonetheless real with tendencies to encompass some parts of South America; and, more speculatively, in Asia, with possible links to the Yen. Further developed, and tied to FTAs, the potential for competing hegemonic blocs would increase, with attendant risks for broader international cooperation.

At a more mundane level, the proliferation of partly overlapping trade agreements gives rise to confusion and complications that can be a breeding ground for conflicting and self-serving rulings and negotiations. Certainly, the authority and prestige of the new WTO, at the nominal center of the system and the specified instrument for dispute settlements, is challenged.

The fact is that it is precisely the WTO that must provide the leadership in maintaining the central thrust of a *multilateral* world system. And to do so, it must have the instinctive and consistent support of the leading trading nations, most of all the United States.

At this stage, it is too late to turn back the existing regional trade arrangements. Nor is that necessary so long as there is a framework of a strong multilateral agreement, updated at regular intervals. Indeed, some can and will argue that in such a context regional free trade and an effective multilateral system can be mutually self-supporting. The point, as I understand it, is that once regional barriers are eliminated, the further step to multilateralism will not seem so forbidding.

That approach nonetheless is bound to be politically and institutionally fragile, given the vested interests involved and the potential competing arbiters of disputes, regional and world-wide. If a constructive balance is to be maintained, then I think we have some homework to do. A good starting point is reconsidering the concerns and interests of the fathers of the Bretton Woods system of trade and finance. And surely there is room for modernization, advancing even beyond the objectives of the Uruguay Round.

The founders of GATT set out rules for customs unions and free trade agreements to minimize conflicts with the basic tenet of most favored nation. Those

---

[3] *Reflections on Regionalism for the WTO*: Report of the Carnegie Endowment Study Group, December 1996

strictures are sound in principle, but they are stated in general terms, subject to varied interpretations. They suffer the defect in practice of having been focused essentially on tariffs.

My sense is that experienced observers who have carefully considered this matter–including the three principal negotiators of NAFTA[4]–agree on some essential points.

- Greater attention must be directed to non-tariff barriers, and most especially rules of origin, so that they do not undercut the progress made in reducing tariffs.
- More emphasis should be placed on an extension of WTO rules to investment, to forestall discrimination in direct investment in particular and in the provision of financial and other services.
- Most important, clarification of the need for, and the authority of, the WTO itself to oversee the practical workings of the regional trade agreements and to insist upon consistency with its rules, existing and new.

I cannot conclude without a further thought, which I have elaborated at length elsewhere.[5]

Surely swings in exchange rates of the size we are experiencing among major currencies–ranging to and beyond 50 percent over a year or two–is destructive of stable and efficient trading patterns in accord with underlying trends in costs and efficiency. Among other things, the volatility encourages defensive investment–producing where you sell rather than where costs are lowest. Perceived overvaluations are a breeding ground for protectionism. As suggested above, one effect is to encourage regional trade and monetary arrangements in an effort to retain islands of stability, providing some sense of insulation from a turbulent financial world.

Exchange rate volatility, at least among the larger countries, has been accepted without much protest. That seems odd when so much negotiating energy and political capital is expended in attacking already low tariffs or other trade barriers of much less significance in terms of trade distortions. Happily, the large market fluctuations, or occasional accusations that depreciated exchange rates are being used as an economic weapon, have not provoked–not yet anyway–the mutual recrimination and economic retaliation characteristic of the 1930s. But surely we are far from the optimum arrangements.

The current financial crisis in Asia–partly provoked and complicated by the distortion in the dollar/yen exchange rate–only underscores these points. Quite understandably, one response will be to strengthen regional financial arrangements as a counterweight to turbulent world markets.

In sum, my sense is that the combined tendency toward trade and currency zones carries implicit dangers. Those interested in an open and efficient trading order need to make their voices heard in asserting the primacy of a multilateral view. Otherwise, the risk is simply too great that the hard work of Arthur Dunkel,

---

[4] Those negotiators - Jaime Serra Puche, Carla Hills and Michael Wilson - were also the primary instigators of the Carnegie Endowment Report cited above.

[5] See, for instance, *The Quest for Exchange Rate Stability: Realistic or Quixotic?*: Paul A. Volcker, Fiftieth Anniversary Stamp Lecture, London University, 1995

and all of those that have preceded and followed in promoting the ideals of trade and economic freedom, will be undercut and eroded away, not by conscious intent but by simple neglect of the need constantly to emphasize and reinforce the essential foundation of a liberal economic order.

The New Regionalism: a Benign or Malign Growth?

Arvind Panagariya and T. N. Srinivasan[1]

1. Introduction

The Most Favored Nation (MFN) provision of Article I of the General Agreement on Tariffs and Trade (GATT), signed in 1947 and subsumed under the agreement of 1994 establishing the World Trade Organization (WTO), requires that:

> *Any advantage, favour, privilege or immunity granted by any contracting party to any product originating in or destined for any other country shall be accorded immediately and unconditionally to the like product originating in or destined for the territories of all other contracting parties* (GATT 1994, p 486).

But the same agreement included several exceptions to MFN, most importantly with respect to preferential trade arrangements (PTAs) through its Article XXIV. This Article gave a legal status to Free Trade Areas (FTAs) and also Customs Unions (CUs) by allowing contracting parties to form such arrangements provided they eliminate, rather than just lower, trade barriers on *substantially all trade* among members and do not make protection against non-members on the whole higher or more restrictive.[2] Article V of the General Agreement on Trade in Services (GATS) signed in 1994 includes provisions that parallel those in Article XXIV.

Until 1965, Article XXIV offered the only provisions for new PTAs.[3] With the addition of Part IV in 1965 and the Enabling Clause in 1979, GATT permitted partial PTAs under two circumstances: developed countries were allowed to grant non-reciprocated and *partial* tariff preferences to developing countries, and two or more developing countries were given the right to conclude agreements extending *partial* trade preferences to each other. Under the former provision, the develop-

---

[1] We thank Jagdish Bhagwati for his penetrating and valuable comments on an earlier draft.

[2] The provisions of Article XXIV rule out partial PTAs.

[3] The existing arrangements involving partial preferences, principally those between former colonies and their colonial powers, were exempted from the general MFN provision within GATT Article I. See Srinivasan (1997a) for details.

ing countries have received very modest benefits from tariff preferences granted by developed countries through the Generalized System of Preferences (GSP).[4] Under the latter provision, developing countries have exchanged partial tariff preferences within arrangements such as the Association of South-East Asian Nations (ASEAN) preferential trading area, converted recently to ASEAN Free Trade Area, and the Southern Cone Common Market popularly known by its Spanish acronym MERCOSUR.[5] Not having been conceived as full-fledged FTAs or CUs at inception, these arrangements would not have been permitted under Article XXIV.

Prior to the early 1980s, PTAs existed within Western Europe, among developing countries and between developed and developing countries. Because the developing-country arrangements were largely ineffective and trade preferences by developed to developing countries limited, effective PTAs were confined to the two arrangements in Western Europe: the European Community (EC) and the European Free Trade Association (EFTA). The limited role for PTAs meant that the architects of the global trading system did not have to fear that regional arrangements might undermine the multilateral process of trade liberalization. Indeed, with the EC negotiating its common external tariffs as a single unit, the United States, which was strongly committed to the multilateral process, was successful in leading the world to reduce trade barriers through seven rounds of multilateral trade negotiations over three decades under the auspices of GATT.

All this changed however when, at the GATT Ministerial meeting in November 1982, the US began efforts to start the eighth round of multilateral trade negotiations. Unable to persuade the EC to go along, the US felt obliged to abandon its long-standing opposition to regional arrangements. Recognizing that PTAs were the only means left for keeping the process of trade liberalization afloat, the US opened negotiations with Canada and concluded the Canada-US Free Trade Agreement in 1989. Though the Uruguay Round was launched in 1986, by the mid-term review in 1988 its success seemed doubtful in part because the EC remained a reluctant player at the negotiating table. This contributed to the United States moving ahead with yet another PTA, this time jointly with Mexico and Canada.[6]

The Uruguay Round concluded successfully in 1994, thereby vindicating the multilateral process and blunting the original rationale for the US pursuit of PTAs. But the apparent success of bilateral negotiations and the preferential access they bring have changed the dynamics of the trade liberalization process. The US has decided to "walk on both legs." The view has gained ground that PTAs are almost

---

[4] It could be argued that by offering developing countries very modest tariff preferences on a few goods, developed countries were able to get away with heavy protection in goods such as textiles and apparel. The cost to developing countries of such protection was arguably much higher than the benefits received under GSP. Thus GSP benefits were no more than crumbs for the poor from the rich man's table.

[5] ASEAN stands for the Association of South-East Asian Nations. Though MERCOSUR now aims to be a full customs union and has progressed substantially towards that goal, all members being developing countries, the arrangement has been concluded under the Enabling Clause rather than Article XXIV.

[6] For a careful discussion of this point, see Bhagwati (1993a).

as good as multilateral liberalization and, at a minimum, an additional instrument of trade liberalization. Thus, at least for now, PTAs have become an integral part of US trade policy. Indeed, President Clinton recently sought, and failed to obtain, fast track authority from the US Congress to negotiate further PTAs with countries in South America.

The shift in US policy has led to a proliferation of regional arrangements around the world. In addition to a revival of PTAs among developing countries, the EEC–now known as the European Union (EU)–has gone on an aggressive campaign for PTAs. The EU, with a core membership of 15, has FTAs with virtually all major Central and Eastern European countries and even some North African countries. As a result, the WTO has been informed of more than 60 regional arrangements since 1985. It is reported by the WTO that virtually all its Members are signatories to one or more regional arrangements.[7]

Because PTAs are inherently discriminatory, their proliferation has led to legitimate fears that they may undermine the multilateral process of trade liberalization. The issue became a key subject of discussions in several WTO working parties which had been looking at the regional arrangements notified to WTO in recent years. In February 1996, recognizing the importance of the issue, the WTO appointed a Committee on Regional Trade Agreements (CRTA) to give coherence to these discussions. A key task of the CRTA is to examine in detail whether regional arrangements are compatible with multilateralism.

Though the Committee's work is still in progress, the Singapore Ministerial Declaration of December 1996 took note of the recent proliferation of PTAs, reaffirmed the primacy of the multilateral trading system and committed the Members to ensure that any proposed PTA is consistent with the rules of the WTO. The paragraph dealing with regional arrangements states:

> *We note that trade relations of WTO Members are being increasingly influenced by regional trade agreements, which have expanded vastly in number, scope and coverage. Such initiatives can promote further liberalization and may assist least-developed, developing and transition economies in integrating into the international trading system. In this context, we note the importance of existing regional arrangements involving developing and least-developed countries. The expansion and extent of regional trade agreements make it important to analyze whether the system of WTO rights and obligations as it relates to regional trade agreements needs to be further clarified. We reaffirm the primacy of the multilateral trading system, which includes a framework for the development of regional trade agreements, and we renew our commitment to ensure that regional trade agreements are complementary to it and consistent with its rules. In this regard, we welcome the establishment and endorse the work of the new Committee on Regional Trade Agreements. We shall continue to work through progressive liberalization in the WTO as we are committed in the WTO Agreement and Decisions adopted at Marrakesh, and in so doing fa-*

[7] Two exceptions are Japan and Hong Kong. The latter has, of course, ceased to exist as an independent country as of 1 July 1997.

> *cilitate mutually supportive processes of global and regional trade liberalization.* (WTO 1997, p 7)

Thus, the view taken by the Singapore Conference and, indeed, by the participating Ministers in their individual statements, is that regionalism is not necessarily incompatible with multilateralism. Given that virtually all Members have been pursuing regional arrangements, this fact should not be surprising.

In this paper, we will argue that economic theory as well as the available evidence do not justify the prevailing complacency towards the proliferation of PTAs. We will first point out key flaws of PTAs and then subject the prevailing concepts of *open* regionalism and *deep* integration to a critical examination. Many pro-free-trade economists, policy analysts and politicians have come to take the view that, in contrast to the regionalism of the 1950s and 1960s, contemporary regionalism is *open* and will strengthen, rather than weaken, the multilateral trading system. Likewise, some analysts have argued that *deep* integration makes PTAs desirable. We will argue otherwise.

2. Dangers of PTAs

As discussed systematically in Srinivasan (1997a), there has always been tension between the principle of non-discrimination which is the cornerstone of the GATT-WTO system, and PTAs, which are inherently discriminatory. With the proliferation of PTAs this tension has become a source of concern for several reasons.

2.1. Trade Diversion

By liberalizing trade among members preferentially, PTAs create new trade between members and divert trade from low-cost, non-member suppliers to high-cost, member suppliers.[8] For example, when Indonesia preferentially eliminates the tariff on Video Cassette Recorders (VCRs) imported from Singapore while maintaining the tariff on others, the reduced protection allows Singaporean suppliers to replace some of the less efficient Indonesian suppliers of VCRs. This change is trade creation and beneficial to the union and the world. Since the tariff reduction does not apply to Korean (and other) suppliers of VCRs, Korean suppliers are placed at a disadvantage vis-a-vis Singaporean suppliers and some of them are forced out of the Indonesian market even though they are more efficient than the latter. The VCRs that were supplied previously by these efficient Korean suppliers are now replaced by those from relatively less efficient Singaporean suppliers. This change is trade diversion and imposes a welfare cost on the PTA and the world as a whole.

---

[8] The analysis in this paragraph assumes increasing marginal costs of production in all countries.

Jacob Viner (1950) who first introduced the concepts of trade creation and trade diversion in his seminal analysis of CUs, considered trade diversion to be a serious problem and was skeptical of PTAs. However, Viner's skepticism has been replaced by indifference–indeed, cynicism–in recent years. Thus, Summers (1991), a passionate supporter of PTAs, dismissed trade diversion altogether with the comment, "I find it surprising that this issue is taken so seriously–in most other situations, economists laugh off second best considerations and focus on direct impacts."

A key argument used by Summers is that when PTA members are *natural trading partners*, i.e., they already trade a lot with each other and are in geographical proximity, the risk of trade diversion is minimal. Bhagwati (1993b), Panagariya (1996) and Bhagwati and Panagariya (1996) have offered detailed critiques of this view. Bhagwati and Panagariya (1996), in particular, show systematically that the *natural trading partners* hypothesis has no analytical basis. Among other things, they note that a large initial volume of trade says nothing about how a tariff preference will affect trade flows *at the margin,* which is what trade diversion is about. They also argue that the natural trading partnership is neither symmetric nor transitive. For example, the US, which is a neighbor of Mexico and with which it trades a lot, may be a natural trading partner of Mexico. But the reverse may not be true since trade with Mexico does not dominate the trade of the US. Similarly, the US may be a natural trading partner of both Mexico and Canada, but Mexico and Canada may not be natural trading partners.

In addition, weaker, uncompetitive industries in a country are more likely to make political contributions to enhance the probability of that country concluding PTAs with other countries in which producers, who would be their competitors in a PTA, are, like themselves, not the most efficient in the world. The reason is that if trade is to be liberalized multilaterally on a MFN basis with all trading partners, they will lose in competition with the most efficient foreign producers. This implies that costly trade diversion is most likely to dominate beneficial trade creation. This point is made forcefully in the recent theoretical contributions by Grossman and Helpman (1995) and Krishna (1995). Similarly, the careful empirical work by Kowalczyk and Davis (1996) on the tariff phase-out in NAFTA shows that the sectors that were allowed the longest phase-out periods in the US were the ones with the strongest import-competing lobbies.

More direct empirical evidence of trade diversion is also beginning to accumulate. A recent, widely publicized, World Bank study by Yeats (1996) provides systematic evidence of trade diversion in MERCOSUR.[9] Similarly, Wei and Frankel (1995, pp 23-27) find that the various stages of expansion of the European Community were accompanied by considerable trade diversion. Referring to the EC expansion during the 1980s, they note: *Overall, the evidence suggests massive*

---

[9] Richard Eckaus of M.I.T. and Robert Scott of the University of Maryland have found that even in the case of NAFTA, there has been substantial trade diversion in the textile industry. A recent report of the WTO is said to reflect "unease among WTO Members about the effects of NAFTA, for instance, rules relating to country of origin of goods, are seen as diverting trade towards NAFTA members and away from more efficient suppliers" (Financial Times, October 9, 1997, page 6)

trade diversion resulted from the membership expansion. (Wei and Frankel 1995, p 24) According to the key finding on which this conclusion is based: *Imports from non-member countries in 1990 were 30 per cent lower than in 1980, after controlling for economic growth.*[10] Thus, the possibility of trade diversion cannot be taken lightly.

2.2. Increased Tariffs on Non-member Countries

As argued originally by Bhagwati (1993b) and modeled formally by Bhagwati and Panagariya (1996) and Panagariya and Findlay (1996), another problem with PTAs is that they can lead to increased protection against non-member countries, turning even an initially trade-creating PTA into a trade-diverting one. In bad times, pressures for protection grow and when a PTA member is unable to raise trade barriers against a partner, the burden of increased trade barriers falls disproportionately on the outside world. This happened in Israel after it concluded FTAs with both the United States and EU, and later in Mexico which, in the aftermath of the Peso crisis, raised tariffs on non-members countries on 503 items from less than 20 per cent to 35 per cent.[11] The same phenomenon has also been observed recently in the Central African Customs and Economic Union (UDEAC) which introduced an across-the-board increase in tariffs on non-members to support trade preferences among member countries. Such increases are possible without invoking WTO censure since many countries either have not chosen to bind their tariffs in the WTO or their bound levels of tariffs are far higher than actually applied rates.

---

[10] It is important to note that even with trade diversion a member of a PTA can under certain circumstances gain welfare, and that, establishing trade creation and trade diversion empirically is a difficult task. As such, empirical studies have to be interpreted with caution. In the case of Yeats (1996), despite pitfalls of specific measures used, the overall evidence of trade diversion is compelling. Wei and Frankel (1996) employ the gravity equation which, despite many modifications by different authors, is likely to remain misspecified and, thus, open to criticism (e.g., see Polak 1996 and Smarzynska 1997).

[11] An argument made frequently by those favoring NAFTA is that compared to the increase in trade barriers in the wake of the macroeconomic crisis in Mexico in early 1980s, the recent tariff increases were minuscule. There are two problems with this argument. First, since the 1980s, there is better appreciation of the economic logic that balance-of-payments (BoP) crises are macroeconomic in origin and, hence, macroeconomic policy adjustment, and not trade policy instruments, should be used to address them. Thus, invoking the BoP provision of GATT/WTO for imposing trade restrictions is no longer accepted without question. As a result, even India, the last major bastion of protectionism, ended up liberalizing its trade regime after a BoP crisis even though it had no PTA with the United States or EU. Second, Mexico was given a massive US$40 billion debt-relief package to deal with the peso crisis of December 1994, which was not available during previous crises. If Mexico had shown a lack of commitment on its reforms, the fate of the package would have been in grave doubt.

Tariffs are, of course, not the only means of making the non-members countries pay for internal preferences. The burden can also be passed on through a more rigorous implementation of administered protection such as anti-dumping. Hindley and Messerlin (1993) found some evidence that internal liberalization in the EC was accompanied by vigorous anti-dumping against non-member countries.

2.3. The Spaghetti-Bowl Phenomenon

In FTAs as opposed to CUs, member countries fear trade deflection, i.e., imports from non-member countries destined to a high-tariff member may enter through a low-tariff member. Or more subtly, the low-tariff country may import a product in almost finished form, add a small amount of value to it and then export it to the high-tariff country duty free. To avoid trade deflection, FTAs usually include rules of origin according to which products receive duty-free status only if a pre-specified proportion of value-added in the product originates in member countries.

With the proliferation of crisscrossing FTAs, the non-discriminatory MFN tariff is being fast replaced by a spaghetti bowl whereby tariffs vary according to the ostensible origin of the product. Figure 1, adapted from Snape (1996) and taken from Bhagwati, Greenaway and Panagariya (forthcoming), depicts this spaghetti bowl for the European Union. Complicated as it looks, the figure actually understates the complexity of the trade regime that prevail among these countries. There are differing rules of origin for different FTAs and differing phase outs of tariffs on identical products in different FTAs (see Bhagwati 1997). As a result, a given product is subject to various tariff rates depending on the origin assigned to it and its stage of liberalization within the FTA.

Quite apart from the complexity of the regimes, the rules of origin themselves can be manipulated by lobbies to keep imports out. The NAFTA rules of origin took as many as 200 pages to codify. The view that the rules of origin were manipulated for protectionist reasons is supported by the fact that they were sought by the US, which had lower tariffs than Mexico for most products. This means that there was little incentive to import goods through Mexico for sale in the US. Trade deflection should have been Mexico's worry, not that of the US.

Overlapping FTAs lead to perverse incentives, opening additional sources of trade diversion. For example, once Chile, which already has an FTA with MERCOSUR, joins NAFTA, a Chilean firm will have to buy components in Brazil if it wants to take advantage of the preferential tariff in MERCOSUR, and in the US if it wants to exploit the preference in NAFTA, notwithstanding the fact that the most efficient supplier of the components may be located somewhere in Asia.

Figure 1: The European Spaghetti Bowl

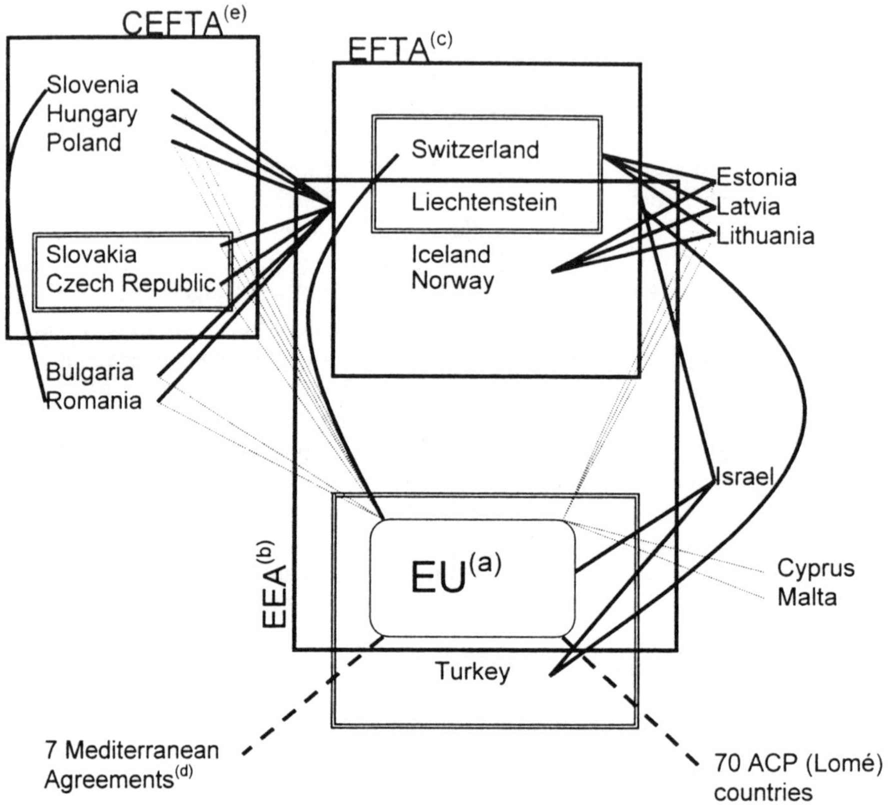

Figure 1 (continued)

NB: Does not include countries of the former Soviet Union other than Baltic countries.

(a) European Union comprises: Austria, Belgium, Denmark, Finland, France, Germany, Greece, Ireland, Italy, Luxembourg, Netherlands, Portugal, Spain, Sweden, and United Kingdom.

(b) European Economic Area

(c) European Free Trade Association

(d) Algeria, Egypt, Jordan, Lebanon, Morocco, Syria, Tunisia

(e) Central European Free Trade Agreement

EU Single Market

Customs Union

Free Trade Area

EU Association Agreements

Non-reciprocal agreements

Source: Adopted from Snape (1996)

2.4. WTO-Illegal Policies in PTAs

Finally, measures that clearly violate the provisions of the WTO are nonetheless practiced in PTAs. One such measure is the trade-balancing requirement within MERCOSUR, which is prohibited under the WTO agreement on Trade-Related Investment Measures (TRIMs). Thus, an Argentine company operating in Brazil must export as much Brazilian goods to Argentina as it imports from the latter. Another example of this kind relates to NAFTA. Mexico agreed to a voluntary export restraint (VER) of tomatoes to the US[12] even though VERs are prohibited under the WTO Agreement on Safeguards. While the use of such WTO-inconsistent measures does not seem to be widespread, and is yet to be challenged in the WTO, it is undoubtedly a problem deserving attention.

3. Is Open Regionalism an Antidote to Discriminatory PTAs?

Advocates of recent PTAs also defend them on the ground they represent *open* regionalism in contrast to the *import-substituting* PTAs among developing countries that proliferated during 1950s and 1960s. The Council of Economic Advisors to the US President under the chairmanship of Dr. Laura Tyson of the University of California, Berkeley, defined open regionalism and its consistency with GATT as follows:

> *Open regionalism refers to plurilateral agreements that are non-exclusive and open to new members to join. It requires first that plurilateral initiatives be fully consistent with Article XXIV of the GATT, which prohibits an increase in average external barriers. Beyond that, it requires that plurilateral agreements not constrain members from pursuing additional liberalization either with non-members on a reciprocal basis or unilaterally. Because member countries are able to choose their external tariffs unilaterally, open agreements are less likely to develop into competing bargaining blocs. Finally, open regionalism implies that plurilateral agreements both allow and encourage non-members to join.* (CEA 1995, p. 220)

They also assert that:

---

[12] This is also an example of a trade policy instrument being used for achieving a domestic political objective. Intense pressure was put on Mexico to agree not to sell their tomatoes in the US (with which it has a Free Trade Agreement) at a price lower than 20.68 cents a pound. David Sanger (New York Times, October 12, 1996) quotes a senior official of the Clinton Administration: *This was Mexico's moment to pay back for the bailout.* (p 1) presumably referring to the US decision to lend Mexico US$12.5 billion following the peso crisis of December 1994. He quotes another official as saying: *The math was pretty simple, Florida has 25 electoral votes, and Mexico doesn't.* (p 9)

Possibly the most distinctive legacy of this Administration in international trade is the foundation it has laid for the development of open, overlapping plurilateral trade agreements as stepping stones to global free trade. The Administration's plurilateral initiatives in North America, the rest of the Western Hemisphere, and Asia embody principles of openness and inclusion consistent with the GATT. (CEA 1995, pp 214-15)

The Eminent Persons' Group (EPG), appointed by the Asia Pacific Economic Cooperation forum (APEC) in their second report, defines open regionalism along the same lines (APEC 1994).[13] Before considering other possible definitions, let us examine closely the one adopted by the CEA and the EPG.

It should be noted that by its very definition any plurilateral free trade agreement provides preferential market access to members and, as such, violates the MFN principle. Even if, in the face of experience to the contrary, such agreements are declared to be in conformity with the updated GATT Article XXIV, any extension to others of any liberalization among parties to the agreement, except on an MFN basis, cannot possibly be viewed as other than conditional and preferential market access. It is available to only those non-members who are willing to meet whatever conditions (e.g., reciprocity) are attached to such an extension.

Although the EPG recommended *unilateral liberalization to the maximum extent possible* and recognized that any individual APEC member can unilaterally extend its APEC liberalization to non-APEC members on an unconditional MFN basis, it does not think that either is likely or even desirable. For example it points out that:

The largest members, including the United States, are unlikely to liberalize unilaterally when they can use the high value of access to their markets to obtain reciprocal liberalization from others. The same view applies in other economies in the region ... we would note ... that the region would give away an enormous amount of leverage ... if its members, especially its largest members, were to liberalize unilaterally to any significant degree.(APEC 1994, p 29)

The EPG candidly admits that:

We rejected the concept of unconditional MFN treatment of non-members as the sole means of implementing open regionalism for the economic and political reasons.... (APEC 1994, p 34)

The main reasons were the familiar *free rider* problem and the claim that it is rare that benefits of politically negotiated trade liberalization, multilateral or regional, have been extended to non-participants on a non-reciprocal basis.

---

[13] The Eminent Persons' Group no longer exists. Its chairman during its existence, Fred Bergsten (1997), has compared five possible definitions of 'open regionalism': (i) open membership, (ii) unconditional extension of regional preferences to non-members on an MFN basis, (iii) conditional extension only to those non-members who are willing to engage in reciprocal liberalization, (iv) simultaneous pursuit of multilateralism and regionalism in order to avoid creating new discrimination, (v) limiting regional liberalization only to those measures, such as trade facilitation, that do not require member countries to decide how to treat non-members. We discuss some of these definitions below.

The free rider argument and the demand for reciprocity reflect a mercantilist view of trade liberalization, namely, that a country's offer of liberalized access to its markets is a costly concession for which it has to be compensated by reciprocal liberalization by its trading partners. Except in cases where significantly adverse terms of trade effects are induced by liberalization (an unlikely event certainly for small countries, and most probably even for as large a grouping as APEC), this argument does not carry much weight. One would have thought that if indeed the goal of the EPG was globally free and open trade, far from bowing to political expediency it should have used its prestige to educate the political leaders of APEC that their fears about extending unconditional MFN to non-members are unwarranted.

It is unfortunate that the regional route to liberalization and a version of open regionalism have been embraced by Mr. Renato Ruggiero, the Director-General of the WTO. He recently suggested that:

> *The regional liberalizing impulse is not in itself cause for alarm among the upholders of the multilateral system. Regional initiatives can contribute significantly to the development of multilateral rules and commitments ... At the most basic level the real split is between liberalization, at whatever level, and protectionism. Viewed from this perspective regional and multilateral initiatives should be on the same side, mutually supportive and reinforcing.* (WTO 1996, p 10)

But he added:

> *However, the sheer size and ambition of recent regional initiatives means we can no longer take this complementarity for granted, if indeed we ever could. We need a clear statement of principles, backed up by firm commitments, to ensure that regional schemes do not act as a centrifugal force, pulling the multilateral system apart. The answer is to be found, I suggest, in the principle which some of the newer regional groupings have enunciated–'open regionalism.'* (WTO 1996, p 10)

Ruggiero contrasted two interpretations of open regionalism. The first essentially required that any regional preferential trade arrangement be consistent with Article XXIV of GATT 1994 and the understanding on its interpretation incorporated in the WTO agreements on Trade in Goods; the second that:

> *... the gradual elimination of internal barriers to trade within a regional grouping will be implemented at more or less the same rate and on the same timetable as the lowering of barriers towards non-members. This would mean that regional liberalization would in practice as well as in law be generally consistent with the m.f.n. principle.* (Ibid, p 11)

He concluded:

> *The choice between these alternatives is a critical one; they point to very different outcomes. In the first case, the point at which we would arrive in no more than 20 to 25 years would be a division of the trading world into two or three intercontinental preferential areas, each with its own rules and with free trade inside the area, but with external barriers still existing among the blocs.* (Ibid, p 11)

He clearly expressed his preference for the second, arguing, in sharp contrast to the CEA, that it:

> *...points towards the gradual* convergence *of regionalism and multilateralism on the basis of shared aims and principles, first and foremost respect of the m.f.n. principle. At the end, we would have one free global market with rules and disciplines internationally agreed and applied to all, with the capacity to invoke the respect of the rights and obligations to which all had freely subscribed. In such a world there could and must be a place for China, Russia and all the other candidates to the WTO.* (Ibid, p 11)

Notwithstanding the Director-General's preference for the second interpretation, it seems a bit odd to call it regionalism. After all, if regional liberalization is to be extended *on the same time table, in practice and in law,* to non-member countries on an MFN basis, it would be multilateral and not regional. If that is the case, there appears to be no particular advantage in initiating such liberalization on a regional basis in the first place.

It is evident that open regionalism as defined by the Council of Economic Advisors and the Eminent Persons' Group is not a particularly new and fruitful concept in the arena of trade liberalization. On the other hand, there appears to be nothing regional or preferential in the Director-General's preferred version of 'open regionalism'. Are there any potentially fruitful definitions?

As noted by many, a distinguishing feature of current regional arrangements is that they are taking place in an environment in which trade barriers have been brought down to low levels through eight rounds of multilateral trade negotiations. This suggests a possible definition of open regionalism as FTAs and customs unions with very low trade barriers against outside countries. While this definition distinguishes recent regionalism from earlier versions, it does not comprise discrimination: barriers against outsiders may be low but nonetheless discriminatory relative to insiders who face no barriers.

Let us suppose for a moment we accept the view that it is possible to discriminate, albeit with low barriers, and still be open. But what is the level of discrimination at which closed regionalism turns into open regionalism? When Mexico maintains a large number of external tariffs in the 15-20 per cent range, keeps open the option of raising them up to 35 per cent, and also has the instrument of anti-dumping at its disposal, can we say that it is pursuing open regionalism under NAFTA? Or should we adopt external trade barriers in the US as the critical level which distinguishes open from closed regionalism? This latter definition is also problematic: even after the Uruguay Round liberalization, more then half of textiles and clothing products will remain subject to 15-35 per cent tariffs in the US and anti-dumping will remain a major trade barrier. To put the matter differently, despite lower, though by no means low, external trade barriers today, the motivating force behind regional arrangements is no different than in the 1950s and 1960s. Now as then, discrimination is the name of the game as member countries continue to be driven by a desire to secure a *preferential* access to the partner country's market. This is clearly the impression conveyed, for example, in the recent report by the United States Trade Representative, Operation and Effect of NAFTA.[14]

Yet another dimension in which open regionalism is claimed to be distinctive is that regional agreements are open to any country wishing to join, presumably as long as it is willing to abide by the rules of the agreement. Almost by definition such arrangements, even those conforming to the requirements of GATT Article XXIV, have to discriminate against non-members for the agreement to have any meaning. In spite of this, it could still be argued that freedom of entry could be potentially substantive if it attracts many countries to join the existing FTAs. If that happens, the world will quickly converge on global free trade. But despite some of the rhetoric, membership in regional arrangements is hardly free. The admission price can include several unpleasant and essentially trade-unrelated side-payments such as acceptance of particular intellectual property regimes, investment rules, labour, environmental and product standards that could make membership onerous (Bhagwati 1995). Also, openness to membership need not necessarily mean automatic and speedy approval of applicants for membership. Mexico's entry into the Canada-US FTA, thus making it NAFTA, was neither quick nor easy. While APEC is not yet a PTA, its membership policy is nonetheless instructive.

> *At the Vancouver summit, APEC leaders decided to accept Russia, Peru and Vietnam as new members, but declared a 10-year moratorium on further entrants. The so-called 'consolidation period' thus forced eight other economies that had applied for membership to be shut out of APEC for a decade. The eight applicants are Columbia, Ecuador, India, Macao, Mongolia, Pakistan, Panama and Sri Lanka.* (BERNAMA, The Malaysian National News Agency, January 17, 1998).

For completeness, we must note that Asian regionalism has been *open* in the sense that liberalization undertaken by members of Asian regional groups has been nondiscriminatory. Specifically, APEC has created no trade preferences and, similarly, despite having signed the ASEAN Free Trade Area (AFTA) agreement, which is in principle a preferential trading arrangement, its members have so far undertaken much of their liberalization on a nondiscriminatory basis. While we approve of this Asian approach and, indeed, recommend its adoption in other parts of the world, to call it *open regionalism* is to confuse the issue. Being fully compatible with the MFN principle of GATT, recent liberalizations by Indonesia or the Philippines, even though ostensibly undertaken to achieve the goals of AFTA, are not only non-discriminatory but also essentially unilateral. The fact that both are members of ASEAN did not play a role.

[14] As discussed in Panagariya (1997), the United States certainly sees APEC as means of gaining increased market access for US goods and has refused to give tariff or other trade concessions under the APEC auspices except on a discriminatory basis.

4. Regionalism and *Deep* Integration

It is sometimes argued that contemporary PTAs and Regional Trade Agreements (RTAs) go beyond *shallow* integration in terms of liberalization of trade among members, and involve *deep* integration such as coordination, if not complete harmonization, of other policies including competition policies, regulatory regimes, investment codes, environmental policies, labour standards and so on. Contrasting deep with shallow integration almost invites one to think of the contrast between deep and shallow analysis in favour of the former! But deep integration is not necessarily good. As is well known, there are no good reasons of economic efficiency or fairness of process for harmonizing labour and environmental standards across trading nations (Bhagwati 1996, Klevorick 1996, Wilson 1996). Even if coordination or harmonization of some non-trade-related policies are desirable, such coordination could be pursued without having to engage in preferential trade. Besides, to the extent that other policies are trade-related, their harmonization as part of a PTA could exacerbate its trade-diversionary impact.

It is one thing to suggest that reform of domestic policies relating to the financial sector, non-traded infrastructure, and so on would be needed if full benefits of integration with the global economy are to be reaped. It is an entirely different thing to argue that such reforms are more likely to be undertaken and credible if the reforming country is a member of a PTA. This so-called *locking-in* of reforms through a PTA has been cited as a reason why Mexico did not raise its tariffs or go back on other domestic reforms when a peso crisis hit in December 1994. This reasoning is not persuasive since Mexico in fact raised its tariffs on imports from non-NAFTA countries. More importantly, the credibility of reforms, and hence the lock-in, would be far more effective if they are undertaken as part of a unilateral external sector liberalization with respect to all trading partners on a MFN basis. Credibility of such MFN tariff reductions would be enhanced if the reduced levels are bound in the WTO. Liberalization on a MFN basis would almost surely be more beneficial than partial and preferential liberalization within a PTA.

5. Resolving the Incompatibility between PTAs and the WTO

Because the enthusiasm for regional arrangements is unfortunately still strong, it is important to ask whether we can minimize the adverse effects of PTAs and if so how. First and foremost, we can consider placing a moratorium on the expansion of PTAs beyond those already in an advanced stage of negotiation, particularly the big FTAs such as the Transatlantic Free Trade Area (TAFTA) and APEC. At the same time, we should move speedily to bring the unfinished agenda of multilateral trade liberalization to a successful conclusion. Such a move will not only promote the cause of multilateral liberalization directly, it will also do so indirectly by neutralizing the impact of trade preferences within PTAs. At the limit, if all external barriers drop to zero, PTAs will be effectively eliminated.[15]

Second, given the demonstrated failure (Srinivasan 1997a) of the working party mechanism for examining the consistency of any proposed PTAs with Article XXIV,[16] another approach is to modify or replace Article XXIV by a better alternative that is precise, transparent and predictable in its application. For example, at a minimum each FTA member could be required to bind tariffs at the actual or applied levels prevailing at the time of negotiating the FTA. This would ensure that tariff protection against non-members was not raised in the future. Had such a provision been in effect, Israel and Mexico would not have been able to raise their external tariffs following FTAs with the US.

Third, as Bhagwati (1991) suggested, any proposed CU could be approved only when its common external tariff is set at the minimum of the pre-union import tariffs of the member countries. One implication of this is that the CU will engage in free trade with *all* non-members, if at least one member had a zero pre-union tariff for each of the traded commodities! Leaving aside this unlikely occurrence, the Bhagwati proposal could *lower* welfare of some members of the CU and *raise* that of non-members (Srinivasan 1997b). Since such a possibility could deter the formation of a customs union, the Bhagwati proposal may still be treated as a desirable reform which in effect could act as a deterrent for WTO Members who wish to enter a customs union and thus compromise the MFN principle.

Fourth, instead of focusing on tariffs, McMillan (1993) suggests that:

> *A proposed RIA [Regional Integration Agreement], in order to get GATT's imprimatur, would have to promise not to introduce policies that result in external trade volumes being lowered. And, if after some years the RIA is seen to have reduced its imports from the rest of the world, it would be required to adjust its trade restrictions so as to reverse their fall in imports.* (p 300)

Measuring trade volumes is certainly more workable. But changes in *aggregate* volumes of trade with non-members need not necessarily indicate changes in global welfare. Besides, by substituting *outcome* variables (viz. trade volumes) for *instrument* variables (viz. tariff rates) when in fact outcomes are impossible to predict with any accuracy, the McMillan proposal runs into problems similar to those afflicting the malodorous *managed-trade* approach.

Fifth, to contain the spaghetti-bowl phenomenon, one could require that there be no rule of origin on a product in a member country with the lowest tariff in the

---

[15] This point was made in a recent letter signed by a number of economists around the world and published in *Financial Times*, June 25, 1996.

[16] In all, 98 agreements were notified under Article XXIV during the life of GATT from 1947 to the end of 1994, including the most enduring of all, namely the European Communities (EC) and the European Free Trade Association (EFTA). A further 11 agreements were notified by developing countries under the 1979 Enabling Clause. Working parties were established to examine virtually all agreements. While 15 working parties had not completed their examinations as of the end of 1994 and five had failed to report for various reasons, out of the 69 that had submitted their reports, only six explicitly acknowledged conformity with GATT Article XXIV, and those did not include the EC or EFTA, and only two of the six are still active! (WTO 1995, p 16).

union on that product. Such a requirement would have eliminated the need for rules of origin in the US in a large majority of products. We could also require that whenever the difference between the highest and lowest external tariff rates in the union is less than a pre-specified limit, say, 5 per cent, no rules of origin are permitted.[17] With multilateral liberalization moving ahead, this requirement could help kill the rules of origin on many products in many FTAs faster than otherwise.

An advantage of the proposals on binding the external tariff and then bringing it down to the levels of the preferential tariff is that it will help arrest the proliferation of trade-diverting PTAs. For in that case only the countries truly interested in eventual multilateral free trade will muster the courage to enter into FTAs.

Sixth, administrative protection through aggressive use of anti-dumping and safeguard measures have emerged as means of offsetting some of the liberalization achieved in the Uruguay Round. The provisions of Article XXIV with respect to protection against non-members do not cover administrative protection. As such, a PTA could be in compliance with it as far as other measures of protection against non-members are concerned, while at the same time raising the bite of administrative protection against them. Greater discipline in the use of administered protection and elimination of asymmetry in anti-dumping procedures against non-members vis-a-vis members would therefore be helpful.

Seventh, there is the set of rather complex proposals by Serra et al (1997), which comprises some of the proposals discussed earlier and goes further by recommending the harmonization of trade rules such as anti-dumping among members of a regional PTA; a requirement that the design and accession conditions of PTAs not have the effect of preventing other countries from becoming members; development of rules to ensure that PTAs have investment provisions or treaties that deflect investment, and so on.

All the alternatives discussed earlier start from the presumption that PTAs are not only here, but should also be allowed to stay forever provided they are in conformity with some form of an amended Article XXIV. A far better alternative is to ensure that PTAs have only a temporary existence. One such alternative is to retain the notification requirements of Article XXIV and lay down a precise time limit (say five years) by which, first, *all* preferences (tariff and non-tariff) within existing or proposed PTAs must be extended to all WTO Members on an MFN basis. Second, in the case of customs unions, if the common external tariff structure results in an increase in tariff relative to what prevailed in any country prior to its becoming a member, such increases are to be rescinded within the same period. Third, in the case of FTAs *any increase* in the applied external tariffs of a member following its formation, even if it is within its previously bound levels, is to be rescinded within the same period. Any disputes relating to the observance of these conditions would be dealt with under the rules and procedures governing the settlement of disputes in the WTO.

This alternative restores non-discrimination within a given time limit and avoids having to examine whether PTAs meet specified conditions for a perma-

[17] See Wonnacott (1996) for proposals along these lines.

nent waiver from MFN.[18] Also, it recognizes the fact that PTAs, such as the EU, are often formed, and certainly sustained, primarily for fundamental geo-political reasons. Indeed, the original purpose of the formation of the European Coal and Steel Community and later the European Economic Community was to reduce the prospects of yet another European war. By leaving the customs union intact, while eliminating within a reasonable time whatever initial trade preferences it contained, this alternative accommodates the political fundamentals while minimizing collateral economic damage.

Bibliography

Asia-Pacific Economic Cooperation (1994), *Achieving the APEC Vision.* Second report of the Eminent Persons Group, APEC. Singapore

Bergsten CF (1997), *Open Regionalism.* The World Economy, Vol 20, October, pp 545-565

Bhagwati J (1991), *The World Trading System at Risk.* Princeton University Press: Princeton NJ

Bhagwati J (1993a), *Beyond NAFTA: Clinton's Trading Choices.* Foreign Policy, Summer, pp 155-62

Bhagwati J (1993b), *Regionalism and Multilateralism: An Overview.* In: Melo and Panagariya (eds). New Dimensions in Regional Integration. Cambridge University Press: Cambridge, Great Britain

Bhagwati J (1995), *US Trade Policy: The Infatuation with Free Trade Areas.* In: Bhagwati J and Krueger AO (eds). The Dangerous Drift to Preferential Trade Agreements. American Enterprise Institute for Public Policy Research. Washington DC

Bhagwati J (1996), *Introduction* and *The Demands to Reduce Domestic Diversity Among Trading Nations.* In: Bhagwati J and Hudec R (eds). Fair Trade and Harmonization. MIT Press: Cambridge MA, pp 1-40

Bhagwati J (1997), *Fast Track to Nowhere.* The Economist, October 18, pp 21-23

Bhagwati J and Panagariya A (1996), *Preferential Trading Areas and Multilateralism: Strangers, Friends or Foes?* In: Bhagwati J and Panagariya A (eds). The Economics of Preferential Trade Agreements. AEI Press: Washington, D.C.

Bhagwati J, Greenaway D and Panagariya (forthcoming), A *Trading Preferentially: Theory and Policy* Economic Journal.

CEA (1995), *Economic Report of the President 1995.* Council of Economic Advisors: Washington DC

GATT (1994), *The Results of the Uruguay Round of Multilateral Trade Negotiations–The Legal Texts.* GATT Secretariat: Geneva

Grossman G and Helpman E (1995), *The Politics of Free Trade Agreements.* American Economic Review, September, pp 667-690

Hindley B and Messerlin P (1993) *Guarantees of Market Access and Regionalism.* In: Anderson K and Blackhurst R (eds). Regional Integration and the Global Trading System. Harvester Wheatsheaf: London.

---

[18] This alternative is a modification of the proposal put forward by Panagariya (1994) that in pursuing regional trade liberalization the countries in East Asia should proceed in a non-discriminatory manner. He suggested that the countries could negotiate reductions in trade barriers regionally and implement them on a non-discriminatory basis.

Klevorick A (1996), *Reflections on the Race to the Bottom.* In: Bhagwati J and Hudec R (eds). Fair Trade and Harmonization. MIT Press: Cambridge MA. pp 459-467

Kowalczyk C and Davis D (1996), *Tariff Phase Outs: Theory and Evidence from GATT and NAFTA.* In: Frankel J (forthcoming). Regionalization of the World Economy. University of Chicago Press: Chicago

Krishna P, *Regionalism and Multilateralism: A Political Economy Approach.* Economics Department, Columbia University, December 1995, mimeo.

Krugman P (1991), *The Move to Free Trade Zones.* Policy Implications of Trade and Currency Zones. Symposium Sponsored by the Federal Reserve Bank of Kansas City

McMillan J (1993), *Does Regional Integration Foster Open Trade? Economic Theory and GATT's Article XXIV.* In: Regional Integration and the Global Trading System, Anderson K and Blackhurst R (eds). Harvester Wheatsheaf: London

Panagariya A (1994), *East Asia and the New Regionalism.* The World Economy 17, No 6, November, pp 817-839

Panagariya A (1996), *The Free Trade Area of the Americas: Good for Latin America?* The World Economy 19, No 5, September, pp 485-515

Panagariya A (1997), *APEC and the United States.* In: Woodland A and Pigott J (eds) International Trade Policy and the Pacific Rim. Macmillan Press: London, (forthcoming)

Panagariya A and Findlay R (1996), *A Political Economy Analysis of Free Trade Areas and Customs Unions.* Feenstra R, Irwin D and Grossman G (eds). The Political Economy of Trade Reform. Essays in Honor of Jagdish Bhagwati. MIT Press: Cambridge Mass

Polak JJ (1996), *Is APEC a Natural Regional Trading Bloc?* The World Economy 19, No 3, September

Serra J, Aguilar G, Córdoba J, Grossman G, Hills C, Jackson J, Katz J, Noyola P and Wilson M (1997), *Reflections on Regionalism: Report of the Study Group on International Trade.* Carnegie Endowment for International Peace. Washington DC

Smarzynska B (1997), *Gravity Model of International Trade Reconsidered.* Yale University, processed

Snape R (1996), *Trade Discrimination–Yesterday's Problem?* Economic Record 72(219), December, pp 381-396

Srinivasan TN (1995), *APEC and Open Regionalism.* Yale University, processed

Srinivasan TN (1997a), *Regionalism and the World Trade Organization: Is Non-Discrimination Passé?* In : Krueger AO (ed), The World Trade Organization as an International Institution. The University of Chicago Press

Srinivasan TN (1997b), *The Common External Tariff of a Customs Union: Alternative Approaches.* Japan and the World Economy, 281, pp 1-19

Summers L (1991), *Regionalism and the World Trading System.* Policy Implications of Trade and Currency Zones. Symposium Sponsored by the Federal Reserve Bank of Kansas City

Viner J (1950), *The Customs Union Issue.* Carnegie Endowment for International Peace. New York

Wei S-J and Frankel J (1995), *Open Regionalism in a World of Continental Trade Blocs.* Presented at the American Economic Association meetings, January 3-6, 1997 at a joint AEA-Korea-American Economic Association session.

Wilson JD (1996), *Capital Mobility and Environmental Standards: Is There a Theoretical Basis for a Race to the Bottom?* In: Bhagwati J and Hudec R (eds). Fair Trade and Harmonization. MIT Press: Cambridge MA, pp 393-427

Winters LA (1996), *Regionalism versus Multilateralism*. Policy Research Working Paper No 1687. World Bank, Washington DC

Wonnacott P (1996), *Beyond NAFTA–The Design of the Free Trade Agreement of the Americas*. In: Bhagwati J and Panagariya J (eds). The Economics of Preferential Trade Agreements. AEI Press: Washington DC

World Trade Organization (1995), *Regionalism and the World Trading System*. WTO, Geneva

World Trade Organization (1996), *The Road Ahead: International Trade Policy in the Era of the WTO*. Fourth Annual Sylvia Ostry Lecture, Ottawa, 28 May 1996. WTO Press/49, Geneva, 29 May 1996

World Trade Organization (1997), *Focus Newsletter*, No 15, WTO, Geneva.

Yeats AJ (1996), *Does Mercosur's Trade Performance Justify Concerns About the Effects of Regional Trade Arrangements? Yes!* World Bank, Washington DC, mimeo.

Trade Linkage and Human Rights

Jagdish Bhagwati

1. Introduction

Arthur Dunkel is widely, and properly, given virtually the entire credit for the success of the Uruguay Round since he nursed it through thick and thin. Without him, his successor Peter Sutherland would not have had the broad shoulders to stand on and grasp the prize soon after Dunkel's retirement from a most distinguished and defining term as Director-General of the General Agreement on Tariffs and Trade (GATT).

The Uruguay Round has now closed. And, as Lester Thurow pronounced with fanfare in Davos in 1989, *GATT is dead.* But it has died, not for his profoundly wrong reasons, but for Dunkel's profoundly right ones: it has been transformed, reborn, as the new and invigorated World Trade Organization (WTO). The important questions that arise now relate principally to the *new issues*, in particular, the linkage of trade with human rights; environmental and labour standards; competition policy; and how WTO obligations interface with national sovereignty.

I propose therefore to address here, so as to clarify an increasingly confused and confusing debate, the key question: should trade liberalisation or market access be linked to human rights, labour standards, environmental behaviour, and a host of 'social' issues? This problem has acquired great salience recently in several contexts.

2. Trade Linkage in New Contexts

Trade with China has received the greatest attention. The renewal of most favoured nation status (MFN) has traditionally attracted flak; now the economic and human-rights preconditions of China's entry to the WTO have also become a bone of contention on the domestic US scene.

But the December 1996 Ministerial meeting of the WTO in Singapore was also marked by a sustained effort by the Clinton administration, allied principally with France and Norway, to insert a Social Clause into the WTO. Such a Clause would specify selected labour standards, like the non-use of child labour, as preconditions for gaining access to markets of WTO Members.

Similarly, regarding the administration's failed request for fast track authority to negotiate future trade agreements, Congressman Gephardt had written to his fellow Democrats in the house that no such authority should be granted unless agreements in regard to environmental and labour standards were built directly into the trade treaties, as distinct from the 'side agreements' written into the NAFTA treaty. Besides, the position of Democrats generally was to stiffen these agreements whereas Republicans wanted to weaken, even delete, them altogether in future trade agreements. It is accurate to say that, in consequence, the administration failed partly because it could not resolve the linkage issue on the political scene.

3. Distinguishing between Linkage Issues

Evidently, if we are to analyse these demands and the appropriate way to deal with them we need to distinguish among them conceptually. For, similar as they are at first blush, and discussed in the media and in the US Congress as if they were identical, they are in fact not so. The main distinction we must draw is between (a) the use of generalised trade sanction against offending countries and (b) the use of tactics such as suspension or denial of market access against specific products that offend a particular human right or standard such as the non-use of prison labour or of sweatshop workers in the manufacture of the product.

- *Generalised Trade Sanctions*: The UN-sanctioned embargoes against South Africa on apartheid or against Ian Smith's Unilateral Declaration of Independence in Southern Rhodesia qualify as generalised trade sanctions against a country whose human rights violations are widely deemed beyond the pale. The suspension or denial of MFN status to the Soviet Union over emigration rights or to China over its denial of multiple human rights to its citizens is another, admittedly less fierce, generalised sanction.
- *Preconditions for Trade in Specific Products*: Conversely, the NAFTA supplemental agreements on labour and environmental standards essentially provide for procedures to eventually fine and even suspend market access rights of firms or products that use proscribed standards or practices. Such agreements generally are not product-specific in content but are applied to specific offending products in practice. This applies also to the proposed social clause at the WTO: it would proscribe practices while a dispute settlement process would evidently apply in general to complaints about trade in specific products produced with the proscribed methods.

These two types of trade linkages to rights, standards and social issues are obviously different in character. They also raise somewhat different questions as to both efficacy and desirability. But, I shall argue here, the case for both is extremely weak, the latter even flawed.

4. Trade Sanctions

When we apply trade sanctions, we may not be deterred by the fact that they may not hurt enough so as to have a corrective, beneficial effect on the offending behaviour of the sanctioned country. In fact, we may even be willing to suffer economic harm ourselves while gaining no results. Thus, a moral absolutist may simply forego supping with the Devil even though the result is that she misses a free meal and the Devil does not shed his horns. There is little doubt that some of the human rights critics of China today, who would suspend China's MFN status and block its entry into the WTO, are in this moral camp. The American journalist Abe Rosenthal's columns in *The New York Times*, bursting with moral indignation at China's human rights violations and our economic engagement nonetheless with her, are certainly in this vein.

But few of us are entirely moral absolutists. Instead, most of us are consequentialists: we seek sanctions so that we get results. Here, there are two questions that an economist must raise: (a) are sanctions going to work; and (b) are there other methods that would work better (in the sense that the cost-benefit ratio is more favourable to us)?

- *Efficacy of Sanctions*: Clearly, anyone who claims that trade sanctions cannot work is wrong: the embargo on South Africa, for instance, is generally agreed to have been successful. What we must remember, however, are a few guiding principles which, if ignored, are likely to guarantee failure. A multilateral embargo, even a widely plurilateral one that includes the principal trading partners of the sanctioned country, is preferable to a unilateral one. It both reduces the likelihood of significant leakage and increases the psychological leverage. Even then, of course, defections are often observed and require extensive monitoring (which can be difficult) and penalties for defection (which can be hard to enforce). The efficacy of the embargo is greater if the target is a small country without leverage (such as Cuba after the collapse of the Soviet bloc and the ruination of the Russian economy) than if it is a large country with huge economic and political leverage (such as China today). It is a lot harder to maintain an embargo when the targeted country can exercise economic and political options to encourage defections: either within countries as when China can drive a wedge between our business and our human-rights groups or between countries as when it can play off the Europeans and the Japanese against the United States. The embargo will work better, therefore, when we target a country for practices that attract widespread condemnation, as with apartheid, as distinct from practices that are culturally specific to limited numbers of nations.[1]

- *Greater Efficiency of Alternative Policies*: But trade sanctions that can conform to these criteria and therefore have the prospect of being even moderately effective are likely to be a very small set indeed. In practice, we must therefore ask: are there not other ways in which we can prod or punish offending countries into changing their behaviour? Indeed, it is a question that must be confronted even when the trade sanctions might be considered to be an effective policy tool: for, the cost to us in terms of trade disruption and the gain in terms of effectiveness must also be evaluated and compared with those attending other ways of influencing the target country. A cost-benefit analysis is as appropriate here as in other areas of public policy.

In the modern world, with the phenomenal recent growth of civil society and of its institutions such as NGOs and media such as the CNN, our ability to zero in on morally offensive practices anywhere has grown hugely. Embarrassment, if not shame and even guilt, follow. Indeed, governments cannot escape scrutiny and the accusing finger from a variety of such quarters in the public domain.

Even international institutions such as the International Committee on Human Rights, the apex body that has its mandate under the international convention on civil and political rights which defines the basic human-rights law agreed upon by signatory states at the United Nations, become focal points at which these states must confront the consequences of their human-rights policies under procedures that, subject to certain conditions, grant standing to individuals against their governments. These international institutions, besides, carry greater weight because they spare no nation, looking symmetrically at all (unlike national governments that often look at others while turning a blind eye to their own warts, a classic example being the annual, official US evaluation of human rights that does not look at non-compliance within the US itself). This impartiality also lends credibility, hence clout, to well known NGOs such as Human Rights Watch and Amnesty International: they report on police brutality in India only to follow up with an exposé of police brutality in New York.

The effectiveness of these institutions in prompting the desired changes cannot be overestimated. Instances abound, crowding our newspapers almost daily. A recent example is the influence exercised by American women's groups on the all-male hiring practice of the Vienna Philharmonic Orchestra by threatening to boycott their imminent US concert tour. Faced with humiliation, if not the threat to the pocketbook, the orchestra caved in and hired a female member, thus changing a dishonourable, time-honoured tradition. By contrast, governmental actions including embargoes are likely to have been less compelling. The US government, for instance, could not have effec-

[1] Thus, the preservation of an endangered species such as the tiger is more likely to attract widespread condemnation than the elimination of dolphin-unsafe tuna fishing, which reflects concern for dolphins that is not grounded in a wider moral principle but reflects simply the fact that many Americans find dolphins cute.

tively levelled the charge of sexism at Austria while its own society is not free from it: NGOs in the US could effectively do so, however, and carry conviction because they equally target domestic sexism.

I would therefore argue that the better, if not the best, way to advance the agenda of human rights is to ask our governments to support NGOs at home and abroad working to advance the rights whose violation we deplore, with the government putting its money where its mouth is. And the vocal cords should indeed be exercised energetically in the existing international human rights groups.

Such a strategy could well find business groups allied in the effort, as contrasted with the case where trade sanctions are used and, because they endanger profits directly, business groups promptly tend to break ranks on human rights issues. The popular concern that détente and engagement change us rather than the offending countries, paralysing us into silence rather than prodding others into observance of human rights, derives wholly from the attempts to use trade sanctions as our weapons. By contrast, détente and engagement will yield results, perhaps slowly but surely, if we use them pro-actively, as I have argued, in the institutions of the new civil society to embarrass, shame and reform. Engagement then brings into the international arena, and hence into continual confrontation with the consequences of their violations, the nations that otherwise can be shielded by their isolation from this powerful process.

5. Setting Preconditions for Trade in Specific Products

The typical demands for fulfilment of particular labour (and often also environmental) standards, failing which market access would be denied or suspended to products utilising the proscribed processes, are of a different character altogether. For instance, they reflect not just moral objectives but a larger dose of *competitiveness* concerns. They are also generally more popular in the US and in some European nations; but they are ill advised nonetheless.

These demands do not only come in the shape of the insertion of a *social clause* into the *multilateral* WTO, the incorporation of agreements on labour and environmental standards into extension of the *plurilateral and preferential* NAFTA to new countries, such as Chile, and the attachment of like strings to the renewal of fast track trade negotiating authority, but also in the shape of calls for *unilateral* enactment of legislation. This is particularly true of the *blue and green protectionism* bill proposed in 1994 by US Congressman Richard Gephardt – blue refers to blue-collar workers and hence to labour standards, and green of course to environmental standards – and of the US journalist Robert Kuttner's occasional demand for congressional approval of a *social tariff* on US imports in the form of countervailing duties to offset the *social dumping* by countries with lower standards.

The principal reasons why these demands are unwise are that (a) they can be regarded, with some credibility, as protectionist in design, even though not necessarily in intent; and (b) a more effective way to pursue such agendas is again not through linkage in trade treaties and institutions such as the WTO but through other non-trade agreements and institutions such as the International Labour Office (ILO) and UNICEF. In addition, there is much to be said for the view that freeing trade is about removing obstacles to trade whereas the demand for linkage is about putting up roadblocks to free trade instead: it is odd and ironic as well as intellectually incoherent, therefore, to introduce linkage into trade treaties and institutions.

5.1. Protectionist Design

The groups that seek such trade linkage are typically either those who fear international competition from countries with *lower* standards or those who want *higher* standards because they genuinely feel a transborder moral obligation to extend such standards to people abroad.[2] It is useful to distinguish the two groups by their primary concern although it is possible for both objectives to be shared by an individual or a group and even though the public pronouncements of groups motivated by different concerns do progressively overlap as they ally with each other in their demands. Thus, if one scrutinises the proponents of the social clause and of labour standards preconditions in regional trade agreements, the labour unions that are most vociferous include those in textiles, an industry exposed to fierce international competition from poor countries. At the same time, although human-rights groups focus on rights, not on competition, the language in which many US Congressmen couch their support for such measures typically betrays a concern for *fair trade* and *unfair competition*, even if some of them speak of transnational moral concerns.

The Princeton economist Alan Krueger has suggested – based on statistical analysis of the constituency characteristics of Congressmen who sponsored the recently proposed Child Deterrence Act – that constituencies with a greater share of workers in his view more likely to suffer from foreign competition were not more likely to have sponsors. But this analysis basically ignores the central fact that, with grossly misleading and persistent propagation of the view that all child labour is automatically exploitative in the same sense as when children work in bondage and under hazardous conditions,

---

[2] These are not the only two motives that matter; but they are the principal ones of relevance to the policy questions discussed here. I have dealt with the question more fully in *Demands to Reduce Domestic Diversity among Trading Nations* in Bhagwati J and Hudec R (eds) (1996), *Fair Trade and Harmonization: Prerequisites for Free Trade?* MIT Press: Cambridge Mass., Chapter 1. Also see some of my writings on this subject in the media, reprinted in Bhagwati J (1998), *A Stream of Windows: Unsettling Reflections on Trade, Immigration and Democracy.* MIT Press: Cambridge Mass

the debate has been cleverly guided by those seeking relief from competition as one that equally derives from overriding morality. Thus, even those who speak from moral concerns have had these concerns aroused by tendentious and misleading characterisation of complex socio-economic phenomena such as child labour in poor countries (whose solution does not lie in denying market access but in joining forces and deploying a set of policies whereby NGOs and governments work with impoverished families, employers, primary school authorities and the children themselves, as has been happening in India for example). It is as if the anti-abortion groups saturated the media with pictures of aborted late-term fetuses to distort and define the debate on abortion rights, to the exclusion of the nuances that are in fact at the heart of the debate. To run a statistical analysis on Congressmen's votes without going beyond the veil to ask pointedly whether their moral concerns have themselves been a result of active lobbying by the protectionist groups is to miss the point since the objective is precisely to investigate whether protectionism is playing a primary role in their vote. Just as Sherlock Holmes asked why the dog didn't bark, we must ask why these Congressmen have acquired the moral concern they have and why that concern takes the form of trade linkage rather than other methods.

The principal driving force behind these linkage demands has clearly been the fear of competition, as was abundantly evident in the United States during the NAFTA debate. Fearful of competition from the poor countries, protectionists such as Patrick Buchanan seek to turn to *isolationism*, withdrawing from the global economy. But an alternative response, equally designed to moderate competition, is what I call *intrusionism*. This takes the form of *unfair* trade demands addressed to the poor nations, seeking to raise their environmental and labour standards: this would presumably raise the production costs of rivals abroad in the South to levels that make their competition more tolerable. An analogy can drive this home. Faced with a charging bull, you may catch it by the horn (as with isolationism) or reach behind the beast and catch it by its tail (as with intrusionism). The intrusionist response however is no less of a folly than the isolationist option, though the foolishness is less transparent. It seeks to restrain trade, but from the other end: it is tantamount therefore to *export protectionism*, the mirror image of the conventional, Buchanan-variety *import protectionism*.

In fact, the protectionist intent, and more so the design, of the trade linkage may also be inferred from the fact that the contents of the social lause, for example, have been reduced to a *core*, where the defendants are fully expected to be only the poor countries, to the exclusion of the 'social' issues where the OECD countries, chiefly the United States, are equally likely to find themselves as defendants. Thus, while the use of child labour *sui generis* (and not just the reprehensible practices of bonded child labour and the employment of children in hazardous occupations such as glassmaking and in cruel conditions of the type that inspired the impassioned writings of Chadwick, Engles and Dickens in 19th century England and the subsequent protective legislation) is to be prohibited by such a clause, there is nothing for example about the rights of migrant labour where conditions of abject abuse are not uncommon in the US itself if investigative TV reports are to be believed. Again, while the *right to unionise* is to be included, there is no mention of restrictions on secondary boycotts for instance or the permitted hiring of replacement workers, which cripple the ability in the US to strike and which doubtless have contributed to the emasculation of unions and to the phenomenal shrinking of unionised labour in the American garments industry. Again, the widespread use of sweatshops by the American garment industry on US soil, with wholly inadequate enforcement, is evidently a violation of US laws and of human rights aspirations, so that inclusion of this issue in a social clause in the WTO, with market access suspended for such an industry, would put the US squarely into the dock, threatening its garment industry with virtual shutdown in world trade. So, where is the US on this issue on the social clause?

5.2. Alternative Ways to Pursue Rights and Social Objectives

The developing countries suspect then that, in pushing relentlessly for a social clause in the WTO, the Clinton administration is invoking ethics to secure relief from foreign firms in the competitive global age, wearing a moral mask on a face furrowed by the fear of competition.

An increasing number of economists, of all political persuasions, share this concern, albeit in a fairly nuanced way. They would de-link labour standards and other social issues from trade and thus terminate attempts at inserting them into the WTO, get away from selectivity aiming at the poor countries to include a far more comprehensive menu of concerns from the human rights agenda, and then address these concerns energetically in appropriate international agencies such as the ILO for labour issues and the UNICEF for children's issues. These economists therefore are not opposed to, and many indeed actively support, the pursuit of a human-rights agenda; they simply do not want to have it captured by intrusionists and protectionists who see this agenda (captured and defined by their extensive lobbying) as a splendid opportunity to advance their competition-moderating objective.

Again, such a de-linking of the moral agenda from trade treaties and institutions would enhance the credibility of the human rights and social-issues NGOs. The alliance with the protectionists distorts the agenda far too obviously in the direction of shielding the producers in the rich countries from competition from the poor countries. By asking for a pro-active pursuit of these goals, they will be able to widen the agenda to a more substantial and symmetric menu of desired rights than a trade-dictated choice of menu must inevitably define.

Again, it is commonly asserted that ILO, UNICEF, and like institutions, do not have teeth. But this is the same as saying that the Pope has no troops. Surely, one does not need the rack to spread Christianity! It is easy to miss the fact that these institutions create the ethos and bring into a coherent framework the information about member states' performance in regard to rights and values that the NGOs seek to advance world-wide. In turn, this enables NGOs and governments to use this information to create the pressure points for progress,[3] thus leading in varying degrees to what I call the Dracula effect: expose evil to sunlight and it will shrivel up and die.

Thus, the ILO has the Committee of Experts on the Application of Conventions and Recommendations, whose distinguished members monitor annually the compliance of member states with the conventions they have ratified, while also taking up (one at a time) individual conventions and examining the member states' conformity to them *regardless of ratification.* The Trade Policy Review Mechanism at the WTO does much the same for Members' trade policy to great advantage, prodding the reviewed countries to move towards reforms even though there is no enforcing power at all. I have suggested that a World Migration Organisation could do the same for countries' overall policies concerning all forms of immigrants, legal and illegal, and refugees.

These are powerful techniques even if applied to others to the exclusion of one's own warts. But their power arises also from the fact that they apply universally to all nations, playing no favourites. Thus, the ILO experts will catch the sweatshops in New York and the *de facto* slavery among migrant workers on American farms as much as they will highlight the prevalence of child labour in hazardous occupations such as rug-making in Pakistan and glassmaking in India.

6. Concluding Observations

All this strongly implies then that trade linkage in the form of a social clause for example is not an efficient way to advance a human rights or social issues agenda. It is also worth emphasising that even the intrusionist lobbies that are fearful of international competition and push for the linkage as a precondition for freeing trade for that reason alone are mistaken in general. The belief in the 1980s that trade with poor countries produces paupers in our midst by hurting the real wages of our workers has been challenged effectively by a great deal of analysis that shows that the basic building blocks of the arguments leading to the fears are unsubstantiated: for example in the 1980s when real wages fell most, the prices of labour-intensive goods in world trade, and in the US, rose instead of falling as required for the gloomy analysis of trade.[4]

---

[3] These can include private boycotts, legally accepted in western jurisprudence. They can also generate voluntary labelling which enables consumers to vote with their dollars against practices they disapprove of.

[4] I have dealt with these arguments in a series of papers, the latest being *Play it Again, Sam: Yet Another Look at Trade and Wages,* Columbia University, mimeographed, February 1997. The occasional assertion that there is now a *consensus* that trade explains around 20 per cent of the decline in real wages is simply nonsense: I, for one, would now argue, on the basis of analytical reflection and study of evidence over several years, that trade *helps* workers. (Bhagwati, ibid)

Nor are the intrusionist lobbies, which fear that our own standards will collapse due to a 'race to the bottom' as firms choose technologies and locations to exploit lower standards and governments compete to get the firms by lowering standards, on more solid ground. Numerous careful studies show that the empirical basis for these fears is hard to find; indeed, it does not exist.[5]

Therefore, it is mere folly to keep pushing for a social clause in the WTO. The proper course of action is to de-link the human rights and social standards issues from the trade agenda, and to pursue the former vigorously in appropriate institutions and by other means.[6]

Bibliography

Bhagwati J (1997), *Fast Track: Not so Fast*, The Wall Street Journal, September 10.

Bhagwati J (1997), *Play it again Sam: Yet Another Look at Trade and Wages*, Columbia University, mimeographed, February

Bhagwati J (1998), *A Stream of Windows: Unsettling Reflection on Trade, Immigration and Democracy*. MIT Press: Cambridge Mass

Bhagwati J and Hudec RE (eds) (1997), *Fair Trade and Harmonization: Prerequisites for Free Trade?* Volumes 1 & 2, MIT Press: Cambridge Mass

Passell P (1997), *Loading the trade agenda with divisive issues could backfire*. The New York Times, October 9

---

[5] See the contributions by Arik Levinson and by Bhagwati and Srinivasan, in Bhagwati and Hudec, op cit, Volume 1.

[6] This is the viewpoint I have advocated as a member of the Academic Advisory Committee of the Human Rights Watch (Asia) and was embodied in my writing and petition opposing linkage in the renewal of fast-track authority that President Clinton unsuccessfully requested from the Congress last year. See, in particular, my: *Fast Track: Not so Fast.* Wall Street Journal, September 10, 1997; and Peter Passell, *Loading the trade agenda with divisive issues could backfire,* New York Times, October 9, 1997.

Trade and Environment

Richard Eglin

1. Introduction

In 1991, the GATT became a target of fierce criticism that it was hostile to the protection of the environment. The immediate cause of the criticism was the report of the tuna-dolphin dispute panel, which was released in September of that year. It ruled against a United States embargo on imports of Mexican tunafish that had been imposed on the grounds that Mexico's tunafishing fleet was drowning dolphins in its nets.[1] The GATT ruling was condemned by environmentalists as evidence that Mexico's commercial interests counted for more in the eyes of the trading system than the lives of dolphins, and *GATT kills dolphins* became a clarion call for a variety of environmental groups and consumer advocates to launch campaigns claiming that GATT rules were undermining environmental policies and standards on a broad front.

The mood created was alarmist, and there followed widespread demands from the environmental community to *green the GATT*.[2] It was claimed that:

- trade liberalisation necessarily brought about increased environmental degradation;
- GATT rules were exercising a chilling effect on the development of new environmental legislation and were forcing countries to lower their environmental standards, for fear of them being challenged on commercial grounds as trade restrictions or to engage in a *race to the bottom* to safeguard the competitive position of their domestic producers;

---

[1] GATT document DS21/R (unadopted) of 3 September 1991, reproduced in GATT - Basic Instruments and Selected Documents (BISD) 39S/155

[2] See Charnovitz S (1992), *Trade negotiations and the environment.* International Environmental Reporter (11 March), Bureau of National Affairs, Washington DC; French H (1993), *Costly Trade Offs: Reconciling Trade and the Environment.* Worldwatch Paper 113. Worldwatch Institute, Washington DC; WWF (1991), *The General Agreement on Tariffs and Trade, Environmental Protection and Sustainable Development.* WWF International Discussion Paper. Gland, Switzerland; WWF (1992), *International Trade, GATT and the Environment.* International Position Paper. Gland, Switzerland

- such serious competitiveness problems would result from differences in environmental standards between rich and poor countries that *green* trade restrictions (eco-dumping duties) would be needed to deal with them;
- the GATT was incapable of dealing sensitively and effectively with environment-related trade disputes.

That autumn, "GATTzilla" posters hung from lampposts in Washington depicting the GATT as a monstrous lizard with a dying dolphin in one hand and a drum of DDT under its arm, one pace away from flattening the U.S. Capitol building; the symbolism was crude, but in addition to its environmental message it played effectively to political concerns in the United States that the GATT meant compromise and loss of national sovereignty.

For Arthur Dunkel, the timing could hardly have been worse. The failure of governments to conclude the Uruguay Round negotiations on schedule in December 1990 had been followed by bitter recrimination (notably between Europe and the United States over the failure to advance on agricultural trade liberalisation) and by a resurgence of demands in the United States for unilateral and regional solutions to trade problems. Dunkel had to rebuild political support for the multilateral trade agenda and find a new basis on which to conclude the Uruguay Round.[3] Environmental issues could not be ignored, yet they were not a subject for negotiation in the Uruguay Round and there could be no question of introducing them at such a late stage.

Moreover, many GATT members were hostile to any notion of acknowledging that a legitimate link existed between trade and environment, and they were suspicious of the motives of those making this claim. Some felt OECD governments were over-reacting to pressure from vocal green lobbies to pursue environmental goals at every opportunity and at any cost and were seeking to weaken the rules of the trading system to allow trade restrictions to be used more easily for environmental purposes. Some feared a new green conditionality would be attached to their overseas market access. Some saw the issue as a dangerous new manifestation of trade protectionism at a time when several OECD countries were having difficulty in agreeing to reduce trade barriers in traditional areas such as textiles and clothing and agriculture.

With little room for manoeuvre on this issue, Dunkel and Rubens Ricupero, the Brazilian Ambassador and Chairman of the GATT CONTRACTING PARTIES in 1991, set about launching a work programme on trade and environment which would allow a structured debate to take place in GATT alongside, but clearly separate from, the Uruguay Round negotiations.[4] In December 1991, the GATT

---

[3] This he did successfully, and the Dunkel Draft of the Uruguay Round results was tabled in December 1991. It served extensively as the blueprint for the Final Act of the Uruguay Round that was signed in Marrakesh in March 1994

[4] In a number of respects environmental concerns were nevertheless addressed, with or without an explicit environmental label, in the results of the negotiations. The Preamble to the WTO Agreement includes for the first time direct references to the objective of sustainable development and to the need to protect and preserve the environment. The Agreements on Technical Barriers to Trade and on Sanitary and Phytosanitary Measures take explicitly into account the use by governments of measures to protect human, animal

Group on Environmental Measures and International Trade was convened for the first time, and the following January Dunkel made a speech in Bangkok which laid out the basis upon which he felt a constructive dialogue could be pursued between those convinced of the importance and urgency of the issue and those still harbouring serious doubts about its legitimacy.[5] In it he appealed to governments at the forthcoming UN Conference on Environment and Development in Rio de Janiero (the "Earth Summit" of June 1992) to avoid viewing the issue as an impossible choice between two popular and politically important policy objectives, and to concentrate instead on developing supportive links between trade and environmental policy-making.

The core of Dunkel's message was that international trade and the protection of the environment are at heart natural allies. Growing market economies are best equipped to take care of their environments properly, and effective protection of the environment is needed if economic growth is to be sustained over the long term. Trade can help governments deliver the greatest increase in the quality of the environment at the least cost by allocating scarce resources, particularly environmental resources, as efficiently as possible and by stimulating technological progress and productivity growth. Trade also generates wealth, which can help finance the expensive task of cleaning up and protecting the environment. Creating the conditions for international trade and investment to prosper by opening markets, particularly to exports from developing countries, and by keeping markets open through clear and enforceable rules is therefore very much part of a comprehensive approach towards the protection of the environment and the promotion of sustainable development. Beyond that, the key to coordinating trade and environmental policies in a market economy lies in pricing environmental resources properly to reflect their real scarcity and true social value. That is largely a question of assigning property rights and putting in place the right structure of taxes and regulations, not of restricting trade. Trade policies may have a supporting role to play in certain well-defined circumstances, but it is up to environmental policies and domestic resource management policies to make the difference in the majority of cases.

---

and plant life and health and the environment. The Agreement on Agriculture exempts direct payments under environmental programmes from WTO Members' commitments to reduce domestic support for agricultural production, subject to certain conditions. The Agreement on Subsidies and Countervailing Measures treats as a non-actionable subsidy government assistance to industry covering up to 20 per cent of the cost of adapting existing facilities to new environmental legislation. And both the TRIPS and the Services Agreements contain environment-related provisions. Although these did not satisfy the more strident calls at the time for the *greening of the GATT*, they did reflect the extent to which environmental considerations had increased in importance in policy-making terms by the time of the end of the Uruguay Round negotiations, as well as the capacity of trade negotiators to accommodate into WTO rules a well-argued case for taking those considerations into account without undermining the open, non-discriminatory foundations of the trading system.

[5] Speech to the Conference of the International Herald Tribune in association with the Thailand Development Research Institute. *Asia and the Pacific: Merging Business and the Environment.* GATT/1527 of 23 January 1992

Dunkel's message is as relevant today as it was in 1991. As the WTO looks towards launching new trade negotiations across a broad front, it needs to concentrate its attention on the one area in which it can claim competence (trade) and not dilute its primary message (reduce trade protectionism). The WTO is not an environmental agency, nor is it equipped to become one. Considerable single-mindedness will be called for if it is to meet its core responsibilities. However, it is important that single-mindedness not be mistaken for narrow-mindedness, or for a belief that improving the functioning of the trading system stands above other important public policy objectives. If governments are to maintain popular support for open trade and the WTO, they must not fail to respond to concerns about the effects of trade liberalization and economic globalization on the attainment of environmental goals. The future success of the WTO in advancing the multilateral trade agenda will be bound up in ways that it never was before with the progress governments make in dealing effectively with non-commercial concerns, nationally and multilaterally.

2. Trade Liberalization and the Environment

One of the most influential factors that has helped to forge the basis for a common approach to the subject of trade and environment in the WTO, particularly between developed and developing countries, has been the elaboration of the concept of *sustainable development*.[6] This replaced the *limits to growth* paradigm that was popularized in the 1970s, through which economic growth was viewed as being a part of the problem of environmental degradation, not part of the solution.[7] Making development sustainable means ensuring that economic growth goes hand in hand with better environmental protection, and it has become a fundamental starting point for developing a coordinated policy approach towards trade and environment at national and multilateral levels.[8] For developing countries in par-

[6] The development of the concept is associated most closely with the Final Report of the UN Commission on Environment and Development (1987), *Our Common Future*. (The Brundtland Report)

[7] See Meadows DH et al (1972), *The Limits to Growth: A Report for the Club of Rome's Project on the Predicament of Mankind.* Universe Books: New York. Not everyone has abandoned that view. See, for example, Daly HE (November 1993), *The perils of free trade*. Scientific American; Daly HE and Goodland R (1994), *An ecological-economic assessment of deregulation of international commerce under GATT*. Ecological Economics. Vol 9, No 1; and Ekins P, Folke C and Costanza R (1994), *Trade, environment and development: The issues in perspective*. Ecological Economics, Vol 9, No 1

[8] The Report of the WTO Committee on Trade and Environment to Ministers in Singapore in December 1996 made the point as follows: *There is a close link between poverty and environmental degradation. An open, equitable and non-discriminatory multilateral trading system and improved market access opportunities can assist developing countries obtain the resources to implement national development and environmental policies, diversify their economies and provide income-generating activities for the poor. They are essential for supporting countries in their efforts to ensure sustainable management of*

ticular, trade provides an economic lifeline. Secure market access abroad has become far more important to their development prospects than reliance upon uncertain aid flows, and their membership in the WTO provides the legal guarantees that the lifeline will not be cut by discrimination or protectionism from their trading partners.

Trade liberalisation is therefore complementary to better protection of the environment. In that, the results of the Uruguay Round negotiations can provide a ready source of inspiration: reducing barriers to trade in environmentally-friendly goods and services; providing developing countries with improved market access for higher value-added production, to relieve the pressure they face to specialise in natural resource exploitation or low value-added, environmentally sensitive activities; disciplining and reducing environmentally-damaging trade restrictions and subsidies; and encouraging the spread of environmentally-sound technology by enforcing intellectual property rights. In this respect, WTO Members are already making an important contribution to sustainable development and better environmental protection worldwide through the implementation of the Uruguay Round results.

The challenge for the WTO is to agree on how those advances can be taken further. The two areas that stand out for particular attention are energy and agriculture. Liberalisation of these sectors generates a good deal of resistance on the part of a number of WTO Members, yet they are cited more often than any other areas of trade as having the potential of yielding clear *win-win* situations in terms of gains for both the trading system and the environment.

Several countries continue to protect domestic energy production (notably coal) through border restrictions and domestic support measures at a high economic cost and at a high cost to both the trading system and the environment, when alternative sources of more environmentally-friendly energy are available from overseas suppliers.[9] Removing the trade restrictions and market distortions can bring both trade and environmental benefits. The energy sector is sensitive for many WTO Members and achieving significant liberalization there will no doubt be difficult. All the more reason, then, for the environmental community to lend its considerable political weight to the task at an early stage and join the trade community in pressing for more rational energy policies in WTO Member countries.

In the case of agriculture, the Uruguay Round results contain a built-in agenda for further negotiations to liberalize trade, beginning in 1999. The difficulties that will be involved cannot be over-estimated, and the case for enlisting the support of the environmental community so as to pursue environmental objectives in tandem with trade objectives is a strong one. The agricultural sector contains many examples of the failure of markets to incorporate environmental externalities, and the

---

their resources. Implementing appropriate environmental policies determined at the national level is also needed in order to ensure that trade-induced growth will be sustainable. WTO document WT/CTE/1 of 12 November 1996

[9] Anderson K (1992), *Effects on the environment and welfare of liberalizing world trade: the cases of coal and food.* In: Anderson K and Blackhurst R (eds), *The Greening of World Trade.* Harvester Wheatsheaf; de Moor A (1997), *Subsidizing Unsustainable Development*, Institute for Research on Public Expenditure, Amsterdam

task of designing proper environmental policies to deal with them is not easy. What has made this sector a matter of such environmental concern, however, is that market failures have been compounded by trade restricting and distorting policies with negative environmental consequences of their own. Studies paint a largely unambiguous picture of direct and often significant environmental harm stemming from market access restrictions, domestic support policies and export subsidies on the one hand, and from high taxation of agricultural production relative to other economic activities on the other (not only directly but also indirectly through exchange rate over-valuation and import protection of other sectors of activity).[10]

> *One of the most potentially constructive effects of the interdependence of trade and environmental issues is that in developed countries, accompanying environmental interventions can help to* sell *trade reform in agriculture to a broader public. In developing countries, on the other hand, the benefits of trade reform including market access, higher prices and expanded exports, can help these nations* buy *needed environmental improvements.*[11]

Beyond traditional sectors such as these, there is considerable scope for the WTO to engage in creative thinking about where new markets for environmental goods and services can be developed and liberalized, to the benefit of both the trading system and the environment. One promising line of examination is environmental services which, although already traded, are not for the time being assigned any market value nor paid for. The most pressing case is the export of greenhouse gas absorption services by countries with large forest resources; these countries are receiving no payment for the environmental services their forests provide to the rest of the world, and for many of them there is consequently little commercial incentive to protect the forests from destruction. Studies are under way in the context of the UN Climate Change Convention of the possibilities for organizing a system of tradeable permits for greenhouse gas emission. At a certain stage the WTO may be able to contribute to the negotiation and practical administration of such a system; bringing it under the rules of the trading system could provide it with a binding quality that would make its implementation all the more effective.

3. Coordinating the Multilateral Trade and Environmental Agendas

Developing constructive linkages between the multilateral trade and environmental agendas is a logical step for governments to take in an era of economic

---

[10] See, for example, Anderson K (1992), *Agricultural trade liberalization and the environment: A global perspective*. The World Economy. Vol 15, No 1; Anderson K (1992), *Agricultural policies, land use and the environment*. The 14th Denman Lecture, University of Cambridge, Granta Editions, Cambridge; and Runge CF (1994), *The environmental effects of trade in the agricultural sector*. In: OECD, *The Environmental Effects of Trade*, Paris, France

[11] Runge CF (1994), op cit

globalization and of more transboundary environmental problems. The fact that over 200 international environmental agreements (IEAs) co-exist with the WTO gives clear cause for believing that multilateral cooperation on the environment is a practical option, and its appeal is quite evident from the point of view of the WTO which is dedicated to finding cooperative, multilateral solutions to problems in the area of trade. Yet there has been little evidence until now of an attempt by trade and environmental negotiators to coordinate their policy proposals and forge a common approach towards trade-related, global environmental problems.

One result is that a number of the most important IEAs contain trade measures whose consistency with the WTO trade rules is questionable.[12] If any of these measures were put to the test through dispute settlement and found inconsistent with WTO obligations, a WTO Member could be faced with the politically unacceptable choice of having to remove a trade measure it is obliged to apply to meet its IEA commitments or to defy the WTO ruling. It is disruptive to both the multilateral trade and environmental agendas for governments to continue to be placed in the position of undertaking binding policy obligations that may be found to be mutually inconsistent under different international legal instruments. Clarification is called for.

Probably more ink has been spilled on this than on any other issue at the interface between trade and environment. The discussion has ranged across legal analysis of how IEAs and the WTO are related under international law and what interpretation should be given to various GATT rules (particularly GATT Article XX) that discipline the use of environmental trade restrictions in IEAs; economic analysis of the efficiency and effectiveness of using trade restrictions in IEAs; analysis of the relative institutional strengths and weaknesses of IEAs and the WTO; and cruder debates about the respective political importance of trade and environmental policy objectives.[13]

None of these lines of analysis has proved conclusive. A move was nevertheless made in the WTO in 1996 by a number of OECD countries, which proposed changing WTO rules (or at least interpreting them differently) so as to accommodate trade measures in IEAs which currently are WTO-inconsistent but which are claimed to be essential to the environmental effectiveness of the IEAs.[14] The trade measures they have in mind primarily are those applied by IEA parties to dis-

---

[12] In particular, the Convention on International Trade in Endangered Species (CITES), the Basel Convention and the Montreal Protocol.

[13] For a summary of the arguments governments have brought to this issue in the WTO, see the 1996 Report of the WTO Committee on Trade and Environment, op cit. For more detailed analysis, see for example the relevant contributions by Bhagwati, Srinivasan, Wilson, Hudec and Farber, among others, in Bhagwati JN and Hudec RE (1996*), Fair Trade and Harmonization: Prerequisites for Free Trade?* MIT Press: Cambridge Mass; and Petersmann E-U (1994), *Settlement of international environmental disputes in GATT and the EC: comparative legal aspects.* In: Towards More Effective Supervision by International Organizatons, Blokker N and Muller S (eds)

[14] In particular the European Communities and Switzerland. Their proposals are summarized in the Report of the WTO Committee on Trade and Environment, op cit

criminate against imports from countries that have not joined the IEA and are not engaged in tackling the environmental problem the IEA seeks to resolve.

The proposal met stiff resistance from many other WTO Members. Their most deep-seated concern relates to the importance of not abusing the WTO as a powerful tool for enforcement in areas outside its specific competence. The environment is not the only area of international affairs where the desirability of more enforceability arises,[15] and trade sanctions are not the only, nor generally the best, enforcement tool available. Furthermore, the obligations in question are those of non-discrimination, the cornerstone of the WTO legal system and the principal means of protecting the rights of weaker members of the multilateral trading system. The use of trade sanctions for breaches of international environmental norms and the use of trade restrictions by one country to try to change the environmental practices of another is very divisive, and largely contradicts efforts to find cooperative solutions to environmental problems that are regarded as having an international dimension. Trade restriction is a blunt instrument which may appear to offer a seductively easy means of action in the short term to those who can wield it most readily. Over the longer term it destroys the basis of international relations and cooperative action, and in the case of the environment it is the long term that matters most.

As long as the WTO continues to operate on the basis of consensus decision-making (and there are strong arguments in favour of it doing so), it is hard to see how agreement will be reached to weaken its non-discrimination provisions and allow discriminatory trade measures to be used for non-trade purposes. A country which has not been persuaded to join a consensus to resolve an environmental problem through an IEA can hardly be expected to join a consensus in the WTO to change the trade rules in ways that would allow it to be punished for its recalcitrance. If trade is indeed the cause of an environmental problem, then trade measures are the appropriate tool for policy intervention and it would follow that the WTO should accommodate them; and in at least one important respect it will, since in such circumstances it would seem unnecessary to apply the trade measures in a discriminatory fashion. If, however, the trade measures are intended to serve some other purpose, for example to penalize countries that do not sign an IEA, it is far more difficult for the WTO to provide the necessary accommodation without undermining its multilateral purpose. It is surely more constructive for environmental agreements to be backed up by financial compensation arrangements and technology transfer, where these are necessary to encourage full participation in an IEA, rather than using trade policy weapons to try to force countries into a course of action which is not of their own choosing.

---

[15] The debate over introducing a so-called social clause into the WTO to enforce ILO labour standards has very similar characteristics to the debate over enforcing IEAs through discriminatory trade restrictions, and recently attention has turned to the possibility of enforcing human rights standards in the same way. For parallels and contrasts between the environment and labour standards issues in the context of trade, see Bhagwati JN (1995), *Trade liberalisation and fair trade demands: addressing the environment and labour standards issues*, The World Economy, Vol 18, No 6

4. WTO Rules, National Environmental Standards, and Competitiveness Concerns

Demand for a cleaner environment and for environmentally-friendly goods and services is increasing worldwide, and it has generated a range of new policy measures, both price-based and regulatory, that are designed to value environmental resources properly in the marketplace, an exercise sometimes referred to as *internalising* environmental costs. This has been most evident so far in the OECD countries, but new environmental legislation and environmental standard-setting is increasing also in developing countries and the trend seems sure to continue.

Environmental policies can have complex and potentially significant trade effects, and it would be naive to ignore the danger that trade protectionists may pursue their commercial interests behind a facade of environmental concern. The WTO has a permanent responsibility towards its Member countries to remain vigilant in that regard. Its role is all the more important because there are serious dangers involved, for the environment as well as for the trading system, in misusing trade restrictions. Important questions arise, therefore, about the adequacy of WTO rules and disciplines to ensure that unnecessary obstacles to trade are avoided.

At the same time it is cynical to suggest that environmental policy-makers faced with pressing environmental problems cannot find an accommodation for efficient and effective policy measures under the WTO. Inevitably, these measures will affect imports as well as domestic products, but the WTO need not get in their way; it does not stand for free trade at any cost. The key requirement from the WTO's point of view is that environmental measures that incorporate trade provisions or that affect trade significantly do not discriminate.

Subject to the requirement of non-discrimination being met, WTO rules place little constraint on the policy choices available to a country to protect its own environment against damage either from domestic production or from the consumption of domestically produced or imported products. By and large, a country can do anything to imports or exports that it does to domestically produced goods, and it can do anything it feels necessary to regulate its own production processes. What a country cannot do under WTO rules, however, is apply trade restrictions to force other countries to change their production methods or otherwise to limit their access to world markets in the event their production methods remain unaltered.

For environmental policy makers, this constraint is one of their principal bones of contention that the WTO rules are insensitive to environmental issues and need changing. From their point of view, life-cycle analysis of a product, including the way it is produced and ultimately disposed of as waste, is important to ensure that the full environmental impact of both production and consumption activities is taken fully into account. The method of production cannot then be divorced from the product's physical characteristics. Is there, in that regard, any legitimate case to be made for using trade restrictions to differentiate among traded goods and services according to how they have been produced?

To answer that question, it is useful first to distinguish measures that address environmental problems and pollution caused by the consumption of a product (e.g., measures favouring the use of unleaded gasoline in cars) from those that address environmental problems and pollution caused by the production process (e.g., measures to reduce air emissions from factories). This distinction underlies the concept of like product, which is of considerable practical and systemic importance in all of the core GATT Articles and related WTO Agreements. Defining whether or not products are like depends to a very large extent upon case-by-case analysis. However, broadly speaking products are like if they have the same or similar physical characteristics or if they can be used more or less interchangeably for the same purpose. It is contrary to WTO rules to discriminate between them, for example by applying different tariff rates to them or an internal tax to an imported product but not to its domestically produced equivalent. Products can be differentiated on the basis of differences in their product characteristics, or on the basis of differences in their production methods if these affect the characteristics of the product (e.g., pesticide residues on fruit), but they cannot be differentiated on the basis of their production methods if these leave behind no trace in the product (e.g., tuna caught in a way that causes the death of dolphins).

The rationale behind this approach lies in the efficient assignment of economic policies to correct market distortions. It is most efficient (first-best) to use the policy instrument that addresses a distortion as close to its source as possible. Policy instruments that are applied further away from the source of the distortion are likely to have less predictable beneficial effects and higher secondary costs associated with their use. In the case of a market distortion that relates to an environmentally damaging process method, the efficient solution is assured through the equalisation at the margin of the costs of pollution abatement and control and the benefits of improved environmental quality. Generally speaking, this implies acting directly on the source of pollution by changing the production method. Even in theory, the equalisation will rarely be achieved by restricting trade at some distant market in the products that are being manufactured in a polluting way; in practice it is unlikely that it will ever be achieved because of the difficulty policy-makers have in designing an optimum policy intervention.

By way of a practical example, consider the reaction of a foreign supplier facing an additional tariff in his export market because it has been determined there that his production process is too polluting. One reaction may be to try to avoid the tariff by changing to a less polluting production method if he has the financial and technological resources to do so. Alternatively, however, he might aim to maintain his market share even after paying the extra tariff by reducing his production costs, for example by lowering his environmental standards still further. The ambiguity of the producer's response suggests strongly a mis-assignment of policies. Trade restrictions cannot be counted on to operate predictably to achieve the policy objective, since they are applied so far distant from the source of the distortion. However, the secondary costs of using them are ever present, in this case because of the misallocation of resources which could result from protecting domestic production and penalizing the foreign producer and from ignoring the fact that different countries have different pollution assimilation capacities and different social preferences as regards the level of pollution they are prepared to tolerate.

This feature of the WTO legal system gave rise to one of the most fiercely argued claims of the environmental community some years ago, that the rules of the trading system were antithetical to the maintenance of high national environmental standards. Producers in *high* standard countries, it was claimed, would incur higher costs of production than their competitors in *low* standard countries. One response might be for those producers to resist any increase in environmental standards at home on the grounds that they would otherwise be forced out of business, a scenario which for obvious reasons caused concern from an environmental point of view. If environmental standards were raised in spite of opposition from domestic producers, market forces would result in the migration of industry from high to low environmental standard locations and encourage the proliferation of so-called pollution havens to attract foreign investment by footloose, polluting industries. The net outcome would be a higher level of pollution per unit of output in the world economy, which again caused evident concern from an environmental point of view. Hence, the argument went, in order to allow producers in high environmental standard countries to remain competitive it would be necessary to permit countries to introduce under new WTO rules some form of offsetting trade restriction (so-called eco-dumping duties) against imports produced abroad at lower cost in a more polluting way to combat unfair trade.[16]

Demands from some environmental groups that eco-dumping duties be imposed on goods produced in a polluting way resulted in one of the most controversial issues in the early stages of GATT work on trade and environment, and brought out more directly than anything else suspicions that the environmental agenda was being driven by barely disguised green protectionism.

Empirical evidence does not support arguments that genuine problems of international competitiveness are created by differing environmental standards in different countries.[17] Even if such arguments were found to be of real concern in business circles, the important question is whether trade restrictions are an effective way of trying to compensate for international differences in environmental standards. If, as was suggested earlier, they will not act predictably to change an overseas producer's methods of production, the argument for using trade restrictions boils down essentially to one of a domestic industry's need for protection against foreign competition. The reason for lack of international competitiveness, whether environmental or something else, is a secondary consideration. The WTO already provides possibilities for protecting domestic industry temporarily against foreign competition, for instance through safeguard action, and it hardly seems necessary to invent and bless a new protective instrument with a specifically green label attached to it.

---

[16] This set of arguments has been reviewed critically by Bhagwati and Srinivasan in Chapter 4, Vol 1, of Bhagwati JN and Hudec RE (1996), op cit

[17] See, for example, Grossman GM and Krueger A (1991), *Environmental Impacts of a North American FreeTrade Agreement.* Working Paper No 3914. National Bureau of Economic Research, Cambridge Mass; Grossman GM and Krueger A (1994), *Economic Growth and the Environment.* Working Paper No 4634. National Bureau of Economic Research, Cambridge Mass

The competitiveness issue has been set aside, for the time being at least, in the trade and environment debate. The Report of the WTO Committee on Trade and Environment to Ministers in Singapore in December 1996 contained the following statement:

> *WTO Member governments are committed not to introduce WTO-inconsistent or protectionist trade restrictions or countervailing measures in an attempt to offset any real or perceived adverse domestic economic or competitiveness effects of applying environmental policies; not only would this undermine the open, equitable and non-discriminatory nature of the multilateral trading system, it would also prove counterproductive to meeting environmental objectives and promoting sustainable development. Equally, WTO Members note that it would be inappropriate for them to relax their existing national environmental standards or their enforcement in order to promote their trade.*

In certain circumstances, a particular production method may be viewed as causing such a high degree of environmental prejudice of a global or transboundary nature that coordinated action at the multilateral level will be required to suppress it. Cooperative negotiations through international environmental agreements are then called for. Attempts to force harmonisation of production methods or compensate for national differences in them through second or third-best policy instruments such as trade restrictions have little to recommend them. Developing the *Polluter Pays Principle* and the notion of environmental cost internalisation into internationally accepted standards could be a helpful way forward, accepting of course that environmental resources do not need to be valued in the same way around the world. It is worth noting, in this context, that it is the policy objectives (standards) that need to be harmonized, not the policies themselves. The same policy can produce different results in different countries, while the same standard can usually be achieved in different ways; it is natural that not all countries will choose to tackle specific policy objectives with the same policy tools.

5. Conclusion

During the next few years the WTO must establish its credentials as the successor to the GATT in managing the multilateral trading system responsibly and effectively. Environmental and sustainable development issues have now been brought into the mainstream of WTO work, and the WTO's handling of its trade and environment work programme will be viewed critically from many points of view as a gauge of its success. As far as the trade community is concerned, the key to moving the WTO work programme on trade and environment along is likely to entail ensuring that it builds on the following points.

- Keep markets open and competitive. Trade liberalisation complements effective environmental policies, not only at a general level but even more importantly through removing specific trade restrictions and distortions that themselves cause direct environmental harm.

- Feed into markets proper price signals. The key to managing environmental resources properly in a market economy is ensuring that their prices reflect as accurately as possible their real scarcity and true social value. A wide range of market-based instruments and regulatory measures is available to serve this purpose, but trade restrictions are unlikely to figure high on the list.
- Respect the fact that different countries do not and will not all have the same environmental standards. The values they assign to environmental resources will not necessarily, or even probably, be the same and there is nothing inherently wrong in finding that the price of a good consequently varies from one country to another, any more than that it varies because of differences in wage levels or corporate tax rates.
- Avoid at all costs the use of environmental measures, purposely or not, for trade protectionist purposes. Slippage there will poison not only the trading system but also national and international environmental agendas.
- Resolve international environmental problems cooperatively, through multilateral negotiation and agreement. Allowing disagreements in the negotiation of IEAs to degenerate into trade disputes, or pressing unilaterally for the resolution of transboundary environmental problems, will not produce the kind of stable solutions to environmental problems that are needed if economic growth and the protection of the environment are to be sustained over the long term.

Building on the Singapore Ministerial: Trade, Investment and Competition

Sir Leon Brittan

1. Introduction

The General Agreement on Tariffs and Trade (GATT) during Arthur Dunkel's time as Director-General made historic moves to sweep away outdated exceptions to open trade rules even in such sensitive sectors as agriculture and textiles. But, arguably more important in the long term, this will also be remembered as the period when GATT decided to catch up with and to get ahead of developments in international economic integration.

Before globalisation had made it into modern English language dictionaries, the Punta Del Este declaration of September 1986 pushed GATT negotiations beyond goods into the fields of services, intellectual property and investment. These negotiations have very largely been successful, and we have sound foundations for the next big push on services liberalisation, due to start no later than January 2000. On intellectual property, too, ground breaking work was done by the Uruguay Round negotiators, although implementation, particularly in developing countries, requires continued technical support and political impetus. Least was perhaps achieved on the investment front, although the Agreement on Trade-Related Investment Measures (TRIMs) marks a useful codification of existing prohibitions on government behaviour likely to distort the world-wide flow of private capital.

The World Trade Organization (WTO), having been born of so innovative a negotiating process, must remain true to its antecedents and continue to anticipate the needs of the world economy. It was in that spirit that the European Union went to the first Ministerial-level meeting of the WTO in Singapore in December 1996. It was for that reason that we were so pleased that our ideas for initial WTO work programmes in the fields of investment and of competition were accepted by the Ministers. And that is why I want to devote these pages to a personal reflection on the work to be done in Geneva on both these themes.

2. Competition

Let me begin with competition, a field where personally I suggested the need for stronger international rules well before the conclusion of the Uruguay Round.[1]

Continued liberalisation in GATT and the parallel globalisation of business behaviour have led, over a number of decades, to a constant growth of trade in goods, services and investment. These developments have changed the nature and workings of the trading system.

As a result, the scope for governmental action to restrain fair international competition is increasingly limited. More attention is therefore inevitably focusing on those private measures that have a similar effect but are not subject to international rules.

Competition rules are one area where government can affect trade but for which no general rules or principles of a binding nature exist. As the international community negotiates a growing body of rules requiring countries to give rights to foreign companies operating within their territory, the issue of international cooperation to deal with possible abuses of those rights is more and more likely to arise.

Should the multilateral system be complemented and strengthened by a set of rules to support the effective application of competition law? And, if so, how could this be done?

Competition law is a basic feature of the market economies and legal systems of many WTO Members. When applied effectively, competition law supports the competitiveness of industries, protects the individual right to compete in a sound and fair manner, and maximises consumer welfare. It thus benefits producers, consumers and society as a whole. It also keeps economies open.

Domestic competition laws usually include a set of rules both for investigating commercial practice (on horizontal or vertical agreements, dominance, mergers) and for identifying whether they have anti-competitive effects and if so proposing remedies, together with an enforcement structure to ensure respect of the law, access to a judicial or administrative body for parties affected by anti-competitive practices and, lastly, a process providing for judicial review.

The multilateral system has been substantially strengthened by the establishment of the WTO. Governments have, through successive GATT Rounds, been made subject to increasing disciplines guaranteeing transparency, non-discrimination and access to markets. But, at a time when business activities and production methods have become global, there are still no general WTO disciplines on the conduct of commercial enterprises.

The stillborn 1947 Havana Charter was based on the concept of comprehensive rules covering both public and private practices. Since the 1970s both the OECD and the UNCTAD have carried out significant work on competition rules. And in the late 1980s, the European Commission and the US Administration did some pioneering work on international cooperation in the competition field.

---

[1] Speech given at the World Economic Forum, Davos, 1992. See bibliography

I would like to describe these bilateral initiatives in some detail, because they have not received very much attention so far and because I think they do serve to show how such cooperation is feasible.

On 23 September 1991 the Commission concluded an Agreement with the Government of the United States of America regarding the application of their competition laws. Following a decision by the European Court of Justice, this Agreement was subsequently approved on behalf of the European Community by a joint decision of the Council and the Commission of 10 April 1995.[2]

In substance, this agreement provides for three things: an extensive exchange of information; a procedure of so-called negative or traditional comity whereby each party within the limits of its legal obligations refrains from measures that could affect the interests of the other party; and a more innovative procedure of positive comity whereby a party may invite the other party to implement the latter's own laws against practices that have a harmful effect on the former's interests.

Positive comity was recognised as one key method of addressing anti-competitive behaviour occurring outside a country's territory, without giving rise to the need to exert extraterritorial jurisdiction. This has been a consistent focus of European attention, reflecting Europe's view that the United States has expanded its extraterritorial jurisdiction more than any other country, thereby creating friction in its bilateral relations.

The principle of positive comity provides that a party adversely affected by anti-competitive behaviour occurring in whole or in part in the territory of another party may request the other party to take action. Positive comity also enables the party within whose territory anti-competitive behaviour is occurring to retain control, if it so wishes, over any enforcement activities addressing that behaviour.

Accordingly, in 1996 the Commission was granted a mandate to seek to reach an agreement that would strengthen the positive comity provisions of the 1991 Agreement. The resulting deal is, at the time of writing, awaiting formal endorsement by EU Member States and by the US authorities.

The Draft Agreement applies where certain anti-competitive activities, which are occurring in whole or in a substantial part in the territory of one party, are also adversely affecting the interests of the other party. In such cases, the party whose interests are affected may request the party in whose territory the conduct is principally occurring to take enforcement action, pursuant to its own competition rules.

The Draft Agreement not only provides guidelines on how such positive comity requests should be dealt with: it raises a presumption that in certain circumstances a party will normally defer or suspend its own enforcement activities.

The presumption of deferral or suspension arises where the anti-competitive activities at issue do not have a direct, substantial and reasonably foreseeable impact on the requesting party's consumers, or where the anti-competitive activities occur principally in and are directed principally towards the other party's territory. In other words the presumption arises where the requesting party is seeking to protect its export trade or where the centre of gravity of the anti-competitive activities is within the territory of the other party.

---

[2] Official Journal of the European Communities : Ref. L 95, 27.4.95, pp 45-50

The Draft Agreement recognises that there may be circumstances where it is appropriate for both parties to undertake parallel investigations, for example when the public interest requires that particularly serious anti-competitive activity is subject to sanction in both jurisdictions. This recognition of the possible appropriateness of parallel investigations only applies where both markets are harmed.

Mergers are not within the scope of the Draft Agreement because US and EC merger legislation would not allow a deferral or suspension of action as envisaged by the Draft Agreement which contains the obligation to adopt a final decision within tight time limits. But the controversy over Boeing's merger with McDonnell Douglas demonstrates clearly that this, too, is an area needing further attention.

Even if not yet an answer to all potential problems, the Draft Agreement is therefore an important development in international cooperation in the field of competition law, and represents a political commitment to cooperate rather than seeking to apply antitrust laws extraterritorially.

There are a number of reasons why, beyond such bilateral experiments, the more general adoption of an international framework of competition rules should be considered in a liberalised and globalised world economy :

- to promote the existence of domestic competition structures in the jurisdictions of all WTO Members;
- to increase the effectiveness and coherence of the national competition policies of WTO Members. Instruments of cooperation can help overcome the obstacles to enforcement caused by the internationalisation of business behaviour;
- to avoid conflicts of law and jurisdiction between countries and to promote a gradual convergence of competition laws. This would increase the legal security of firms operating in different jurisdictions, as well as reduce their costs of compliance with competition laws;
- to strengthen the multilateral trading system and promote more equal conditions of competition and market access world-wide.

Let me take these issues in turn. Many countries or regions that have implemented comprehensive competition policies nonetheless lack the necessary instruments where the information central to the investigation may be located outside their jurisdiction and thus beyond their reach. Absent the necessary proof of anti-competitive conduct, competition authorities are unable to take remedial action.

Certain practices are difficult to tackle under present rules by any agency. For example, export cartels have, for trade reasons (the wish of countries to improve the terms of trade) not been subject to competition law in exporting countries. For legal and practical reasons too, competition law has not been applied. Absent an effect on the exporting country's markets, the competition authority has no jurisdiction over export cartels. For the importing country, export cartels have an effect on the market and so jurisdiction can be established, but the evidence needed to prove the existence of the cartels is located outside the importing country's jurisdiction.

As important as avoiding situations where no one can act is avoiding conflicting jurisdictions. This is a real risk. The 1980s and 1990s have seen a significant increase in international mergers, strategic alliances, joint ventures, licensing agreements etc. These arrangements may face examination by different authorities at the same time with a potential for a conflict in the law or remedy applied to the same case. In an extreme example, divergences in the laws applicable to the same set of facts may result in conflicting conclusions as to the legality of the behaviour under review. The Boeing case is too fresh in the public mind for comment to be needed here. The key point is that, even where there is a common view as to the anti-competitive nature of the conduct, the remedies imposed in each jurisdiction may be incompatible. Greater convergence of laws and cooperation between competition authorities would therefore reduce the likelihood of such conflicts and promote greater legal certainty for business.

Finally, the review of commercial practices involves considerable work and costs, both for competition authorities and for the businesses whose conduct is subject to review. If the same commercial practice falls within several jurisdictions the costs increase accordingly. Greater cooperation and the elimination of unnecessary duplication of effort can reduce costs to competition authorities and business alike.

Beyond these competition-based arguments, it is essential for trade liberalisation purposes, too, that there be an external dimension to competition policy. Anti-competitive practices affect the balance of access opportunities negotiated between WTO Members. They are the next serious set of barriers to trade. The application of competition law contributes to creating accessible markets and to assuring the overall openness and stability of the trading system. Competition policy is now clearly trade related, and the application of competition law principles on export markets will help level the playing field and promote equal conditions of competition for firms competing on international markets.

While governments today are subject to very strict international disciplines in respect of the laws they make or the measures they apply, as soon as these have an effect on trade, no rules exist at the international level to control anti-competitive commercial practices. Such practices can replace formal governmental barriers that have been reduced or eliminated. Arguably, the incentive for firms to engage in anti-competitive behaviour impeding market access (such as cartels combined with boycotts, exclusionary abuse of a dominant position, exclusionary vertical restraints) increases with the reduction of tariffs and other barriers. Also, as industrial structures in emerging economies increase in sophistication, so will the devices used by firms to protect the market from foreign competition. Finally, governments, whose freedom of action to support domestic industries through administrative measures has been curtailed by international rules, may be tempted to maintain lax standards of enforcement of competition regulation, or to grant exceptions to protect specific industrial sectors.

Although competition rules do exist in many countries, anti-competitive practices are often impossible to tackle without active enforcement by the domestic competition authorities. In the absence of international rules, firms have to rely exclusively on the commitment and tenacity of the agencies of the country where they operate to have their concerns addressed.

Recent history, notably concerning the markets for cars and photographic film in Japan and the US, confirms that real or perceived anti-competitive practices can generate trade friction. So far, we have muddled through, but I fear that the trading system will be unable to effectively resolve a growing number of such disputes in the absence of agreed rules of conduct.

Against that background, I am confident that the working group set up by the Singapore Ministerial will succeed in establishing a broad consensus over the next year or two to the effect that competition activities do need to be more closely coordinated, and that the impact of these national activities on world-wide access to markets justifies a leading role for the WTO.

I would not expect the next round in the WTO to result in the establishment of a comprehensive set of common rules as ambitious or as detailed as those incorporated into the TRIPS Agreement by reference to existing international intellectual property codes. But some meeting of minds should be possible on at least the key issues.

The European Union has proposed a multilateral framework of rules. The first key element would be a commitment that the principle of fair competition would be inscribed by all WTO Members in domestic law, and adequately enforced. This would be a clear parallel to the first principle of the TRIPS Agreement. Its implementation would necessarily be rather more difficult than for the latter, because the concept of competition is less widespread in today's public administration than was intellectual property protection in 1986. I hope that adequate technical assistance could help to close that gap.

The second building block would be to establish some basic common principles as to what fair competition was. All practitioners have agreed on the negative effects of certain horizontal restrictive practices, such as market sharing, price agreement, exclusive distribution agreements or boycotts on foreign firms. So-called vertical restrictions such as distribution or supply agreements are also universally condemned. In such areas it should not be difficult to identify those practices that are not only universally condemned but also constitute major obstacles to market access, and then to agree that their regulation (and generally prohibition) would constitute a key element in common rules around the world.

Similarly, in the field of mergers, it may be premature to propose the adoption of world-wide substantive norms, but it would not be inappropriate to harmonise procedures so that, where several territorial authorities have interest in a single proposed merger, duplication and conflict can be avoided. Even if we only succeeded in moving towards more compatible timetables for review of mergers, that would be a step in the right direction.

Beyond the areas where, even in a first round of talks, limited common rules might be established, the third building block in an international agreement would be more general provisions for cooperation between competent authorities. Here, the US models described above are directly relevant.

Finally, but not the least important, even the first steps towards an international instrument on competition should include firm dispute settlement provisions. The principle of allowing dispute settlement to apply in novel areas of WTO rule-making was particularly controversial in the field of intellectual property a decade ago. The Uruguay Round enabled us to reach a consensus in favour of the application of dispute settlement even to such sensitive matters. I am sure that dispute settlement is also essential in the field of competition, because without dispute settlement the WTO would lack teeth. Clearly, dispute settlement would not be expected to create in Geneva a court of appeal against the detail of national competition decisions. But the need to limit the scope for WTO review of national decision-making has been successfully met already in other fields, such as the prudential regulation of services, so it should not be too difficult to negotiate appropriate boundaries to WTO dispute settlement in the competition field either.

In a first stage, the more ambitious parts of this package might be applied only by a limited number of countries. Cooperation might provide for a series of levels of activity, starting with the exchange of information not restricted by national confidentiality requirements and by consultations on cases of common interest. But this is exactly the sort of area where flexibility is essential to get the process started, and I am sure that we should accept a degree of flexibility in order to ensure that we do indeed make a start soon.

Even set about with such qualifications, I am conscious that these may seem to be very ambitious objectives. I would certainly concede that they are far-sighted, but I believe that the GATT proved itself capable of just this sort of far-sighted endeavour, and I am confident that the WTO will match its predecessor's record.

3. Investment

Turning to investment, I may say that it was no coincidence that the liberalisation of world-wide flows of foreign direct investment (FDI) was the first theme I addressed publicly following the ratification of the WTO Agreement and the beginning of the post-Uruguay Round era. For the liberalisation of FDI could unleash enormous new opportunities for growth and prosperity in developing and developed countries alike.

Because developed countries share a commitment to the pursuit of prosperity in open markets, they share a conviction that the free flow of world-wide investment is a good thing. For their business people, FDI has always been a tool to break down barriers. It can secure access to raw materials. It can overcome barriers to market access, such as distance from markets and ignorance of local tastes.

For the host economy, however, investment was for too long regarded with suspicion. Developing countries, to be blunt, feared economic colonisation. Even in many developed countries, in Europe and elsewhere, foreign investment was regarded as an unwelcome challenge to local firms.

This earlier ambivalent attitude has now substantially changed. The issue of foreign investment has been largely divested of the ideological overtones of the 1960s. Investment is recognised for what it is: a source of extra capital to supplement domestic savings, stimulate the domestic banking sector and deepen the stock market; a boost to big-budget projects faltering for lack of official finance; a vehicle for export market access, rational production, technology transfer, and managerial know-how. In the wake of a surge in FDI, there may also be risks to manage, be it the over-valuation of the host country's currency, a growing current account deficit or the danger of over-easy decisions to make the wrong investments. But despite these (perfectly manageable) risks, FDI as such is no longer seen as a threat; transplants are no longer Trojan Horses. On the contrary, capital is recognised as a scarce resource that no country can afford to drive away.

Unsurprisingly, perhaps, as host countries have increasingly welcomed inward FDI, there has been a growth of popular fear in Europe, the United States and Japan that outward FDI cannot be as good for the home country as it is for the host country. Fortunately, however, the populist view that outward FDI is a self-wounding search for cheap labour is very far from reality. In most industries, labour costs account only for 5 to 10 percent of overall production outlays, as against 25 per cent as recently as the 1970s. Foreign direct investment tends not to occur in industries with a high labour content.

Nor are wage costs alone likely to determine any company's investment-location decisions. The quality of labour, the quality of infrastructure and the level (and growth potential) of local demand for a product are much more important. Very often, outward investment generates additional demand for exports of capital equipment, technology and sub-assemblies from the home country. Research into the subject very rarely suggests any adverse effect of outward investment on activity or employment levels. In short, investment is not a zero-sum game: there is no *sucking sound*, whether across the Rio Grande, across the borders of Europe or across the North-South divide.

The facts and figures suggest that the benefits of investment have been long understood by business, although not always by politicians. During the 1980s, world FDI increased at around 30 percent annually, more than 3 times the rate of world exports and 4 times as fast as world GDP. Investment is spreading as well as growing. It is no longer only large North American, European and Japanese transnational corporations (TNCs) that are driving these impressive investment figures:

- Large TNCs no longer have a monopoly of FDI. Small and medium-sized enterprises now account for one in ten of international investments made.
- Nor do the companies of Europe, North America and Japan dominate as of old. Newly industrialised economies are becoming outward investors in their own right, albeit from a low base. Four out of ten of the largest investors in China, for example, are East Asian. Nor are the *tigers* investing only in their own region. Indonesia will build its new regional passenger aircraft in Europe. Samsung is making a European investment worth US$700 million in consumer electronics. Indeed, the Republic of Korea is now the biggest foreign investor in Romania.
- Developing countries have become very attractive hosts to FDI. The share of investment going into OECD countries has been slashed in half during the past decade. Over half of world FDI now goes to developing countries, compared to less than one fifth as recently as 1989.
- The sectoral composition of FDI is changing too. The shift from goods to services-related investment is even faster than the growth of services in world trade, because many services require a commercial presence as a pre-condition of effective market access. In the United States, for example, services already account for over half of all FDI.

If investment is a desirable and desired thing, administrations may still sometimes find it threatening, because free FDI flows limit officials' ability to control and shape their countries' economic destiny. This disadvantage, if it is a disadvantage at all, is in my view massively outweighed by the advantage of allowing private sector decision-makers to generate economic benefits world-wide. But it is a price that some governments in some sectors still find difficult to pay. That is a tragedy. Investment is good for us all. It is not merely of economic but also of overwhelming political benefit. To trade is one thing, but to invest in each others' economies implies a lasting political involvement, a stake that we take in each other's societies, however distant or apparently different. Investment relies on, and helps to create, stability and prosperity world-wide. It is a critical building block in lasting international friendships and is an important guarantee to the sustainability of trade flows themselves.

That is why I attach enormous importance to further freeing the scope for investment world-wide, and welcome the long-standing commitment of companies of the developed countries to a better climate for investment. European employers put investment high on their agenda in their 1995 inauguration memorandum to President Santer, making clear that they wanted the investment regimes of Europe, as well as those of others, to be made as attractive as possible to world-wide investors.

What then are the problems that investors face, and what can one do to resolve them?

The most obvious obstacle to would-be investors is lack of opportunity: an embargo on FDI, whether economy-wide or in a single industry. Such wholesale restrictions are increasingly rare, particularly now that the tide of communism has receded so far. Remaining investment bans, which exist even in developed countries, may relate to what are presented as over-riding national security considerations, but are actually in some cases the unjustifiable hangover from a dirigiste past.

More widespread than a total ban and equally damaging is secrecy. Governments seem too often reluctant to publish clear guidelines as to who can invest and under what conditions. Would-be European investors in a number of countries, for example, do not know to whom to apply for an investment licence. Even if they do, they have no means of knowing whether their application is being processed, what considerations are being applied by those examining it, or when they might expect a reply. Clearly, in investment as in other areas where multilateral rules exist, transparency will be a minimum requirement.

The next requirement is non-discrimination. There must be no discrimination by host countries between foreign investors of different nationality. Once established, foreign investors as a whole should be treated no less favourably than national companies. In other words, we need a most favoured nation principle and a national treatment obligation.

Agreeing the precise scope of these rules may not be easy. For example, they would need to make clear that preferential regional investment arrangements are acceptable, subject to the usual sort of WTO safeguards against abuse of the process of regional integration. The European Union is of the view that new investment rules–like all the rules that already exist for agriculture, goods, intellectual property and services–should allow members of regional groupings such as the European Union to open up more rapidly among themselves than they may be doing multilaterally, if the multilateral pace of investment liberalisation is not adequate. This rule is not a tool of protectionism in investment any more than elsewhere. Nor need it be used extensively. Indeed, because the European Union has an open policy on establishment and treats all companies alike, the regional integration clause should not be seen as a threat at all. But it is a necessary guarantee of our future freedom, and I hope our partners will recognise this.

Beyond these key issues, foreign investors need to know that they can take the risk of investing in a given country free at least from unreasonable and uncompensated expropriation. They will invest only if they can have access to a fully convertible currency, can bring in key personnel, can repatriate their profits at will and are free from unduly onerous performance requirements.

Companies, being in existence to make profits, will also want to have reasonable treatment from tax authorities. The principle of non-discrimination must however be balanced against the legitimate aim of restricting tax evasion.

Solutions to all these problems are conceivable, and precedents exist in the agreements already made on related issues in WTO. The most difficult question is a more general one: how to resolve disputes about the application of such rules to real life? Detailed rules on these matters will be worthless unless they are backed by expeditious, fair and effective dispute settlement procedures that bind the parties and provide clear penalties for non-compliance.

The experience of the WTO shows that the world has come to accept the need for strong dispute settlement procedures. Should such disputes procedures in the investment field apply only between states or also between investors and host states? I am inclined to want to see both. Where a company's problems reflect a pattern of failure in the host-state's system, WTO-style dispute settlement has a key role to play in ratchetting down the obstacles to investment flows. But it may not be the only solution. Where a country's investment culture is already on the right lines, investor-state arbitration is enough to correct occasional departures from normally sound host-state behaviour.

Although this is a somewhat daunting list of issues, there are rules already in place that provide some answers to some of the problems. The most widespread and promising solutions to these problems are found in existing bilateral investment protection treaties. OECD countries as a whole have signed nearly 600 such agreements, mostly with non-OECD partners. European countries are particularly active. The geographical coverage of these treaties is uneven, but is growing. The problem now indeed is that there are just too many such treaties, that they differ one from another, and that they foster both a complex and an uneven basis for investment operations.

Regional agreements have also addressed investment liberalisation of late, but have yet to make much of an impact. The investment principles of Asia-Pacific Economic Cooperation forum (APEC), for example, seem entirely laudable, at least as far as they go. But they are non-binding and are couched in best-endeavours language, allowing any exception provided for in current domestic laws, regulations and policies. This does not detract from their significance as a step in the right direction by a group of countries not all of which had made any moves at all before now. But APEC is still without binding rules and without any dispute settlement.

The same goes for the developed world's regional organisation. The OECD national treatment instrument is similarly non-binding. Other OECD commitments relevant to investment also leave much to be desired, not least in their lack of effective enforcement procedures.

This survey of current rules need to be rounded off with a brief description of the substantial investment-related content of the Marrakesh package. To begin with, the TRIMs Agreement itself has made a number of useful contributions. It incorporates specific investment disciplines in the multilateral system for the first time. It secures full transparency, with an obligation to notify existing TRIMs, an obligation that will extend automatically in the future as the list of prohibited investment measures is lengthened. For non-conforming TRIMs, the agreement sets a strong standard of liberalisation by prohibiting the maintenance of those measures at the end of agreed transitional periods. All these requirements are backed by WTO dispute settlement. Most important of all, the agreement acknowledges that broader future work on investment will be needed in WTO.

On the investment protection front, the TRIPS Agreement marked a huge step-change in the climate for international investment in a range of knowledge-based industries.

The General Agreement on Trade in Services (GATS) also has widespread implications for investment. Establishing a commercial presence through FDI is often essential to effective market access in the services field. The GATS fully recognises this, and creates a positive liberalisation dynamic for investment and commercial presence. But this is not a perfect solution, although it does define categories of restrictions, for example, limitations on branching, that are generally prohibited. As with the TRIMs Agreement, consultations and dispute settlement on services will be governed by the new tougher dispute settlement discipline of the WTO. Both agreements provide Members with the right to compensation if their benefits are damaged by breaches of these obligations.

Where next? Without going further into detail, it is clear that there are already a lot of rules on investment. But they overlap and may contradict each other. They give less than complete coverage of the problems. They do not always have real bite. Their enforcement provisions are often lax.

What should happen next, to improve and strengthen current rules in a world in which the countries involved are ever more numerous, the ever smaller companies invest abroad and the industries involved are ever more complicated?

I take it for granted, first, that bilateral investment treaties will continue to play an important role for developed countries. Alongside bilateral arrangements, regional arrangements will have their place. They must be subject to proper oversight. But I do not see why regional investment arrangements should not be allowed on the same sort of basis as preferential regional trade arrangements are allowed in the WTO.

Neither regional nor bilateral action can match the need for broader efforts at investment liberalisation. The OECD for one has already done a lot of work on new investment rules. But this does not remove the ultimate need for world-wide investment rules. That is why the Commission proposed that the WTO be involved, starting now, in discussions of investment issues. I welcome the Singapore Ministerial decision to launch such discussions. We have no guarantee at this stage that the WTO will write binding WTO investment rules. Nor did we seek such a guarantee. But I am confident that there would be great advantage for all in a WTO investment agreement:

- First, it would cover everyone, including the newly industrialised countries which played such an active part in the Uruguay Round rule-making and which are playing an ever more active part in world-wide investment.
- Second, WTO rules are real rules, binding for all Members and subject to strict dispute settlement. Those are the sort of rules that business people recognise. They are of infinitely greater value than looser understandings binding narrower groups of countries.
- Third, in WTO, investment rules will take their place in a balanced package of disciplines. So, for example, more openness to investment could be accompanied by stronger WTO competition rules; this should neutralise fears of big multinationals abusing their position in emerging economies.

While I am optimistic that a consensus in favour of WTO negotiations will emerge, it would be wrong to pre-empt the period of confidence-building that has just begun among WTO Members by prescribing in great detail the sort of rules that would be needed. I do however wish to record one personal hunch, which is that the nature of the rules needed may be different for FDI than for past targets of WTO liberalisation.

The reason is simply that, whereas in the past we have very largely been regulating the trade-impeding instincts that arise all too frequently in the political processes of the nation state, we are here trying to bolster some rather more positive trends. Despite the continued camouflage of anti-investment rhetoric, developing countries without exception are striving to create an investment-friendly environment at home, and are striving to do so very largely by benchmarking themselves against their more successful competitors: i.e., by measuring their own policies against those of their peers. The experience of the European Round Table in over a decade of detailed and scientific analysis of developing country investment procedures is that the differences between regimes are narrowing and that the host countries are eager to demonstrate how much progress they are making towards liberalisation.

In these circumstances, objective and enforceable rules on issues such as national treatment, non-discrimination, transparency, due process and so on are certainly going to be needed, if only because they constitute themselves the fundamental benchmark policies for a successful FDI framework. Beyond that, however, we may need to be a little more imaginative than usual and perhaps in this field to consider whether WTO should become not only the body making the rules but also the body encouraging peer review and benchmarking. The two processes would be mutually reinforcing: benchmarking should lead to improvements in individual investment regimes which in turn could be notified and then bound as elements of the WTO obligations of a member.

Such flexibility would probably be helpful in bringing all countries to accept a first set of disciplines in a field that raises questions of sovereignty even in the sophisticated administrations of the developed world. It would also allow the sort of flexibility over time and between sectors that would enable all countries to make a start now where they felt able to do so, even if in some sensitive sectors full liberalisation was not immediately feasible. These are questions more than prescriptions, but it is not out of place to raise them here.

4. Conclusion

The tentative nature of these final remarks serves to demonstrate that the adventure of international economic liberalisation is far from over. The obstacles we face in competition, investment and other fields are novel and the answers too must be imaginative. As we tackle this new agenda, I am confident that the spirit of ambition and flair that enabled us to make a success of the Uruguay Round, pushed on so effectively by Arthur Dunkel, will be needed more than ever to keep the world economy on the liberal path set by GATT as its central bequest to the WTO world.

Bibliography

Brittan L (1992), *A Framework for International Competition.* Mimeograph

Commission of the European Community (CEC) (1994) *The Uruguay Round, a Global Agreement, Global Benefits*, Office for Official Publications of the European Communities (EurOP)

CEC (1995), *GATS: The General Agreement on Trade in Services: A Guide for Business.* EurOP

CEC (1995), *A Level Playing Field for Direct Investment World-wide.* COM(95)42 final. EurOP

CEC (1995), *Competition Policy in the New Trade Order: Strengthening International Cooperation and Rules: Report by a Group of Experts.* EurOP

CEC (1996), *Towards an International Framework of Competition Rules.* COM(96)284 final. EurOP

CEC: Directorate General for External Economic Relations (DG) (1993) *International Economic Interdependence : A discussion paper.* Mimeograph

CEC.DG (1994), *Trade and Investment: A discussion paper.* Mimeograph

CEC and UNCTAD Division on TNC and Investment (1996) *Investing in Asia's Dynamism. European Union Direct Investment in Asia.* EurOP

European Round Table of Industrialists (ERT) (1996), *Investment in the Developing World, New Openings and Challenges for European industry.* ERT, Brussels

Various (1995) *The Stockholm Trade Policy Seminar*, Ministry for Foreign Affairs, Stockholm

International Competition Policy and the WTO

*Merit E. Janow**

1. Introduction

In December 1996, at the Singapore Ministerial of the World Trade Organization (WTO), the world's trade ministers agreed to establish a working group to study and discuss the relationship between trade and competition policies.[1] Those consultations got under way despite a lack of consensus on the appropriate focus of the discussions and on whether or not competition policy was a subject matter that had a place under WTO rules or dispute settlement procedures in the future.

This lack of consensus should hardly surprise us, given the limited history of multilateral discussions on competition policy and the many differences among countries with respect to the structures and purposes of their competition laws and policies–if indeed they have them at all. For some countries, consumer welfare and efficiency are the highest competition policy priority, for others, social goals such as protection of small and medium sized industries are among the central purposes of competition policy. This discussion uses the term competition policy to encompass those national laws (such as US antitrust laws) and policies designed to promote competition in the marketplace and to deter and punish restrictive or abusive business practices. The main concern of competition law and policy is therefore private firm actions.[2]

---

* The author wishes to thank Jagdish Bhagwati and Eleanor Fox for their extensive comments and helpful suggestions. The views expressed herein are, of course, purely personal.

[1] The Singapore Ministerial Declaration stated that a working group would be formed *to study issues raised by Members relating to the interaction between trade and competition policy, including anticompetitive practices, in order to identify any areas that many merit further consideration in the WTO framework...The General Council will...determine after two years how the work of each body should proceed. It is clearly understood that future negotiations, if any, regarding multilateral disciplines in these areas will take place only after an explicit consensus decision is taken among WTO Members regarding such negotiations.* See Ministerial Declaration, 13 December 1996, available at: http://www.ustr.gov

[2] Competition law can also apply to the abusive conduct exercised by authorized monopolies or state enterprises. Many countries have developed complex rules to address the conduct of

By contrast, a central focus of trade policy is on *government* policies or practices that adversely discriminate between domestic and foreign goods and services and block access to markets. Non-discrimination, fairness, and transparency in the treatment of foreign goods and services are among the central objectives of multilateral trade policy. Competition policy is expected to be blind to the nationality of firms; trade policy in contrast is charged with seeking to eliminate distinctions in treatment even though some areas of trade policy permit such distinctions to be made, e.g., in anti-dumping and safeguard measures, which are designed to help domestic firms.

Although the core concerns of trade policy are not identical with the core concerns of competition policy, there are areas of overlap, and with increased globalization the two policy areas have become more intertwined. Why is this?

First, as formal barriers to international trade and investment have been reduced and international trade and investment have grown, this has brought renewed attention to private business practices that can nullify the effects of trade liberalization. Exclusionary practices on the part of private firms can adversely affect competition in a relevant market and raise costs not only for domestic consumers but also for foreign firms and consumers. Such arrangements may be between local firms or they may be transnational in nature and take the form of market allocation agreements, cartels and the like across national boundaries.

Second, government practices are often implicated in the mix. Governments can act affirmatively in ways that distort the operation of private markets and provide advantages to local firms. Examples include: discriminatory competition policy enforcement patterns; government authorized exemptions to national competition laws; the use of competition laws for industrial and trade policy purposes; or trade policy measures that more directly affect cross-border sales such as anti-dumping measures and voluntary export restraint arrangements. Alternatively, government practices can affect competition through acts of omission, e.g., by tolerating anti-competitive arrangements and failing to enforce competition laws if such laws are in place. Both areas referenced here–exclusionary or anti-competitive business practices and government practices that affirmatively or otherwise undermine inter-firm competition–lie largely outside international rules.

For some, this is a clear indication of weakness in the multilateral trading system that warrants the formal inclusion of competition policy into WTO rules and dispute settlement procedures. Others see the WTO as ill-suited for that purpose. This paper examines both sides of that debate. It concludes that new and expanded initiatives at the international level *are* needed, and it suggests incremental steps that could be undertaken bilaterally, regionally as well as multilaterally. This is not to say, however, that the logical next step is to develop international competition policy rules nor that the WTO itself would be strengthened if such rules were subject to WTO dispute settlement.

In making this argument, the paper takes a backward glance in time so as to review multilateral and other experiences with international competition policy

---

such enterprises. For example, under US law the state action doctrine immunizes some private action that is taken pursuant to articulated state government policies and that is actively supervised by the state.

issues; reviews sources of international economic tensions centering on business practices; and considers the pros and cons of possible different approaches looking ahead.

2. Evolution of Multilateral Coverage of Private Restraints and Competition Issues

Although the early architects of the International Trade Organization (ITO) were concerned about the pernicious effects upon the world trading system that could arise from international cartels, a review of history reminds us that the early efforts to identify and proscribe certain business practices within the ITO charter contributed to the quiet demise of the ITO.[3]

Opposition within the United States to the Havana Charter focused in no small measure on its provisions governing restrictive business practices. Particularly troubling to some was the notion of ceding antitrust jurisdiction to a nascent international organization whose governing charter was viewed as being less rigorous than US antitrust law and of uncertain application. In addition, there was considerable suspicion that foreign countries (especially the European nations) had different standards of business behavior from those practiced in the United States, and had a greater tolerance of cartels and other industrial agreements.[4]

Although the ITO never materialized, the issue of multilateral coverage of private anti-competitive business practices was not buried along with it. In the late 1950s, a group of 12 experts was convened at the General Agreement on Tariffs and Trade (GATT) to take another look at this question. That group could not reach a consensus opinion. While more has changed in the global economy than ever could have been imagined when that expert group met, the central arguments at the core of both the minority and the majority opinion remain relevant to our day.

The majority opinion recommended that business practices be left outside of dispute settlement (in particular, Article XXIII); rather, the majority advised parties to enter into bilateral consultations. The majority contended that the absence of consensus and experience in this policy area made it unrealistic to try to arrive at any multilateral agreement vis-a-vis the control of international restrictive business practices. One way of remedying this deficiency, they argued, would be to develop a supra-national body vested with broad powers of investigation, but this option was seen as unrealistic if countries had not yet addressed the problem at the domestic level.[5] In contrast, the minority expert view argued that Article XXIII of the GATT should be an available tool and that it was imperative that some measures be taken to counteract restrictive business practices having harmful effects upon international trade.

---

[3] Wilcox C (1949), *A Charter for World Trade*. Macmillan: New York, p 105

[4] Diebold W (October 1952), *The End of the ITO*. Essays in International Finance. Princeton University, No 16, p 18

[5] See GATT, Basic Instruments and Selected Documents (BISD) 7S/29

One consequence of this expert report was a GATT 1960 resolution calling for the GATT to provide a forum in which the Contracting Parties could confer on restrictive business practices, on an ad hoc basis and upon request.[6] This resolution existed in relative obscurity until it was invoked in 1996 by the United States in the context of a film dispute with Japan.

Some experts have argued that there remains some scope to apply the GATT rules to competition policy-based claims; however, the complaint would have to be based upon some measure applied by a government in contravention of an existing GATT obligation with respect to national treatment or a quantitative restriction, for example. A government measure that *creates* conditions by which business interests discriminate against foreign goods and services could give rise to a violation claim. Several GATT panels reviewing disputes involving Japan have elaborated the range of informal measures that could be deemed a government measure.[7] Then too, GATT's non-violation provisions provide some scope for a complaint of competitive foreclosure of a market, if, for example, non-application of national antitrust or competition laws were adjudged to be a government measure.[8]

Still, at least two other conditions would have to be satisfied: the measure would need to have altered the competitive conditions established by other GATT undertakings, and the government measure taken would have to be one that could not reasonably have been anticipated at the time that the tariff or other concession was made. Each of these conditions is a high hurdle that has rarely been brought to the test, and never directly with respect to competition issues as such.

Whatever the legal possibility of such claims under GATT rules, it is clear that the GATT served as a forum neither for the negotiation of common rules pertaining to business practices nor for the resolution of disputes that have arisen out of some mix of private and governmental practices. To put it another way, the GATT was used neither as a sword to reach private anti-competitive business practices, nor as a shield to protect private parties from the unilateral reach of foreign competition laws.

This state of affairs did not change fundamentally with the expansion of commitments that came out of the Uruguay Round. The important development that has occurred, however, is that selective new provisions in the WTO agreements now more directly address private practices seen as trade-restricting, and hold governments responsible to a degree for those practices. A few examples follow.

The *basic telecommunications services* agreement requires countries to liberalize market access and national treatment restrictions, and to implement regulatory

---

6 Specifically the recommendation states that ...*the party addressed should accord sympathetic consideration to and should afford adequate opportunity for consultations with the requesting party, with a view to reaching mutually satisfactory consultations, and if it agrees that such harmful effects are present it should take such measures as it deems appropriate.* See BISD (9th Supp, 1961) p 28

7 Japan Trade in Semiconductors, adopted in 4 May 1988. L/6309, BISD 35S/153-4, along with the recent film dispute between the United States and Japan (for which the panel report was not yet made public at the time of this writing).

8 For a comprehensive treatment of this subject, see. Hoekman BM and Mavroidis PC (March 1994), *Competition, Competition Policy and the GATT*. The World Economy. Vol 17, p 141

principles intended to guide domestic regulatory practices. These principles are not intended to serve as a comprehensive competition policy code for the telecommunications sector. They are selective, yet bespeak a recognition that telecommunications remains a heavily regulated sector and that in many jurisdictions regulatory authorities are not independent of telecommunications providers. Since domestic suppliers usually are dominant suppliers, whether they be private or public entities, such entities, if left free to make decisions about how to treat other suppliers, would be capable of thwarting the market access and national treatment commitments made by governments. The principles seek to support competition in the telecommunications sector by means of competitive safeguards designed to prevent major suppliers from engaging in anti-competitive practices.

The *General Agreement on Trade in Services (GATS)* also contains a number of provisions that seek to deal with anti-competitive practices of domestic service providers. For example, the GATS provides that monopoly service suppliers must not act in a fashion inconsistent with the most favored nation obligation under the Agreement, or with their scheduled commitments. Further, the GATS requires WTO Members to ensure that domestic monopolists do not abuse their monopoly positions in respect of markets in which they do not hold a monopoly position.[9] The accord requires mandatory consultation on alleged restrictive business practices upon the request of another WTO Member. It is not self-evident from the text what standards a panel would apply to determine whether such abusive conduct occurred.

Those examples are not a full recounting of the undertakings now part of the WTO agreements that address private business practices and competition policy matters. There are additional relevant undertakings as part of the new rules on investment, intellectual property, safeguard measures, technical barriers to trade, and others. They serve to illustrate several points: first, that some aspects of what might be considered competition policy have on a selective basis found their way into the WTO framework; and second, that these undertakings can enhance market access commitments, perhaps particularly in service sectors of economies that remain heavily regulated.

3. Some Problems, and Proposals for Addressing them

Let us now consider more directly some of the problems that have brought discourse on competition policy onto the world stage and then evaluate possible alternative approaches for addressing those problems.

- A first set of challenges has stemmed from enforcement and litigation of international cases. Cases have shown that international cartels and other abuses of international markets do occur and can be detrimental to firms and consumers whether located in developed or developing countries.

[9] See Article VIII(1) of the GATS in *The Results of the Uruguay Round of Multilateral Trade Negotiations: The Legal Texts.* WTO (1995), Geneva Switzerland, Annex 1B, pp 325-364

Uncovering such abuses is itself difficult. Additionally, enforcement or litigation of international cases often raise substantial procedural and evidentiary challenges, particularly when evidence and parties are located in multiple jurisdictions. Unilateral enforcement actions on competition policy occur against a backdrop of longstanding tensions vis-à-vis the extraterritorial application of national competition (or antitrust) laws.

US actions have been especially controversial in this regard. US case law at the turn of the century suggested that the reach of US antitrust law extended no further than the water's edge. By the mid-1940s, however, US case law had established that the Sherman Act applied to conduct occurring abroad when the participants intended to and did adversely affect US commerce and the effects were deemed to be more than minor. This came to be called the *effects* test.

At present, it is relatively undisputed as a jurisdictional matter that the reach of US antitrust laws covers foreign business practices perceived as having adverse consumer effects in the United States. And indeed, most industrialized countries now apply some form of effects test.[10] However, what distinguishes US antitrust law from competition law in many countries is that it carries both civil and criminal penalties, high fines, and private rights of action. In years past, a number of countries introduced so-called *blocking* and *claw-back* statutes, their specific raison d'être being to thwart US discovery practices and to ameliorate the effects of treble damages.

More recently, the locus of controversy has been the reach of US antitrust laws with respect to foreign private practices seen as limiting US exports and hence principally harming US producers as distinct from US consumers. In such *market-access* cases, the competitive harm is experienced by consumers in the foreign market as well as by the would-be foreign market entrant. Although officials from several governments expressed their strong objections to such market access cases, to date, few US antitrust cases have been brought under this theory. Indeed, this fact has itself led some members of Congress to the belief that US trade laws should be enhanced so as to provide greater potential coverage of foreign business practices.

Recent years have also seen efforts at improved cooperation between enforcement authorities of competition policy. For example:

- In 1991, the *United States* and the *European Union* entered into an agreement which facilitates discovery, and implements the notion of *positive comity*. In cases where both parties believe themselves to have an interest in pursuing enforcement actions, the agreement identifies comity factors to be considered in any effort to accommodate the claims of rival interests.[11] The notion of positive comity bespeaks an effort not only to ease or at least to manage tensions with respect to extraterritoriality, but also to raise cooperation to a new level.

---

[10] See American Bar Association, *Report of the Special Committee on International Antitrust*, September 1, 1991.

[11] See Agreement Between the Government of the United States of America and the Commission of the European Communities Regarding the Application of Their Competition Laws. Article IV. Available at: http://www.doj.gov

- In 1995, the *United States* and *Canada* replaced an earlier non-binding memorandum of understanding by entering into a Mutual Legal Assistance Agreement (MLAT). This agreement provides guidance for those situations in which a party requests that another party's competition authority initiate activities. It contains a lengthy list of factors for each party to consider, when the actions of one may affect important interests of the other.
- In 1994, the US Congress passed a statute authorizing US antitrust enforcement agencies to share confidential information and evidence, on a reciprocal basis, with foreign enforcement authorities. In 1997, the *United States* concluded its first comprehensive bilateral accord under this statute with *Australia*, covering both civil and criminal matters.

Implications from this review of recent cooperation agreements include the following: First, while international consultations between enforcement authorities have been taking place for many years, enforcement cooperation across international boundaries appears to be still at an early stage of development. Second, recent bilateral accords represent a further step towards making the compulsory process of one jurisdiction available for use by another requesting jurisdiction. The expanded positive comity notions, for example, provide the parties in question with the means to more systematically consider whether to exercise or to forgo jurisdiction over a case. These accords however do not seek to achieve substantive legal harmonization, nor do they contain binding dispute settlement mechanisms. As a result, policy conflict stemming from differing legal standards and national policy priorities are not clearly resolved by virtue of such accords.

- A second source of international economic tension, notably between trade authorities, has been engendered out of perceptions that countries are not enforcing their competition laws, are enforcing them in a discriminatory fashion, or are otherwise tolerating private, exclusionary practices on the part of local business to the detriment of foreign market entrants.

These types of allegations have clouded US-Japan trade and economic relations for more than a decade, and have resulted in a number of bilateral trade accords in areas such as glass, paper, automotive, construction services, and other sectors. Many of the challenged business practices focus in part on distribution (or vertical) business practices, where it has been alleged that unilateral and joint activities of domestic producers have effectively foreclosed foreign firms and other new entrants from using existing or developing new distribution channels. These problems have arisen in the trade context and solutions, however unsatisfactory, have been embodied in trade agreements.

In those instances where the Government of Japan has been prepared to make specific sectoral commitments, those usually encompass commitments to proactively encourage imports and to vigorously enforce its Anti-Monopoly Act. Responses by Japan's competition policy agency have appeared, for the most part, defensive and limited. In few, if any, sectoral disputes that have been the subject of bilateral trade/market access tension has Japan's Fair Trade Commission found a domestic antitrust violation.

The bilateral trade accords that speak to the issue of Japanese business practices have generally been unpopular in Japan and have produced mixed results. In Japan, US trade objectives have commonly been characterized as US government advocacy for non-transparent and unwelcome administrative guidance on the part of Japanese bureaucrats in favor of imports. Furthermore, although some sectors (notably semiconductors) have witnessed significant increases in foreign market penetration in Japan, overall these bilateral trade accords have not established a durable trade policy framework within which can be addressed market access disputes centering on exclusionary business practices.

- A third source of international economic tension has emanated from those legal conflicts that have arisen in the context of multi-jurisdictional review of mergers.

Large international mergers typically require review by multiple competition authorities. Disclosure requirements, timetables, and legal standards differ a great deal, depending on the jurisdiction. The proposed merger of McDonnell Douglas and Boeing in 1997 made these points in a dramatic fashion. In that case the US Federal Trade Commission decided to close the investigation of Boeing's proposed acquisition of McDonnell Douglas, since it had concluded that the acquisition would neither substantially lessen competition nor tend to create a monopoly in either the defense or the commercial aircraft markets.[12] The European Commission took issue with the merger, raised concerns about the effect of the merger on Boeing's dominance, and threatened to reject the merger and impose large fines unless some specified adjustments were made by Boeing.

Despite the fact that neither of the two merging firms had production assets within the European Union, few competition law experts took issue with the authority of the EU to review the proposed merger, given the global commercial aircraft market. Rather, at issue were the different legal conclusions reached by US and European authorities. This case generated a great deal of heated public comment on both sides of the Atlantic to the effect that the respective conclusions reached by the EU and US competition authorities were informed not so much by competition law as by national champion and trade policies hiding behind competition law. At any rate, this case offers a generous crop of lessons. We learned, and not for the first time, that:

- In a global economy, two or more nations can lay jurisdictional claim to the same business transaction.
- Major competition authorities can come to sharply different substantive legal conclusions, even when they have the same facts before them.
- The European Union (like the United States) is fully prepared to apply its own laws when a foreign transaction is thought to have effects within the European Union. This pattern of extraterritorial application is in fact likely to proliferate. For example, there were press reports at the time of the Boeing case that Japan too was considering the implementation of domestic measures to allow Japan to

[12] See, Statement of Chairman Robert Pitofsky and Commissioners Janet D. Steiger, Roscoe B. Starek III and Christine A.Varney in the Matter of The Boeing Company/McDonnell Douglas Corporation. File No. 971-0051. At http://www.ftc.gov/opa/9707/boeingsta.htm

legally express its judgement on foreign mergers having potentially significant effects upon the Japanese market.

Surely, this range of tension suggests that more international attention to competition policy and its enforcement is needed. What might be done, and what role might be played by the WTO? These questions have produced a robust body of literature and considerable expert debate. Many interesting proposals have surfaced; here we shall focus on two major alternative models that have been advanced by some experts and policymakers.[13]

Some leading European experts and officials have proposed the development of a comprehensive multilateral framework of rules and procedures governing competition policy. Sir Leon Brittain in particular has been a forceful advocate of a new round of multilateral negotiations focusing on developing competition and merger rules and holding governments responsible for the implementation of those rules. This view received support in an influential 1995 report submitted to DG-IV by a group of leading European experts. They called for movement on two fronts: first, a further deepening of existing forms of bilateral cooperation; second, the gradual construction of a plurilateral agreement inclusive of a *dispute settlement procedure based on a set of jointly determined competition rules.*[14] The expert group argued in favor of establishing minimum rules and then gradually expanding the number of countries signing on to those rules.

A second viewpoint, expressed frequently by US officials, has opposed efforts to develop multilateral rules and instead urged the adoption of more effective bilateral and plurilateral cooperation agreements. Let us consider each of these alternative proposals.

Quite distinct from the question of whether international competition policies could be effectively administered at the WTO is the threshold matter of whether the development of international competition rules, enforced at the international level, is desirable and achievable. I think generally not. Such a formulation presupposes either a degree of convergence of underlying laws or a move toward formal harmonization of competition laws.

As for the benefits of formal harmonization of competition laws, they certainly have long been debated. At this juncture, neither the need for that step nor the requisite trust to undertake that step has shown itself to be evident.

The considerable variation that exists among even apparently similar national competition laws is likely to mean that a new overarching set of binding rules might have to be drafted at such a level of generality as to make the effort of questionable value. There may be broad agreement in many OECD jurisdictions on disallowing horizontal agreements among competitors to fix prices, engage in group boycotts, and allocate markets. Yet, once we move outside the narrow area of hardcore offenses, differences in national standards as to permissible business practices become substantial.

---

[13] A particularly nuanced treatment of this subject and proposal was advanced by Professor Fox. See Eleanor M. Fox (January 1997), *Toward World Antitrust and Market Access.* American Journal of International Law. Volume 91, No 1, pp 1-25

[14] EC DG-IV, *Competition Policy in the New Trade Order: Strengthening International Cooperation and Rules.* Report of the Group of Experts. (Brussels: July 1995) p 23

For example, the application of national laws with respect to abuse of dominance (or what is called monopolization under US law) often require that there be a finding of market power in relation to a defined market. For the United States and the European Union, market share is a common proxy or first screen. However, there are significant differences as to the level of shares that can be considered problematic–high shares are required in the United States whereas lower levels could suffice in the European Union.

The treatment of vertical restraints differs significantly across jurisdictions–and has undergone substantial modifications within countries, over time. The Chairman of the US Federal Trade Commission noted recently, for example, that some of the anti-competitive effects identified by the European Union would not be given much weight in an American court; indeed, they might be regarded today as efficiencies rather than anti-competitive effects.[15]

Thus, while some degree of soft harmonization is occurring as a result of increased interaction between firms and legal regimes, formal harmonization, especially by means of a set of international rules, seems problematic and unlikely to be productive.

Then too, the case for an international body reviewing international merger cases under binding dispute settlement procedures is even harder to imagine. In this sense, the concerns raised by the majority opinion in the 1960 GATT expert study group remain alive today: there is likely to be considerable objection in some countries to the idea of an international body attempting to sit in judgement over the complex decisions rendered by national competition authorities and courts.

Only the member states of the European Union have been prepared to confer jurisdiction over competition policy to EU authorities with respect to transactions seen as having EU-wide effects. This record of economic integration is an extraordinary and unique one. It doubtless reflects the interest in using Community-wide law to address the economic fragmentation of Europe and its war-torn history. One wonders if European nations would have been prepared to integrate their competition policy regimes even if there was no overall integration scheme.

What possible role then for the WTO? The dilemma is this: the WTO has shown itself capable of addressing trade restricting and discriminatory government practices and of serving as a forum for negotiating the reduction and elimination of such trade distortions. With its wide membership including both developed and developing economies, enhanced dispute settlement capabilities, and broad coverage of issues, the idea of taking additional problems in international commerce to the WTO is appealing. The need for more international policy engagement on competition policy is now also obvious.

At the same time, however, the WTO has a number of limitations of relevance for competition policy that need to be considered. As noted earlier, the goals of competition and trade policy are not identical, and it is not clear whether the WTO

---

[15] See Robert Pitofsky, *Vertical Restraints and Vertical Aspects of Mergers–A US Perspective*. Fordham Corporate Law Institute. Paper presented at the Twenty-Fourth Annual Conference, International Antitrust Law & Policy. 16-17 October 1997

can prove to be an environment in which competition policy goals can survive a trade dispute.

As succinctly stated by the head of the US Antitrust Division, the negotiation of competition rules within the context of a multilateral trade negotiation could result in the codification of the politically most feasible as opposed to the economically most efficient or the most consumer welfare enhancing outcomes.[16] It is possible that such a process could, over time, gradually ratchet up an improved appreciation for competition policy and its enforcement, but this is uncertain.

Further, if competition policy disputes were to become subject to WTO dispute settlement, what standard of review would be applied by a dispute settlement panel? Most of the areas of possible expansion of the WTO's agenda involve an expansion of international rules into areas of national policy. Hence, although this question of standard of review is not confined to competition policy, it is particularly critical given the evolving legal doctrine of competition policy. Surely, in the competition policy context this bespeaks a need to accord a high degree of deference to the decisions of national authorities. (This point of view has been stressed in the EU expert report and emphasized in the earlier 1960 GATT expert committee report). Determining appropriate standards of deference to national authorities when the suspect practice is government bias (e.g., in competition policy enforcement practices) would be a major challenge.

It may also suggest that the scope of WTO review, if it were to take place at all, should be kept narrow. One expert has suggested that dispute settlement or its equivalent should consider procedural issues such as the conditions whereby a country is obliged to undertake an investigation, transparency of process, and the like.[17] Although that might be constructive, these procedural screens, while serving some purposes, may still not ensure that there is an effective competition policy regime in place. For example, there are environments where the legal and institutional competition policy infrastructure is in place, largely transparent, etc. but the end result is not an effective regime.

These complexities and others all suggest the benefit of developing a positive international vision for competition policy in the next century. But we are also suggesting that such positive vision needs to encompass incremental measures that build domestic and international cooperation and enforcement capabilities. Let us consider a few alternatives:

- Promoting the further development of effective competition laws, policies and enforcement capabilities at the national level.

Many more countries now have competition legislation and national agencies in place than when the GATT experts convened in 1960; yet their conclusion still seems apt. Namely, that international cooperation on competition policy matters is likely to have as a prerequisite the development of laws and institutions at the national level. In some environments, competition authorities are weak or belea-

---

[16] Remarks by Joel I. Klein, Assistant Attorney General, Antitrust Division, Department of Justice. Presented at Fordham Law Institute, 24th Annual Conference on International Antitrust Law and Policy. New York, 16 October 1997

[17] Frederic Jenny, *The Interface Between Competition Policy and Trade, Investment and Economic Development.* Conference paper presented in New Delhi, 17-18 March 1997

guered by powerful other interests. In part for this very reason, there may be a role for multilateral, regional as well as bilateral discussion of the structural and analytical features that regulatory and competition enforcement agencies need in order to establish effective regimes. Expanding links with other international organizations more technically versed in competition law and policy that can also offer analytical support may provide one means of increasing the WTO's general capabilities to serve as an advocate for competition policy and institutional development.

- Considering additional and expanded procedural cooperation agreements in the area of enforcement cooperation as well as mergers.

To some degree, cooperation agreements may serve to require countries to internalize, or at least to consider more fully, the important interests of the other party. Additional bilateral or even regional cooperation agreements may be constructive incremental steps. Such arrangements appear to have few of the downside risks that can be associated with bilateral trade accords. Cooperation agreements between enforcement agencies are likely to be viewed as risky by business interests if there is a perceived risk of leakage of confidential information, requiring careful attention to safeguards.

In the merger area, additional efforts at procedural harmonization could reduce transaction costs for business and interject a higher degree of predictability. This too, is not a new idea, and much work has been undertaken, including at the OECD, on steps that could be taken to develop common filing forms, harmonize deadlines, disclosure requirements, etc. Looking to future initiatives, it may also be constructive to further consider the conditions under which deference or positive comity could be appropriate in the merger context.

- Considering selective additional competition policy commitments in the context of new and future multilateral negotiations is also important.

As negotiations get under way for new or existing areas of sectoral coverage, integrating competition policy objectives explicitly in those sectoral agreements should be considered, e.g., in areas such as the rules governing government procurement practices, investment restrictions and service sectors of an economy.

- Considering new or enhanced consultation mechanisms among trade and competition enforcement officials at the WTO and elsewhere could prove useful.

This might entail, for example, using the 1960 consultation provisions of the GATT or some other mechanism both as an early warning device when disputes involving a mix of government/business practices are looming as well as a place for holding consultations when such conflicts are under way.

4. Concluding Observations

Although the core concerns of trade policy are not identical with the core concerns of competition or antitrust policy, there are areas where these two policy areas are congenial and indeed are mutually reinforcing. A near-term challenge for early discussions on competition matters at the WTO is to focus on those areas where some meeting of the minds might well prove possible and constructive.

A world where there is more extensive international cooperation on competition enforcement and more engagement on the relationship between private business practices and access to international markets will represent a significant step forward. It is unlikely, however, to be synonymous with effective access to international markets. Improvements in competition rules and their enforcement may be a necessary but not sufficient condition for effective market access; many areas will require additional initiatives in terms of trade liberalization and regulatory reform. While it is not obvious that all roads lead inexorably to the World Trade Organization as a forum for settlement of competition related disputes, the WTO still has an important role to play in strengthening international engagement on competition issues.

The Uruguay Round Results and National Sovereignty

John H. Jackson

1. Introduction

It is a privilege to participate in a volume of writings to honor Arthur Dunkel, former Director-General of the GATT. Arthur Dunkel's efforts were central to the development and successful conclusion of the most massive international trade negotiation ever held–the Uruguay Round. The results of this Round, and most notably the establishment of a new institutional framework for international economic relations through the World Trade Organization (WTO) and its reformed dispute settlement procedures, are already having a significant impact on the way trade diplomacy is conducted. This is raising questions in the minds of national political leaders and diplomats, and among those questions is the one addressing the concept of sovereignty.

This issue was critical for the final implementation and acceptance by national governments of the Uruguay Round. In particular, during the 1994 debates in the US Congress about accepting the Uruguay Round, there were many hearings and other discussions about whether the new WTO Charter would be too constraining and intrusive on national government sovereignty. This brief article explores some of those arguments about the WTO and the question of its impact on sovereignty, whatever that word means.

2. Meaning of Sovereignty

One of the problems is the very word sovereignty, which has been used in a variety of contexts and often in a very loose sense to designate any situation where international treaty norms, or other international organization decisions and activities, appear to legally constrain what national governments would like to do.

Much older concepts of sovereignty are clearly out of date, but the word is still widely used in a variety of settings, which often imply different sub-meanings.[1]

In broad brush, I see the antiquated definition of sovereignty as something like the notion of absolute power of a nation state's supreme authority over its subjects and territory, unfettered by any higher law or rule (except perhaps ethical or religious standards) unless that nation state consents in an individual and meaningful way. It could be characterized as the nation state's power (embodied in the monarch?) to violate virgins, chop off heads, arbitrarily confiscate property, and all sorts of other colorful actions.

No sensible persons today would agree that such sovereignty legitimately exists anywhere in the world. A multitude of treaties and customary international law norms impose international law constraints (at least) on extreme forms of arbitrary actions even by a sovereign as to his or her own citizens. Of course some theories can explain these constraints as having been consented to by sovereigns, but they cannot always explain the observable phenomena of modern day international law applications. Furthermore, policy advocates and political representatives sometimes argue that their nation should decline to accept a treaty *because* it takes away its sovereignty by consent. Indeed, in this sense all treaties take away sovereignty and so the argument of some would seem to deny the validity of any treaty acceptance.

But then what does sovereignty in today's usage signify? I will suggest a tentative hypothesis: most of the time when sovereignty is used in current policy debates, it really refers to questions about the allocation of power; normally government decision-making power. I would argue that most of the sovereignty objections to joining an international treaty are basically arguments about the allocation of power among different levels of governmental and other institutions. That is, when someone argues that the US should not accept a treaty because it takes away US sovereignty to do so, what that person most often means is that a certain set of decisions should, as a matter of good government policy, be made at the nation state level, and not at an international level.

Often this meaning is not articulated and the objection to a treaty is stated in generic terms, sometimes with religious fervor, so that the argument seems easy to dismiss. When stated so broadly, opaquely and categorically, the sovereignty argument indeed appears unrealistic; it assumes a degree of independent action for a nation state that hardly exists today. However, when viewed as a question of

---

[1] Portions of this manuscript are adapted from an earlier manuscript by this author, as follows: Jackson JH, *The Great 1994 Sovereignty Debate: United States Acceptance and Implementation of the Uruguay Round Results.* In: Essays in Honor of Louis Henkin. (Kluwer Publishers, forthcoming). At the time of this writing also to be published in the Columbia Journal of Transnational Law, October 1997 issue. Other works relevant to the subject of this article include: Jackson JH (1996), *Reflections on Constitutional Changes to the Global Trading System.* Chicago Kent Law Review. Vol 72, No 2; Jackson JH (1997), *The World Trading System: Law and Policy of International Economic Relations*, 2nd ed, MIT Press: Cambridge Mass; Jackson JH (1995), *The Uruguay Round, World Trade Organization, and the Problem of Regulating International Economic Behaviour.* Hyman Soloway Lecture Ottawa: Centre for Trade Policy and Law

allocation of power, the debate only begins with the sovereignty objection; it must continue with an analysis as to why it is better or worse for such a power shift to occur in certain specified circumstances.[2]

To go further, I suggest that the allocation of power issue, as often embraced by an invocation of a sovereignty argument, is part of a very complex landscape of issues relating to the allocation of power for all types of government (and non-government) decisions in our world today. First there is a question of *vertical* allocation of power: At what level should a decision be made? An international body? A national body (the federal level)? A sub-federal entity? A local neighborhood? What are the elements to consider in deciding such questions?

Second there are also *horizontal* power allocation questions. Should a certain decision be under the control of the legislature, the executive, the judiciary or some other government entity, or even a non-government entity?

When sovereignty objection arguments are decomposed and examined for underlying reasons, then it becomes clear that there is merit to examining closely what is at stake for a nation to accept the constraints of an international treaty.[3] Clearly what is at stake will differ with the size, power, population, economic circumstances, etc. of the nation state. A large and powerful state would more likely be hesitant to accept obligations to an international decision-making procedure which would most probably result in decisions contrary to the national goals of such a powerful state. This might be because of a one-nation one-vote voting structure with a large membership of mini-states whose national goals are inconsistent with those of the large state. Consequently, what often becomes important is the actual constitutional structure of the international institutions put in place by the treaty obligations.

By way of contrast, small countries might find that membership in certain types of treaty-based international institutions actually enhances sovereignty in certain real senses. By such membership, they may feel less threatened by other nations

---

[2] It is evident that the concept of *subsidiarity*, currently the subject of intense debate in Europe, is closely related to this discussion. I do not intend here, however, to get into the middle of the European debate.

[3] Statement of John H. Jackson: (Hessel E. Yntema Professor of Law, University of Michigan) The World Trade Organization and US Sovereignty: Hearings Before the Senate Committee on Foreign Relations. 103d Cong. (June 14, 1994): *This does not mean that it is frivolous to carefully study the question, as this hearing is designed to do. It is important to assure ourselves that if there develops the rare situation when an international body or rule system operates in a manner to abuse the rules or abuse the procedures of an organization so as to threaten the vital interests of the United States, that the US will still retain the tools to take appropriate counter measures. In the case of the WTO, I believe that the US and other nations are protected in that respect. Among other protections, the WTO Charter allows for withdrawal with a brief six month notice. It is also the case that this Congress is likely to specify in the implementing legislation that the WTO Charter and the Uruguay Round rules are not 'self-executing', so again in the rare case of serious abuse of international procedures the US would maintain its own constitutional freedom to act even if inconsistent with international rules. In such a case, of course, the US could be in breach of its international legal obligations and might face counter-measures.*

which are much larger and more powerful. For example, a dispute settlement mechanism might, in the eyes of a small country, redress some of the imbalance of power when it comes to handling disputes or sources of tension about the way either nation has been applying its international economic policies (such as trade barriers).

3. The US Uruguay Round Implementing Act: Decomposing the Sovereignty Arguments

The Uruguay Round results were signed on April 15, 1994. During the ensuing months the Office of the US Trade Representative and its officials worked with the Congress to develop a proposed statute. The votes were held in the House of Representatives on 29 November 1994, with approval by 288 to 146. In the Senate the vote was 1 December 1994 with approval by 76 to 24. During 1994 many congressional hearings in a large number of different committees were held on the Uruguay Round results and the proposed statute (including some ancillary issues). In a number of these hearings the issue of sovereignty was an important focus in one way or another. Combined with a general public debate in all the various media, as well as many academic, business and other public fora, 1994 witnessed in the US a truly major and historical debate about questions of US economic treaty participation and their relation to various concepts of sovereignty.[4]

I now look more closely and specifically at some of the various issues discussed in the Great 1994 Sovereignty Debate. I will not attempt to present an exhaustive inventory of all the varied arguments relating to sovereignty. The question on which I will focus is: What did the opponents of the Uruguay Round mean when they argued that the US should not accept the Uruguay Round results because it "detracts from or takes away US sovereignty?" And what did the proponents mean when they said that such arguments do not lead to the opponents' conclusions?

It should be immediately noted that although the conclusion (to accept or not to accept) is basically bipolar, the arguments are not necessarily so. Specific sovereignty considerations may add up to a conclusion one way or the other, but merely because a small bit of sovereignty is taken away does not mean that no treaty should be accepted. Offsetting policies may make it appropriate to give up some sovereignty in order to achieve some important policy results. A classic situation is represented by the prisoner's dilemma, in which independent actions by a group of players can result in worsening the situation for all; but cooperation can prevent such a result. (This is a classical trade policy argument).[5] Likewise it should be noted that sovereignty loss can have a number of different meanings, which dif-

---

[4] See generally: *Uruguay Round Agreements Act: A Legislative History of Public La.* No. 103-465, 1994 U.S.C.C.A.N (108 Stat. 4809) 3773

[5] Jackson JH, Davey W and Sykes A (1995), *International Economic Relations*, 3rd ed, West Publishing Co 1995, p 33; Kenen PB (1989), *The International Economy.* 2nd ed, p 125

ferent persons weigh differently in their policy advocacy. For example, loss of sovereignty could mean that:

A nation's right/power to pursue certain domestic policies is diminished because of:

- interference by international law constraints, regardless of whether these operate effectively or whether they cause domestic law changes which in turn pose constraints
- practical or real constraints (for example because of international economic interdependence)
- interference by international law institutions in a manner that changes domestic law and the constraints it offers
- constraints of international treaty law norms which, although ignorable, can result in retaliation, compensation, or other counteractions by other nations or players

Treaty acceptance causes external influences on domestic policy in certain ways disadvantageous to the opponent of the treaty. For example, an opponent may fear that certain domestic special interests (such as large corporations) may have greater abilities than most groups to influence the international body, and thus achieve results by the remote pressure of international decisions or norms that could not otherwise be achieved at the national government level. (For different subjects, this can operate in difference directions, so it is not impossible to find a particular domestic interest opposing some treaties and favoring others, even though both diminish national sovereignty).

3.1. General Implications of Accepting Substantive Treaty Norms

Some of the sovereignty arguments are aimed at the mere fact of accepting treaty obligations for certain subject matters. Other objections may relate to the implications of becoming part of the treaty institutions.

Focus for the moment on the question of acceptance of a treaty with various substantive norms, but no institutions; that is, no joint decision-making powers or dispute settlement procedure is contained in the treaty. When opponents to such acceptance argue that the treaty *takes away* sovereignty, what are they likely to mean?

Clearly acceptance of any treaty reduces the freedom of scope of national government actions in some sense. At the very least, certain types of actions inconsistent with the treaty norms would give rise to an international law constraint, and the amount of constraint will then vary with the institutional mechanisms for enforcement as also with the national domestic government structure or political attitude towards international norms. Some skeptics might dismiss an international norm as ineffective and thus not constraining. But if a treaty norm were *self-executing* or *directly applicable* in a domestic legal system, it could have a greater constraining effect. Even without such effect, a treaty can have important domestic legal effects, such as influencing how domestic courts interpret domestic legislation. Beyond that, a treaty norm even without domestic legal effect can have weight in some domestic policy debates where some advocates will stress that positions contrary to their views would raise serious international or treaty concerns.[6] Thus the sovereignty *objection* can be seen to be directed more to the question where should a decision be made, and what influences on that decision should be permitted.

It can also be observed that the lack of direct effect of a treaty in domestic law is considered a possible protection against sovereignty *diminution*. This is because, without direct effect, a nation normally can decide how to respond to a complaint that its actions have breached international law, and one possible response is to ignore the complaint and live with the breach. This may not be particularly admirable but it can act as a sort of buffering process, safety valve, or check and balance against international action that might be deemed overreaching or otherwise inappropriate.[7]

Finally, it should be noted that the legal ability to withdraw, within a defined period of time, arguably reduces the worry about infringement *on* sovereignty. This option seemed to be interesting to some of those worried about the sovereignty arguments. The Uruguay Round treaty provisions allow withdrawal upon six months notice. Whether this is a realistic option for nations today, in the light of their considerable dependence on international trade and the trade system of the WTO, is a somewhat different question that can be considered also.[8]

Related to the considerations mentioned above, some general objections to a treaty are driven by the substance of particular issues. Many environmentalist advocates and groups in the 1994 debate were concerned that specific treaty clauses would trump US environmental law, or even state law such as that of California, in a way to harmonize downward the more stringent US law about which the environmentalists were justifiably proud. Thus important questions were raised about the legal and practical effect of the WTO and Uruguay Round treaty norms on particular subjects, and sovereignty *objections* became objections to the substance of the international norms, at least to the extent that those norms appeared not to give enough leeway to domestic US political institutions to decide more appropriate higher standards.

3.2. WTO Decision-Making Procedures–Risk to Sovereignty

Some of the sovereignty objections in the 1994 debate were targeted towards the institution of the WTO. Various opponents to the treaty argued that the WTO posed risks to US sovereignty because decisions could be made in the WTO that would override US law. This objection engages a number of particular clauses of the WTO, as well as relating to the legal effect of potential WTO decisions on US

---

[6] See, e.g., *Restatement (Third) of the Foreign Relations Law of the United States* §114 (1986)

[7] Jackson JH (1992), *Status of Treaties in Domestic Legal Systems: A Policy Analysis*. 86 AJIL 310

[8] See WTO (1995), *The Results of the Uruguay Round of Multilateral Trade Negotiations, Legal Texts*. The World Trade Organization, Geneva, Switzerland, Article XV

domestic law. As to the latter, testimony pointed out that WTO decisions did not have self-executing or direct legal effect in US law, so once again there was an element of buffering protection which in realistic terms gave the national government some opportunity to resist inappropriate international decisions.[9]

But more significant, perhaps, is the fact that the decision-making procedures of the WTO have been significantly circumscribed by negotiated treaty text. In fact, by comparison to the loose language of the GATT–which would have remained in effect if the WTO had failed to emerge–the WTO had many more protections for national sovereignty. These protections were significantly enhanced in the treaty drafting that went on during the fall of 1993, spurred by the US negotiators and other countries who worried about some of the general treaty text of the previous Uruguay Round drafts.

Without here going into these matters in depth,[10] an examination of a series of specific decision-making powers for the WTO general bodies shows protections such as super majorities (often three-fourths requirement of all the Members, not just those voting–a very difficult target to achieve), and prohibitions against changing the substantive rights and obligations of the Members without more difficult amending or treaty negotiation procedures. In addition, an emphasis on consensus decision-making is manifested in a number of provisions, sometimes with fall backs to voting only after a period of time for an attempt to achieve consensus. Indeed, some of these provisions could be seen to give a *de facto* veto power to a few of the most powerful trading entities. These features can be seen in the texts relating to:

- Amending the WTO and subsidiary agreements (Article X)
- Adopting a formal *interpretation* (Article IX:2)
- Adopting waivers (Article IX:3 & 4)
- Adding plurilateral agreements (optional agreements) to Annex 4 (Article X:9)
- Changing the Dispute Settlement Understanding in Annex 2 (Article X:8)

Most sovereignty objections clearly were aimed at power allocation. Members of Congress were concerned whether the allocation of power regarding WTO decision making was an inappropriate infringement on US sovereign decision making. Certainly this allocation was more protective of national government decision-making than of the GATT, and many other international organizations in today's world (although few of those organizations have such an extensive impact on national economies). It was clear in the Uruguay Round negotiation that there was

---

[9] *The World Trade Organization and US Sovereignty: Hearings Before the Senate Committee on Foreign Relations*, 103d Cong. (1994) (June 14, 1994, statement by Rufus Yerxa, Deputy USTR)

[10] Jackson JH (1995), *The World Trade Organization: Watershed Innovation or Cautious Small Step Forward?* The World Economy. 11; Jackson JH (1996), *The Uruguay Round and the Launch of the WTO–Significance and Challenges*. In: The World Trade Organization–the Multilateral Trade Framework for the 21st Century and U.S. Implementing Legislation, 5 (Terence P. Stewart, ed). See also, Jackson JH, *The Uruguay Round and the Launch of the WTO–Significance and Challenges*. Chapter 1 of American Bar Association Book on the Uruguay Round (1996), reprinted from World Trade Organization. See also *Hearings, supra* notes 3, 4 and 9

no chance to achieve any sort of formal, weighted voting (such as in the IMF or in the World Bank), or even a small special body with added power like vetoes or special competence (such as the United Nations Security Council). Thus the negotiators greatly restricted the decision-making powers of the WTO bodies, even to the point that there can be worry that the WTO will be hamstrung by inaction derived from its consensus culture.

3.3. The Uruguay Round Treaty and US Law: Implications for Sovereignty Issues

Several significant issues of US constitutional and other law also, sometimes oddly, became embroiled in the sovereignty debate. A few examples will be discussed.

3.3.1. The Famous US Section 301

A considerable amount of hostility has been expressed by US trading partners towards US "Section 301".[11] This statute has a special role in the US constitutional division of power between the Congress and the President, delegating to the President the authority to retaliate with trade sanctions against certain *unreasonable* or *unfair* foreign government actions that damage US commerce. This statute has sometimes been used by the US to apply trade sanctions against other nations in a manner inconsistent with US treaty obligations, and major Uruguay Round participants were determined to reign in US unilateralism. This determination was part of the impetus for improved dispute settlement procedures and for the WTO charter itself.

However, the US Congress made it very clear that it would not tolerate changes in Section 301, and the Executive negotiating position followed that mandate. So except for some minor procedural amendments, Section 301 remains intact. Yet it was explained in ways (too complex to recount here) that argued that Section 301 could not be found inconsistent with US WTO obligations (in the absence of some specific action). Indeed, the Section 301 statute does call for the use of WTO dispute procedures. This statute, however, was perhaps the most important political judication of the sovereignty considerations in the Congress during the 1994 debate.

3.3.2. The Treaty Clause and the Fast Track Statutory Approach

Another intriguing manifestation of sovereignty concerns was the subject of some interesting debates about the constitutionality of the Fast Track procedure for approving the Uruguay Round and the WTO. Two levels of sovereignty concerns were raised in this context (demonstrating that the allocation of power concept

[11] United States Trade Act of 1974, Section 301, 2411 (1994). See e.g., *Services of the European Commission.* Report on U.S. Barriers to Trade and Investment, 11-12 (1994)

goes deeper than just the federal level of a nation state).[12] It was argued that, despite various precedents to the contrary, when an international agreement involved major national commitments and membership in an international organization which might involve yielding US sovereignty to global institutions, the constitutional treaty clause requiring approval by two-thirds vote of the Senate was the only appropriate procedure, and the statutory procedure would be unconstitutional. In addition, regarding the second level of sovereignty arguments, it was argued that one purpose of the Senate treaty clause procedure of the constitution was particularly to protect the sovereignty of US sub-federal states. The Senate, it was argued, was a better protector of such states' rights since each state had equal representation there (two senators) and traditionally, it was claimed, was more assiduous in protecting states' rights.

This portion of the 1994 debate also involved various other constitutional arguments, and an interesting Senate Commerce Committee hearing in October 1994 with two debating law professors.[13] In the end, the Fast Track procedure was followed, and the Senate voted 76 to 24 in favor of the statute with its delegation to the President. It can thus be argued that this was yet another precedent for following the statutory procedure (at least for trade treaties or other matters related to the "commerce clause" of the US Constitution), and was also an opinion by three fourths of the US Senate favoring the constitutionality of the statutory approach.

3.3.3. Sub-Federal States in the United States

The question of sub-federal states of the US received considerable attention in the 1994 Uruguay Round debate. This and the prior NAFTA (North American Free Trade Agreement) were the first times since the origin of GATT that such attention was given to state interests. A major concern by the states was the potential for a broad scope treaty like the Uruguay Round results to invalidate many different state laws governing economic regulation, environmental affairs, product safety and health standards, etc. (insofar as these were left to the states by Congress or other federal bodies). An organization of state Attorneys General posed

---

[12] See *S.2467, GATT Implementing Legislation: Hearings Before the U.S. Senate Commerce, Science and Transportation Committee*, 103d Cong. (Oct. 18, 1994, Statements and discussion of Laurence H. Tribe and Bruce Ackerman). See also, Ackerman & Golove, *Is NAFTA Constitutional?* 108 HARV. L.REV. 4 (1995); Laurence Tribe, *Taking Text and Structure Seriously: Reflections on Free-Form Method in Constitutional Interpretation,* 108 Harv. L. Rev. 6 (1995). Finally see, *Statutory Procedure for Approval of the Uruguay Round Trade Negotiations and the WTO.* Treaty Clause Memorandum sent to various members of Congress and Executive Branch officials, dated November 11, 1994. Signatories included: Professors Bruce Ackerman, Yale University; Abram Chayes, Harvard University; Kenneth Dam, University of Chicago; Charles Fried, Harvard University; David Golove, Arizona University; Louis Henkin, Columbia University; Robert Hudec, University of Minnesota; John H. Jackson, University of Michigan; Harold Hongju Koh, Yale University; Myres McDougal, Yale University

[13] See footnote 12

sub-federal sovereignty objections to the Office of the US Trade Representative, and this Office worked with the state officials to include language in the 1994 Uruguay Round Agreements Act designed to protect state interests, particularly interests of states in potential dispute proceedings that might be brought at the WTO against certain state laws. Already, state laws had been subject to such proceedings under GATT in the Canadian challenge to state alcoholic beverage regulations. A GATT panel concluded that many of these state laws were inconsistent with GATT obligations such as the national treatment obligations requiring that imports be treated no less favorably than domestic products.

The result for the Uruguay Round Implementing Act was several lengthy sections giving state government officials various procedural rights to participate and provide inputs into US handling of WTO disputes affecting them. After this text was negotiated state officials indicated satisfaction with the approach and removed their objections to US acceptance of the Uruguay Round treaty.[14]

3.3.4. The Proposed WTO Dispute Settlement Review Commission

One of the more explicit manifestations of sovereignty concerns relating to power allocation in the 1994 debate was a compromise proposal between the US President and Senator Dole (then Senate Majority Leader).

A democratic President needed votes in a Republican-dominated Senate to achieve passage of the Uruguay Round Agreements Act; and in late November 1994, a few days before the congressional votes were scheduled, Senator Dole proposed the idea of later enacting a statutory commission composed of five US federal judges which would review adopted WTO panel reports that were adverse to the US, judging them against a list of four particular criteria.[15] The commission would then advise Congress whether it found any panel report to be contrary to any one of these criteria. If the commission were to make determinations of the contrary nature for three reports, then Congress would consider a resolution to withdraw from the WTO (giving the requisite six-month notice required by the Uruguay Round agreements.) This proposal (as of this writing in November 1997) has not become law, and appears unlikely to become law. Nevertheless the

---

[14] See Jackson JH, Davey W and Sykes A (1995), *International Economic Relations*, p.1168 (3rd ed). Schaefer M and Singer T (December 1992), *Multilateral Trade Agreements and U.S. States: An Analysis of Potential GATT Uruguay Round Agreements*, 26 Journal of World Trade, p 31. Statement of Administrative Action for the Uruguay Round Trade Agreements, Title I, Section 102, H.R. Doc. 103-316, at 15 (1994). Letter from Michael Carpenter (Attorney General of Maine), Heidi Heitkamp (Attorney General of North Dakota), Charles W. Burson (Attorney General of Tennessee) to Michael Kantor (USTR) (July 27, 1994) (on file with author)

[15] The proposed bill sets forth four criteria for evaluating WTO dispute reports, asking whether the panel had 1) exceeded its authority or terms of reference; 2) added to the obligations of, or diminished the rights of, the United States; 3) acted arbitrarily or capaciously or engaged in misconduct, etc.; or 4) deviated from the applicable standard of review including that in the antidumping text set forth in Article 17.6 of that text.

proposal, its findings and its criteria all reveal an explicit concern for various aspects of the sovereignty objections discussed above.

4. Broader Sovereignty *Implications* of the WTO Dispute Settlement System

Among the most important issues are the implications of the new dispute settlement procedures. Under the Uruguay Round text, these procedures are much more rigorous and legalistic than previously. No longer can a panel report be blocked. An appellate process is changing diplomatic thinking about trade problems. Likewise, we are now seeing a large number of cases brought, suggesting the possibility that the procedures are viewed with favor and as an opportunity to be pursued. There are indications already that many nations and particularly diplomats are finding the processes of the WTO in some ways substantially different from those of the previous GATT. In some ways this is worrisome. However, many of these matters will not become apparent until after we have a larger body of experience and jurisprudence under the dispute settlement system.[16]

5. Conclusions

Sovereignty, in practical terms, is still an important argument in many government policy debates. It has an emotional appeal and is often used in a blunt and undifferentiated way as a convenient argument by those who simply wish to oppose some specific government proposal. Yet when the context of the sovereignty arguments is analyzed it can often be demonstrated that they reflect some important policy concerns and issues that deserve scrutiny and resolution. In this article, I have done this and suggested that these issues seem to relate principally to the allocation of power, particularly as between international institutions and norms, compared to national or even sub-federal levels of government.

In the context of treaty acceptance, for example, questions are raised about the domestic-law effect of international norms, about the nature of international decision-making processes that can generate secondary norms obligating the nation state, about details of dispute settlement procedures affecting the credibility and efficiency of those procedures, and about questions of internal domestic allocation of power that are raised by international treaties, other norms and institutions. When we examine some of these details in a decomposed or disaggregated way, we can more easily determine how to weigh some of the disadvantages of those details against the advantages of strengthened international norms and institutions. This process in turn may then assist governments in evaluating the important policy considerations involved in participating in international institutions. Possibly

[16] Jackson JH (forthcoming) *The WTO: Constitution and Jurisprudence.* Chatham House (Royal Institute of International Affairs) London UK.

this approach to sovereignty arguments will lead to better government decisions, and force those who use sovereignty objections to policy proposals to be more concrete and explicit about their objections, enabling a more informed and constructive resolution of conflicting positions.

About the Authors

Jagdish Bhagwati

Jagdish Bhagwati is the Arthur Lehman Professor of Economics and Professor of Political Science at Columbia University, and was the Ford International Professor of Economics at MIT for several years. Between 1991 and 1993, he was Economic Policy Adviser to the Director-General, GATT. He is the recipient of several honorary degrees and Prizes, among them the Bernhard Harms Prize (Germany), the Seidman Distinguished Award for Political Economy (USA), the Mahalanobis Memorial Medal (India), and the Kenan Award (USA). Three volumes of essays in his honour have been published in the United States, the United Kingdom and the Netherlands. Aside from his scholarly work, he is also a frequent writer on public policy issues in leading newspapers and magazines.

Leon Brittan

Sir Leon Brittan is Vice President of the European Commission. In Brussels, Sir Leon has been responsible both for competition policy and, since 1993, for external relations, including multilateral trade policy. After a distinguished career at the Bar in London, and a series of senior ministerial posts in the UK government (1979-86), Sir Leon Brittan has been a member of the European Commission since 1989.

Willy de Clercq

Minister de Clercq became Chairman of the European Parliament's Committee on Legal Affairs and Citizens' Rights in January 1997. He was the European Commissioner for External Economic Relations (1985-89) at start of negotiations for the Uruguay Round of GATT. He was elected twice as Chairman of the Interim Committee of the International Monetary Fund. From 1973 to June 1977 he was Minister of Finance. In 1973, he became Deputy Prime Minister. He is Honorary President of the European Liberal Democrat and Reformist Party.

Jean-Pascal Delamuraz

Jean-Pascal Delamuraz, Swiss Minister of Economy, has been a member of the Swiss Federal Council since 1984. He first headed the Federal Military Department and since 1987 has been in charge of the Federal Department of Economic Affairs. Mr. Delamuraz was President of the Swiss Confederation in 1989 and again in 1996. Prior to his elected Government positions he was a member of the National Council (Lower House of Parliament) from 1975 onwards.

Richard Eglin

Richard Eglin is currently Director of the Trade and Development Division, which also covers regional agreements in the WTO Secretariat. He received a Ph.D. in Economics from Jesus College, Cambridge University, in 1977 and subsequently became a staff member of the International Monetary Fund in Washington. Mr. Eglin joined the GATT in 1985 and was given responsibility for Trade and Environment in 1991, when Mr. Dunkel first created the division. He was Director of that division until February 1997.

Geza Feketekuty

Geza Feketekuty is the director of the Center for Trade and Commercial Diplomacy at the Monterey Institute of International Studies. As director of the Center, he has developed both a research program in international trade and investment, and an innovative master's degree program in commercial diplomacy. He came to the Center with more than 20 years of experience in the Office of the United States Trade Representative and as Senior Assistant to the US Trade Representative. For several years he chaired the OECD Trade Committee. He has written numerous articles and books on trade policy issues, including: International Trade in Services: An Overview and Blueprint for Negotiations and The New Trade Agenda.

Robert E. Hudec

Robert E. Hudec is the Melvin C. Steen and Corporate Donors Professor of Law at the University of Minnesota. He served as a lawyer in the Office of the US Trade Representative during the Kennedy Round (1963-67), and as a member of several dispute settlement panels under GATT, NAFTA and the WTO. Professor Hudec is the author of: *The GATT Legal System and World Trade Diplomacy; Developing countries in the GATT Legal System*; and *Enforcing International Trade Law.*

John H. Jackson

Professor Jackson is University Professor of Law at Georgetown University, Washington DC and Hessel E. Yntema Professor of Law Emeritus at the University of Michigan. After graduating from Princeton (1954) and the University of Michigan Law School (1959), he practiced and taught law, later joining the Michigan faculty in 1966. In 1973-74 he was General Counsel of the Office of the US Trade Representative in Washington DC. He has authored many books and articles concerning GATT (and WTO). In 1992 he received the Wolfgang Friedmann Memorial Award for life-long contribution to the field of international law, at Columbia University Law School. He has taught in ten countries, and counselled many governments on matters of international economic law.

Merit E. Janow

Merit E. Janow is a Professor in the Practice of International Trade at Columbia University's School of International and Public Affairs. In November 1997 she also became Executive Director of the International Competition Policy Advisory Committee to the Attorney General and Assistant Attorney General for Antitrust at the Department of Justice. She was Deputy Assistant to the US Trade Representative for Japan and China in 1990-93. Previously, she practised corporate law in New York with a major Wall Street law firm. She has a J.D. from Columbia University School of Law and a B.A. in Asian Studies from the University of Michigan, Ann Arbor. She has written numerous articles and two books on trade policy issues.

Roy MacLaren

The Honourable Roy MacLaren, High Commissioner for Canada to the United Kingdom, was Canada's Minister for International Trade from 1993 to 1996. He served as Canada's Minister of National Revenue, Minister of State (Finance) and Parliamentary Secretary for Energy, Mines and Resources. Prior to entering politics, he held senior positions with Massey-Ferguson Ltd., Ogilvy and Mather (Canada) Ltd. and Canada Business Media Ltd. He was also Canadian diplomat from 1957 to 1969 and was educated at the Universities of British Columbia, Cambridge, Harvard and Toronto.

Helmut Maucher

Dr. h.c. Maucher has spent almost his entire career with Nestlé SA, the Switzerland-based international food company. From 1981 until June 1997 he was CEO of the Nestlé Group, of which he has been Chairman since 1990. He is on the

Board of Directors of various companies. Currently he is President of the International Chamber of Commerce (Paris), and Chairman of the European Roundtable of Industrialists (Brussels). Mr. Maucher has received many prizes and is the author of *Leadership in Action* (Marketing ist Chefsache).

Arvind Panagariya

Arvind Panagariya is Professor of Economics and Co-director of the Center for International Economics at the University of Maryland, College Park, MD. He received a Ph.D. in Economics from Princeton University in 1978. He was a staff member of the World Bank from 1989 to 1993 and has served as a consultant to various international institutions including the WTO, the World Bank and the Asian Development Bank. He has written extensively on trade theory and trade policy, and his articles have appeared in the leading professional journals. His two recent books are *The Economics of Preferential Trade Agreements* (edited with Jagdish Bhagwati) and *The Global Trading System and Developing Asia* (edited with M.G. Quibria and N. Rao). He also edits (with Dani Rodrik) the Journal of Policy Reform.

David de Pury

David de Pury has had a career in legal practice, diplomacy and business. At present he is chairman of de Pury Pictet Turretini & Co Ltd, a company specializing in asset management and international investment, which he co-founded in 1996. Between 1986 and 1991, he was the Swiss Government Representative for Trade Agreements. David de Pury was the chief negotiator for Switzerland in the Uruguay Round. He was also Chairman of the OECD Trade Committee and Governor for Switzerland of the Inter-American Development Bank. Between 1992 and 1996 he was Chairman of BBC Brown Boveri Ltd and Co-chairman of the ABB Asea Brown Boveri Group. In that capacity, he was a member of the European Roundtable of Industrialists (ERT). He serves on the board of directors of several multinational companies including Nestlé Group.

Marcelo Raffaelli

Marcelo Raffaelli was Chairman of the Textiles Surveillance Body of the Multi-Fibre Arrangement at GATT from 1982 to 1994. He worked with the Brazilian Foreign Service between 1952 and 1982 and was posted to Venezuela, the Netherlands, the United Nations (New York), Washington DC, Montevideo, London and the Ivory Coast. Between 1973 and 1977 he was Brazil's representative to the Cocoa, Coffee and Sugar Organization in London and led the Brazilian delegations in the negotiation of several multilateral agreements.

Rubens Ricupero

Mr. Ricupero was appointed as UNCTAD's fifth Secretary-General in September 1995. Previously, in the course of a long Brazilian government career, he was Deputy Head of the Presidential staff in 1985, before being promoted to Special Advisor to the President in 1986. In 1987 he was sent to Geneva as Ambassador to the United Nations and Brazil's Permanent Representative to the GATT. In 1991, he was named Ambassador to the United States. In 1993, he was appointed Minister of Environment and Amazonian Affairs by President Itamar Franco, before becoming Minister of Finance in 1994. He supervised the launching of the current Brazilian economic stabilisation programme. His positions in the GATT from 1989-91 included: Chairman and Spokesman of the GATT Informal Group of Developing Countries, Chairman of the GATT Committee on Trade and Development, Chairman of the GATT Council of Representatives and of the GATT CONTRACTING PARTIES.

Renato Ruggiero

Mr. Ruggiero assumed the post of Director-General of the World Trade Organization in Geneva on 1 May 1995. Renato Ruggiero graduated in law from the University of Naples in 1953 and has been as a professional diplomat much of his career: Mr. Ruggiero was Chef de Cabinet to the President of the European Commission (1969 to 1978), Ambassador and Permanent Representative of Italy to the EEC in Brussels (1980-84), and Director-General for Economic Affairs (1984-85), and Secretary General (1985-87) at the Foreign Ministry. During this period he also served as the Personal Representative of the Prime Minister at seven G-7 Economic Summits, and as Chairman of the Executive Committee of the OECD. Between 1987 and 1991, as Italy's Foreign Trade Minister, he launched and implemented the programme for the liberalisation of foreign trade and capital movements. Upon leaving government service, he was on the Boards of various Italian, European and American companies either as a director or in an advisory capacity.

T. N. Srinivasan

T. N. Srinivasan is the Samuel C. Park, Jr. Professor of Economics and Chairman of the Department of Economics at Yale University. He has published extensively on International Trade, Development, Agricultural Economics and Microeconomic Theory. His most recent book is entitled *Developing Countries and the Multilateral Trading System: From the GATT (1947) to the Uruguay Round and the Future Beyond.* Professor Srinivasan is a Fellow of the Econometric Society and the American Academy of Arts and Sciences and holds a Ph.D. in Economics from Yale University.

Peter Denis Sutherland

Peter Sutherland, born on 25 April 1946 in Dublin, is Chairman of Goldman Sachs International and also Chairman of the British Petroleum Company Plc. From July 1993 to May 1995, he was Director General of GATT and, upon its creation in 1994, the World Trade Organization. Between 1981 and 1984 he was Attorney General of Ireland and from 1985 to 1989 was a Commissioner of the European Communities.

Paul A. Volcker

Paul Volcker currently is serving as director and consultant to a number of corporations and non-profit organizations. He recently retired as Chairman and Chief Executive Officer of Wolfensohn & Co. Inc. upon the merger of that firm with the Bankers Trust company, of which Mr. Volcker will become a director. Previously Mr. Volcker was Chairman of the Board of the Federal Reserve System from August 1979 to August 1987. Initially appointed to that position by President Carter for a four-year term, he was reappointed in 1983 by President Reagan. Upon completion of his second term as Chairman, Mr. Volcker returned to private life.

Clayton Yeutter

Ambassador Clayton Yeutter is Of Counsel to Hogan & Hartson, one of America's largest law firms. Between 1985 and 1988, he served as US Trade Representative. In 1989, President Bush named him as Secretary of Agriculture, where he served as the Administration's point man in steering the 1990 Farm Bill through Congress. In 1991, Secretary Yeutter was named Republican Chairman. In 1992 he returned to the Administration to coordinate domestic policy in the Cabinet level post of Counselor to the President. Prior to 1985 he was President and Chief Executive Officer of the Chicago Mercantile Exchange and held various subcabinet positions in the Nixon and Ford Administrations.

B. K. Zutshi

Mr. B.K. Zutshi superannuated from the Indian Administrative Service after a distinguished career of nearly 35 years and is currently working as Vice-

Chairman, Telecom Regulatory Authority of India. He was India's Chief Textile Negotiator in the early 1980s, and from 1989 to 1994, India's Ambassador and Permanent Representative to the GATT. He served as Chairman of the GATT Council (1992) and as Chairman of the CONTRACTING PARTIES (1993).

List of Acronyms

AMS	Aggregate Measure of Support
APEC	Asia Pacific Economic Cooperation forum
ASEAN	Association of South-East Asian Nations
ATC	Agreement on Textiles and Clothing
BISD	Basic Instruments and Selected Documents
CAP	Common Agricultural Policy
CEA	Council of Economic Advisors
CITES	Convention on International Trade in Endangered Species
CRTA	Committee on Regional Trade Agreements
CU	Customs Union
DG	Directorate General
EC	European Communities
EEC	European Economic Community
EFTA	European Free Trade Association
EPG	Eminent Persons' Group
EEP	Export Enhancement Program
ERT	European Round Table of Industrialists
EU	European Union
FTAs	Free Trade Areas
GATS	General Agreement on Trade in Services
GATT	General Agreement on Tariffs and Trade
GBT	General Agreement on Basic Communications Services
GSP	Generalized System of Preferences
IASC	International Accounting Standards Committee
IBRD	International Bank for Reconstruction and Development
ICC	International Chamber of Commerce
IEA	International Environmental Agreement
ILO	International Labour Office
IMF	International Monetary Fund
IPRs	Intellectual Property Rights
ITA	Information Technology Agreement
ITO	International Trade Organization
LDCs	Less-Developed Countries
MAI	Multilateral Agreement on Investment
MERCOSUR	Southern Cone Common Market
MFA	Multi-Fibre Arrangement
MFN	Most Favoured Nation

MIT	Massachusetts Institute of Technology
MTAs	Multilateral Trade Agreements
NAFTA	North American Free Trade Agreement
NGO	Non-Governmental Organizations
NTBs	Non-tariff Trade Barriers
OECD	Organisation for Economic Co-operation and Development
OPEC	Organisation of Petroleum Exporting Countries
PTAs	Preferential Trade Arrangements
RTAs	Regional Trade Agreements
SADEC	South African Development and Economic Cooperation
TNC	Trade Negotiations Committee
TNCs	Transnational Corporations
TRIMs	Trade-Related Investment Measures
TRIPS	Trade-Related Aspects of Intellectual Property Rights
TSB	Textiles Surveillance Body
UDEAC	Central African Customs and Economic Union
UNCTAD	United Nations Conference on Trade and Development
UNDP	United Nations Development Programme
UNIDO	United Nartions Industrial Development Organization
US	United States of America
USTR	United States Trade Representative
VCRs	Video Cassette Recorderes
VERs	Voluntary Export Restraints
WHO	World Health Organization
WIPO	World Intellectual Property Organization
WTO	World Trade Organization

STUDIES IN INTERNATIONAL TRADE POLICY

Studies in International Trade Policy includes works dealing with the theory, empirical analysis, political, economic, legal relations, and evaluations of international trade policies and institutions.

General Editor: Robert M. Stern

John H. Jackson and Edwin Vermulst, Editors. *Antidumping Law and Practice: A Comparative Study*

John Whalley, Editor. *Developing Countries and the Global Trading System.* Volumes 1 and 2

John Whalley, Coordinator. *The Uruguay Round and Beyond: The Final Report from the Ford Foundation Project on Developing Countries and the Global Trading System*

John S. Odell and Thomas D. Willett, Editors. *International Trade Policies: Gains from Exchange between Economics and Political Science*

Ulrich Kohli. *Technology, Duality, and Foreign Trade: The GNP Function Approach to Modeling Imports and Exports*

Stephen V. Marks and Keith E. Maskus, Editors. *The Economics and Politics of World Sugar Policies*

J. Michael Finger, Editor. *Antidumping: How It Works and Who Gets Hurt*

Horst Herberg and Ngo Van Long, Editors. *Trade, Welfare, and Economic Policies: Essays in Honor of Murray C. Kemp*

David Schwartzman. *The Japanese Television Cartel: A Study Based on* Matsushita v. Zenith

Alan V. Deardorff and Robert M. Stern, Editors. *Analytical Perspectives and Negotiating Issues in the Global Trading System*

Edwin Vermulst, Paul Waer, and Jacques Bourgeois, Editors. *Rules of Origin in International Trade: A Comparative Study*

Alan V. Deardorff and Robert M. Stern, Editors. *The Stolper-Samuelson Theorem: A Golden Jubilee*

Kent Albert Jones. *Export Restraint and the New Protectionism: The Political Economy of Discriminatory Trade Restrictions*

Alan V. Deardorff, James A. Levinsohn, and Robert M. Stern, Editors. *New Directions in Trade Theory*

Robert Baldwin, Tain-Jy Chen, and Douglas Nelson. *Political Economy of U.S.–Taiwan Trade*

Bernard M. Hoekman and Petros C. Mavroidis, Editors. *Law and Policy in Public Purchasing: The WTO Agreement on Government Procurement*

Danny M. Leipziger, Editor. *Lessons from East Asia*

Tamin Bayoumi. *Financial Integration and Real Activity*

Harry P. Bowen, Abraham Hollander, and Jean-Marie Viaene. *Applied International Trade Analysis*